Proceedin

MW01275160

Second Annual IEEE International Workshop on Horizontal Interactive Human-Computer Systems

10-12 October 2007
Newport, Rhode Island, USA

Proceedings

Second Annual IEEE International Workshop on Horizontal Interactive Human-Computer Systems

10-12 October 2007
Newport, Rhode Island, USA

Los Alamitos, California

Washington • Tokyo

IEEE Computer Society Order Number P3013
ISBN-10: 0-7695-3013-3
ISBN-13: 978-0-7695-3013-0
Library of Congress Number 2007932993

Additional copies may be ordered from:

IEEE Computer Society
Customer Service Center
10662 Los Vaqueros Circle
P.O. Box 3014
Los Alamitos, CA 90720-1314
Tel: + 1 800 272 6657
Fax: + 1 714 821 4641
http://computer.org/cspress
csbooks@computer.org

IEEE Service Center
445 Hoes Lane
P.O. Box 1331
Piscataway, NJ 08855-1331
Tel: + 1 732 981 0060
Fax: + 1 732 981 9667
http://shop.ieee.org/store/
customer-service@ieee.org

IEEE Computer Society
Asia/Pacific Office
Watanabe Bldg., 1-4-2
Minami-Aoyama
Minato-ku, Tokyo 107-0062
JAPAN
Tel: + 81 3 3408 3118
Fax: + 81 3 3408 3553
tokyo.ofc@computer.org

Individual paper REPRINTS may be ordered at: <reprints@computer.org>

Editorial production by Patrick Kellenberger
Cover art production by Alex Torres
Printed in the United States of America by Applied Digital Imaging

IEEE Computer Society
Conference Publishing Services (CPS)
http://www.computer.org/cps

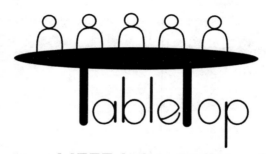

Second Annual IEEE International Workshop on Horizontal Interactive Human-Computer Systems

Table of Contents

Far & Away: Remote and Distributed Tabletop Collaboration

Out & About: Tabletops in the Real World

Reading, Writing & More: Tabletop-User Experiences

WIMP!: Bringing Traditional Interactions to the Tabletop

Inside & Out: Novel Tabletop Interactions and Infrastructure

Gadgets & Gizmos: 'Notable' Tabletop Hardware

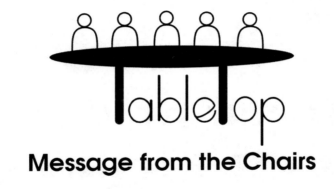

Message from the Chairs

We would like to welcome you to TABLETOP 2007, the Second Annual IEEE International Workshop on Horizontal Interactive Human-Computer Systems.

Over the next few days, it is our hope that you, the workshop attendees, will benefit from the bringing together of geographically diverse experts from a wide range of domains. It is our goal that you will leave TABLETOP 2007 more informed, inspired, and connected than when you arrived. Additionally, it is our hope that future tabletop researchers will return to these proceedings to read the papers and notes that helped define their field.

This year we were pleasantly surprised to receive a total of 86 submissions across the papers, notes and posters categories. The program committee accepted 21 full papers and 7 notes that span a number of exciting topics with tabletops as the common ground. Posters and demos will round out the technical program, providing a more interactive and hands-on opportunity for discussions. The final program incorporates research from university, industrial and government labs from around the world; thirteen different countries from Asia, Europe, North America, and Australia are represented. We have supplemented the proceedings with a DVD containing video figures for many of the posters, notes, posters and demonstrations.

As with any workshop, TABLETOP 2007 required a great effort made by many people. The exciting program that you will experience over the next few days was only possible with the hard work of the program committee and external reviewers, all of whom volunteered their time and effort. We would also like to thank the many area chairs for their efforts and for their patience in dealing with two novice general chairs. Finally, it is the corporate and government sponsors as well as the support of IEEE that make organizing and running such a workshop possible.

One cannot have an "annual" event until there is a second meeting, and we are happy to help TABLETOP establish itself as the premier event in the field of tabletop interfaces.

Andy Wilson and Clifton Forlines
TABLETOP 2007 Chairs

Kathy Ryall and Stacey Scott
TABLETOP 2007 Program Chair and Co-chair

Program Committee

Mark Billinghurst, University of Canterbury
Andreas Butz, University of Munich
Hal Eden, University of Colorado at Boulder
Michael Haller, Upper Austria University of Applied Sciences
Karrie Karahalios, University of Illinois
Judy Kay, University of Sydney
Carsten Magerkurth, SAP Research CEC St. Gallen
Ali Mazalek, Georgia Tech
Meredith Morris, Microsoft Research
Kumiyo Nakakoji, University of Tokyo
David Pinelle, University of Nevada, Las Vegas
Yvonne Rogers, Open University
Sriram Subramanian, Philips Research Eindhoven
Bruce Thomas, University of South Australia
Fred Vernier, University of Paris 11
Daniel Wigdor, University of Toronto
Massimo Zancanaro, Bruno Kessler Foundation (formerly ITC)

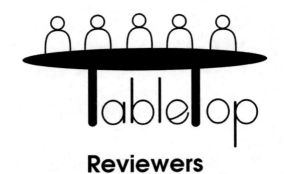

Reviewers

Abdullah Al Mahmud, User-System Interaction, Eindhoven University of Technology
Dima Aliakseyeu, Technical University Eindhoven, Department of Industrial Design, User-Centered Engineering Group
Christopher Andrews, Virginia Polytechnic Institute and State University
Trent Apted, University of Sydney
Francois Berard, LIG/IIHM, University of Grenoble
Tony Bergstrom, University of Illinois at Urbana-Champaign
Mark Billinghurst, Human Interface Technology Lab New Zealand
Sebastian Boring, University of Munich
Peter Brandl, Upper Austria University of Applied Sciences
Andreas Butz, University of Munich
Anthony Collins, University of Sydney (USYD)
Nicholas Dalton, Open University
Paul Dietz, Mitsubishi Electric Research Labs
Joan Dimicco, IBM
Florian Echtler, Technische Universität München
Hal Eden, University of Colorado at Boulder
Danyel Fisher, Microsoft Research
Morten Fjeld, Chalmers TH
Coldefy François, Orange Labs
Raphael Grasset, HIT Lab NZ
Michael Haller, Upper Austria University of Applied Sciences
John Halloran, Coventry University
Mark Hancock, University of Calgary
Otmar Hilliges, Ludwig-Maximilians-Universität München
Paul Holleis, Nokia Research
Eva Hornecker, Open University
Kori Inkpen, Dalhousie University
Pourang Irani, University of Manitoba
Shahram Izadi, Microsoft Research
Karrie Karahalios, University of Illinois
Judy Kay, University of Sydney
Matthias Kranz, Technische Universität Braunschweig
Andreas Kunz, Inspire AG
Celine Latulipe, UNC Charlotte
Taehee Lee, University of California, Santa Barbara

Darren Leigh, Mitsubishi Electric Research Laboratories
Chiara Leonardi, FBK- Bruno Kessler Foundation
Carsten Magerkurth, SAP Research
Regan Mandryk, University of Saskatchewan
Paul Marshall, Open University
Jean-Bernard Martens, TU Eindhoven
Masood Masoodian, The University of Waikato
Mitsunori Matsushita, Nippon Telegraph and Telephone Corporation
Ali Mazalek, Georgia Tech
Meredith Morris, Microsoft Research
Christian Müller-tomfelde, CSIRO ICT Centre
Miguel Nacenta, University of Saskatchewan
Kumiyo Nakakoji, RCAST, University of Tokyo/SRA-KTL Inc.
Petra Neumann, University of Calgary
Tim Pattison, Defence Science and Technology Organisation
Fabio Pianesi, FBK-irst
Wayne Piekarski, University of South Australia
David Pinelle, University of Nevada, Las Vegas
Susan Robinson, Georgia Institute of Technology
Yvonne Rogers, Open University
Nicolas Roussel, Univ. Paris-Sud
Kathy Ryall, MERL
Christian Sandor
Kosuke Sato, Osaka University
Michael Schmitz, DFKI GmbH
Stacey Scott, University of Waterloo
Hartmut Seichter, Human Interface Technology Laboratory New Zealand, HITLabNZ
Stefan Seipel, Department of Mathematics, Natural and Computer Science, University of Gävle
Yoshinari Shirai, NTT Corporation
Sriram Subramanian, Philips Research Eindhoven
Jim Sullivan, Center for Lifelong Learning and Design
Akio Takashima, Hokkaido University
Masahiro Takatsuka, ViSLAB, The University of Sydney
Lucia Terrenghi, Ludwig-Maximilians University of Munich
Bruce Thomas, University of South Australia
Daniel Tomasini, FBK-irst
Edward Tse, University of Calgary
Philip Tuddenham, University of Cambridge
Brygg Ullmer, Louisiana State University
Elise van den Hoven, Eindhoven University of Technology
Frederic Vernier, University of Paris 11
Fernanda Viegas, IBM Research
Daniel Wigdor, University of Toronto
Andy Wilson, Microsoft Research
Chris Wren, MERL

Takashi Yoshino, Wakayama University
Massimo Zancanaro, FBK-irst (formerly ITC)
Guillaume Zufferey, Ecole Polytechnique Fédérale de Lausanne

Far & Away: Remote and Distributed Tabletop Collaboration

C-Slate: A Multi-Touch and Object Recognition System for Remote Collaboration using Horizontal Surfaces

Shahram Izadi, Ankur Agarwal, Antonio Criminisi,
John Winn, Andrew Blake, Andrew Fitzgibbon
Microsoft Research Cambridge, 7 JJ Thomson Avenue, Cambridge, CB3 0FB
{shahrami, ankagar}@microsoft.com

Abstract

We introduce C-Slate, a new vision-based system, which utilizes stereo cameras above a commercially available tablet technology to support remote collaboration. The horizontally mounted tablet provides the user with high resolution stylus input, which is augmented by multi-touch interaction and recognition of untagged everyday physical objects using new stereo vision and machine learning techniques. This provides a novel and interesting interactive tabletop arrangement, capable of supporting a variety of fluid multi-touch interactions, including symmetric and asymmetric bimanual input, coupled with the potential for incorporating tangible objects into the user interface. When used in a remote context, these features are combined with the ability to see visual representations of remote users' hands and remote physical objects placed on top of the surface. This combination of bimanual and tangible interaction and sharing of remote gestures and physical objects provides a new way to collaborate remotely, complementing existing channels such as audio and video conferencing.

1. Introduction

Interactive tabletops can very naturally support co-located face-to-face collaboration [24, 25, 26]. This is a product of both their physical form, allowing users to view a large horizontal workspace whilst maintaining awareness of others, and their ability to support more fluid and direct interaction with digital content using touch, hands, gestures, and potentially other sensed physical objects [21, 23, 37]. Although the use of tabletops for co-located collaboration is well established, the role that such systems can play in remote collaboration has only very recently become a theme of investigation [6, 10, 32, 38].

Rich physical interactions occur over and around the tabletop surface during co-located collaboration. For example, we use our hands to refer to virtual or physical artifacts on the surface and use gestures to express actions.

We constantly use the physical affordances of the tabletop [30], placing artifacts such as documents onto the surface to share and refer to them.

These physical interactions form important visual cues for collaboration, providing awareness of other peoples' actions and intentions, and facilitating fine grained coordination amongst members of the group. These interactions are clearly lost when we move to the remote case, and are often overlooked by current CSCW and groupware tools such as video and audio conferencing or remote desktop systems.

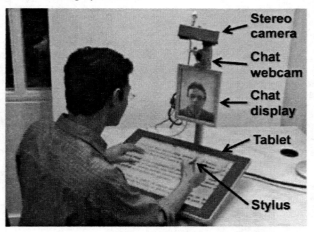

Figure 1: The C-Slate hardware setup comprising of a top-down stereo camera attached to a large tablet workspace, with a video conferencing display at eye-level to the user.

We introduce the Collaborative Slate (or C-Slate), a new vision-based system which utilizes a stereo camera attached above a commercially available horizontally mounted tablet technology as shown in Figure 1; with a second smaller display and web camera attached at eye-level to the user, supporting video and audio conferencing. The tablet supports high resolution stylus input, for fine grained inking and cursor control. Images captured from the stereo camera are processed using new vision and machine learning algorithms to allow high precision

IEEE computer society

fingertip and touch detection, enabling both stylus and multi-touch interaction on the tablet surface.

New stereo vision and machine learning techniques are also used to recognize a variety of physical objects placed on the display, without the need to tag these with visual markers. This allows ordinary everyday objects such as post-its, documents, stationery or mobile devices to be sensed in order to invoke particular UI actions. This recognition system is also capable of detecting a user's hand poses, allowing these to also be mapped onto UI actions. These features provide a new and interesting interactive tabletop configuration, enabling a variety of fluid multi-touch interactions, including symmetric and asymmetric bimanual input, coupled with the potential for incorporating tangible objects into the UI.

The use of a top-down camera also allows images of hands and objects on top of the tablet surface to be rapidly captured, segmented and transmitted over the network to other C-Slates where they are rendered on the tablet display. This provides a virtual embodiment of the remote participant's hands, and allows remote parties to share images of physical objects with each other, such as written notes, drawings or game pieces, simply by placing them on the surface. This combination of bimanual and tangible interaction and sharing of remote gestures and physical objects provides a new way to collaborate remotely, complementing already established channels such as audio and video conferencing.

2. Related work

Our system relates to a large body of work within multi-touch and object sensing, direct input and tangible tabletops, and remote gesturing tools. We shall cover these aspects in turn within this section.

Multi-touch has received a great deal of attention recently through the widely disseminated research of Wilson [36, 37] and Han [13], and products such as the Apple iPhone [2] and now the Microsoft Surface [21]. Multi-touch has an even longer history however, and the first systems appeared well over two decades ago (see [5] for an overview of the major landmarks).

One technique of detecting multiple fingertips on a display is to build custom sensing electronics into the surface itself [8, 18, 23, 35]. These systems are typically based on capacitive sensing, although other sensors can be utilized [18, 27]. They usually sense at low resolutions and are visually opaque, relying on projection for display. Even with this low-resolution sensing, rich sets of interactions have been demonstrated [23, 40]. What is harder with such systems (as they are non-optical) is to image the entire hand or other arbitrary physical objects close to or touching the surface. Rather, other objects aside from the hand need to be actively tagged to be detected by the surface [9, 23].

Camera-based systems allow more flexibility in sensing, providing a higher resolution optical system for capturing richer information about arbitrary objects in proximity to the display. Wilson [37] clearly highlights the tradeoffs of this flexibility, in terms of the high computational costs, the difficulty in achieving real-time interactive rates, ambiguity of data (particularly detecting when an object is hovering as opposed to touching the surface), and susceptibility to occlusion and adverse lighting conditions. This makes developing such systems an interesting and challenging problem.

2.1 Camera based Multi-touch Systems

One common approach to building a multi-touch and object sensing tabletop is to place a camera on top or underneath the display surface, and use computer vision algorithms to process the captured images. These top-down and bottom-up configurations carry various tradeoffs. Top-down approaches [20, 34, 37, 39] tend to capture richer data regarding the interactions occurring on the surface as the camera is directly pointing at the display, although occlusion can be an issue. The camera can feasibly image and process all objects on or near the surface – e.g. hands, individual fingertips, and other objects such as documents. Early examples are Krueger's VideoDesk [16] and Wellner's DigitalDesk [34].

Bottom-up approaches [13, 21, 36] place the camera underneath or behind the surface, and typically employ rear projection onto a diffuse surface material. In most cases, the use of the diffuser attenuates the camera signal, and consequently requires Infrared (IR) techniques [13, 21] to sense IR reflective objects such as fingers on the other side of the surface. This makes sensing arbitrary objects difficult, unless IR visual markers [21] are used to passively identify objects placed on the surface. Conversely, this reduced signal also improves the accuracy of such systems, reducing ambiguities, for example caused by an object far from the surface being accidentally detected by the camera.

This issue of detecting the proximity of objects to the surface is a real challenge for top-down camera systems, particularly in the context of detecting when fingers are touching as opposed to hovering on the surface. In DigitalDesk a microphone was used alongside the camera to coarsely detect when fingers were touching the surface; other techniques (e.g. [19]) often rely on the finger dwelling or other gestures to detect when a user is touching the display.

As demonstrated by Wren et al. [39], TouchLight [36] and the Visual Touchpad [20], stereo vision can assist in detecting the depth of objects in a scene, using various algorithms to compute the disparity between the images captured by the stereo pair. By setting appropriate thresholds it is feasible to detect contact with the surface to within a few centimeters of accuracy.

PlayAnywhere [37] uses a single top down camera and projector set off-axis to detect multi-touch and tangible objects. The system uses an IR camera and IR source to illuminant the foreground objects of interest. The projector plus illuminant guarantees that shadows will be cast on the surface in a variety of lighting conditions. PlayAnywhere uses this shadow information to detect when a single finger from each hand is touching the surface. This can be achieved with millimeter accuracy, and combined with an optical flow technique for bimanual interaction. Tangible objects can also be supported using a fast visual bar-coding scheme.

Although the Visual Touchpad is an indirect input device for interacting with large displays in the same space, it shares many commonalities with C-Slate. A stereo camera is employed over a large opaque and darkly colored touchpad to detect touching fingers. Vision techniques are used to track the position and orientation of the hands and make informed guesses as to the identity of each finger to calculate particular gestures. Further UI feedback is provided by segmenting the hands from the images and augmenting them transparently onto the large display. A similar user experience is provided in the TactaPad [28], using optical sensors embedded in the touchpad. A logical progression from Visual Touchpad and TactaPad is to consider how superimposing of hands can be used for feedback in remote collaboration.

2.2 Remote Gesturing Systems

Remote gesturing within CSCW is a growing area of research (see [15] for a detailed review). Early examples are VideoDraw [31] and Clearboard-1 [14], which overlaid analogue video of hands (and in the latter case, upper bodies) of remote participants on a horizontal workstation. Clearboard-2 [14] provided a digital instantiation of the shared workspace, using rear-projection for display, and a camera above the surface. A half mirror and polarizing film were placed above the display surface, which ensured only images of the top half of the participant (and not the screen) would be captured and relayed onto remote parties.

This seminal work combined video conferencing output (focusing on the face) and the surface interaction space (focusing on the hands and arms) into a single display. The system overlaid digital ink on top of this video. In experiments, users found this approach visually overloading at times. Clearly, rendering the video conferencing session underneath the digital content can be distracting. The two channels can interfere with one another, causing difficulties in perceiving the digital content. Further, with this overlaying scheme, occlusion issues exist if the digital content is extended beyond ink, to other types such as documents, images or video. This makes sharing of rich media difficult with Clearboard.

VideoArms [29] combines audio conferencing with a camera pointing at a large surface to capture and segment forearms of people as they interact on screen. These are sent over the network to remote displays where they are overlaid over the shared workspace. The system uses simple computer vision techniques to extract out forearms based on skin tones. Tang et al. describes various revealing experiments with VideoArms where various transparency and rendering effects of virtual arms are evaluated.

Agora [17] and Kirk [15] describe two physical setups using projectors and cameras over a table. Video of physical interactions occurring on a table are captured, and overlaid remotely by projection. Video conferencing facilities are also provided. Kirk [15] and Luff et al. [17] provide quantitative and qualitative evidence as to why such systems can benefit remote collaboration.

Even more recently, the DiamondTouch [8] multi-touch technology has been used for remote collaboration [6, 10]. For example, Digitable [6] combines this multi-touch ability with cameras to provide virtual embodiments of remote users' hands and arms. T3 [32] provides similar mechanisms but uses a camera and projector array with support for input using multiple Anoto pens. These recent systems, share a common goal: to support remote collaboration across horizontal multi-touch surfaces. We aim to explore the combination of this with the power of sensing a variety of tangible objects for both local and remote interactions. Our system shares this motivation with PlayTogether [38], an extension of the PlayAnywhere tabletop system to support remote interactions. Wilson's work serves as an exemplary case that highlights the use of remote gestures and object sharing for gaming.

3. Introducing C-Slate

The C-slate provides fluid techniques for interacting both with the remote collaborator and with the digital workspace. The system is intended to be used in a diverse set of scenarios, from collaborative group work through to gaming. One of the primary goals however is to support collaborative reviewing and annotation of shared electronic documents, for example maps, architectural plans or academic papers. This focus suggests the need for a stylus based interface. For our purposes, we chose to utilize a large commercially available tablet surface, capable of high resolution display and stylus input. This provides new interactive, form factor, and display possibilities when compared to projection.

As shown by [6, 14, 15, 17 29, 31, 32] providing virtual embodiments of arms and hands alongside audio and video conferencing channels can provide much utility for remote collaboration. We therefore attach a camera above the tablet, which faces the surface and captures images of hands and other objects placed over the display. The foreground objects are segmented out from the captured images, and transmitted over the network to remote C-Slates, where they are visually overlaid on the tablet workspace. Unlike some existing remote gesture systems, our approach scales to physical objects as well as forearms, allowing both virtual representations of the users' hands and physical objects to be shared with remote participants. Based on findings of Clearboard, we avoid visually overloading the tablet UI by physically demarcating the video conferencing output from the interaction space using a second display at eye level.

Like PlayTogether, Digitable and T3 we further extend the utility of remote gesturing systems by adding an additional sensing step before transmitting the video for remote rendering. New computer vision and machine learning techniques are applied to each segmented image in order to extract out information regarding recognizable physical object classes. Upon recognition, these objects can be used to carry out local UI actions, which are also relayed onto the remote workspace. This is a key novelty of C-Slate, allowing automatic real-time detection of untagged everyday objects, and allowing online addition of arbitrary new object classes. This recognition system is extended also to distinguish a user's hand from other objects, and further, recognize hand poses, allowing these to also be mapped onto UI actions.

Like [20, 36, 39] we also employ a stereo setup using disparity to estimate when objects are touching the surface. However, for many multi-touch applications, more detailed and high-precision finger touch detection is necessary. The use of a tablet rather than projection makes it difficult to employ a shadow based technique such as in PlayAnywhere. Instead C-Slate provides a new real-time stereo vision and machine learning technique for accurately detecting fingertips and touch. Unlike PlayAnywhere and Visual Touchpad touch is detected for each fingertip, and at a higher level of accuracy than systems that use disparity alone. This allows very fine grained gestures based on individual fingertip data to be integrated into the UI, and additionally allows these gestures to have a remote visual embodiment and effect.

This provides C-Slate surfaces with both multi-touch sensing and high resolution stylus input. Although systems [8, 11] have provided pen and multi-touch input, our configuration provides higher resolution and non-tethered use. This coupled with the ability to detect untagged objects on the surface provides for an exciting new tabletop technology. Additionally, these features are coupled with remote gesturing and object sharing allowing us to explore new remote collaborative scenarios exploring document writing, annotation and editing tasks.

3.1 Shared Workspaces

As shown in Figure 2, the tablet screen provides a window onto a large digital workspace, which is shared across the network with other connected C-Slates. Within the workspace, media items such as images, video, web pages and documents can be opened, reviewed and annotated.

Figure 2: A screenshot of the shared workspace UI. Far left, the media items that can be opened. Far right, controls for switching between pen, highlighter and eraser, and starting a whiteboard session. A selected document is reviewed & annotated in the middle.

By default everything in this digital workspace is shared remotely, i.e. every UI event generated locally is transmitted over the network and rendered remotely. However, the shared workspace is just another application on the user's private desktop, and can be quickly minimized and reactivated to switch between private and public work.

Once connected to other C-Slates, an audio and video conferencing link is also established. Audio in particular has been found to be critical in remote collaboration [15, 17]. Either of these channels can be disabled by the user during collaboration.

3.2 Image Segmentation

Segmenting out the foreground objects in the overhead camera images allows us to selectively overlay content on the remote user's workspace. We make use of a very simple and low-cost optical technique for segmentation, inspired by [14]. This exploits the fact that light emitted by an LCD screen is polarized. We place linear polarization filters on our camera lenses and rotate these so that they suppress the light exiting from the LCD but let other light through (for example from foreground objects). This essentially 'switches off' the display to the cameras, providing a black uniform background which greatly simplifies foreground object extraction.

This approach works more effectively than skin tone analysis used in VideoArms and preserves foreground

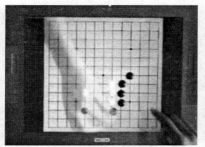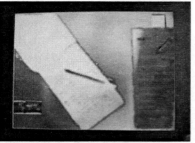

Figure 3: Phantom presence allows each remote user to see the other's hands and objects: (Left) A remote hand holding a pen fading into view on the tablet, whilst the other hand rests on the surface remaining opaque; (Centre) a game of GO being played with a remote participant with a mixture of remote Virtual (white) and local Physical (black) counters. (Right) A real notepad and document placed on the surface are rendered remotely.

color unlike PlayTogether. The technique also scales to segmentation of physical objects placed on the surface.

Before segmentation, the images from the two cameras are first rectified – in our current implementation this is achieved through the camera hardware. Additionally, before rendering objects on the remote screen, the skewed images from the top-down camera are transformed via a homography that is computed beforehand by automatically detecting the corners of the screen in the two images. This allows the overlaid objects to be aligned with the contents of the screen.

3.3 Phantom Presence

The remote gesturing part of C-Slate allows for interactions and objects on the tablet surface to be captured and rendered across remote workspaces. Figure 3 (left & center) shows examples of a remote user's hands being rendered on the shared workspace.

The transparency and blurring of any object (such as hands) is determined by the height of the object from the tablet surface – the closer the object gets to the display the more opaque and sharp it becomes. This gives objects a ghostly effect as they approach the surface, which we call Phantom Presence. This extends the transparency functionality provided in VideoArms, allowing users to get a sense of depth of the remote object. This acts as another peripheral channel for fine-grained coordination whilst also allowing users to mitigate occlusion issues rapidly by controlling the transparency of the object e.g. users may wave their hands high above the surface to gain floor control without completely disturbing the user interacting in the workspace, they may see an approaching hand and coordinate their interactions, or move an object placed on the surface higher up, to allow others to see the content underneath it.

We use stereo vision to calculate the depth of any object. After segmentation of the images from the two cameras, a matching process is used to compute disparity values for each pixel in the foreground. Subtracting the disparity value of the screen at each pixel from this then gives a relative disparity measure that increases directly

with height from the screen. These disparity values can be normalized and used to create an alpha mask for the object.

Depending on the application, the users may see exactly the same, or flipped or mirrored versions of the workspace e.g. when used for playing a game of GO, the workspace is flipped on one of the tablets so that the two players see the board from their respective sides. The image of the overlayed hands and objects is also correspondingly flipped to simulate the physical setting where the players would sit on opposite sides of the board.

Phantom presence allows users to share physical objects across the network by rendering images of the artifacts on remote workspaces. Figure 3 (right) shows a document and notepad placed on top of the surface being rendered remotely, thus providing a mechanism for participants to show each other physical artifacts that they are referring to in conversations.

3.4 Object Recognition

Current tabletop systems have demonstrated the utility of using tangible objects for invoking UI actions [21, 23, 37]. Such systems typically require a priori active or passive tagging of objects. We use stereo vision and machine learning to recognize different object classes, by training with labeled images of appropriate untagged objects. Object recognition opens up a new range of possible actions and extends the interactive possibilities of our system. For instance, placing a camera on the surface may enable the pictures to be transferred to disk and shared with the remote participant. Recognizing documents could automatically switch the top-down camera to high-resolution image capture mode intermittently, in order to capture a higher definition image of the document for remote rendering or OCR. Objects could also be used alongside gestures for rapid UI actions, e.g. placing down scissors on the surface and defining a region could cut the text from the document.

The recognition system is adaptive and capable of learning new object classes at run-time. It can also be manually corrected through the UI, to be retrained. The system recognizes objects classes as opposed to particular

Figure 4: Enabling multi-touch sensitivity using stereo vision. Our detailed analysis of fingertips allows for symmetric and asymmetric bimanual interaction: scaling, rotation, translation with simultaneous use of the stylus and also single handed rotation and scaling.

instances of these objects – this has particular tradeoffs as discussed later.

For the automatic classification of an image into one of several possible objects, we use a dataset of pre-labeled images of the various object classes that we support (up to 24 classes at present). A model based on random forests [4] is learnt in order to optimally discriminate between the different objects. This involves automatically learning a set of tests (rules) in the form of a number of decision trees [7]. Having segmented the image, each foreground connected component is taken as a separate object. At test time each foreground pixel undergoes the tests encoded in each of the learnt trees and a histogram distribution over leaf labels given by the random forest is computed for each object. The final classification step is performed by nearest neighbor comparison of each such histogram with exemplar (training) histograms using a distance metric which is invariant to rotation or mirroring of the object.

Our classification algorithm combines appearance, shape and depth cues to achieve accurate class discrimination in real-time. In particular, stereo features (expensive in general) are computed on an on-demand basis, only if necessary for discrimination. Our current automatic algorithm achieves recognition accuracy around the 99% mark on 24 object classes. More details are provided in [7].

A coarse level touch-detection is also obtained for these objects using the disparity cues. The classifier can also be trained to identify hands and particular hand poses. For example, hand poses being could be used for actions such as virtual object selection by pointing and closing a window using a fist. These events are only generated when the user's hand is touching the surface (computed from depth information from the stereo camera). The system is also capable of recognizing the hand holding an object. For example, the system can recognize an eraser and highlighter in the hand, and allows simple interactions to be mapped to these e.g. highlighting or erasing the text underneath the hand when the object makes contact with the surface.

3.5 Gesture and Bimanual Interaction

The pose recognition does not work at a precision level of individual fingertips, and although this is suitable for many simple UI actions, more fine-grained analysis is required to support other common multi-touch gestures [3, 40]. We again use the stereo camera to enable multi-touch on the tablet, coupling this with simultaneous high resolution stylus input. This allows us to support asymmetric interactions [12] using the stylus in the dominant hand whilst carrying out peripheral actions with the non-dominant hand [11, 12], as well as symmetric interactions more classically associated with bimanual interfaces [3].

Figure 4 shows some of the potential interactions: two handed symmetric scaling and rotation (note the stylus, though present, is not used in this case); asymmetric action involving rotation with the non-dominant hand while using the stylus with the dominant hand; and finally zooming into a document with a single hand.

Once the system recognizes a hand, a more detailed analysis is carried out to detect individual fingertips and accurately determine if they are touching the surface. Visible finger tips are detected in the image via a two step process. Individual points on the edge of the segmented hand are first classified as lying on a finger tip or not, and then a clustering phase combines evidence from multiple points to detect the finger tips. The classifier is built again by using a training database of images of hands, labeled with the fingertip positions. Each point is robustly encoded as a 64 dimensional signature vector computed from a local image patch around it and a Support Vector Machine [22] is trained to distinguish between tip and non-tip points based on these signatures.

Detected fingertips are further processed to detect touch. In our setup, conventional stereo algorithms that compute disparity images (e.g. [20, 39]) fail to meet the level of precision for our requirements – we found often when a finger hovers above the screen it can be falsely detected triggering unexpected behavior in the UI. We have developed an algorithm that probabilistically aggregates stereo cues from several points at each fingertip and uses a finger-specific geometric model to resolve this. The method returns a probability value for the touch detection of each finger and allows multi-touch sensing with several millimeter precision. Details of the approach are described in full in [1].

4. Implementation

The C-Slate is realized using off-the-shelf hardware, although the frame attaching the various components together has been custom built. Wacom's Cintiq 21UX is used for the tablet display, providing a large 21" display size and 1600x1200 screen resolution with a digitizer capable of detecting strokes, hover and pressure from a single stylus. We use the Bumblebee 2, a stereo camera from Point Grey Systems, capable of providing high framerate, hardware synchronized and rectified stereo images. We have also tested our algorithms with a pair of standard web-cameras to form a stereo camera. These are found to work satisfactorily although they provide slightly lower framerates and accuracy. Our applications are built using a combination of Win32 and WPF. Phantom Presence video is streamed as encoded low-res PNG images over UDP preserving per-pixel alpha values. UI updates, such as mode switches, ink strokes, or changes in the transform matrix of a virtual object, are sent between shared workspaces using a proprietary protocol again using raw sockets.

5. Discussion and Future Work

In this paper, we have focused on describing the underlying technology of C-Slate. As demonstrated we have used new stereo vision techniques in various ways including remote gesturing, touch detection, and object recognition to create a new tabletop technology that also supports remote collaboration. There are of course interesting issues and observations associated with the use of our computer vision based systems. Adverse lighting is clearly an issue for vision systems. This is in part mitigated by attaching a light source to the C-Slate stand, but other approaches are also being explored. Occlusion is also an often cited problem of using overhead cameras on interactive surfaces. However we have found it to be far less of an issue than we originally anticipated. Perhaps telling is that the majority of the users so far have thought it the tablet is in fact a touchscreen rather than a camera-based system. We partly attribute this to the fine-grained touch detection enabled on the surface, but would attempt to quantify this in our future studies.

System robustness could be further improved for touch detection by supporting automatic online addition of new training examples. For example, we could couple our camera-based technique with a single-point touch overlay on our tablet screen, which allows us to unambiguously determine if a user is touching the surface and remove any false positives from our classifier.

Sharing of paper documents appears to be an important aspect of remote collaboration. Our cameras do not have the resolution to sufficiently capture detailed images of documents but we anticipate integrating a high resolution stills camera to the setup to improve image clarity. Automatic detection of a paper document could programmatically trigger the camera to take an image. This high resolution image could be incorporated into the Phantom Presence video in a lightweight manner by transmitting the high resolution image once, and using paper tracking techniques [37] to render this onto the outline of the object.

For a full assessment of our system, we are planning to run extensive user studies. In the interim, we have begun deploying the system in our workplace to get initial feedback. Although not quantified, people have expressed how C-Slate offers a natural and expressive way of collaborating remotely. For example, at a glance users can see if a remote participant is interacting on the screen, writing, pointing and referring to something, waiting for a response and so forth. The transitions between these states are also easy to perceive e.g. switching from writing to pointing. The visual impact of seeing the hand makes it easier to draw peoples' attention and less prone to being lost on visually noisy backgrounds. The transparency effect allows users to gain more peripheral awareness of when peoples' hands are approaching the surface. This appears to make coordination tasks much easier.

Users have also been enthusiastic about the bimanual interaction techniques. The asymmetric and symmetric bimanual input enabled by simultaneous touch and stylus input indeed opens up another channel for interaction – the non-dominant hand is frequently used for both local and remote interactions. It is very intuitive for a user to be writing with one hand and gesturing with the other. Rotation and translation with non-dominant hand seems particularly important during writing tasks while scaling seems secondary and sometimes distracting during writing.

The ability to detect object classes presents a novel and potentially powerful feature for users, allowing them to quickly invoke UI actions using physical objects that already have strong meanings and affordances associated with them. E.g. a user is likely to readily understand the actions to expect when bringing a physical highlighter or eraser to the digital surface. This however indicates the need for careful UI design, as physical objects could potentially cause unanticipated UI behavior.

Finally we are investigating other interactive arrangements for remote group work, for instance where multiple co-located participants are interacting with remote parties using C-Slate. These will require new tabletop configurations, for example tiling two tablet displays together to increase the size of the physical workspace for group interaction.

6. Conclusions

We have presented a novel set of technologies designed to improve remote collaboration on horizontal surfaces.

Initial user feedback on the system has been positive and extensive user studies are on our agenda. The contributions of this paper are a new multi-touch and object sensing system called C-Slate that supports multimodal input from untagged objects, high precision multi-touch, hand poses, and high-resolution stylus input on a large tablet surface, thus providing a new interactive and interesting tabletop technology; and the exploration of these tabletop systems for remote collaboration combining and extending the work carried out by the tabletop, multi-touch, and remote gestures communities.

Acknowledgements

We thank Andy Wilson, Abigail Sellen, Bill Buxton and Dave Kirk for all their inspiration and feedback.

7. References

1. Agarwal, A. et al. High Precision Multi-touch Sensing on Surfaces using Overhead Cameras, In Tabletop'07.

2. Apple iPhone Multi-touch, http://www.apple.com/iphone

3. R. Balakrishnan and K. Hinckley. Symmetric bimanual interaction. In ACM CHI, pages 33–40, 2002.

4. L. Brieman. Random Forests. Machine Learning, 2001.

5. W. Buxton. Multi-Touch Systems that I Have Known and Loved. http://www.billbuxton.com/multitouch

6. Coldefy, F.; Louis-dit-Picard, S., DigiTable: an interactive multiuser table for collocated and remote collaboration enabling remote gesture visualization, In ProCams '07.

7. T. Deselaers et al. Incorporating On-demand Stereo for Real Time Recognition. In CVPR, 2007.

8. Paul Dietz and Darren Leigh. DiamondTouch: a multi-user touch technology. 2001.

9. P.H. Dietz et al. DT Controls: Adding Identity to Physical Interfaces. In Proceedings of UIST, 2005.

10. Esenther, A., and Ryall, K., RemoteDT: Support for Multi-Site Table Collaboration. In CollabTech 2006.

11. Y. I. Gingold, et al. A Direct Texture Placement and Editing Interface. In UIST 2006.

12. Y. Guiard. Asymmetric division of labor in human skilled bimanual action: The kinetic chain as a model. The Journal of Motor Behavior, 19(4):486–517, 1987.

13. J. Y. Han. Low-Cost Multi-Touch Sensing through Frustrated Total Internal Reflection. In UIST, 2005.

14. H. Ishii, M. Kobayashi, and J. Grudin. Integration of Interpersonal Space and Shared Workspace: ClearBoard Design and Experiments. ACM TOIS, 11(4), Oct 1993.

15. David Kirk. Turn It This Way: A Human Factors Treatise on the Design and Use of Remote Gestural Simulacra. PhD Thesis, University of Nottingham.

16. Krueger, M, Videoplace: an artificial reality. In CHI 1985, pages 35–40.

17. H. Kuzuoka, J. Kosaka, K. Yamazaki, Y. Suga, A. Yamazak, P. Luff, and C. Heath. Mediating Dual Ecologies. In Proceedings of CSCW 2004.

18. JazzMutant Lemur. http://www.jazzmutant.com/lemur_overview.php.

19. J. Letessier and F. Berard. Visual Tracking of Bare Fingers for Interactive Surfaces. In UIST 2004.

20. Shahzad Malik and Joe Laszlo. Visual Touch-pad: A Two-handed Gestural Input Device. In ICMI 2004.

21. Microsoft Surface, http://www.surface.com

22. John Platt. Probabilities for Support Vector Machines. Advances in Margin Classifiers, pages 61–74, 1999.

23. J. Rekimoto. SmartSkin: an infrastructure for freehand manipulation on interactive surfaces. In CHI 2002.

24. Y. Rogers and S. Lindley. Collaborating around vertical and horizontal displays:which way is best? In Interacting With Computers, pages 1133–1152, 2004.

25. K. Ryall et al. Exploring the Effects of Group Size and Table Size on Interactions with Tabletop Shared-Display Groupware. In CSCW 2004, pages 284–293.

26. S. D. Scott, K. D. Grant, and R. L. Mandryk. System Guidelines for Co-located, Collaborative Work on a Tabletop Display. In Proceedings of ECSCW, 2003.

27. Tactex Controls Inc. Array Sensors. http://www.tactex.com/products_array.php.

28. TactaPad. http://www.tactiva.com/tactapad.html.

29. Tang, A., Neustaedter, C. and Greenberg, S. VideoArms: Embodiments for Mixed Presence Groupware. In BCS-HCI 2006.

30. Tang, John C. Findings from Observational Studies of Collaborative Work. International Journal of Man-Machine Studies, 34(2):143–160, 1991.

31. Tang, John C. and Scott L. Minneman. VideoDraw: A Video Interface for Collaborative Drawing. In Proceedings of CHI, pages 313–320, 1990.

32. Tuddenham, P. Distributed tabletops: territoriality and orientation in distributed collaboration. In CHI '07 Extended Abstracts.

33. V. Vapnik. The Nature of Statistical Learning Theory. Springer, 1995.

34. Pierre Wellner. Interacting with Paper on the Digital Desk. Communications of the ACM, 36(7):86–96, 1993.

35. Wayne Westerman. Hand Tracking, Finger Identification and Chordic Manipulation on a Multi-Touch Surface. In PhD dissertation, University of Delaware, 1999.

36. Andrew D. Wilson, 2004. TouchLight: An Imaging Touch Screen. In ICMI 2004.

37. Andrew D. Wilson. PlayAnywhere: A Compact Interactive Tabletop Projection-Vision System. In Proceedings of UIST, 2005.

38. Andrew D. Wilson and D. Robbins. PlayTogether: Playing Games across Multiple Interactive Tabletops. 2007.

39. Wren, C. and Ivanov Y, Volumetric Operations with Surface Margins, In CVPR 2004.

40. Wu, M. et al. Multi-finger and whole hand gestural techniques for tabletop displays. In UIST 2003.

T3: Rapid Prototyping of High-Resolution and Mixed-Presence Tabletop Applications

Philip Tuddenham and Peter Robinson
University of Cambridge Computer Laboratory
15 JJ Thomson Avenue, Cambridge CB3 0FD, UK
{firstname}.{lastname}@cl.cam.ac.uk

Abstract

Multi-person tabletop applications that require a high display resolution, such as collaborative web-browsing, are currently very difficult to create. Tabletop systems that support mixed-presence collaboration, where some collaborators are remote, are also hard to build. As a consequence, investigation of some important tabletop applications has been rather limited. In this paper, we present T3, a software toolkit that addresses these challenges. T3 allows researchers to rapidly create high-resolution multi-person tabletop applications for co-located or remote collaborators. It uses multiple projectors to create a single seamless high-resolution tabletop display, and allows multiple tabletops to be connected together to support mixed-presence collaboration. This engineering is hidden behind a simple, flexible API. T3 also supports existing user interface components, including buttons and spreadsheets, allowing the rapid creation of complex tabletop applications.

1. Introduction

In recent years, interactive tabletop interfaces have emerged as a key tool for co-located collaboration over digital artifacts. Yet, in spite of much promising research, there has been little investigation of tabletop interfaces to support the collaborative tasks for which people currently use their desktop computers, such as collaborative web browsing, spreadsheets and document review. These are compelling applications to which tabletop interfaces may bring significant benefits. However, this area remains largely unexplored because, with very few exceptions, the display resolution of today's tabletop interfaces is too low to support such applications.

A further area that remains largely unexplored is the extension of tabletop interfaces to remote groups of collaborators. In this mixed-presence setting, each remote group would sit at its own tabletop. As shown in Figure 1, all the tabletops would then be linked together to provide a shared workspace for collaboration in which collaborators could interact with, position and orient digital artifacts. All the tabletops would show the same artifacts, along with remote embodiments (such as arm shadows) of the participants. Such a system could well offer remote collaborators some of the benefits of tabletop interaction, such as a greater awareness of each other's actions, and space to explore both personal and group work [13], both longstanding problems in conventional groupware. However, despite promising early results, investigation of these mixed-presence systems has been rather limited [16, 7, 4].

The significance of these two gaps in the research should not be underestimated. If we are truly to believe that these interfaces will be adopted then we must begin to explore the benefits that tabletop interfaces can offer over and above conventional physical tabletops.

Recent tabletop research has been fuelled by software toolkits that address the core engineering involved, allowing researchers to concentrate on interaction techniques and applications. As we shall show, the reason for these two gaps in the research is that these kinds of systems pose unique engineering challenges that cannot easily be solved using today's toolkits. From our own experiences, and from discussions at a workshop [17], we know that it is presently very difficult for researchers to overcome these issues.

In this paper we present T3, a software toolkit that we have implemented to address these problems. It uses multiple projectors to create a single seamless high-resolution tabletop display, and allows multiple tabletops to be connected together. T3 allows researchers to rapidly prototype high-resolution tabletop interfaces for applications such as collaborative spreadsheets and collaborative web-browsing, both for co-located and mixed-presence collaboration. It is freely available for academic research and will allow rapid exploration of this field. Furthermore, through our experiences, we have been able to investigate the challenges in creating these interfaces.

0-7695-3013-3/07 $25.00 © 2007 IEEE
DOI 10.1109/TABLETOP.2007.16

In the next section, we review recent work to identify the challenges in engineering these applications and establish design goals for our work. We then present T3, showing how it meets these goals, and outline a simple worked example. We illustrate its utility through five novel research projects and conclude by discussing its limitations.

2. Background and Design Goals

2.1. Tabletop Collaboration

A great number of projects have investigated various aspects of tabletop interfaces for co-located collaboration [e.g. 15]. Much of the work has been possible because of reusable software toolkits, notably DiamondSpin [14], and the more recent Buffer Framework [6], that handle the core engineering such as:

- Allowing collaborators to arbitrarily position and orient digital artifacts, and groups of digital artifacts.
- Allowing multiple users to interact concurrently.
- Supporting direct interaction using bare-hands or stylus.

DiamondSpin is particularly useful because it allows researchers to rapidly prototype complex tabletop applications by reusing existing Java Swing user interface components, such as buttons and file choosers. This feature is essential if we are to investigate complex applications such as collaborative spreadsheets or web-browsing, because it is not within the scope of a research project to engineer such applications from scratch.

The Buffer Framework demonstrates a novel architecture that provides responsive performance when hundreds of digital artifacts appear on the tabletop. Unfortunately, it does not allow the reuse of existing user interface components, and so creating new applications is difficult.

2.2. Higher-Resolution Displays

The key problem in supporting applications such as collaborative web-browsing or spreadsheets, is in creating a

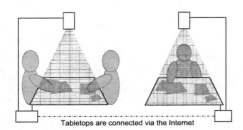

Figure 1: Mixed-presence collaboration.

display surface with a sufficiently high resolution. In order to use the unique affordances of tabletop collaboration, we wish each web-page or spreadsheet to appear no larger than an ordinary sheet of paper, so that they can be passed between collaborators as one might with paper documents. However, to accomplish this, we need to be able to legibly display small text and user interface components, which is impossible on most of today's tabletop displays.

We aimed to display 12pt text legibly (i.e. text that appears the same size as 12pt text that comes out of the printer). We have found that this requires a resolution of at least 60dpi, so that a fairly modest 85cm × 85cm table requires a 4 Megapixel display. By contrast, almost all today's tabletop displays provide at most 2.6 Megapixels using at most two projectors.

Higher-resolution projectors are extremely expensive and unsuitable. By far the easiest way to create a higher-resolution display using is to tile multiple projectors. For example, we have tiled 6 projectors to create a 4.7 Megapixel display using modest, inexpensive equipment. Such multi-projector designs are commonplace in the display walls used in visualisation research. However, tiling introduces further problems.

Firstly, the huge number of pixels and multiple graphics outputs can lead to unresponsive applications if a naïve rendering architecture is used. Secondly, it can be very difficult to align the projectors to the degree of precision required for a seamless display, and so these displays can suffer from small overlaps, mismatches and keystoning. Even using the precision mechanical alignment mountings that have been designed for this purpose, aligning 6 projectors to the required accuracy is time-consuming, requires careful engineering, and often relies on rear-projection, which precludes the use of some direct-touch and stylus technologies.

Large multi-projector display wall systems address both of these issues. Hardware-acceleration and selective updating speeds up the rendering process, using commodity graphics cards and interfaces such as OpenGL. These systems also automatically compensate for small projector misalignments by applying small adjustment transformations and blending masks to each frame before it is sent to the projectors [9, 18, 1]. These adjustments are usually calculated using a quick calibration procedure, avoiding the need for precise mechanical alignment. Unfortunately, these display wall toolkits are not designed to afford tabletop interaction or rapid prototyping; they typically do not, for example, support rotation of artifacts.

The DiamondSpin toolkit is unlikely to extend easily to a multi-projector tiled display. It does not yet use hardware-accelerated rendering, so performance would be limited, and there is not scope to add adjustment transformations or blending masks. By contrast, the Buffer Framework uses

OpenGL rendering, performed well on a 4 projector tiled display using mechanical alignment, and could easily be modified to support adjustment transformations and masks.

2.3. Mixed-Presence Collaboration

We also wish to investigate mixed-presence collaboration, whereby two geographically-separated tabletops are linked together to allow two remote groups to collaborate as though co-located around the same tabletop. Prior research in this area has investigated mixed-presence drawing surfaces [e.g. 16] and tangible interfaces [e.g. 2, 19].

There has, however, been little mixed-presence investigation of applications in which collaborators interact with, position and orient digital artifacts like spreadsheets or text documents. TIDL [7] and RemoteDT [4] both allow mixed-presence collaborators to position and interact with digital artifacts on large horizontal displays (much as GroupKit [10] does for remote collaborators on conventional desktop computer interfaces). However, none of these systems allow collaborators to reorient artifacts. Orientation serves several important roles in co-located tabletop collaboration, such as allowing transitions between personal and group work [13, 8], and it should not be overlooked when designing mixed-presence tabletop systems.

Creating a mixed presence system that allows participants to reorient artifacts is desirable but technically difficult: firstly because standard remote display protocols are not designed to handle artifact rotation; and also because the existing tabletop toolkits, DiamondSpin and Buffer Framework, cannot easily be extended to support mixed-presence collaboration. The very recent DigiTable work [3] supports mixed-presence tabletop collaboration, including orientation, remote arm shadows and existing Java Swing components but is not widely available and, to our knowledge, does not support multiple projectors, precluding high-resolution applications.

2.4. Design Goals

Having reviewed the literature, we now establish several design goals. The system should:

- provide abstractions to support the core tabletop interaction functionality provided by other tabletop toolkits, such as rotation of artifacts. Such requirements have been discussed in prior work [11, 14], and in Section 2.1 we have enumerated the most salient given the space available.
- allow creation of higher-resolution tabletops by supporting multiple projectors in a tiled array, using hardware-accelerated rendering for performance, and applying small transformations and masks to create the illusion of a seamless display.

	Diamond Spin	Buffer F'work	Display walls	TIDL/ RemoteDT	DigiTables	T3
Tabletop interaction (e.g. rotation, etc.)	✓	✓			✓	✓
Higher-resolution		✓	✓			✓
Two linked surfaces (mixed-presence)			Some	✓	✓	✓
Reuse existing UI components	✓		✓	✓	✓	✓

Table 1: Comparing tools and design goals.

- allow geographically-separated tabletops to be connected together to create a shared workspace for mixed-presence tabletop applications.
- allow researchers to rapidly create complex tabletop applications like spreadsheets by reusing existing user interface components.

Table 1 summarises our design goals and the limitations of existing tools.

3. The T3 Toolkit

Having established these design goals, we now provide a brief overview of the T3 architecture, followed by a description of each component, example applications, and a discussion of the implementation.

Figure 2 outlines the T3 architecture. Applications are created using a simple, well-documented Java API. The API is based around the notion of a single seamless large display, in which the application programmer can create rectangular tiles to represent interactive draggable digital artifacts such as spreadsheets or web-pages. The application programmer uses T3 to arbitrarily position and orient the tiles within a single large coordinate space.

Importantly, tiles can be filled with existing Java Swing user interface components, which function as expected without any extra code required on the part of the applications programmer. This includes buttons and text boxes, and even third-party components such as spreadsheets and web-browsers, allowing rapid creation of complex applications. T3 works behind the scenes to ensure that the application programmer is never required to consider the effects of tile rotation or scale, nor how to distribute the information to multiple tabletops, nor multi-projector blending techniques, nor simultaneous input event streams.

Each multi-projector tabletop display is controlled by a local computer running a T3 client. This client communicates with the application, receiving tile updates and sending back user input events. If desired, multiple clients can connect to the same application via the Internet to allow

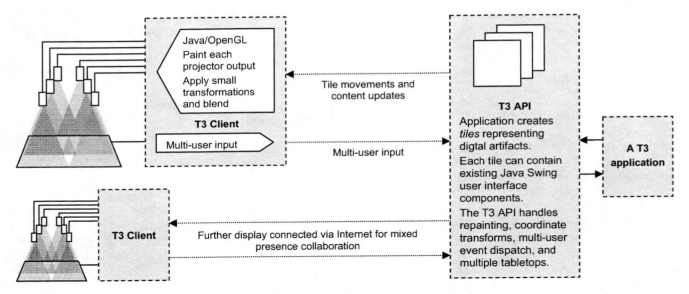

Figure 2: T3 system architecture to support multi-projector tabletops and mixed-presence collaboration.

mixed-presence collaboration, as proposed in the Introduction. The client automatically creates the correct images to send to each of the projectors in the multi-projector display. It positions and orients the tiles, applying small warps and masks to correct for projector misalignment and create the illusion of a single seamless display.

3.1. Physical Apparatus

T3 is easily configurable to support any number of projectors connected to a single PC. We have created three tabletop displays:

- Six projectors and a single 2.4GHz PC with three NVIDIA GeForce 7600 dual-head graphics cards to create a 4.7 Megapixel display.
- Four projectors and a single PC with two dual-head graphics cards to create a 5.7 Megapixel display.
- One projector to create a 0.8 Megapixel display.

All the components are available off-the-shelf, and neither multi-projector display cost more than $13,000, including mountings. We have tested the toolkit using 3 brands of graphics cards. For multi-user input, we use standard graphics tablet styluses and Anoto streaming styluses, and the system could easily be extended to multi-touch surfaces.

3.2. API and Swing Applications

The application programmer creates tiles by instantiating T3's tile class. The programmer specifies how each tile should be positioned, rotated and scaled on the tabletop by specifying coordinates and dimensions in millimetres, and an angle in radians. Collaborators move tiles around the display surface by dragging with their stylus using Rotate 'N' Translate [8]. The application programmer determines which tiles are draggable and can group tiles so that they are then dragged together, allowing creation of mobile container elements like Storage Bins [12].

Each tile functions as a Java Swing window in which existing user interface components can be used without any modification required, as we illustrate later with a worked example (Section 4). Multiple collaborators can interact simultaneously to drag these tiles and manipulate the components within. The vast majority of Swing components work as expected without any modification, though components that use popup windows currently require special attention.

This mechanism works by opening the necessary Swing windows off-screen. Swing repaint events are then trapped by the T3 toolkit which renders the windows into images that are sent to the T3 clients. Similarly, user input events received from the T3 clients are translated into Swing input events and dispatched to the appropriate Swing window. T3 uses geometric transforms to determine the tile immediately "underneath" the event on the tabletop and then transforms the event from tabletop coordinates (in millimetres) into Swing window coordinates, "undoing" the effects of tile rotation, translation and scaling, similar to Diamond-Spin's transformation engine.

T3 also provides an alternative API to support more customised applications that avoid the constraints of Java Swing. This allows implementation of more complex designs like Storage Bins [12], and both APIs can be mixed within the same application to produce, for example, a Storage Bins design that supports web browsing using a Java Swing web browser component. In this alternative API,

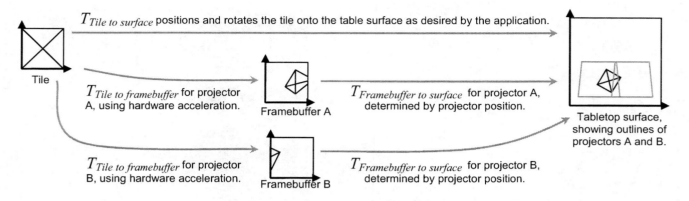

$T_{Tile\ to\ surface}$ positions and rotates the tile onto the table surface as desired by the application.

Tile

$T_{Tile\ to\ framebuffer}$ for projector A, using hardware acceleration.

Framebuffer A

$T_{Framebuffer\ to\ surface}$ for projector A, determined by projector position.

$T_{Tile\ to\ framebuffer}$ for projector B, using hardware acceleration.

Framebuffer B

$T_{Framebuffer\ to\ surface}$ for projector B, determined by projector position.

Tabletop surface, showing outlines of projectors A and B.

Figure 3: Transformations between coordinate spaces in the T3 client.

the application programmer simply overrides a paint routine and an input event processing routine for each tile.

T3 uses a multi-threaded architecture to handle the simultaneous input event streams from multiple users and multiple tabletops. This provides responsive performance and allows multiple collaborators to interact simultaneously to drag or manipulate tiles. The multi-threading and object locking are handled automatically by the toolkit.

Tiles are rectangular by default, but other shapes can be created by painting parts of the tile with transparent pixels. An ordering for the tiles determines occlusion when tiles overlap. T3 also provides a mechanism to smoothly animate groups of tiles between two specified positions and orientations, which can be used, for example, to zoom out to a thumbnail overview. A further mechanism allows the creation of translucent lines that join different tiles, which can be used, for example, to illustrate dependencies between artifacts.

3.3. Rendering and Performance

Each multi-projector display is controlled by a local T3 client, which receives tile information from the application, via the Internet if necessary, and performs the actual rendering.

The client uses OpenGL (via the JOGL library) to exploit hardware-accelerated rendering provided by modern graphics cards. Tile images are stored in the texture memory within each graphics card. The client then renders each frame for each projector by transforming tile images into the framebuffer. Figure 3 illustrates the transformations between the tile coordinate space, the frame buffer, and the display surface. The transformation, $T_{Tile\ to\ framebuffer}$ consists of two parts:

$$T_{Tile\ to\ framebuffer} = T^{-1}_{Framebuffer\ to\ surface} \cdot T_{Tile\ to\ surface}$$

The first part, $T_{Tile\ to\ surface}$, positions, scales and rotates the tile onto the display surface as desired by the ap-

plication. The second part, $T^{-1}_{Framebuffer\ to\ surface}$, is a small transformation that compensates for projector misalignment. It is obtained using a short calibration procedure, which calculates the relationship between points in the framebuffer and points on the display surface, and then performs a matrix inversion. As described previously, the misalignment problem is difficult to solve mechanically for high-resolution displays, and such software solutions are well understood in the display-wall community.

We have tested T3 using a range of applications (Section 4) using the 6-projector apparatus. In all cases, T3 performed responsively and achieved a frame rate of 60fps (the maximum rate supported by the projectors).

We have also tested T3 to the limits of its performance by filling the display with large numbers of draggable, partially overlapping, 100x100px images, all moving simultaneously along predetermined paths. Using the 6-projector apparatus, T3 achieved a frame rate of 40fps when animating 400 such images, and 30fps when animating 800 such images, and remained responsive throughout both tests. These results are similar to the reported performance of the Buffer Framework [6] in comparable tests, though precise comparisons are not possible.

3.4. Multiple Tabletops

The client and the application can run on the same computer to create a single high-resolution multi-projector tabletop interface. Alternatively, as described earlier, multiple clients can connect to the application via the Internet for mixed-presence tabletop collaboration. In this case, the clients and the server use a protocol to communicate tile content updates, tile movement and user input events.

This protocol is optimised so that the most frequent operations, such as dragging tiles, use low bandwidth and provide responsive performance. The system also uses a basic adaptive scheme to avoid overwhelming lower-performing clients. We have tested our system using both a high speed

```
public static void main(String[] a) throws Exception {

// Create a new tabletop, d.
PortfolioServer d = new PortfolioServer(
    new ServerSocket(2000),
    new ServerSocket(2001), false);

// create a new tile of 500*500 pixels on d
SwingFramePortfolio myTile = new SwingFramePortfolio(
    d, d.rootPortfolio, new RotateNTranslate(),
    500,500);

// add a JSpreadsheet and menu bar to the tile
myTile.getFrame().add( new JSpreadsheet(80,40) );
myTile.getFrame().setJMenuBar(menuBar);

// make the tile appear a physical size 200mm*200mm
myTile.setTileWidthAndHeightInPORT(200.0, 200.0);

// position the tile 300mm from the top and left of
// the tabletop, rotate it by 0.17 radians  and set
// scale factor 1.00.
myTile.setPORTtoPPORT(300.0, 300.0, 0.17, 1.00);

// make the tile visible
myTile.setVisibleWhenParentVisible(true);
}
```

Figure 4: Complete sample code (top) using T3 to create an editable tabletop spreadsheet (bottom) that appears on the multi-projector tabletop, can be passed using Rotate 'N' Translate and can be used in mixed-presence collaboration.

Figure 5: Collaborative web-browsing. Pages appear small yet legible, can be passed around the table (top) and browsed in a tree (bottom).

LAN and a lower bandwidth wireless network, and it performed responsively in both cases.

In mixed-presence collaboration, we display remote embodiments on the tabletops in order to convey presence and to allow remote participants to gesture to each other. We currently use telepointer traces [5] that follow each participant's stylus . Traces are a starting point in our investigation of remote embodiments: they are easy to implement, allow rich gestures, and are robust to network jitter. They allow participants to convey shapes, routes and indicate groupings. However, they may not convey presence as well as alternative embodiments such as arm shadows [16].

4. T3 Applications

We now describe a range of projects that rely on T3 to explore new tabletop applications. The projects are all being undertaken by five students in our Laboratory.

Worked Example. Figure 4 illustrates a short program that creates a tile and fills it with a third party Swing JSpreadsheet component. The result is a working tabletop spreadsheet application. The spreadsheet appears as a legible rectangular 20cm × 20cm tile on the table. It is sufficiently small that multiple spreadsheets can be viewed simultaneously by collaborators around the table, and can be passed between collaborators using the Rotate 'N' Translate technique. Columns and rows can be selected, and formulae can be entered into cells. Without requiring modification of this program, mixed presence collaborators can connect over the Internet and can similarly interact with the spreadsheet. Further development will allow participants to collaborate over multiple interdependent worksheets to perform different analyses of the same data set.

Collaborative Web-Browsing. A second project investigates finding and sharing information from the web (Figure 5). The high-resolution capability of T3 allows web pages to appear legible yet sufficiently small that multiple collaborators can each read their own pages and pass them around. T3 also allows us to reuse a third party Java Swing web browser component for rapid development; the basic tabletop web browsing application was implemented by a student in 60 lines of Java in around 1 hour. Collaborators can open web pages, follow links, and pass pages between each other.

Remote Document Review Meetings. Our third project investigates mixed-presence document review meetings, in which remote collaborators discuss and collaboratively an-

Figure 6: Remote review meetings using T3. Documents containing size 12pt text can be read (top-left), browsed (top-right), and used for remote collaboration (bottom).

Figure 7: Mixed-presence command and control interfaces using T3. Two co-located participants (left) collaborate with a remote participant (right).

notate draft text documents. Our interface allows multi-page text documents to appear rather like an open book on the tabletop (Figure 6). We use the high-resolution feature of T3 to project legible text at size 12pt. The interface allows remote collaborators to use styluses to pass documents to each other, to browse within a document using a thumbnail view, and to annotate pages. T3 allowed us to rapidly create the interface, which was implemented by a graduate student in 650 lines of Java in around three days.

Command and Control Interfaces. A further student project uses T3 to investigate map-based command and control tasks, comparing co-located collaboration to mixed-presence collaboration (Figure 7). T3 has allowed us to create a single interface and then switch easily between co-located collaboration and mixed-presence collaboration to conduct the study.

Large-Format Collaborative Programming Interfaces.

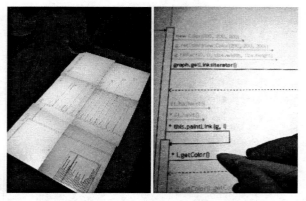

Figure 8: Interactive UML sequence diagrams with annotations using T3.

Students have used T3's high-resolution capabilities to generate interactive tabletop UML diagrams annotated with source code (Figure 8).

5. Discussion and Conclusions

At the outset of this paper, we highlighted two important areas of tabletop research that remain largely unexplored: applications that require higher-resolution displays, such as collaborative web-browsing; and mixed-presence applications, whereby geographically-separated tabletops are linked together. We showed that such applications are particularly difficult for researchers to create, because they present engineering problems that are not addressed by existing tools. By integrating recent research from co-located tabletop interfaces, multi-projector display walls and distributed groupware, T3 goes a significant way towards addressing these problems.

T3 addresses the core engineering required to use multi-projector displays and to connect remote tabletops together. However, it nevertheless provides a simple, flexible API that allows researchers to rapidly prototype new tabletop applications, without having to consider the engineering realities of multi-projector transformations or distributed rendering. Existing Java Swing user interface components, including buttons and spreadsheets, can be used without modification, allowing researchers to rapidly create complex applications. We have shown that T3 achieves responsive performance in a variety of applications, even when animating hundreds of digital artifacts.

We believe that the combination of these features will enable novel tabletop research that has not previously been possible. For example, the combination of high-resolution, tabletop interaction and complex applications allows rapid prototyping of tabletop web browsing interfaces. Similarly, mixed-presence collaboration and tabletop interaction permits interfaces in which mixed-presence collaborators can reorient artifacts, a behaviour which serves important awareness roles in co-located collaboration.

The ability to reuse existing Java Swing user interface components, such as buttons and spreadsheets, is not without its limitations. The components are designed only for a single user and so, for example, in our tabletop spreadsheets it is not possible for two users to simultaneously select two different columns within the same spreadsheet. Furthermore, we do not believe that applications designed for a single user at a desktop PC are by themselves sufficient to support tabletop collaboration. Nevertheless, the ability to use existing components will undoubtedly lead to rapid development of more complex tabletop applications, such as collaborative web-browsing. T3 also supports more radical application designs by providing an alternative API that is not constrained by Java Swing.

Tabletop research has advanced considerably over the last 8 years, and we would be foolish to think that the abstractions provided by T3 are by themselves sufficient to support the tabletop interaction techniques of the future. Nevertheless, we have illustrated the versatility of T3 with a wide range of applications, and we believe that it will be of utility to researchers wishing to explore these new areas. We believe that T3 could be used to implement the vast majority of today's tabletop applications, and we expect the abstractions to develop over time to reflect new research.

T3 is freely available to academic researchers, along with documentation and example applications, at http://www.cl.cam.ac.uk/t3/.

Acknowledgements

We gratefully acknowledge the support of Rowan Hill, Tom Matthews, Richard Russell and Stephen Williams, who are undertaking projects using T3; members of the Rainbow Group and the anonymous reviewers, for useful comments; and Thales Research and Technology (UK) and the EPSRC, who jointly funded this work.

References

[1] Ashdown, M., Flagg, M., Sukthankar, R., and Rehg, J. A flexible projector-camera system for multi-planar displays. In *Proc. Conf. Computer Vision and Pattern Recognition (CVPR) 2004*, vol. 2, 165–172.

[2] Brave, S., Ishii, H., and Dahley, A. Tangible Interfaces for Remote Collaboration and Communication In *Proc. CSCW 1998*, 169–178.

[3] Coldefy, F. and Louis-dit-Picard, S. DigiTable: an interactive multiuser table for collocated and remote collaboration enabling remote gesture visualization. In *Proc. PROCAMS 2007*.

[4] Esenther, A., and Ryall, K., RemoteDT: Support for Multi-Site Table Collaboration. In *Proc. Int. Conf. Collaboration Technologies (CollabTech)*, 2006.

[5] Gutwin, C. and Penner, R. Improving interpretation of remote gestures with telepointer traces. In *Proc. CSCW 2002*, 49–57.

[6] Isenberg, T., Miede, A., and Carpendale, S. A buffer framework for supporting responsive interaction in information visualization interfaces. In *Proc. Int. Conf. Creating, Connecting and Collaborating through Computing (C5'06)*, IEEE Computer Society (2006), 262–269.

[7] Hutterer, P., Close, B. S., and Thomas, B. H. Supporting Mixed Presence Groupware in Tabletop Applications In *Proc. TABLETOP'06*, 63–70.

[8] Kruger, R., Carpendale, S., Scott, S.D., and Tang, A. Fluid integration of rotation and translation. In *Proc. CHI 2005*, 601–610.

[9] Li, K., Chen, H., Chen, Y., Clark, D.W., Cook, P., Damianakis, S., Essl, G., Finkelstein, A., Funkhouser, T., Housel, T., Klein, A., Liu, Z., Praun, E., Samanta, R., Shedd, B., Singh, J.P., Tzanetakis, G., and Zheng, J. Building and using a scalable display wall system. *IEEE Comp. Graphics and Applications 20*, 4 (2000), 29–37.

[10] Roseman, M. and Greenberg, S. Building Real Time Groupware with GroupKit, A Groupware Toolkit. *ACM Trans. Comp. Human Interaction 3*, 1 (1996), 66–106.

[11] Scott, S., Grant, K., and Mandryk, R. System guidelines for co-located collaborative work on a tabletop display. In *Proc. ECSCW 2003*, 2003.

[12] Scott, S.D., Carpendale, M.S.T., and Habelski, S. Storage bins: Mobile storage for collaborative tabletop displays. *IEEE Comp. Graphics and Applications 25*, 4 (2005), 58–65.

[13] Scott, S.D., Carpendale, M.S.T., and Inkpen, K.M. Territoriality in collaborative tabletop workspaces. In *Proc. CSCW 2004*, 294–303.

[14] Shen, C., Vernier, F.D., Forlines, C., and Ringel, M. Diamondspin: an extensible toolkit for around-the-table interaction. In *Proc. CHI 2004*, 167–174.

[15] Shen, C., Ryall, K., Forlines, C., Esenther, A., Vernier, F.D., Everitt, K., Wu, M., Wigdor, D., Ringel Morris, M., Hancock, M., and Tse, E. Informing the Design of Direct-Touch Tabletops *IEEE Comp. Graphics and Applications 26*, 5 (2006), 36–46.

[16] Tang, A., Boyle, M., and Greenberg, S. Understanding and mitigating display and presence disparity in mixed presence groupware. *J. Res. and Practice in Inf. Tech. 37*, 2.

[17] Terrenghi, L., May, R., Baudisch, P., MacKay, W., Paterno, F., Thomas, J., and Billinghurst, M. Information visualization and interaction techniques for collaboration across multiple displays. In *Ext. Abstr. CHI '06*, 1643–1646.

[18] Wallace, G., Anshus, O.J., Bi, P., Chen, H., Chen, Y., Clark, D., Cook, P., Finkelstein, A., Funkhouser, T., Gupta, A., Hibbs, M., Li, K., Liu, Z., Samanta, R., Sukthankar, R., and Troyanskaya, O. Tools and applications for large-scale display walls. *IEEE Comp. Graphics and Applications 25*, 4 (2005), 24–33.

[19] Wilson, A. D., and Robbins, D. C. PlayTogether: Playing Games across Multiple Interactive Tabletops *IUI'07 workshop on Tangible Play*.

Distributed Tabletops: Supporting Remote and Mixed-Presence Tabletop Collaboration

Philip Tuddenham and Peter Robinson
University of Cambridge Computer Laboratory
15 JJ Thomson Avenue, Cambridge CB3 0FD, UK
{firstname}.{lastname}@cl.cam.ac.uk

Abstract

Mixed-presence tabletop interfaces aim to support collaboration between remote groups. However, it is unclear why tabletop interaction techniques should be important for mixed-presence or remote collaboration, and recent projects in this area differ as to which elements of tabletop interaction they choose to support. In this paper we discuss the benefits of tabletop interaction for mixed-presence and remote collaboration. In particular, we wish to support the natural tabletop awareness mechanisms of territoriality, orientation and consequential communication. We derive design guidelines for such systems and present Distributed Tabletops, a novel system that can be customised to investigate various mixed-presence tasks. Our early observations of Distributed Tabletops in use validate our design guidelines.

1. Introduction

Interactive tabletop interfaces have emerged as an effective tool for co-located collaboration over digital artifacts. Collaborators sit around a horizontal multi-touch surface that displays digital artifacts such as photos, documents and web pages. They can then interact simultaneously to move, reorient and manipulate the artifacts, as they might with paper artifacts on a conventional tabletop.

Several recent projects have investigated the possibility of linking together geographically-separated tabletop displays in order to create a shared workspace for remote collaboration [1, 5, 9, 3]. Each of the geographically-separated collaborators sits at his or her own tabletop display. The displays are then linked, perhaps via the Internet, so that these remote collaborators can each interact with the shared artifacts and see each other's actions, as if co-located around the same tabletop.

Previous efforts to support remote collaboration over digital artifacts had tended to use conventional monitor- and mouse-based interaction to create shared workspaces, but this approach encountered well-documented problems [4, 6, 7]. For instance, on a conventional monitor there is often insufficient space for collaborators to work in different parts of the workspace without losing an awareness of each other's actions. Large horizontal displays and tabletop interaction techniques might allow these problems to be overcome, so that remote collaborators can communicate as though sat around the same table. Furthermore, by using multi-touch surfaces at each remote site, we can also support collaboration between geographically-separated groups of collaborators, namely mixed-presence collaboration [23].

The recent remote tabletop collaboration projects have set out to investigate these issues but, surprisingly, some important questions remain unanswered:

- Why might tabletop interaction, so effective for co-located collaborators, be similarly appropriate for remote and mixed-presence collaboration?

- Which elements of co-located tabletop collaboration are important for remote and mixed presence tabletop collaboration? Some recent remote tabletop collaboration projects differ on this issue and, for instance, very few systems allow remote collaborators to reorient digital artifacts as they can in the majority of co-located tabletop systems.

- What additional factors must be considered in the design of tabletop systems for mixed-presence collaboration, as opposed to just remote collaboration?

In the first half of this paper we review literature (Section 2) and discuss the above questions in the context of prior work (Section 3). In particular, we believe that supporting natural tabletop awareness mechanisms of orientation, territoriality and consequential communication will greatly benefit remote and mixed-presence tabletop collaboration, and we suggest design guidelines for achieving these goals.

0-7695-3013-3/07 $25.00 © 2007 IEEE
DOI 10.1109/TABLETOP.2007.15

We then present *Distributed Tabletops*, a novel system that we have created, following these guidelines, to support remote and mixed-presence collaboration over digital artifacts (Section 4). By using direct input mechanisms, preserving a co-located-style seating arrangement among distributed collaborators, allowing them to move and orient artifacts, and projecting remote arm embodiments, Distributed Tabletops supports the natural awareness mechanisms posed above. We report our early experiences with Distributed Tabletops and discuss the design trade-offs in such systems (Section 5).

2. Background

Systems for synchronous collaboration (i.e. where all participants collaborate at the same time) traditionally support either co-located collaboration or remote collaboration. Mixed-presence groupware is a recent addition to this dichotomy [23] and must support both. This paper draws on work in each of these areas.

2.1. Co-located Collaboration

Single Display Groupware (SDG) [21] describes systems that allow co-located collaborators, each with their own input device, to interact simultaneously using a shared display. Tabletop interfaces are a form of SDG that use a large horizontal display and multi-user direct input mechanisms such as styluses or a multi-touch surface. Early systems [e.g. 22] took inspiration both from augmented paper, such as Wellner's DigitalDesk [30], and studies of co-located tabletop collaboration [26]. Recent research focuses on studies of human behaviour [e.g. 12, 19, 17] that can inform tabletop interaction techniques [e.g. 13].

2.2. Remote Collaboration using Monitor/Mouse Systems

In these systems, each remote collaborator uses their own conventional desktop computer. The computers are then linked to create a shared workspace for remote collaboration. Such systems tend to be characterized by a lack of awareness among collaborators about each other's actions in the workspace, with collaboration suffering as a result [6, 7, 4]. The problem is particularly acute in systems in which each collaborator can manipulate their view of the workspace independently of others, for example to scroll to a different region of the workspace. Some of these awareness problems seem rooted in the combination of small display and impoverished input and remote embodiments that characterize these systems. Another area of research has taken an alternative approach using large-format displays.

2.3. Remote and Mixed-Presence Collaboration on Large Displays

In large-format remote collaboration systems, each remote collaborator uses their own large display, either horizontal or vertical, usually with direct input mechanisms (styluses or touch). The displays are then linked together to provide a shared workspace for remote collaboration.

The earliest such systems were shared drawing surfaces, such as VideoWhiteboard [27]. Remote collaborators could interact simultaneously to sketch, while shadows of their arms and bodies were projected onto the remote workspace to allow gesture and to maintain awareness and a sense of presence. Clearboard [10] additionally allowed collaborators to make eye contact "through" the drawing surface. Tang et al. [23, 24] used a shared drawing surface to investigate remote embodiments in mixed-presence collaboration.

Other projects investigated remote collaboration over tangible artifacts using a similar approach. DoubleDigitalDesk [30] was an early such system for remote collaboration over paper documents on desks. A camera mounted above each surface captured an image of the tangible artifacts and the user's arms; this image was then projected onto the remote collaborator's surface. More recent systems use similar techniques for collaboration over paper documents [14], board games and sketching [33], single physical objects [31], and collaborative physical tasks [11].

In these tangible remote collaboration systems, a given artifact is only ever tangible for one collaborator; other collaborators see mere video projections and cannot interact directly. This effect is unavoidable, even desirable, in tasks such as remote bomb disposal, but can be problematic in other domains. Brave et al. [2] present an alternative approach whereby each remote collaborator has a complete set of tangible artifacts. When the system senses that a user has moved an artifact, local actuators move the corresponding artifact on the remote collaborators' displays. In practice, however, this approach constrains collaboration.

This has led to systems that use purely digital artifacts to investigate large format displays for remote collaboration, for tasks other than sketching, and without the asymmetry problem of remote tangible systems. Escritoire [1], RemotEDT [5], ViCAT/TIDL [9] and the very recent DigiTable work [3] all address technical challenges in this area. They present each remote collaborator with a shared workspace of movable interactive digital artifacts on a large horizontal display, rather like co-located tabletop interfaces. For instance, Escritoire is designed for remote collaboration over images that can be arranged using styluses, while RemotEDT and TIDL both support legacy applications in mixed-presence collaboration using, respectively, a multitouch surface and multiple mice.

These remote tabletop projects take inspiration from co-located tabletop research, but are selective about the elements that they adopt. For instance, orientation serves key roles in co-located tabletop collaboration, as we shall discuss later, and yet only DigiTable allows collaborators to reorient digital artifacts. We were also surprised to find that none of these works justify their decisions about supporting orientation. Similarly, all these systems allow remote collaborators to share the same virtual "seat" at the table, without explaining this decision, and yet this situation would never occur in co-located tabletop collaboration. We shall further discuss these projects later in the paper.

3. Designing for Mixed-Presence and Remote Tabletop Collaboration

As we have seen, recent attempts to create mixed-presence tabletop collaboration systems have differed as to which characteristics of co-located tabletop collaboration they choose to support, and why these might be relevant to remote collaboration. We begin by enumerating the salient characteristics of co-located tabletop collaboration over digital artifacts in order to discuss the relevance of each to mixed-presence and remote collaboration.

3.1. Co-located Tabletop Interaction

We draw on observational studies of tabletop collaboration [26, 12, 19], requirements for tabletop collaboration [18] and various tabletop interfaces [e.g. 20, 13]. We aimed to avoid focusing on particular tasks by choosing characteristics of collaboration around digital artifacts, regardless of what the artifacts actually represent. We enumerate the characteristics as follows:

- A large horizontal display surface.
- Collaborators sit in different positions around the edge of the surface.
- Direct input mechanisms (stylus or touch).
- Digital artifacts can be moved and freely reoriented.
- Collaborators can see each other's arms.
- Simultaneous interaction by multiple collaborators.
- Collaborators can see each other's bodies and faces.
- Collaborators can talk to each other.

Allowing collaborators to talk to each other and to interact simultaneously is clearly important for any kind of collaboration, and does not warrant discussion.

Supporting adequately the ability of remote collaborators and mixed-presence collaborators to see each other's faces and postures is technically challenging. Work in this area has only recently shown promising results [16]. Though desirable, it is outside the scope of this research.

The remaining characteristics (the first five) are essential for three natural tabletop awareness mechanisms that are central to co-located tabletop collaboration: territoriality; orientation of artifacts; and consequential communication. We now discuss in turn the relevance of each of these mechanisms to remote tabletop collaboration.

3.2. Territoriality

Tse et al. [28] studied spatial partitioning in SDG applications using conventional monitor/mouse interaction and found that collaborators used spatial partitioning to avoid interfering with each other's actions. Scott et al. [19] observed that co-located collaborators naturally partition the space on a tabletop to serve different roles:

- A personal territory is the area directly in front of a collaborator. It allows them to reserve a particular area of the table for themselves. They can then use it as a place to reserve artifacts for themselves and to conduct individual work as part of the group task. People also monitor the progress of work in the personal territories of their collaborators.
- Group territory occupies space that isn't considered personal territory. It is used for the main group task and also to transfer artifacts, for example to signal availability by depositing them there.
- A storage territory is an area in which collaborators store and organize artifacts into related groups or piles.

Territoriality can be considered a natural awareness mechanism that allows participants to reserve resources for themselves and to transition between individual and group work during a collaborative task. This is particularly important in *mixed focus tasks*, which require people to transition frequently between individual and group work to complete the task [6, 7]. By contrast, monitor/mouse remote collaboration systems perform badly in these mixed-focus tasks because it is difficult for collaborators to accomplish individual work while also maintaining an awareness of each others actions. For instance, for many tasks, the screen is not large enough to allow two collaborators to work side by side on different parts of the workspace and so collaborators must scroll their views of the workspace independently, losing an awareness of each other's actions [6, 7].

The large physical size of remote and mixed-presence tabletops may go some way to solving these problems, but we believe that if such systems are truly to permit both individual and group work in the manner of co-located collaboration then they must support the corresponding awareness mechanisms, such as territoriality.

These remote and mixed-presence systems will therefore need to be sufficiently large to incorporate territories. Different collaborators will have to sit at different positions around the edge of the "virtual table" so that they each have space for a personal territory in the shared workspace. This "virtual seating arrangement" must mimic co-located seating arrangements and be preserved across the different connected tabletops if we are to promote a sense of spatial arrangement of people. Direct input mechanisms would ensure that even remote collaborators would have to reach across the table if they are to access artifacts in another collaborators' personal territory. Finally, all collaborators must be able to see each other's arm movements on the table in order to emphasise the seating arrangement and therefore the locations of the personal territories. For remote and mixed-presence collaboration, this could be accomplished by projecting arm shadows that extend from each collaborator's seat as a remote embodiment in a similar style to the systems reviewed earlier. Other remote embodiments, such as the telepointers, do not extend from the seat and hence do not emphasise the seating arrangement as we would desire.

3.3. Orientation of Artifacts

Kruger et al. [12] investigated the roles of artifact orientation in tabletop collaboration:

- Comprehension. People often orient artifacts to be most readable for themselves.
- Coordination. The orientation of an artifact indicates its ownership and availability. When people orient an artifact towards themselves it suggests that they have personal use of it. Collaborators can also establish personal and group territories by appropriately orienting artifacts in these spaces.
- Communication. Orienting an artifact to another person indicates that the artifact and accompanying talk and gestures are directed at that person, whereas orienting an artifact to yourself signals that you are doing personal work.

Hauber et al. [8] briefly discuss a remote tabletop system that allowed remote collaborators to position and orient digital photos as part of a wider study of presence. They report the use of orientation for comprehension, but, perhaps because of their task, not for coordination or communication.

Orientation is another natural awareness mechanism that allows participants to reserve resources for themselves and to transition between individual and group work; roles which, as we noted previously, should not be overlooked in the design of remote collaboration systems. Orientation also allows collaborators to establish an audience for their utterances, aiding turn-taking, a noted problem of group-to-group collaboration systems.

If remote and mixed-presence collaboration systems are to support orientation in the manner of co-located tabletops, then once again we need a consistent "virtual seating arrangement" among the connected tabletops so that artifacts that are oriented to one collaborator are not oriented to any other collaborators, co-located or remote. Collaborators must be able to reorient digital artifacts in the workspace, perhaps using a technique like Rotate 'N' Translate [13]. Use of direct input mechanisms and arm shadows would aid awareness of the seating arrangement and of who is orienting to whom.

3.4. Mixed-Presence Embodiments

If we are to support mixed-presence collaboration, as opposed to just remote collaboration, then we must address the associated human factors. In particular, naïve use of embodiments like telepointers leads to a disparity in the conversation dynamic whereby a user is much more likely to interact with their co-located collaborators than with their remote collaborators, with a negative effect on collaboration. Tang et al. [23, 24] observed the use of a mixed-presence whiteboard and show that richer embodiments, such as arm shadows, mitigate this effect. They review the roles played by physical bodies in collaboration and suggest that remote embodiments for mixed-presence collaboration should:

- Be controlled by direct input mechanisms and allow remote collaborators to interpret current actions and the actions that led up to them. By contrast, impoverished indirectly-controlled embodiments, such as telepointers, do not adequately convey the awareness information that is unintentionally communicated in co-located collaboration, such as arm position ("consequential communication").
- Allow remote collaborators to interpret gestures by capturing and rendering fine-grained movements and postures.
- Appear in the workspace in order to convey gestures as they relate to the workspace.
- Be visible not only to remote collaborators but also provide local feedback so that we might infer how our actions are interpreted by remote collaborators.

If we are to support mixed-presence collaboration without experiencing a conversation disparity then we must support rich arm shadow embodiments that follow these design guidelines, rather than impoverished telepointers.

3.5. Design Guidelines

Based on this analysis, we believe that by supporting natural tabletop awareness mechanisms like territoriality, orientation and consequential communication, remote and mixed-presence tabletops can provide effective support for both individual and group work. This addresses some of the

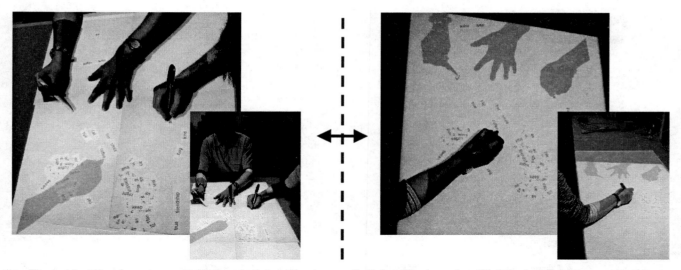

Figure 1: Mixed presence tabletop collaboration over digital artifacts using Distributed Tabletops. In this application, participants interact simultaneously to move and reorient the words to create poetry. Visible in the photos are arm shadows, personal territories, and artifacts at arbitrary orientations.

shortcomings of conventional monitor/mouse remote collaboration.

We have discussed ways in which remote or mixed-presence tabletops can support these mechanisms and we now summarise this with a series of design guidelines for such systems:

1. Large horizontal display surfaces.

2. Consistent "virtual seating arrangement" among the connected tables.

3. Direct input mechanisms (stylus or touch).

4. Digital artifacts can be moved and reoriented using a technique such as Rotate 'N' Translate [13].

5. Collaborators are represented remotely by arm shadow embodiments with local feedback.

6. Simultaneous interaction by multiple collaborators.

7. Collaborators can talk to each other.

Of the prior work, Escritoire [1], RemoteDT [5] and Vi-CAT/TIDL [9] do not support a consistent "virtual seating arrangement", arm shadow embodiments or reorientation. The very recent DigiTable work [3] does support these guidelines, but also has a feature that allows remote collaborators to violate the consistent seating arrangement. The rationale for the features we have highlighted is not discussed, beyond a need for remote embodiment, and the system is not evaluated, so we do not know whether it supports the awareness mechanisms we have drawn upon.

We now put these guidelines into practice to create Distributed Tabletops.

4. Distributed Tabletops

Distributed Tabletops is a prototype system that we have created, following our design guidelines, to investigate mixed-presence and remote tabletop collaboration over digital artifacts. In this section we present an overview, showing how the system addresses each of the design principles. We then briefly explain the implementation and describe our early observations of the system in use.

Figure 1 illustrates our Distributed Tabletops system. We connect two or more geographically-separated large horizontal displays, with multiple collaborators sat around each. Our system then links the displays so that they all display exactly the same contents at all times, creating a shared workspace for collaboration. Each collaborator has a stylus and can interact simultaneously with digital artifacts that are displayed. We use a reusable toolkit in order to support various tasks and artifacts, such as virtual puzzle pieces, virtual pages of text, or virtual spreadsheets. Unlike prior work in this area, participants sit at different locations around the edge of the "virtual table" and can use their styluses to move and reorient components using the Rotate 'N' Translate [13] technique, as they might at a co-located tabletop.

We use arm shadows as remote embodiments. A video camera mounted above each tabletop captures collaborators' arm gestures in the workspace. The system identifies the arm outlines, which are then displayed as translucent "shadows" on the other tables. The arm shadows are displayed in the correct place in the workspace and appear at the correct time with respect to artifact manipulations in the workspace. Collaborators also see their own arm shadows, to provide local feedback. All participants can gesture and interact with the workspace simultaneously.

The system supports a variety of artifacts and we chose to test a "magnetic poetry" task, in which collaborators create poetry by moving and reorienting words that appear as artifacts on the table. We chose this fairly simplistic task for a variety of reasons: interaction is constrained to just moving and reorienting, so there is little scope for problems; collaborators can carry out both individual work and group work in the context of the task; and there are many small artifacts, so it is easier to observe use of orientation and the roles of territory. Nevertheless, the natural awareness issues identified earlier are not only relevant to this simplistic task but also generalize to real-world tasks.

4.1. Implementation

Much of the necessary software infrastructure is encapsulated in our T3 software [29], which is freely available for academic research. T3 is a Java toolkit designed to allow two tabletop displays to be linked together in the manner described above. Each display is controlled by a local computer running the T3 client software, which performs the rendering and controls the Bluetooth Anoto styluses used by the local participants. All the clients connect to a central T3 server, which runs the actual application. All the clients receive update messages from the server about artifact location, size, orientation and contents, and send back user input messages detailing stylus position, etc.

T3 applications create rectangular artifacts which collaborators can move, orient and interact with using their styluses. T3 supports rapid prototyping by allowing creation of artifacts containing legacy Java Swing components such as buttons, web-browsers and spreadsheets. In order to support responsive rendering of oriented components, the T3 clients store the image of each artifact as an OpenGL texture, which can then be rendered into the framebuffer at the correct location and orientation using hardware-acceleration provided by commodity graphics cards.

On top of T3, we have added the functionality to extract arm outlines from video camera images, and to render them as translucent shadows on the workspace at each tabletop. A commodity webcam is positioned above each table and sends images to the local computer, which identifies the outlines of any arms present on the tabletop surface. These contours are then sent to the other clients, which render the outline on their own displays.

The arm segmentation process is particularly difficult for front-projected displays like ours because the projected light discolours the hands and creates extra shadows. The majority of arm-shadow work uses rear-projected displays from which arms can easily be segmented using background subtraction and/or skin-colour segmentation [e.g. 24]. Nevertheless, we have managed to use a simple algorithm to re-

liably segment arms and hands on a front-projected display. It is well known that skin is a poor reflector of blue light, and thus by controlling the colours displayed on the tabletops we can perform the segmentation using background subtraction in the blue colour plane. We then find the contours in the segmented image, after first filtering out small shapes that represent noise. To reduce network and processing bandwidth, we approximate the contour by a polygon before transmitting it to the other clients. More complex segmentation algorithms [e.g. 32] may well produce reliable results without the need to control the colour, but our goal here was to produce a simple prototype that would allow us to investigate our design guidelines.

Camera images at a resolution of 640x480px are received, processed and rendered at 15fps with no noticeable delay. This frame rate is limited by the camera, rather than the system. The artifacts themselves are rendered at 60fps, the highest rate supported by the projector, with no noticeable delay. We use the OpenCV computer vision library, and each client is controlled by an Intel Core 2 2.4GHz PC.

4.2. Early Observations

We have not yet conducted formal user studies of Distributed Tabletops, but early observations of the system in use are promising.

We tested the system using the poetry application in two sessions with 6 participants in total. In each session two participants sat at one tabletop and one participant at the other. Participants reported that the system felt responsive to use. None of them had any problems interacting with the interface, and all easily managed to string words together.

Even in this very limited trial, there was some evidence to suggest that participants were using the notions of territory and orientation. In both sessions, all participants were observed establishing personal territories by orienting words towards themselves in these regions of the table, and subsequently used these regions to construct fragments of poetry away from the other members of the group.

All participants in both sessions were observed taking words from each other's personal territories. However, this was not unintentional; rather they were enjoying themselves and began deliberately and playfully "stealing" words from each other and moving them into their own personal territories, resulting in exclamations like "Give that back!". Participants would also move words away when they thought they were about to be "stolen". This suggests that participants were aware of the personal territories of their collaborators and also that they felt a sense of ownership over the words in their own personal territories. Furthermore it indicates that, through the embodiments, participants had a good awareness of each other's actions and intentions.

Overall, all the participants enjoyed interacting with each

other in both sessions, and we did not observe a conversation disparity between the two tabletops.

5. Design Trade-offs in Groupware

Our design principles and the Distributed Tabletops system are motivated by the need for natural awareness mechanisms in tabletop collaboration. This aids mixed-focus tasks, which involve both individual and group work.

In monitor/mouse remote collaboration systems there are well-known trade-offs between supporting individual work and group work. Gutwin and Greenberg [6] show that allowing individuals to interact in a powerful way often prevents the group from maintaining an awareness of each other's actions in the workspace. They identify three areas where such trade-offs occur, and in this section we discuss each of these in the context of Distributed Tabletops.

Workspace navigation. For many tasks, conventional screens are too small to allow two collaborators to work side by side and to display a reasonable-sized workspace. Accordingly, collaborators must scroll independently in the workspace to accomplish individual work, leading to a lack of awareness. By contrast, Distributed Tabletops provides a large display with high awareness. There is sufficient space for collaborators to work side by side and, although the workspace cannot be scrolled, the size is presumably sufficient for the tasks currently carried out on physical tables. Furthermore, unlike monitor/mouse interaction, the task is split into multiple artifacts which can then be grouped into piles, allowing efficient use of the display space without resorting to scrolling. For example, a newspaper article layout task might use artifacts representing pages and articles which can be overlaid, so that the task can be completed effectively even though there is not sufficient space on the display to view all pages and articles at once. That said, the trade-off still arises when collaborators work on the same artifact at the same time: making copies of artifacts makes individual work easier but limits group awareness [25]. We believe, therefore, that this trade-off can be mitigated if the task is partitioned in a way that reduces the need for collaborators to work on the same artifact at the same time.

Artifact manipulation. In monitor/mouse remote collaboration a trade-off exists between allowing powerful artifact manipulation for individuals and providing awareness information to the group. The authors suggest powerful individual actions be made more perceivable to the group using techniques like animation and sounds. This design trade-off undoubtedly applies to Distributed Tabletops, such as in the location of controls [15]. However, we believe that the effect will be mitigated by support for natural awareness mechanisms like territoriality and orientation.

Workspace representation. The authors consider the problem of providing a shared workspace for collaborators who each wish to view different representations of the same underlying data. The same problem applies both to co-located tabletop interfaces and to Distributed Tabletops, and has yet to be explored in either.

6. Discussion and Conclusions

We believe that our design guidelines are an appropriate foundation for mixed-presence and remote tabletop collaboration over digital artifacts. Even in our early observations of Distributed Tabletops, we have seen evidence to suggest that participants were using mechanisms of territory and orientation as they would in a co-located setting, had a good awareness of each other's actions and intentions, and collaborated in a mixed-presence setting without a conversation disparity between the two tabletops.

Further work will involve formal user studies to investigate the differences between the roles of territory and orientation in co-located and mixed-presence collaboration, and the roles that they can play in different tasks.

Further development of the computer vision algorithm is also required if the system is to support tabletop applications that use unrestricted colours, and other more complex algorithms may be more appropriate in these cases [e.g. 32]. However, many applications are nevertheless possible using our algorithm, and we are currently using the Distributed Tabletops system to investigate remote and mixed-presence document collaboration and command and control tasks. It may also be possible to combine this kind of interface with systems that investigate other aspects of group-to-group collaboration such as faithfully conveying eye-gaze and body posture [16].

This paper makes three contributions. Firstly, we observe that previous work investigating mixed-presence and remote tabletop collaboration over digital artifacts seems to be uncertain as to what constitutes tabletop collaboration and why these techniques might be important in such a different setting. We begin by discussing the various aspects of co-located tabletop collaboration and show that supporting natural awareness mechanisms like territoriality, orientation, and a careful choice of remote embodiment are all crucial to remote and mixed-presence tabletop collaboration over digital artifacts.

Secondly, based on this discussion, we pose design guidelines for systems to support such collaboration. Finally, we present the Distributed Tabletops as a method. Unlike prior work, Distributed Tabletops preserves a consistent "virtual seating arrangement" between tables, uses direct input mechanisms, allows orientation of artifacts, and uses arm shadows as remote embodiments. Early observations indicate that our design principles are valid, and we discuss trade-offs in groupware design.

In summary, Distributed Tabletops represents a first step

towards design principles and a system for remote and mixed-presence tabletop collaboration over digital artifacts.

Acknowledgements

We gratefully acknowledge Mark Ashdown, members of the Rainbow group, and the anonymous reviewers, for useful comments; and Thales Research and Technology (UK) and the EPSRC, who jointly funded this work.

References

[1] Ashdown, M. and Robinson, P. Escritoire: A Personal Projected Display. *IEEE MultiMedia* 12, 1 (Jan. 2005), 34-42.

[2] Brave, S., Ishii, H., and Dahley, A. Tangible Interfaces for Remote Collaboration and Communication. In *Proc. CSCW 1998*, 169–178.

[3] Coldefy, F. and Louis-dit-Picard, S. DigiTable: an interactive multiuser table for collocated and remote collaboration enabling remote gesture visualization. In *Proc. PROCAMS 2007*.

[4] Dourish, P. and Bellotti, V. Awareness and coordination in shared workspaces. In *Proc. CSCW 1992*, 107-114.

[5] Esenther, A., and Ryall, K., RemoteDT: Support for Multi-Site Table Collaboration. In *Proc. Int. Conf. Collaboration Technologies (CollabTech)*, 2006.

[6] Gutwin, C. and Greenberg, S. Design for individuals, design for groups: tradeoffs between power and workspace awareness. In *Proc. CSCW 1998*, 207-216.

[7] Gutwin, C. and Greenberg, S. A Descriptive Framework of Workspace Awareness for Real-Time Groupware. *Comput. Supported Coop. Work* 11, 3 (Nov. 2002), 411-446.

[8] Hauber, J., Regenbrecht, H., Billinghurst, M., and Cockburn, A. Spatiality in videoconferencing: trade-offs between efficiency and social presence In *Proc. CSCW 2004*, 413–422.

[9] Hutterer, P., Close, B. S., and Thomas, B. H. Supporting Mixed Presence Groupware in Tabletop Applications In *Proc. TABLETOP'06*, 63–70.

[10] Ishii, H. and Kobayashi, M. ClearBoard: a seamless medium for shared drawing and conversation with eye contact. In *Proc. CHI 1992*, 525-532.

[11] Kirk, D. and Stanton Fraser, D. Comparing remote gesture technologies for supporting collaborative physical tasks In *Proc. CHI 2006*, 1191–1200.

[12] Kruger, R., Carpendale, S., Scott, S. D., and Greenberg, S. Roles of Orientation in Tabletop Collaboration: Comprehension, Coordination and Communication. *Comput. Supported Coop. Work 13*, 5-6 (Dec. 2004), 501-537.

[13] Kruger, R., Carpendale, S., Scott, S.D., and Tang, A. Fluid integration of rotation and translation. In *Proc. CHI 2005*, 601–610.

[14] Luff, P., Heath, C., Kuzuoka, H., Yamazaki, K., and Yamashita, J. Handling documents and discriminating objects in hybrid spaces. In *Proc. CHI 2006*, 561-570.

[15] Morris, M. R., Paepcke, A., Winograd, T., and Stamberger, J. TeamTag: exploring centralized versus replicated controls for co-located tabletop groupware. In *Proc. CHI 2006*, 1273-1282.

[16] Nguyen, D. T. and Canny, J. Multiview: improving trust in group video conferencing through spatial faithfulness. In *Proc. CHI 2007*, 1465-1474.

[17] Ryall, K., Forlines, C., Shen, C., and Morris, M. R. Exploring the effects of group size and table size on interactions with tabletop shared-display groupware. In *Proc. CSCW 2004*, 284-293.

[18] Scott, S., Grant, K., and Mandryk, R. System guidelines for co-located collaborative work on a tabletop display. In *Proc. ECSCW 2003*, 2003.

[19] Scott, S.D., Carpendale, M.S.T., and Inkpen, K.M. Territoriality in collaborative tabletop workspaces. In *Proc. CSCW 2004*, 294–303.

[20] Shen, C., Vernier, F.D., Forlines, C., and Ringel, M. Diamondspin: an extensible toolkit for around-the-table interaction. In *Proc. CHI 2004*, 167–174.

[21] Stewart, J., Bederson, B. B., and Druin, A. Single display groupware: a model for co-present collaboration. In *Proc. CHI 1999*, 286-293.

[22] Streitz, N. A., Geissler, J., Holmer, T., Konomi, S., Mller-Tomfelde, C., Reischl, W., Rexroth, P., Seitz, P., and Steinmetz, R. i-LAND: an interactive landscape for creativity and innovation. In *Proc. CHI 1999*, 120-127.

[23] Tang, A., Boyle, M., and Greenberg, S. Understanding and mitigating display and presence disparity in mixed presence groupware. *J. Res. and Practice in Inf. Tech. 37*, 2.

[24] Tang, A., Neustaedter, C., and Greenberg, S. VideoArms: Embodiments for Mixed Presence Groupware. In *Proc. HCI 2006*, 85-102.

[25] Tang, A., Tory, M., Po, B., Neumann, P., and Carpendale, S. Collaborative coupling over tabletop displays. In *Proc. CHI 2006*, 1181-1190.

[26] Tang, J. C. Findings from observational studies of collaborative work. *Int. J. Man-Mach. Stud. 34*, 2 (Feb. 1991), 143-160.

[27] Tang, J. C. and Minneman, S. VideoWhiteboard: video shadows to support remote collaboration. In *Proc. CHI 1991*, 315–322

[28] Tse, E., Histon, J., Scott, S. D., and Greenberg, S. Avoiding interference: how people use spatial separation and partitioning in SDG workspaces. In *Proc. CSCW 2004*, 252–261.

[29] Tuddenham, P., and Robinson, P. T3: Rapid Prototyping of High-Resolution and Mixed-Presence Tabletop Applications. In *Proc. IEEE TABLETOP 2007*.

[30] Wellner, P. Interacting with paper on the DigitalDesk. *Commun. ACM 36*, 7 (Jul. 1993).

[31] Wesugi, S. and Miwa, Y. "Lazy Susan" Communication System for Remote, Spatial and Physical Collaborative Works. In *Proc. IEEE TABLETOP 2006*, 35–42.

[32] Wilson, A. D. PlayAnywhere: a compact interactive tabletop projection-vision system. In *Proc. UIST 2005*, 83–92.

[33] Wilson, A. D., and Robbins, D. C. PlayTogether: Playing Games across Multiple Interactive Tabletops *IUI'07 workshop on Tangible Play*.

TableTops: worthwhile experiences of collocated and remote collaboration

A. Pauchet   F. Coldefy   L. Lefebvre   S. Louis Dit Picard   L. Perron
A. Bouguet   M. Collobert   J. Guerin   D. Corvaisier
Orange Labs: 2, Av. Pierre Marzin, 22300 Lannion, France
francois.coldefy@orange-ftgroup.com

Abstract

Tabletops incite people to collaborate around shared documents. We propose DIGITABLE, a platform for collocated and remote collaboration which attempts to preserve the fluidity of interactions and the mutual awareness of copresence. DIGITABLE combines a multiuser tactile tabletop, a video-communication system and a robust computer vision module for distant users' gesture visualization.

From an experiment, we show that DIGITABLE improves the efficiency of a collaborative task in remote configuration. We also show that remote gesture visualization facilitates coordination as it provides to local participants important information such as intentionality and pointing. Thus, collocated and remote configurations are both worthwhile experiences: remote collaboration is not seen anymore as a poor ersatz of collocated collaboration, although presence feeling is not uniformly perceived by participants.

1. Introduction

This paper addresses remote groupware collaboration and communication. We strive to design a remote collaboration platform which preserves as far as possible the fluidity of the interaction and the mutual awareness provided by co-presence. Mutual awareness refers to human ability to maintain and constantly update a sense of social and physical context. Being aware of others has an important role in the fluidity and the naturalness of collaboration. Our approach is founded on Gutwin's Workspace Awareness [7]. Gutwin provides precious guidelines to design such a platform as he clearly identifies what perceptual information mutual awareness involves, how it is gathered and used by people, and finally, how it may be conveyed and rendered to a remote site. This descriptive framework helps to decide the kind of display to choose and the type of perceptual information to transmit between distant sites.

Among the perceptual information involved in mutual awareness, we focus on the visual channel and especially on the gesture visualization of distant users, as it provides to local participants information facilitating distant coordination and communication such as intentionality (who is intending to do what), action identity (who is doing what) and pointing [9] [10] .

We present DIGITABLE, a collaborative platform which includes a computer vision system to render remote gestures on a shared workspace. We design an experiment to evaluate how our collaborative platform performs in terms of task efficiency, coordination and user experience in collocated and remote uses. We explore several gesture visualization modes to identify how the remote gesture embodiment and the shared desktop orientation affect the task. A further work will complete this study which compels users to focus on the task domain [2] by evaluating DIGITABLE with a more social activity.

2. Related Work

VIDEOPLACE [11], VIDEODRAW [17] and VIDEOWHITEBOARD [18] were among the very first video based attempts to capture participant's gesture and to fuse it with graphic images. Later, CLEARBOARD [8] enabled eye contact between distant participants by using a half mirror polarizing projection screen whose transparency allows rear video projection, while user's reflected image is captured by a camera.

In 2004, Takao proposes TELE-GRAFFITI [14], a remote sketching system for augmented reality shared drawings on real paper sheets. It allows two distant users to contribute to a virtual page, fusing the marks each participant has written on his/her own sheet. A very accomplished work in the domain of remote gesture visualization is VIDEOARMS [15]. The authors designed a collaborative system with effective distant mutual awareness by coupling a sensitive SMARTBOARD with a video capture of participant's gesture overlaid on the remote desktop image. Users can easily predict, understand and interpret distant users' actions or intents, as their arms are visible whenever they want to interact with the tactile surface or show anything on it.

ESCRITOIRE [1] and VICAT [4] both associate a tabletop with a vertical screen for remote collaboration. VICAT is designed for remote and collocated groups' interaction, whereas Escritoire focuses on a personal desktop support-

0-7695-3013-3/07 $25.00 © 2007 IEEE
DOI 10.1109/TABLETOP.2007.13

ing bi-manual interaction. Both systems use conventional video-communication tools and remote gesture is embodied in tele-pointers and traces.

Experiments on platform providing remote gesture visualization are still few [9] [10] and mostly focused on interaction with physical objects of the real world. Our main contribution is to give hints of how a collaborative platform combining remote gesture visualization and full-size video communication affects a collaborative task.

3. DIGITABLE platform

We propose DIGITABLE[5], a platform for collocated and remote collaboration combining a multiuser tactile tabletop, a video-communication system enabling eye-contact and full size remote user visualization, a computer vision module for remote gesture visualization and a spatialized sound system (see Fig. 1 and Fig. 2).

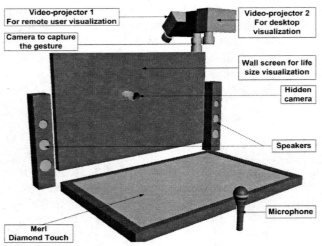

Figure 1. DIGITABLE is a platform combining a Diamond Touch, a video communication system, a spatialized audio system and a computer vision module to provide remote gesture visualization.

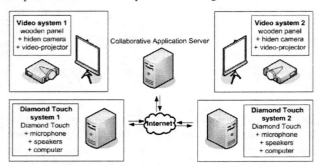

Figure 2. DIGITABLE Architecture: shared application, video communication and remote gesture analysis is implemented at each distant site on a single work station.

We use Merl Diamond Touch [6] tactile surface on which a desktop image is projected from a ceiling mounted video-projector (video-projector 2 in Fig. 1). Diamond Touch

supports up to four users simultaneously. A collaborative application server manages the collaboration between the connected sites and provides the replication of events occurring on window containers on both sites in order to keep the shared desktop consistency. We use an *ad-hoc* software based on Java and JOGL (Java Binding for OpenGL) to implement the interactive window containers.

The video communication system uses a camera hidden behind a wood-screen and peeping through an almost unnoticeable 3mm wide hole. A second video-projector (video-projector 1 in Fig. 1) beams on the wall screen the video of the distant site captured by a symmetric remote spy camera (see Fig. 2). Eye-contact is guaranteed by approximately placing the camera peep-hole at the estimated eyes' height of a seated person and beaming the distant video on the screen such that the peephole and the distant user's eyes coincide. Fine tuning of hole's design and video-projector beam's orientation is performed to avoid camera's dazzle.

Audio and video channels are compressed using respectively the TDAC and the H263 codecs and are sent to the remote site using RTP (Real-time Transport Protocol) over UDP/IP. Note that the video quality is currently limited by the spy camera peep-hole resolution (420 lines expanded to 4CIF - 704x576).

The computer vision module [5] uses a camera placed at the ceiling and pointing at the tabletop. The module consists of a segmentation process detecting any object above the table by comparing, at almost the frame rate, the captured image and the desktop image, up to a geometric and color distortion. The geometric deformation model between the camera images and the desktop images is automatically estimated with an off-line procedure. The color transfer functions are computed on-line to cope with external lightning changes. The computer vision module provides an image mask of the detected objects (hands, arms, or any object above the table) extracted from the camera image. The compressed mask is sent to the distant site and overlaid on the current desktop image. Semi-transparency is used to visualize the desktop "under" the remote partner's arms.

Fig. 3 shows users' gesture and its visualization on the remote site. The left bottom image shows the overlay of the detected hand of site 2 (upper right image); the right bottom image shows the overlay of the detected hand of the user in site 1 (upper left image).

The system runs at about 17 Hz on dual-core Inter Xeon 3.73 Hz with 2Gb of RAM.

4. The present study: Comparison between collocated and remote collaboration

4.1. Objectives

We aim at understanding how the DIGITABLE platform affects collaboration and interaction between users. Many

Figure 3. Remote gesture visualization: view of both distant tables in action (upper line) and of both overlaid desktops (lower line); the left bottom image shows the overlay of the detected hand of site 1 (upper right image); the right bottom image shows the overlay of the detected arms of site 2 (upper left image); the remote gesture is overlaid in transparency with the desktop image.

parameters may impact a group activity: the type of the task which makes users focus more or less on the task and on the personal spaces [3], the position of the participants around the table and the functionalities of the application. More precisely, we focus on how remote gesture visualization influences a distant collaboration task on a tabletop.

4.2. Design

Six different conditions

In remote configuration, the user communicates with his/her remote partner through the life-size video communication system projected on the wall screen in front of him/her (Fig. 1 and 3). We evaluate different embodiments of the remote gesture. Gutwin [7] identifies two main axes for remote awareness representation on a shared workspace: the visual information may be *literal* (it is displayed in the same form as it is gathered) or *symbolic* (particular information is extracted and synthesized when shown), and *situated* within the workspace (placed at the same place of the shared workspace, on both distant sites) or *separated* from it. We propose three implementations of the remote gesture visualization, moving along the *literal/symbolic* axis in an 'original' way described below:

- *Remote face-to-face:* this configuration corresponds to the *literal/situated* embodiment of the collocated face-to-face situation (see upper right image in Fig. 4 and upper image in Fig. 5). We mimic the reality: it is as if users are on both sides of a table. They do not share the same view of the document on the table as the shared workspace is upside down for them;

- *Remote side-by-side:* the users share the same point of view of the desktop. The remote gesture is rendered as if people were side-by-side (or even on each other's laps), in contradiction to the face-to-face visualization of the remote user on the wall screen (see bottom left image in Fig. 4 and middle image in Fig. 5). This configuration corresponds to the *literal* and partly *situated* embodiment of the remote gesture visualization.
- *Reconstructed gesture:* the users share the same point of view of the workspace, while the remote gesture of the distant user is rendered on the desktop to recreate a face-to-face configuration. The remote gesture image is reversed and overlaid on the distant desktop in respect to the contact point on the table (see lower-right image in Fig. 4 and bottom image in Fig. 5). The discontinuity which exists in the side-by-side configuration is reduced since the distant gesture is oriented as if it were coming from the wall screen. The reconstructed gesture configuration has however two drawbacks: firstly, although people "feel" as if they are in a face-to-face configuration, the remote gesture image is mirrored (the distant user's right hand is seen as his left hand); secondly, we may lack of information to complete the full gesture image on the remote site because of the symmetry: this is especially noticeable on the lowest image in Fig. 5, which shows that the remote gesture is incomplete in the upper part of the table.

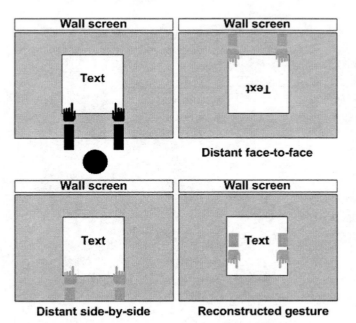

Figure 4. The various configurations to represent the remote gesture; the arms on the upper-right, lower-left and lower-right images stand for the gesture visualization of the user from upper-left image, user whose full size video is projected on the wall screen.

The three reference conditions to which we compare these previous implementations are:

- for the remote configurations: remote collaboration without gesture visualization when the users share the same view of the shared desktop,
- face-to-face and side-by-side collocated situations.

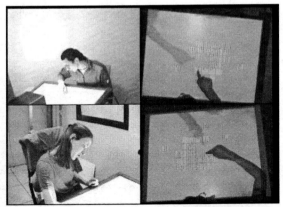

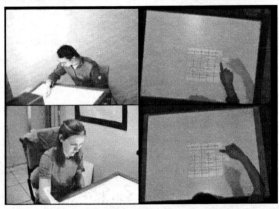

Figure 5. The various embodiments of remote gesture. The upper, middle and bottom images correspond to face-to-face, side-by-side and reconstructed gesture configurations.

A mosaic completion task

We choose a digital mosaic completion task as experiment. In comparison with puzzles, mosaics are composed of square pieces. Puzzles and mosaics have the advantage

to be a friendly application which needs a very short learning stage. The task goal is obvious and the learning process is limited to piece manipulation. Secondly, it has the benefit to make users focus on tactile interaction afforded by the tabletop. Manipulating graphical objects may be one of the most pertinent interactions on a tabletop comparing to text editing for instance. Finally, mosaic completion is clearly identified as allowing users to concentrate on the task space [3]. The users feel challenged to perform the task as fast as possible, although no particular instruction has been given to them in that way.

The type of mosaic has also a significant effect on the completion task: whereas abstract images can be interpreted or understood from any viewing direction, figurative and especially textual mosaics induce a favored orientation for completion. The manipulation of pieces during a session, their orientation and positioning give a lot of information about implicitly private, shared and storage spaces created by participants [13] [16].

From preliminary tests we performed before the present study [12], it appears that textual mosaics lead to a tighter collaboration between users than abstract and figurative ones. As textual pieces cannot be easily read in an upside-down position, participants have first to negotiate the general orientation of the mosaic. Moreover, whereas the orientation of textual pieces can be obviously deduced from its content, its positioning within the mosaic is difficult and needs more coordination and communication between users. To limit the number of sessions during the experiment, we choose textual mosaic (see Fig. 6) among all the three different possibilities (textual, figurative or abstract).

Figure 6. Textual mosaic

Experiment design

To sum up, we want to evaluate

1. how the task completion is affected by the remote configuration,

2. what is the contribution of the remote gesture visualization in terms of task efficiency and user experience.

We have experimented 6 conditions with pairs of users for a textual mosaic completion task: 4 in remote situation (face-to-face, side-by-side both with remote gesture visualization, side-by-side with reconstructed gesture visualization, and a side-by-side remote configuration without gesture visualization), 2 in collocated situation (face-to-face and side-by-side).

4.3. Participants

A total of 30 subjects participated to the study, randomly put in pairs. There were one female pair, six male pairs and eight mixed pairs. Eight pairs gathered persons who knew each other well, two pairs a little and the last five pairs not at all. All participants were postgraduates, had normal or corrected to normal vision. Participants were not paid for the experiment.

4.4. Procedure

The participants completed a series of 6 textual mosaics, 4 in the remote situation and 2 in the collocated situation. For all the remote configurations, the interactions are mediated by the DIGITABLE platform.

During the experiment, the order of the mosaic completions was counter-balanced in collocated situations (face-to-face and side-by-side), in remote conditions (remote face-to-face, remote side-by-side, reconstructed gesture and no gesture visualization) and in situation (collocated and remote). The participants completed an individual training period before the 6 collaborative mosaic completions.

At the end of the session, participants were asked to fill in a questionnaire and were shortly interviewed about how they felt the experiment. The experiment evaluation is guided by objective criteria (completion times, actions performed, collisions) and subjective criteria.

4.5. The mosaic application

We have designed a dedicated Java application for mosaic completion, running locally and/or remotely on the DIGITABLE platform. All the mosaics are composed of a 5x5 grid of square pieces (see Fig. 6). Three types of action are allowed: rotating a single mosaic piece, moving one piece or moving a group of pieces. A mosaic piece can be rotated but in 90° steps, as its edges have to remain parallel to the table sides. A user has to touch one of the 4 piece corners, and to perform a rotational motion. A single piece can also be moved by a user along an invisible grid by touching it near its center and dragging it from one place to another. To move a group of pieces, a user defines an invisible bounding box with a multiple contact on the table and drags it from one place to another. A visual feedback is given to let users identify the currently performed action:

a cross pointer for dragging a single piece (Fig. 7, upper left image), a circular arrow for rotation (Fig. 7, upper right image) and the colored piece contours inside the selected bounding box (Fig. 7, bottom row images).

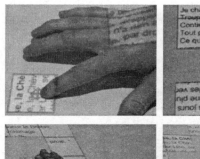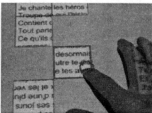

Figure 7. Mosaic application: piece move (upper left image), rotation (upper right image) and bounding box for moving several pieces at the same time (bottom row images).

4.6. Event recording and analysis

The DIGITABLE platform is particularly convenient for experiment recording. The ceiling camera used for remote gesture visualization is also used to record an aerial view of the users' interactions above the table. The full-size video communication system enables to record all the communications between users for all the configurations except for face-to-face collocated condition which needs another camera. Furthermore, the position of the spy camera at the user eyes' height in the wood screen allows us to identify precisely when the participants are looking at each other in the remote configuration.

All the users' actions on the mosaic pieces are saved in a log file by the Java application (piece number, placement and orientation on the table, action type when touched - rotation, moving or bounding box). The mosaic completion times are also collected.

5. Results

5.1. Task efficiency

Table 1 sums up the mean completion times for all the 6 configurations, *i.e* collocated side-by-side, collocated face-to-face, remote conditions (side-by-side with and without gesture visualization, side-by-side with reconstructed gesture and finally face-to-face with gesture visualization). The values in the cells correspond to the mean completion time M in seconds and the standard deviation SD.

When comparing the 4 remote configurations as a whole with the 2 collocated configurations also as a whole, mosaics are completed faster in remote (M=292s, SD=96s) than in collocated conditions (M=339s, SD=149s) according to the significant difference obtained by the ANOVA test with repeated measures (F(1,14) = 4.8, p<0.046).

When comparing more precisely collocated and remote situations, the remote side-by-side condition with gesture visualization is performed significantly faster (M=268s) than the collocated side-by-side condition (M=324s). The ANOVA test with repeated measures on completion times gives a significant difference (F(1,14) = 5,6, p<0.033). The remote side-by-side condition with remote gesture is also more efficient than the collocated face-to-face condition (M=354s): F(1,14) = 6.8, p<0.020.

	Collocated	Remote no G.V.	Remote R.G.V.	Remote G.V.
Side-by-side	324 (108)	291 (100)	287 (82)	268 (108)
Face-to-face	353 (182)	-	-	321 (94)

Table 1. Mean completion times performed by the 15 user pairs; each cell contains the mean completion time and the associated standard deviation in seconds; the columns 'Remote no G.V', 'Remote R.G.V.' and 'Remote G.V.' correspond to the remote configurations without gesture visualization, with reconstructed gesture visualization and gesture visualization respectively.

However, with such a mosaic task, early errors on tile positioning have a huge influence on completion times. The large variations of the intra-subject completion times do not enable other significant findings. For instance, we cannot undoubtedly confirm the apparent ordering of the side-by-side conditions, which gives hints that in remote configuration, the gesture visualization (M=268s) makes the collaboration more efficient (M=291s without gesture visualization). No significant difference was observed between both face-to-face collocated and remote configurations although the remote condition has the shortest mean completion time. There is no significant difference between collocated face-to-face and side-by-side conditions. This may be due to the high standard deviation observed for the collocated face-to-face conditions.

5.2. Coordination

Table 2 sums up the mean numbers of collisions for all the configurations. A collision occurs when both users are acting on a same piece or when they move simultaneously different pieces to the same place.

The collisions are significantly different for all the configuration types and are ordered as follows, with decreasing values: remote configuration without gesture visualization (M=10.9), remote side-by-side configuration (M=6.7), remote face-to-face configuration (M=5.4), reconstructed gesture visualization (M=3.5), collocated face-to-face configuration (M=2.3), and collocated side-by-side configuration (M=1.5) (ANOVA test with repeated measures: F(5,70) = 65.7, p<0.001).

	Collocated	Remote no G.V.	Remote R.G.V.	Remote G.V.
Side-by-side	1.5 (1.4)	10.9 (3.7)	3.5 (1.9)	6.7 (2.3)
Face-to-face	2.3 (2.5)	-	-	5.4 (2.2)

Table 2. Mean numbers of collisions during the experiment; each cell contains the mean number of collisions and the associated standard deviation (in parenthesis); the columns 'Remote no G.V', 'Remote G.V.' and 'Remote R.G.V.' correspond to the remote configurations without gesture visualization, with gesture visualization and with reconstructed gesture visualization respectively.

Pair comparisons between each condition are conducted using ANOVA with repeated measures and significant differences are observed.

5.3. Subjective evaluation: user experience

After a session, participants were asked to fill in an open questionnaire and to cite words which they think suit at best the different conditions, from the following list: frustrating, interesting, nice, individual, joyful, pleasant, stressful, inhibiting, communicative, cooperative, strange, and boring. The participants were allowed to complete the list with their own words, but none of them used this possibility.

Remote configuration: No significant difference in the cited words is detected when comparing remote or collocated configurations. The most frequent cited words when cumulating both configurations are "cooperative" (70 citations), communicative (50), pleasant (50), nice (47) interesting (42), *i.e.* 259 citations over 355 (73%). The platform is actually identified as a fun device for group activities.

Remote gesture visualization: We detect differences in the cited words when comparing remote configurations with and without gesture visualization. Although "collaborative" is still the most cited word, the list of the chosen words is much more positive for the gesture visualization configuration: "pleasant, nice, communicative, interesting and joyful" are equally cited, the others words being very rarely used. This top list covers 89% of the most cited words. This same list, which is also the top list for remote configuration without gesture visualization, covers only 66% of all the cited words. To the question ("Do you think the visualization of the distant gesture is important?"), 13 subjects find it useful, 12 are indifferent and 7 think it is disturbing. Let us note that 4 participants spontaneously found the gesture visualization useless until they experiment the remote configuration without it. Then, they change their mind and deplore the lack of it. Some users also deplore the low quality of the visualization of the remote gesture. The computer vision module runs at almost the frame rate but at the price of low image resolution. Furthermore, the ceiling camera is in some way dazzled by the desktop image projected on the tabletop. As a consequence, the user's arms are in black-lighting, and are captured with relatively low colors contrast by the camera. Finally, another remark was the lack of visual informational feedback when the remote user was touching the table for interacting with a piece. The gesture visualization does not enable to perceive if a remote user has his/her hand above the table or if he/she has yet selected a piece but is actually thinking what to do with it. This lack of information is sometimes misleading and induces conflict in piece manipulation. Some participants (5 over 32) say they would prefer a visual feedback to remote gesture visualization (piece underlined when remotely manipulated, similarly to local interaction).

Collaboration and presence feeling: Two questions were about the feeling the participants have had of working together ("Was the task performed in common? Were your actions depending on your partner?"). From a 10 level rating, we obtain indifferently for collocated and remote configurations the same value 7. In contrast, questions referring to the presence feeling betray that remote configuration does not give sufficient embodiment of the remote partner, whose presence may be forgotten for a while.

Full size video communication system: when asked about their overall impression about DigiTable, 15 over 32 participants spontaneously considered that the video of the remote user was useless.

Mosaic interaction: some users had difficulty to rotate the pieces by selecting the corner, even with the improvement we made in comparison with the first version of the application [12]. Furthermore, this interaction appears to be not intuitive to some people who tried several times to rotate a piece by giving a little impulse with the finger, as if each impulse should rotate it from 90°. Some people also deplore that they could not move and rotate simultaneously a group of mosaic pieces. It demonstrates that our container which only enables translation of groups of pieces is insufficient to respond to the user demand.

6. Discussion

From objective criteria, we have shown that remote and collocated configurations on the DigiTable platform are comparable in terms of task efficiency. Furthermore, the task achieved in the side-by-side remote configuration with gesture visualization is even performed faster than in the side-by-side collocated condition. Although our measures do not provide all the wished statistical evidences, we present hints that remote gesture visualization improves distant collaboration. Participants do not hinder each other in remote configuration: even without taking into account the social problem of proximity, participants' arms do not physically cross. Each user has equally access to the whole table without impeding his/her remote partner. Moreover, contrary to collocated configurations, mosaic pieces are not hidden by the partner's arms as the remote gesture is overlaid in transparency.

Secondly, we have also proved that remote gesture visu-
alization is useful in terms of object manipulation. The coordination between remote users is better when the remote gestures are rendered: significantly less conflicts about object manipulation occurs. Among the remote conditions, the reconstructed gesture configuration is the most efficient to avoid collisions. It outperforms side-by-side remote gesture visualization because, even with a shared view of the workspace, it simulates a face-to-face situation and therefore reduces the discontinuity which exists in the side-by-side configuration. Moreover, in the side-by-side configuration, a user can mistake the remote gesture image overlaid on the desktop for the shadow of his/her own arms. In the reconstructed gesture configuration, as in the face-to-face configuration, participants can interpret a virtual hand coming into their work zone as a visual alarm and so they can prevent any upcoming conflict in piece manipulation. In contrast, in the remote side-by-side configuration with gesture visualization, the remote gesture are always overlaid in the same work zone.

From subjective criteria, we have shown that remote configuration is more appreciated when associated with remote gesture visualization. All in all, participants find the remote gesture visualization rather useful, although 7 over 32 perceived it as disturbing.

Presence feeling is not totally satisfying as reported by most users: the presence of a remote user may be forgotten for a while, when participants are working independently. This may be caused by the fact that we respect most of the Gutwin's recommendations about workspace awareness (we provide tools for intentional and consequential communication) but the artefacts and feedthrough [7]. Visualization is obviously not a sufficient embodiment of the remote user 's gesture. Although seeing the arms of a remote partner, a user still has the liberty to work as if being alone because no unintentional touch can occur. The remote user's embodiment would probably be efficiently enhanced with sound effects of piece manipulations while not overloading users with unceasing noise effects.

Almost half of the participants found the video-communication system useless. This is due to the mosaic task which challenges the participants: they focused on the task to perform as fast as possible. The audio channel was sufficient to communicate and looking at each other was considered as a waste of time. A further investigation will be to count how many eyes contacts between users occurred during sessions. It will help us to evaluate if this assertion is totally founded. But more interesting will be testing the platform with other applications, in which user communication is essential to the completion of the task.

The obtained findings have to be considered in respect to the presented experiment which was focused on the task domain. A textual mosaic completion task actually impacts the results: the orientation problems were increased and the collaboration between participants was tighter than it would have been with abstract and figurative mosaics; the evaluation of the video-communication system is also specific to the task. We will complete our analysis with a complementary storytelling experiment in which task and person spaces would be equally important. With this activity, in which the quality of the constructed story is the main goal, life size video and eye contact will probably be more relevant.

7. Conclusion and future work

In this paper, we address the design of a collaborative multiuser platform and propose DIGITABLE which strives to preserve most of the perceptual elements that are essential to mutual awareness between remote sites.

An experiment on DIGITABLE shows two main elements. Firstly, although DIGITABLE does not provide the same presence feeling in remote and collocated situations, distance does not hinder efficient collaboration anymore. For a particular application, a mosaic completion task, it appears that the remote configuration is even more efficient in terms of task duration than the collocated situation. This is mainly due to the fact that remote participants can reach the whole workspace without impeding each other. Secondly, users clearly favor remote gesture visualization. It greatly facilitates the coordination as the users can easily perceive and anticipate their remote partners' actions.

However, DIGITABLE needs a few technical improvements to enhance the presence feeling: the remote user's action needs to be more embodied. This can probably be obtained by adding feedthrough [7] such as rubbing noises when interacting. This audio feedback may also be completed by a visual one to help a user understand if a remote partner, whose hand is above a mosaic piece, has already seized it or is just hovering. Another point concerns the improvement of the container so that users can rotate a group of pieces to fit it to another completed part of the mosaic.

Further work will complete our present analysis by studying a more social activity in which human to human interaction prevails upon computer human interaction. We hope it will confirm our first findings that remote and collocated collaborations appear to be both worthwhile experiences. Remote work is not perceived anymore as a poor ersatz of collocated activities. And we will end by a frequent comment made by users very nice to be heard about DIGITABLE: "It's Fun! It's Fun!".

Acknowledgments: this work is supported by the French government within the RNTL Project DIGITABLE and the Media and Networks Cluster.

References

[1] M. Ashdown and P. Robinson. Remote collaboration on desk-sized displays. *Journal of Visualization and Computer Animation*, 16(1), 2005.

[2] W. Buxton and B. A. Myers. A study in two handed input. In *Proceedings of CHI'86 Human Factors in Computing Systems*, Boston, USA, 1986.

[3] W. A. S. Buxton. TELEPRESENCE: integrating shared task and person spaces. In *Proceedings of the conference on Graphics interface*, Vancouver, Canada, 1992.

[4] F. Chen, P. Eades, J. Epps, S. Lichman, B. Close, P. Hutterer, M. Takatsuka, B. Thomas, and M. Wu. VICAT: Visualisation and interaction on a collaborative access table. In *Proceedings of the IEEE Workshop on Horizontal Interactive Human-Computer Systems*, Adelaide, Australia, 2006.

[5] F. Coldefy and S. Louis Dit Picard. Digitable: an interactive multiuser table for collocated and remote collaboration enabling remote gesture visualization. In *IEEE workshop on Projector-Camera Systems*, Minneapolis, USA, 2007.

[6] P. H. Dietz and D. Leigh. DIAMONDTOUCH: A multi-user touch technology. In *Proceedings of UIST*, 2001.

[7] C. Gutwin and S. Greenberg. A descriptive framework of workspace awareness for real-time groupware. *Special Issue on Awareness in CSCW*, 2002.

[8] H. Ishii and M. Kobayashi. CLEARBOARD: A seamless media for shared drawing and conversation with eye-contact. In *Proceedings of CHI*, Monterey, California, USA, 1992.

[9] D. Kirk, D. Stanton, and T. Rodden. The effect of remote gesturing on distance instruction. In *Proceedings of CSCL*, Taipei, Taiwan, 2005.

[10] R. E. Kraut, S. R. Fussel, and J. Siegel. Visual information as a conversational resource in collaborative physical tasks. *Human Computer Interaction*, 2003.

[11] M. W. Krueger, T. Gionfriddo, and K. Hinrichsen. VIDEOPLACE : an artificial reality. In *Proceedings of CHI*, San Francisco, USA, 1985.

[12] A. Pauchet, F. Coldefy, L. Lefebvre, S. Louis Dit Picard, A. Bouguet, L. Perron, J. Guerin, D. Corvaisier, and M. Collobert. Mutual awareness in collocated and distant collaborative tasks using shared interfaces. In *Proceedings of Interact*, Rio de Janeiro, Brasil, 2007.

[13] S. D. Scott, M. S. T. Carpendale, and S. Habelski. Storage bins: mobile storage for collaborative tabletop displays. *IEEE Computer Graphics and Applications*, 25(4), 2005.

[14] N. Takao, J. Shi, and S. Baker. TELE-GRAFFITI: A camera-projector based remote sketching system with hand-based user interface and automatic session summarization. *International Journal of Computer Vision*, 53(2), 2003.

[15] A. Tang, C. Neustaedter, and S. Greenberg. VIDEOARMS: embodiments in mixed presence groupware. In *Proceedings of the BCS-HCI British HCI Group Conference*, London, United Kingdom, 2006.

[16] A. Tang, M. Tory, B. Po, P. Neumann, and S. Carpendale. Collaborative coupling over tabletop displays. In *Proceedings of CHI*, Montréal, Canada, 2006.

[17] J. C. Tang and S. L. Minneman. VIDEODRAW: a video interface for collaborative drawing. *ACM Transactions on Information Systems*, 9(2), 1991.

[18] J. C. Tang and S. L. Minneman. VIDEOWHITEBOARD: video shadows to support remote collaboration. In *Proceedings of the CHI*, New Orleans, USA, 1991.

Out & About: Tabletops in the Real World

Put That There NOW:

Group Dynamics of Tabletop Interaction under Time Pressure

Xianhang Zhang, Masahiro Takatsuka
School of Information Technology, The University of Sydney
IMAGEN Program, National ICT Australia
xianhang@u.washington.edu; masa@vislab.usyd.edu

Abstract

Collaborative user applications such as tabletop applications are a challenge to develop because user behaviour is affected not only by the software interface but also by group dynamics. Feedback loops abound in this system so even relatively minor changes in the software can lead to large changes in user behaviour. Designing such interfaces with any degree of predictability requires a thorough understanding of the user's behavioural patterns.

Much of the current research on enhancing group collaboration have focused on so called "non time-critical" applications in which the group is free to take as long as they want to perform a task. This is contrasted with "time-critical" applications like disaster management or surgery where the timing of each step affects the eventual outcome. This paper investigates how behaviour patterns for time-critical scenarios differs from reported behaviours for non time-critical scenarios and how these differences have implications for the design of time-critical, collaborative tabletop software. An observational study was performed to investigate those specific differences are and what implications this has for the design of time critical software. Several findings were discovered which contradict the previous research done on non-time-critical applications, leading to new implications for social software design. A behavioural model based on scarce cognitive load was found to be a useful model of thinking about designing time critical applications.

1. Introduction

The use of groupware is different from single user software because group dynamics strongly affect how the software will be used. One important area in which groupware can be of great benefit is in so called "time critical" scenarios. Horvitz's definition of time-critical interaction is:

"In time-critical contexts, the utilities of outcomes diminish significantly with delays in taking appropriate action." [6]

Examples include such things as military planning, disaster response and surgical procedures. Tabletops have great potential to support time critical collaboration because if it can enhance the rapidness and quality of decisions made during time critical scenarios. Tabletop computing is especially well suited to enhancing time critical collaboration because the primary mode of interaction is synchronous and co-located so rich communication involving facial expressions and pointing is possible.

Supporting time critical tasks may be one of the primary "killer apps" for tabletop computing. At the same time, designing for time critical scenarios is difficult and a poorly designed tabletop application that does not take into account the nature of the task will degrade performance and will not be used.

Collaboration only happens if the benefits of collaborating outweigh the costs and a highly significant cost in time-critical collaboration is the time and effort it takes to communicate. If communication cannot be done quickly and effectively, then it is not done at all and the group splinters into a collection of individuals working largely independently and barely communicating.

While there has been much research done on time critical work in general, very little has focused on *computer supported time critical collaborative work* and how technology such as tabletop computing can be used to enhance time critical work.

The aim of this study was to investigate what sorts of behaviours occurred a computer mediated collaboration device and how altering the situation under which the group operates affects their interaction patterns. From this study, it was possible to gain an understanding of the nature of time critical collaboration and form a useful model of user behaviour.

2. Related Work

2.1 In Group Decision Making

Group Decision Making research focuses on "task performing groups" [5] which focus on making one or a series of decisions. Research into this field has revealed a number of different important dimensions of both group makeup and task environment that affect the decision making process.

Groups which elect their leaders tend to give more responsibility to the leader when stress was low but this effect diminished and even slightly reversed as the stress level increases [9]. Groups with prior history tend to utilize more communication channels and come to consensus faster but they do not necessarily make better decisions depending on the task[17]. Decentralised groups allow an even sharing of information and discussion since each member has access to relevant information. In centralised groups, members at the bottom of the hierarchy are mainly responsible for gathering and communicating information up the ladder and decisions are made by fewer people at the top of the hierarchy[13]. Larger groups took longer to come to consensus than smaller groups but when they did, the consensus was more extreme [13].

Routine tasks and tasks of low complexity lead to less communication and more autonomy among group members while those of high complexity lead to a structural, centralised decision making process[3]. Tasks with higher uncertainty lead to more open discussion and a more even participation between group members. Stress decreases the number of communication channels and makes the network more centralised, placing more powers into the hands of fewer people[4][14]. However, Lanzetta [10] found that stress fragments the decision making process and leads to a more equal power structure. Time pressure plays an important role when it exists. Time pressure can be viewed as a special type of stress but also introduces its own complexities. The work on time pressure is not as developed as those of other fields, even though many decision making groups operate under considerable time pressure and the effects are not as clear cut. Isenberg [7] found that groups under time pressure tended to utilize less communication channels and become more centralised while Kelly & McGrath [8] found the opposite and groups would communicate less and fragment more. Brown & Miller [2] found no effect of time pressure on group behaviour. This variance in findings suggests that time pressure affects different groups in different ways and that the effect of time pressure differs strongly based on the other conditions of group decision making. Time pressure appears to be strongly interrelated with other factors and acts as an intensifier.

2.2 In Tabletop Behaviour

A number of different observational studies have shown certain tabletop behaviours occur under non-time critical scenarios.

Scott [12] found that users delineated tabletop space fairly sharply into a personal working space close to the user, a shared space that supports collaboration between two users and several pockets of storage space around the periphery of the table used to sort and store currently unneeded elements. Locations on the table took on ad-hoc, user defined representational meaning. For example, if one user were to create a pile of photos at one location on the table, this would serve as a social cue to all other users that this place was meant for storage. This notion of territoriality is a common theme in current tabletop research and has informed several designs, most notably, of Apted [1] and Morris [11] which features explicitly zones with different access controls.

Morris [11] shows that, in the context of gestural systems on tabletops, due to the collaborative nature of the system, users on the system would naturally teach each other new techniques and perceive if any other user was having difficulty using the interface. This helps significantly with the problem that gestural systems are hard to make discoverable and therefore, hard to learn.

Tang et al [16] investigate coupling around a standing tabletop device and how people's positioning of themselves relative to their group members has social meaning. He discovered that close physical coupling indicated a desire to collaborate while physical separation acted as a cue that the person preferred to work alone. This propensity for movement was previously not recognized since previous studies have primarily focused on people sitting around the table.

3. Design

Based on previously reported work on tabletop behaviour, we wanted to investigate whether such behaviours would also be present under a time critical situation and also whether the reported effects of environmental factors on group makeup would translate across to tabletop interaction. To this end, we have designed a custom made game called the SheepGame which is designed to elicit the desired behaviours.

3.1 Hardware

Figure 1: The ViCAT Table

Figure 2: An example of a Puck on the right and the internals on the left

Our experiment was run on the ViCAT table which consists of a 164cm diagonal, back projected display Interaction with the ViCAT table is achieved via "Pucks" which are small round, cylinders with an IR LED on the bottom. An IR camera is mounted on the underside of the table which can then detect the position of the pucks.

3.2 SheepGame

Figure 3: A screenshot of the sheepgame

The game requires users to herd flocks of sheep using these pucks. Three different tribes of sheep are present on the map, differentiated by Red, Green and Blue coloured wool. Sheep of the same colour would flock together and sheep of different colours would try and avoid and all sheep would try and avoid the pucks when they were placed on the table. The combination of these behaviours gave the sheep a life like quality and also made them difficult to control. The goal of the game was to make sheep run over "money bags" that would randomly appear on the map as well as avoid running over "bombs" that would also randomly appear.

Since sheep would move away from the pucks, sophisticated herding behaviours have to be established in order to herd the sheep in the right direction. The difficultly in controlling the sheep meant that users had to figure out effective strategies of figuring out how to move the sheep and also meant that the use of more than one puck made the task of moving the sheep significantly easier. This was done in order to encourage co-operation between users.

The main reasons why this application was chosen were that it tried to highlight certain possibilities and restrictions of the tabletop interface. SheepGame forces the users to think about the table space in a spatial manner which meant that users needed to cooperate to move the sheep across the table. None of the users can reach the full extent of the table which means that any request for sheep has to pass through multiple users.

We also investigated whether users prefer to constantly move their physical positions around the table. Most previous tabletop research has either concerned users sitting down at a table or tables in which user positions are clearly assigned. However, Tang el al [16] found that when users were working on an architectural task standing up at a table, users constantly shifted positions around the table and that this shift had social meaning. When users wanted to collaborate, they moved closer together but when they signalled they wanted to work alone, they would move so there was physical separation. Whether users prefer to stay still or shift positions has important implications about the importance of building in intelligent user tracking features into tabletop interfaces.

Finally, we investigated how users deal with scarce physical resources and negotiating for resources. By varying the number of pucks given to the users, the availability of pucks could be either scarce or abundant. Users might need a varying number of pucks depending on how many sheep or bombs they had in their area and what other users were doing.

In total, there were several behavioural features that we wanted to investigate and we tried to build the application software so that they would emerge. Table 1 shows a summary of these links.

Behaviour	Feature
Movement around the table	Large table size
Passing off of responsibility between users	Large table size
Negotiating for resources	Limit number of pucks
Users teaching each other	Make herding difficult to master
Cooperation between users	Make herding easier with more people
Fast learning curve	Use simple and intuitive behaviours

Table 1: A list of behaviours that was hoped to be observed and features designed to reveal these behaviours

4. User Study

We conducted a 4 factor, partially within subjects study among 38 subjects. The factors we chose to vary included:

- **Group Size:** Groups were between 1 and 4 people to compare how different sizes would affect the interaction style
- **Pace:** The slow paced version of the game had relatively few moneybags which appeared for long periods of time, leading to a more relaxed game with more time to strategise. The fast-paced version consisted of much more frequent moneybags which lasted only a short time, leading to a more fast paced game.
- **Pressure to win:** The "with pressure" group would be provided a score and told that their task was to beat the score of the previous team. The "no pressure" group would play the game with no score displayed and instead, a random inspirational picture would pop up for every captured money bag. The inspirational picture is a very poor incentive to succeed so there was little pressure put on them to succeed
- **Pucks used:** Puck number varied from between $n+1$ to $2n-1$ pucks where n is the group size.

These factors were chosen either because previous research indicated that they were important determinants of group behaviour or because they helped probe how user behaviour might change.

4.1 Procedure

Participants were split into groups of between 1 and 4 people. All groups completed a series of 6, 2 minute sessions of the SheepGame split into 3 blocks of two. In each block of two, one run was of the high paced game and one was the low paced game. Between each block of 2, participants within the group were allowed to discuss strategies and general issues. This session was designed to see if people would notice each other's actions. A questionnaire was given both before and after the session which asked about various aspects of user behaviour. Additionally, all sessions were recorded and later coded for communication and co-operation patterns.

5. Results & Discussion

5.1 Directed vs. Group Comments

Directed comments were comments from one group member which was clearly directed towards another member. Examples include "Could you pass me that puck" or "Give me that group of red sheep". Group Comments were comments directed towards no user in particular and were meant for the whole group to hear.

Examples include "Try and keep the flocks separated" and "there's lots of reds on the left".

There was a very strong correlation between the size of the group and the frequency of group comments (p < 0.001) as well as a moderate correlation to directed comments (p < 0.02). Group comments became much more frequent in the largest groups while directed comments decreased slightly. This suggests that the effort taken to use directed comments increase with the size of the group. When group sizes increase, the amount of mental load required to keep track of everyone's movements also increases which makes it harder to use directed comments. Users instead switch to group comments which require less mental effort to co-ordinate for the speaker. There were also more of both comments in the fast paced condition compared to the slow paced condition which can be attributed to there being more things to comment on.

5.2 Teaching

One thing that was only very rarely present was users "teaching" other users better methods of achieving goals. There are three main requirements that need to happen for teaching to occur. First, the user must be aware of how other users are performing an action, secondly, they must realize that they know a better way and finally, they must be able to effectively communicate their better method. We found the time criticality affected all three of these steps.

5.3 Movement

Users very rarely changed physical position around the table. The lack of movement can be partially explained by the fact that there was very little advantage to be gained from moving around the table. Because of the unpredictability of when a money bag/TNT would appear and the relatively long time it would take to move and then reorient yourself, moving to shift to a better position was rarely a useful action. However, what is not explained is why users did not move while trying to flock the sheep across the map. Instead, users would stretch themselves as far as they could reach rather than move to a position in which reach is more comfortable. This is contrary to previous work on tables where reaching was something largely avoided and movement was frequent.

5.4 Sharing

One thing the application & experiment design was specifically built to do was to see how users handled the allocation of scarce & uneven resources and to see if users would negotiate for pucks based on perceived need. In reality, this almost never happened. Either one of two different strategies occurred; users would decided the allocation of the pucks at the start of the round and then not change it for the duration of that round or there would be a set of floating pucks on the table which users could grab at will. In retrospect, it seemed fairly obvious that any overly elaborate protocol to negotiate for sharing resources would fail under time-critical scenarios. The pooling solution has many deficiencies, a careless or inconsiderate user could hog the pucks for example, but it is simple and lightweight enough to be practical. Even still, there were at least two groups who found the pooling concept too cumbersome and eventually moved to static allocation of pucks in later trials.

5.5 Reach

One thing we did find which was at odds with previous tabletop work was that users frequently extended themselves across the table to reach for objects at far ends of the table. In previous tabletop literature, it was generally assumed that reaching was something that was only rarely done. However, under our study, reaching was done by all groups a significant portion of the time. Furthermore, reaching tended to be more frequent in the slow paced condition, perhaps because the consequences of missing a moneybag were comparatively much higher so more effort was put into making sure none were missed.

5.6 Cooperation

Two types of co-operation were noted. The first and more common type was when two people worked together to herd sheep towards a moneybag.

This type of cooperation was more common with less pucks and also more common in the no pressure condition. Users who had two pucks were found to very rarely co-operate. Because using two pucks to herd the sheep is vastly more effective than trying to use one, users with one puck stood to gain something by trying to co-operate which overcame the co-ordination necessary in order to achieve it. Users with two pucks still saw some gain with co-operating since 3 or 4 pucks works better than two but the gain was smaller and not worth the effort.

Figure 4: An example of lack of co-operation. The user on the bottom left must reach around the other two users to achieve his goal.

Figure 5: An example of co-operation. The two users on the left are co-operating to herd sheep towards the moneybag at the top (bottom in the picture) of the screen.

The second type of co-operation involved one person divining the intention of another user and trying to help them fulfil that intention. For example, seeing that another person wanted to grab a moneybag and helping them by clearing the path. Often, sheep of the wrong colour would mill around a moneybag which made it very hard for the sheep of the right colour to move in and displace them. In this situation, the only way to collect the money bag is to simultaneously move the wrong sheep out of the area and move the right sheep in. This is very hard with one person but fairly easy to do with two people. Despite this, almost no groups did this and nobody ever asked a team member to help them to do this. In order to divine the intention of another team member, close observation and a careful understanding of the other user are needed. In time-critical scenarios the amount of effort required to do this is simply not available so this form of co-operation happened very rarely, even though it would have been potentially very useful and would have lead to higher scores.

6. Analysis

Our results point to a model of user behaviour in which users have fixed cognitive assets and they act in a way so as to keep behaviour within their cognitive load. When presented with situations which demand more cognitive load to be placed on the task, for example when the pace is faster or when the groups are larger, users will degrade to communication channels which are less effective but are of lower cognitive cost. Additionally, actions which were cognitively costly like noticing other users actions or negotiating for shared resources were very rare under time critical interaction.

7. Conclusions & Future Work

Time critical interaction represents an important and fertile area for tabletop research and there is much scope for developing new methods to enhance previous work. However, we have demonstrated that group behaviour is very different under time critical situations and that this difference needs to be taken into account of when designing such interfaces. Users consistently abandoned collaboration methods which required high degrees of co-ordination or cognitive effort and would adjust their collaboration patterns based on the cognitive demands of the task at hand.

However, this study only looks at time critical interaction under a single application and it is unclear what aspects of the behaviour studied are peculiar to this application and what can generalise over all time critical interaction, More study is needed for time critical work under a variety of circumstances so the confounding factors can be teased out.

8. Acknowledgements

This research was funded by the National ICT Australia program under the IMAGEN project. We would like to thank Ben Close for his assistance in creating the Puck hardware and Julian Epps, Serge Lichman and Mike Wu for their assistance.

9. References

[1] T. Apted, J. Kay, and A. Quigley, "Tabletop sharing of digital photographs for the elderly," in Proceedings of the SIGCHI conference on Human Factors in computing systems, Canada, ACM Press, 2006.

[2] T. M. Brown and C. E. Miller, "Communication Networks in Task-Performing Groups: Effects of Task Complexity, Time Pressure, and Interpersonal Dominance." vol. 31, pp. 131-157, 2000.

[3] B. R. Burleson, B. J. Levine, and W. Samter, "Decision making procedure and decision quality," Human Communication Research, vol. 10, pp. 557-574, 1984.

[4] J. E. Driskell and E. Salas, "Group decision making under stress.," Journal of Applied Psychology, vol. 76, pp. 473-478, 1991.

[5] C. Gersick and J. Hackman, "Habitual routines in task-performing groups." Organizational behavior and human decision processes., vol. 47, pp. 65-97, 1990.

[6] E. Horvitz and G. Rutledge, "Time-dependent utility and action under uncertainty," in Proceedings of the seventh conference on uncertainty in artificial intelligence Los Angeles, California, United States: Morgan Kaufmann Publishers Inc., pp. 151-158, 1991.

[7] D. J. Isenberg, "Some effects of time-pressure on vertical structure and decisionmaking accuracy in small groups," Organizational Behavior and Human Performance, vol. 27, pp. 119-134, 1981.

[8] J. R. Kelly and J. E. McGrath, "Effects of time limits and task types on task performance and interaction of four person groups," Journal of Personality and Social Psychology, vol. 49, pp. 395-407, 1985.

[9] A. Klein, "Changes in leadership appraisal as a function of the stress of a simulated panic situation.," Journal of personality and social psychology., vol. 34, pp. 1143-1156, 1976.

[10] J. T. Lanzetta, "Group behavior under stress," Human Relations, vol. 8, pp. 29-52, 1955.

[11] M. Morris, "Supporting Effective Interaction With Tabletop Groupware," in Computer Science. Horizontal Interactive Human-Computer Systems, TableTop 2006. First IEEE International Workshop,vol. PhD: Stanford, pp.55- 56,
.

[12] 2006. S. D. Scott, M. Sheelagh, T. Carpendale, K. M. Inkpen,"Territoriality in Collaborative Tabletop Workspaces," in Computer Science. in Proceedings of the 2004 ACM conference on Computer supported cooperative work- SESSION: Tabletop design, Chicago, Illinois, USA, pp. 294 - 303, 2004.

[13] M. E. Shaw, in Group dynamics: The psychology of small group behavior, 3 ed New York: McGraw-Hill., 1981.

[14] D. Ebert-May, C. Brewer, and S. Allred, "Innovation in Large Lectures--Teaching for Active Learning," Bioscience, vol. v47 no. 9 pp. 601-607, Oct. 1997.

[15] B. M. Staw, L. E. Sandelands, and J. E. Dutton, "Threat rigidity effects in organizational behavior: A multilevel analysis," Administrative Science Quarterly, vol. 26, pp. 501-524, 1981.

[16] A. Tang, M. Tory, M. Po, P. Neumann, and S. Carpendale, "Collaborative coupling over tabletop displays," in Proceedings of the SIGCHI conference on Human Factors in computing systems, Montréal, Québec, Canada, ACM Press, pp. 1181 - 1190, 2006.

[16] E. P. Torrance, "The behavior of small groups under the stress conditions of "survival."" American Sociological Review, vol. 19, pp. 751-755, 1954

Affective Tabletop Game: A New Gaming Experience for Children

Abdullah Al Mahmud[1], Omar Mubin[1], Johanna Renny Octavia[1], Suleman Shahid[1], LeeChin Yeo[1],
Panos Markopoulos[2], Jean-Bernard Martens[2], Dima Aliakseyeu[2]

[1]*User-System Interaction Program,* [2]*Department of Industrial Design*

Eindhoven University of Technology, Den Dolech 2, 5600 MB Eindhoven, The Netherlands

{a.al-mahmud, o.mubin, j.r.octavia, s.shahid, l.c.yeo, p.markopolous, j.b.o.s. martens, d.aliakseyeu}
@ tue.nl

Abstract

In this paper, we discuss various options for enhancing the gaming experience in augmented tabletop games. More specifically, we propose to incorporate psychophysiological measurements as a part of the gaming experience, and to integrate a desktop game within its real surrounding (i.e., the entire room) in order to promote more physical activity. Such design options, together with other game rules, aim at promoting social interaction between participating players, as this is considered to be a major characteristic of any good multi-player game. We concretized and informally evaluated the above aspects within a specific tabletop game that we designed for children aged 7 to 11 years. Our findings indicate that psychophysiological feedback in a tabletop game does indeed facilitate social interaction and adds to the fun element. Our results also reveal that children appreciate the involvement of the real world environment in a tabletop game.

1. Introduction

Augmented tabletop technology is an approach towards multi-player gaming that combines traditional board games with computing technology. It is a way of offering richer gaming experiences that are well-established in the realm of computing technology [8], and presenting them in a context that is more socially binding, as is for instance evidenced by the popularity of traditional board games. Tabletop games provide co-located, collaborative and face-to-face interaction, while the tangible interaction elements that are often part of such an environment provide an enjoyable user experience through more natural interactions. However, the static nature of conventional tabletop games limits the scope of realizable games [7], so that further extensions of the augmented tabletop concept are worth exploring.

The potential of tabletop gaming has been well substantiated within several research prototypes [15]. Most existing applications are however targeted towards adult (experienced) players. In order to better illustrate the

potential impact of augmented tabletop gaming, and in order to improve accessibility for a broader audience, more applications that appeal to non-expert users, such as children, are required. There are some recent examples of tabletop applications for children within research prototypes such as READ-It [16] or SIDES [10]. The READ-It game was created to enhance the development of reading skills of five-to-seven-year-old children. The SIDES tool was designed to provide social group therapy for adolescents having Asperger's syndrome. It is evident that most tabletop games have been built either for educational purposes or for social skills development within special groups of children. We are aware of relatively less established work in the area of tabletop gaming for children, solely for the purpose of entertainment and fun. Therefore, we feel that there is uncharted potential for utilizing tabletop technology within such a context.

In traditional games where players sit face-to-face, individual players interpret the facial expressions and physical behavior of their co-players. It could be beneficial if, as part of the gaming experience, this subjective judgment could be complemented by a prediction of the other player's emotional state, for instance based on breathing or heart rate. The use of skin conductance response (SCR) for lie detection within the polygraph is of course well-known [2, 3]. It has been established that psychophysiological signals are also potentially useful within entertainment computing [14]. More specifically, physiological data have been used to objectively measure human enjoyment and fun when playing games [9], i.e., as an evaluation metric. We however do not know of any examples where physiological signals have been used as explicit input into a game environment [7], i.e., as an extra input modality that can augment the interaction and hence the overall game experience. Currently, there is no existing research in the game domain that analyzes the use of real time physiology as an element of fun. Most of the work focuses on game metrics or applications for adults whereas computer games for children that incorporate real-time physiological feedback are yet to be explored.

0-7695-3013-3/07 $25.00 © 2007 IEEE
DOI 10.1109/TABLETOP.2007.30

The goal of the reported study was to explore novel ways of designing a game for children, based on the technical options afforded by augmented tabletop technology that could lead to a more engaging and social gaming experience. Early on in the study it was suggested that social interaction and fun could possibly be promoted by using bluff in combination with physiological feedback, as bluff and deception in theory should be influential to physiological data. This was motivated by a wish to capture how an individual player is feeling at any given moment and to integrate this very personal representation of the context into the game. From the start, the target users in our design were children aged 7-11. It is known from child development literature that, children at this stage start structured learning; they are able to understand rules and engage in structural game play [17].

The prototype that we built has a three-fold contribution towards children's game design. First, designing a tabletop game for children using psychophysiological feedback is, as far as we know, new. Second, our study reveals that bluff enhances fun and social interaction in collaborative tabletop game play. Last but not least, the study provides evidence for the fact that integration of the real world within the context of a tabletop environment leads to a more absorbing gaming experience.

The structure of the paper reflects and reports on the different stages in the design process. After an initial enquiry into game play, several rounds of iterative conceptual design ensued. The resulting prototype, its implementation and evaluation will all be described in detail. The major lessons learned from developing and evaluating the design will be explained at the end in conjunction with possible directions for future work.

2. Game design process

2.1. Conceptual design

The game concept was developed as a result of several user studies with children [13]. Next to the game rules, the roles of bluffing and physical activities had to be developed in depth. Bluffing is an obvious attempt to mislead opponents in hope of gaining an advantage over them. Bluffing can potentially add tension and animosity to a game and seems to be widely appreciated as an exciting aspect of games. Physical Incorporation of the real world within the game environment is highly promising as well. This is especially evident in young children, who like to be physically active, adding activities away from the gaming environment was also considered potentially interesting. The rules of the game were drawn up in a participatory manner, which meant

that feedback and suggestions from the children guided the design choices. The game rules also needed to be outlined in such a manner that an appropriate level of difficulty was maintained throughout the game.

The design process started with a sequence of sessions that aimed at establishing the key aspects that we wanted to incorporate into our tabletop game. Bluff, the use of pyschophysiology and various modes of social interaction were therefore analyzed with several groups of children. This was done by slightly altering the rules of traditional and common games such as Ludo, Liar's Dice [6], Pacman 3D [19], Journey of the Wild Divine [18] and Snakes and Ladders. Various insights were gained in this initial phase that further led to new conceptual designs that were subsequently evaluated with the children via a peer tutoring strategy [4]. The concepts were extensions of the games that we had tested in the earlier round. They included Ludo supplemented with bluffing and physiology and a new mobile game called Save the Princess. In Save the Princess the children had to retrieve resources from the environment.

An intermediate game concept, called Pachisi, was composed by synthesizing the rules from Ludo and Save the Princess. The rationale was that both games comprised of elements that the kids enjoyed. A brief evaluation session was conducted with four kids. The objective of the session was two-fold. One was to test this refined game concept and the other one was to test the 'ping' concept for physiological measurements. To know the physiological measurement of a player's opponent he/she could 'ping' a limited number of times for his/her opponent's physiological data. The test revealed that the game-board in Pachisi was perceived as too linear by the children and they expressed a desire for an overall greater challenge in the game board path. Therefore, a new game concept called aMaze was developed that included pictures of various mazes and labyrinths.

The aMaze game concept was tested against Pachisi before settling on the final game concept SaP: Save aMazed Princess. This new game SaP shares the game rules composed for Pachisi, including the aspect of bluffing, but, inspired by the aMaze game, the game board was more challenging in order to incite some puzzle solving skills in the children. A session was also arranged in which the SaP game concept was evaluated (prior to final implementation) with children. The children rated the SaP game positively in terms of the difficulty level in comparison with earlier game concepts. They reported that the SaP game is more challenging, as they have to think and logically decide which path to choose.

2.2. Game rules of SaP

The game rules of the SaP game are intended to encourage individual effort and involvement as well as teamwork amongst members. The game is played with four players, using two dice. Each team is divided into two players; with teammates sitting opposite each other (see Figure 1, where Player 1 and Player 3 constitute one team).

Movement of a player's token on the game board is enabled by throwing two dice. Player 1 starts the game with the first throw of the dice. He or she hides the dice during the throw and calls out aloud the total score on the dice. Starting from the second round in the game, a player is allowed to bluff about his/her score on the dice. A physiological device that continuously records and interprets physiological data is attached to the player that is throwing the dice. In the context of our game, two types of physiological readings, the galvanic skin response (GSR) and the heart rate, are used. The opponent player that is next in line (player 2, in case player 1 has thrown the dice) is given the option of calling the opponent's bluff. If the player who threw the dice is caught bluffing, a penalty is inflicted. As a rule, the penalty is to retreat the player's token back five positions (the last five squares in the path followed up till then, as there is no orientation due to the game board being a maze). If this is not possible (for example, the throw is only the second throw and/or the player hasn't advanced far enough yet), then the penalty is to move the player back to the starting position. If the player is not caught bluffing (for example his/her opponent does not wish to challenge the throw, or the reported number on the dice is actually correct, i.e., the current player is not bluffing), the player can take whatever number of steps based on the number he/she had reported out loud in any direction he/she desires.

Player 1   Player 2

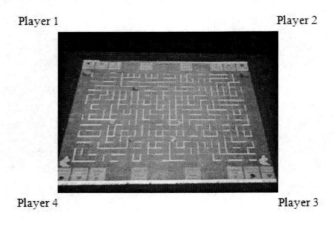

Player 4   Player 3

Figure 1. The game board

In order to judge whether or not a player is bluffing, the challenging player can acquire the assistance of physiological feedback by pinging the player who threw the dice. This is simply done by activating one of two possible menu buttons on the game board, which gives feedback on the current state of the physiological measurements (either GSR or heart rate). The result is an overall estimate from the system of the likelihood of the throw being a bluff. Pinging is only allowed for a fixed number of eight tries and hence cannot be used on every turn. There is no penalty for the player who uses the physiological device when challenging the throw, besides losing one of his tries (wildcards).

The game is structured as a story, having stages (or chapters). The rules of the complete game are as follows. In the first stage of the game, each player has to reach an iconic resource on the maze board (for example, for the first team, player 1 needs to find a river, while player 3 needs to find a mountain). The dice throwing annex bluffing process discussed above is used to move across the board. In order for a player to progress pass a resource; a key that is hidden within the environment is required. Players hence need to leave the game board and retrieve resources from the real world in order to proceed past their current position on the game board. While a player is locating a resource, other players may continue with the game. If Player 1 is looking for a resource, the game can continue until Player 4 throws a dice. Once a player has found the relevant resource he/she can register the retrieval of the resource key, with the system by placing activating a designated menu button on the game board. To create a degree of uncertainty and surprise, the game board supported hidden resources. If a player arrived at certain squares on the game board, a hidden resource popped up. The player would then have to retrieve that resource from the environment before being allowed to move ahead.

In the second stage of the game, both players in a team are given a common target resource (a palace). This means that both players from a team have to meet somewhere on the maze and coexist, after which they can head off together towards the resource target (the palace). The aim of the last stage in the game is to find a princess, in a manner similar to finding the palace. The first team to find the princess is declared the winner. Needless to say that the resources required in a particular stage of the game are only displayed on the game board after the previous stage has been successfully conquered. The flexible way of controlling resources and changing the layout of the game board (to another maze in every round) were of course made possible by the fact that the game was implemented as a virtual tabletop game.

3. Implementation

3.1. Gaming platform

The prototype was implemented on the Build-It [12] hardware platform, using the Visual Interaction Platform (VIP) software [1] (see Figure 2). The setup consists of several artifacts: a data projector, a table supplemented with several tangible checkers (used to represent player's tokens, and for activating the menu buttons on the game board). The light from a data projector mounted above the table is directed towards the table surface, using a mirror. The projector has a resolution of 1024 X 768 pixels and is bright enough for projecting the maze on the table. Interaction on the game board is primarily a selection task. The interaction devices used are square tiles with infrared reflecting tape. A pattern of holes in the reflecting tape provides each tile with a unique identity (and orientation). The center coordinates of the tiles are used as the localization parameters in the selection task. Corner coordinates can be used to track individual checker pieces on top of the intelligent game board, e.g. in order to find out if hidden resources need to be displayed.

Figure 2. The gaming platform

3.2. Software

The tracking system is provided by the VIP platform. Existing software libraries (implemented in C++) that offer vision-based tracking in 2D are incorporated into our application. The VIP platform is designed in order to support a server-client architecture. The server is the tracking system and it sends reports to the client application whenever they become available. Such reports include various parameters and attributes of the tangible checkers, such as their ID, the coordinates of the center and corners of the checker, height, width, etc.

The game engine was visualized in OpenGL (see: http://www.opengl.org/) and C++, and developed using Visual Studio.NET IDE. Animated 2D/3D sounds were implemented using OpenAL (see http://www.openal.org/).

The entire system was a multithreaded application as the tracking and game engine were executing concurrently. In order to generate the maze the Depth First Search (DFS) algorithm was used. It was slightly adapted to render mazes that were a) sufficiently simple and b) had four starting points, one for each player. For each game session a new random maze was generated.

Images and icons in the game were simple bitmap images designed externally in Macromedia Fireworks and texture mapped in OpenGL. The images and icons were primarily comical depictions or caricatures. These images were attached to menu buttons, resource pictures and outputs of physiological measures (see Figure 3).

Figure 3. The representation of sweating, heart rate and bluff probability by Pinocchio on the game board

3.3. Game interface

Each player had a personal interface that was rendered into his or her corner of the maze/tabletop (see Figure 4). This interface included 5 buttons. By employing the tangible tiles, players could activate those buttons. From these 5 buttons, only 3 could actually be activated. Those 3 buttons were pinging for heart rate ("Show me heart rate"), GSR ("Show me sweating") and reporting the retrieval of a physical resource from the environment ("Team A or B found resource"). The other two buttons were meant to be for information display purposes only. One of them was the resultant output of the bluff estimate: a corresponding image of Pinocchio. This same button would display the number of ping tries left when it was not activated. The last button was an image of the current resource target.

Figure 4. Psychophysiological ping output, use of the Tangible Tile, and the interface corner

3.4. Communicating with the Mobi device

For measuring the two physiological readings (GSR and heart rate), the Mobi system is used [11] (see Figure 5). The Mobi system is a multi-channel system that can measure different (electro)-physiological signals such as GSR, ECG, EEG, EMG, temperature, force, movements, respiration etc. For viewing and processing the real-time physiological data captured by the Mobi system, the Portilab signal processing software, which is delivered together with the Mobi system, can be used. It can assist in viewing and processing data in real-time and can store data in a database for offline analysis. We for instance used it to apply filters on the GSR and heart rate signals and to categorize the filtered signals based on signal strength.

Communication between the Mobi device (see Figure 6) and the Portilab software is accomplished using a Bluetooth connection. The processed signals are transmitted by the Portilab software to the game engine, so that this information is available whenever a player wants to "ping" for it.

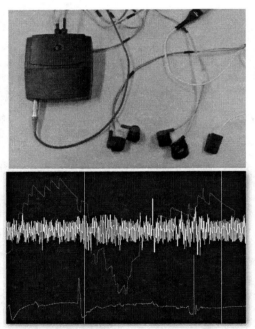

Figure 5. The Mobi system (top) and some psychophysiological outputs in Portilab (bottom)

3.5. Visualizing psychophysiological data

Baseline readings for each player were recorded prior to the start of the game. Players were instructed to be calm and inactive while baseline readings were collected. The physiological data was categorized into three levels (low, medium and high). For heart rate, the most recent five readings were averaged out and compared to the baseline reading. Based on a simple threshold scheme, a low, medium or high level was determined. For GSR, however, the most recent readings were compared amongst each other and similarly a corresponding level was established. The level of physiological arousal was derived either based on the prevailing heart rate or skin response. The level of physiological arousal was directly mapped and a corresponding low, medium or high-level Pinocchio image was displayed as a result.

The icons in Figure 4 depict a high probability of the throw being a bluff, given the length of the nose of Pinocchio and the corresponding high levels of the physiological data. The image of Pinocchio was a pictorial description of the likelihood of the concerned throw being a bluff. The longer the nose of Pinocchio, the more likely was that the other player bluffed. The renderings of the two physiological measures were intended to be equally intuitive.

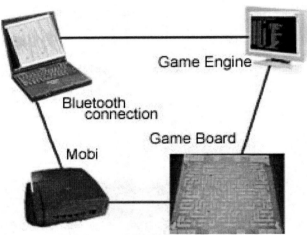

Figure 6. System architecture

4. Prototype evaluation

The final step in the design process was an evaluation of the implemented prototype. The game was evaluated with 8 children within two sessions. Each session lasted for 30 minutes and the teams of children were formed randomly. All the children were acquainted with their teammates before the study and none of them had prior experience in tabletop gaming. Each child in the sessions was given a game board as a gift for their participation.

We aimed to evaluate the usability of the tabletop game, as well as ascertain the impact of our three fold add-ons to tabletop gaming. The key issues were as follows. Would psychophysiological input be understood as a part of the game by children? Would psychophysiological feedback add fun to the game and contribute to a new gaming experience? Would it enhance social communication and social bonding, across and within teams? How would children react to bluff and psychophysiological measurement? How would children react to leaving the game board and carrying out some game play in the environment?

To minimize the risk of technical problems, such as with the calibration of the tracking system, we tested the game in the same laboratory where the prototype was developed. The game table was set in one corner of the lab. The children were seated on two sides of the table (see Figure 7). The physical resources were hidden in different parts of the lab inside paper cups. There were more cups than number of resources. Inside some cups, pictures of resources taped to door keys were hidden. Children were instructed to quickly retrieve the correct resource from the environment and return to the game board.

Each evaluation session comprised of two phases, where we evaluated our game with and without psychophysiological input. Each evaluation session had several parts: training on how to play the game, a free play session, followed by group and individual interviews with card sorting. Physiological baseline measurements were taken for each player before the game started.

One of the experimenters explained how to play the game, the rules and interaction with the game board with respect to the tangible tile and activating the various menu buttons on the game board. The others were video recording, observing, note taking and managing data from the Mobi device.

Figure 7. A play session

5. Results and discussion

5.1 Subjective impressions

We report our analysis based on observations, interviews and videos. It is evident that the children understood that the psychophysiological output and bluff are important and crucial components of the game. They mentioned that they grasped the (ordinal) mapping of physiological data to cartoon drawings. The image of Pinocchio, which was the summarized representation of

the current psychological condition (heart rate, sweating), was ranked higher than the other features/drawings in card sorting by most children. One child said 'Pinocchio helped a lot more than heart rate and sweating because it's the conclusion of both. Most of the time I only see the picture of Pinocchio'. Overall, the gaming experience was enthralling for the children and they appreciated the visualization of the game. Their fascination with the game was evident when one child commented: "The game came from the sky" (referring to the projection). The children also expressed satisfaction with the fact that the game was based on a story with stages or chapters.

In the session when children were playing the game without psychophysiological measurement, children reported that they either looked into the eyes of their opponent or blindly guessed if the other player was bluffing. Later, they expressed during interview that in the game with psychopsychological enhancement it was easier to guess when a player was bluffing. There were more excited during the game with psychophysiological measurement. One child said 'knowing heart rate and nervousness is new and fun' and 'I can see into the heart and body of the others and its cool'. The children also expressed that to ensure sufficient challenge and interest within the game, there should not be too many ping tries. The figure of eight possible tries were deemed to be adequate by the children.

When the psychophysiological measurement device was working properly children had dependency on it and one player said 'sometimes it's too good'. The children reported that psychophysiological measure should not be entirely accurate. It was obvious that there is a need for maintaining a delicate balance between the guessing element and the accuracy of the reading. Moreover, it should not be too easy to fool the system. On the other hand, the system should not be too accurate since this would ruin the challenge in the game, as players would be caught bluffing rather easily. We found out that the data from the Mobi device was partially noisy at times, which would mean that it would not always be accurate.

We only collected qualitative observations on how children compared the two game variations, i.e., with and without psychophysiological feedback. It was evident from their remarks and comments that they enjoyed the version of the game which incorporated the Mobi device and the physiological elements of the game. However, they did at times criticize the Mobi device since it was not ergonomically suited for them, and the earplug for measuring heartbeat was a bit painful and uncomfortable.

Tabletop games today are mostly restricted to audiovisual means, up and around the table [7]. Our evaluation shows that finding resources in the environment, triggered by clues in the tabletop game, is exciting for the children. Children all agreed that collecting resources is a real part of the game and this activity matched with the theme of the game (see Figure 9). During the interviews, children appreciated the game and, interestingly, immediately recognized that it was a combination of technology and other artifacts in the real world. One child stated: "This game is different from others, because you not only use the computer; you also use the real world". Another team said: 'finding the keys is like hunting and that's why we liked it'. The children appreciated the fact that the surrounding environment of the game board was also used as a part of the game. Their approval is validated from the following quote: 'The nice part is clues that are on the board and then you actually move to find the keys in the room on the basis of the clues'.

5.2. Technical observations

From the technological perspective, there were some limitations in the prototype. Tracking of the square tile that was used as the main interaction device in the game was sometimes insufficiently accurate to guarantee successful activation. This was especially a problem when positioning tiles in the corner of the game board. Several children for instance experienced problems when "pinging" (i.e., calling another player's bluff). They sometimes needed several attempts before being successful (see Figure 8). The (unwanted) consequence was that they lost some of their tries (wildcards). The children were able to adjust to this, since they made fewer placement errors in the second game session. We had to compensate for this and for one of the game sessions, we removed the limit of eight tries, consequently providing the children with unlimited tries.

Figure 8. Using tangible tile to check psychophysiological reading

A constraint on the game play was the limited set of GSR electrodes of the Mobi device. During the test, we had only four electrodes, two for each player. Therefore, children had to swap their electrodes with other players, when their turn was over. However, it did not introduce any delay in the game play.

Since the tabletop was not very big, throwing dice on the table was a problem for the children as the dice would occasionally drop from the table and they would have to repeat their throw. Implementing digital dice could help to solve this issue. This could also aid in preventing children from cheating and/or accidentally turning the dice at the time of revealing them to other players. However, there is a trade off, as tangible dice provide children with physical game-play. The children were observed to exhibit peculiar traits with respect to throwing the dice. At times, children would blow into their palms before throwing the dice (as a good luck charm), or extensively shake the dice before throwing it on the table.

Handling and processing of physiological data from the Mobi device was a challenge. The Mobi device was able to record data when it was operating in stationary mode. However, we observed that at times, the device produced noisy data that had to be normalized during transmission to identify which part corresponded to a peak. The peak would then directly represent and determine the bluff probability. Though it is possible to reduce noise by using appropriate filters; yet the transmission of real time psychophysiological data into any game engine faces considerable challenges, primarily due to the limitation of technology. This would be an important direction of future exploration, especially in terms of incorporating physiology in a real time and mobile setting.

Figure 9. Winning (left) and finding resources on the ground (right)

It is common in tabletop systems that the orientation of a shared object causes problems for its users who are located differently around the table [5]. While projecting and designing the game and images we tried to overcome the orientation issue. The maze game board was projected as it is, whereas the interaction buttons on the game board were oriented based on a player's point of reference. The only text that appears during the game is at the start. Here players have to choose the difficultly level of the maze, number of players etc. The children who were seated on the wrong side of the table did not report any problems in interpreting the startup text. Overall children did not mention any problems that could be attributed to the orientation of any of the representations.

6. Conclusion and future work

We have investigated how to design and build an affective tabletop game for children. The evaluation of the designed prototype revealed that children appreciated it as a new gaming experience. The addition of psychophysiologiacal data into a tabletop application provided an extra modality for the game environment. From a research perspective, this work could inspire other ways of utilizing psychophysiological measurements, especially in mobile gaming environments. We also explored the potential of incorporating a tabletop game within a broader context, with the intention of enhancing social interaction and fun within and around the game. The implications for game design of this latter aspect also need to be developed further.

7. Acknowledgement

We would like to thank the children for their active participation and valuable comments. A special mention to their parents for extending their cooperation and for granting permission to use the photos and videos of their children for educational purposes.

8. References

[1] Aliakseyeu D., Martens J.B., Subramanian S., Vroubel, M. and Wesselink, W., "Visual Interaction Platform", In *Proc. Interact 2001*, Tokyo, pp. 232-239.

[2] Geddes, L.A., "History of the polygraph: An instrument for the Detection of Deception", Biomed. Eng., 1973, vol. 8, pp. 154-156.

[3] Gross, J.J and Levenson, R.W., "Emotional suppression: self report and expressive behavior", Journal of Personal and Social Psychology, 1993, vol. 64, pp. 970-986

[4] Höysniemi, J., Hamalainen, P., and Turkki, L., "Using Peer Tutoring in Evaluating Usability of Physically Interactive Computer Game with Children", Interacting with Computers, 2002, vol.15, no.3, pp. 203-225.

[5] Kruger, R., and Carpendale, M.S.T., "Orientation and Gesture on Horizontal Displays", In *UBiCOMP workshop on collaboration with Interactive Walls and Tables*, 2002.

[6] Liar's dice. http://en.wikipedia.org/wiki/Liar's_dice/

[7] Magerkurth, C., Memisoglu, M., and Engelke, T., "Towards the next generation of tabletop gaming experiences", In *Proc. Graphics Interface 2004*, pp. 73-80.

[8] Mandryk, R. L., Maranan, D. S., and Inkpen, K. M., "False prophets: Exploring hybrid board/video games", *Proceedings of CHI 2002*, pp. 640-641.

[9] Mandryk, R.L. and Inkpen, K., "Physiological Indicators for the Evaluation of Co-located Collaborative Play", In *Proc. CSCW 2004*, Chicago, IL, USA.

[10] Marie Piper, Anne., O'Brien, Eileen., Morris, M.R. and Winograd, T., "SIDES: A Cooperative Tabletop Computer Game for Social Skills Development", In *Proc. CSCW 2006*, November 4-8, 2006.

[11] Mobi system. http://www.tmsi.com/?id=5

[12] Rauterberg, Matthias., Bichsel, Martin., Leonhardt, Ulf., Meier, M., "BUILD-IT: a computer vision-based interaction technique of a planning tool for construction and design", In *Proc. Interact 1997*, pp. 587-588.

[13] Salen, K. and Zimmerman, E., *Rules of Play: Game Design Fundamentals*, The MIT Press, Massachusetts, 2003.

[14] Sakurazawa, Shigeru., Yoshida, Naofumi., Munekata, Nagisa, "Entertainment feature of a game using skin conductance response", In *ACM SIGCHI International Conference on Advances in Computer Entertainment Technology*, June 3-5, 2004.

[15] Scott, S.D., Grant, K.D., & Mandryk, R.L., "Systems guidelines for Co-located, Colaborative work on a Tabletop Display", In *Proc. ECSCW'03*, Helsinki, Finland, September 14-18, 2003.

[16] Sluis, R. J., Weevers, I., van Schijndel, C. H., Kolos-Mazuryk, L., Fitrianie, S., and Martens, J. B., "Read-It: five-to-seven-year-old children learn to read in a tabletop environment", In *Proc. IDC '04*.

[17] Wertsch, J.V., *Vygotsky and the Social Formation of Mind*, Harvard University Press, Cambridge, 1985.

[18] Wild Divine. http://www.thelaboroflove.com/wild-divine/

The TViews Table in the Home

Ali Mazalek
*Georgia Institute of
Technology, Atlanta, GA*
mazalek@gatech.edu

Matthew Reynolds
*Georgia Institute of
Technology, Atlanta, GA*
msr@gatech.edu

Glorianna Davenport
*MIT Media Lab
Cambridge, MA*
gid@media.mit.edu

Abstract

The past several years of computer interaction research have shown an increasing interest in tabletops for shared user interactions through touch or tangible objects. Digital media tables offer the potential to expand our digital interactions into casual social settings that are not appropriate for desktop platforms, such as home living rooms. We have developed a tangible media table called TViews, which provides an extensible architecture to enable multi-user interactions with a range of media applications and content via tagged tangible objects. The TViews object positioning utility functions on the surface of an embedded display and enables real-time tracking of a virtually unlimited set of uniquely identified wireless objects that can be used on the surface of any similar table. These objects can be physically customized in order to suit particular applications, and can provide additional functionality through external input and output elements on the objects themselves. In this paper, we present a first field trial of TViews to gain some initial insight into how such a device could be adopted in a real-world home.

1. Introduction

As digital media content and applications grow and spread, human-computer interaction researchers are designing and refining the interface technologies through which we can experience them. Research fields such as tangible interfaces and ubiquitous computing seek to better integrate the lives we lead in the digital realm with our physical environment and social human interactions. In particular, the past several years have shown an increasing interest in the area of tabletop computing, which explores how tabletops can be used as a shared display space for interaction with media content and applications via touch or tangible objects. By providing multiple points-of-control for multi-user interactions around a shared horizontal display, digital media tables (also called digital tabletop platforms) have the potential to enhance and transform the way we share, interact with and socialize around digital applications and content.

At our research lab, we have developed a digital media table with tangible interaction called TViews, which provides an extensible architecture to enable multi-user interactions with a broad range of media content and applications via tagged tangible objects. Two instances of the TViews platform have been constructed in the form of coffee tables for the home. In this paper, we describe our first small-sized field trial of the TViews Table in the home. Through this test, we hoped to discover how the platform would hold up under prolonged use and to see if and how media tables can be adopted in a real-world home.

2. Related work

This section provides a brief overview of some notable and relevant work in tabletop computing.

Some of the research has focused on the development of tabletop sensing technologies, such as the multi-touch sensing DiamondTouch [2] and the tangible object tracking Sensetable [11]. Other examples of digital tabletops include the Philips Entertaible [5] and Microsoft's recently announced surface computing platform [9], both of which can track multiple touches as well as tangible object interactions on an embedded display surface.

There has also been a variety of work on tabletop application designs. Examples include the Urp urban planning system [16], Personal Digital Historian for building digital group histories on the DiamondTouch [14], the SharePic photo application [1], and role-playing games on the STARS platform [6].

In addition to novel application concepts, a number of researchers have been exploring novel interface metaphors and the display and interaction issues particular to tabletops. For instance, the DiamondSpin API provides a means of accommodating the different

0-7695-3013-3/07 $25.00 © 2007 IEEE
DOI 10.1109/TABLETOP.2007.19

viewing angles that users have when seated around a table display [15], while "interface currents" support shared access to content pieces by flowing them around the edge of the horizontal display surface [4].

There have also been a number of research studies seeking to understand collaboration and group dynamics around digital tabletops in order to inform interface design. Examples include work on territoriality [13] and social protocols [10] in tabletop workspaces, as well as studies of the effects of group and table size on collaboration [12]. To date, most studies done on digital tabletops have been conducted in research labs, and there have been limited attempts to deploy interactive media tables into the real-world. Some exceptions include design case studies done with the Drift Table in real homes to discover how such environments support ludic activities [3] and tabletop storytelling workshops in a clubhouse and art school using the Tangible Viewpoints system [7].

3. The TViews Table

TViews is an interactive tabletop display platform that provides multi-user interaction through an extensible set of tagged tangible objects that can be tracked on its surface in real-time. The following subsections provide a brief overview of the TViews platform and describe some of the media applications that have been developed for the table. For more information on the TViews architecture, please see [8].

3.1. System Overview

The TViews Table is based on custom-built acoustic sensing technology that works through the surface of a glass panel placed above an LCD screen embedded in the surface of the table. The technology allows the table to scale to different sizes, and enables an extensible set of interactive objects called pucks to be tracked on its surface and moved from one table platform to another. TViews also provides a scalable framework so that many different applications can run on the same platform or on many connected platforms at once. The compact sensing and display design of the TViews table allows it to be set up in everyday living environments where there is little or no support for infrastructure that is external to the table itself.

TViews interactive objects can be associated to a particular application or used as generic controls for multiple applications. The functionality of the pucks can be extended via externally attached input/output devices, such as buttons, lights or small displays. The current generic puck design includes a top-mounted button and snap-in acrylic pieces that enable color-

customization. In contrast to touch-based tabletop displays, interaction through tangible objects allows application designers to create customized physical objects for different applications, such as the building models in Urp [16]. Using the extensible I/O feature, TViews tags could eventually be embedded into existing devices, such as cameras or cell phones.

3.2. Applications

Over ten different applications have been developed for the TViews platform over the course of our development and testing. We describe here the four applications for media content management and tabletop gameplay that were used during our first field trial of the TViews table.

3.2.1. Picture Sorter. This picture management application allows users to organize their digital photos in a manner similar to sorting physical photos on a tabletop. New images appear in a pile at the center of the table, and the pucks are used to sort them into smaller clusters. The application currently provides only basic sorting functionality, however we plan to incorporate tagging and intelligent sorting features similar to those found in desktop photo applications.

3.2.2. Map Browser. The Map Browser uses GPS metadata to automatically organize images on a geographical map based on the time and location at which each picture was taken. A timeline view provides a temporal means for browsing larger collections on the map. Users attach the pucks to different days on the timeline and drag them around the map to reveal the images, which appear clustered around the puck.

3.2.3. Pente. Pente can be played with two or three players on a single table or in networked mode across two tables. Each player uses their own color-coded puck to drop yellow, red or blue stones onto the playing grid. The goal is to place five stones in a row or capture five pairs of an opponent's stones.

3.2.4. Springlets. Virtual spring objects (masses connected by springs) are controlled by the pucks, leaving colorful trails behind them as they bounce around the display area. Users latch onto the masses with a button press, and drag them around the table causing the attached masses to follow behind. A second button press drops the masses, propelling them forward on their own. Once the spring objects are in motion, users can engage in improvisational play as they try to trap the masses to control the movement and display of colorful trails on the tabletop.

4. TViews in the Home

In this section, we describe our first field trial of the TViews Table in a real-world apartment. Our motivations for conducting a trial of the TViews Table in an actual real home setting were three-fold:

- To evaluate how the technology and system design would hold up when put under prolonged real-world use.
- To examine the use of the interactive objects for controlling media applications and to assess the ease-of-use of the TViews design across our two types of leisure-oriented applications: media sharing and gameplay.
- To see if and how interactive media tables adapt to existing social practices within a real-world home in the context of casual media sharing and gameplay.

The informal and situated nature of this preliminary trial allowed us to observe how one particular home environment assimilated the physicality and playful intent of the table. In this section, we provide and overview of the demographics and methods of the trial, and discuss observations and user feedback.

4.1. Demographics and Methods

We situated the TViews Table in the home of a volunteer user, a technology-related project manager in his early 30s, for a one month period. During this time, he hosted a series of six small social gatherings for his friends and family, during which guests were invited to interact with the table.

In addition to the host, sixteen other users came to try the table, in groups of one to four at time. Larger groups were difficult to accommodate given the small size of the apartment. Nine of the sixteen participants were young professionals in the 25-35 year age-range, whose professions ranged across consulting, software engineering, law, landscape architecture, industrial design, library services, publishing and marketing. Five of the participants were graduate students aged 25-35, in computer science, design and media studies fields. One participant was a filmmaker and academic, and one was an older family member who had worked in nursing (both were over 50). Nine of the participants considered themselves to be digitally savvy. Finally, four of the sixteen participants were family members, four were very close friends, seven were casual friends and one was a work colleague.

We tried to provide a casual atmosphere for the interaction sessions that fit into the ordinary lifestyle of our volunteer host and other users. Since many participants were young professionals with full-time jobs, the interaction sessions were typically held in the evening or on weekends, with two sessions each week for the duration of the month. Participants were invited to the apartment of the host as guests, for a social evening that could include gameplay and hearing about the host's recent travels. They were also made aware in advance that they would have the opportunity to engage in these activities using the host's newly (and temporarily) acquired digital media coffee table, and that a researcher would quietly observe and videotape the social event from the sidelines.

Each interaction session consisted of an informal dinner or snacks, following by casual chatting and social interaction in the living room. Participants sat on a couch and chairs around the TViews Table and were invited to try out the different applications. Over the course of the session, the host casually introduced participants to the range of applications and activities that were available on the table: viewing and organizing personal photos (using the Picture Sorter), browsing a collection of recent travel photos (using the Map Browser), playing a game of Pente, or playful interaction with the Springlets application. Each session lasted around three hours. The guests would try out the different applications on the table, often choosing to interact more or less with certain ones depending on their interests. Details about the actual usage of the table and different applications are provided in the following section. As the evening wound down, we engaged the users in informal brainstorming to gather their feedback about the table and potential applications.

We observed user interactions with the table, and used video and audio recording for data collection purposes during the interaction and brainstorming sessions and to keep track of the applications used by each group. Participants were also asked to complete a questionnaire before leaving. This was used to gather background information about each participant's level of media and technology use, and to get some specific comments and feedback about the interaction sessions. The following section presents our observations of the table and application usage and user feedback.

4.2. Usage Observations and Feedback

The informal and situated nature of the trial allowed us to observe how one particular home environment adopted the physicality and playful intent of the table. The natural setting and relatively long duration of each interaction session (~3 hours per session, a typical duration for an evening social gathering at the host's apartment) drew the focus of participants away from the novelty of the platform. Parallel to our goals described above, we present our observations from three perspectives: the table's technical performance, the interactions with different applications, and the assimilation of the table into the home environment.

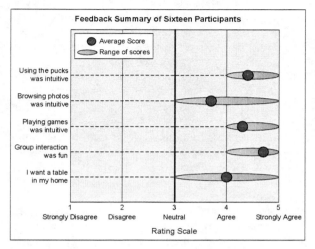

Figure 1. Results of user feedback questionnaires.

4.2.1. Technical Performance. In addition to sharing media and playing games, our TViews users put the table through the usual everyday coffee-table usage, such as placing a wide assortment of objects on its surface and eating food on the display while playing games. Additionally, we observed that the host would slightly rearrange the furniture in his living room at times, for example to make space for a larger group of guests. On two occasions, this took place during the interaction session itself, in order to accommodate more people sitting around the TViews table. In these cases, the table did not require any kind of recalibration of the sensing technology.

Overall the system performed well, and participants were able to use the table and pucks without difficulty. The only significant technical issues that came up were position errors resulting from poor contact of the acoustic sensor to the surface of the glass and a lag in positioning if a puck was moved too quickly. Unlike our past experiences with the table in lab-based tests, users at home (even the non-technically-oriented ones) were not particularly cautious with the interaction objects, often pressing them hard or repeatedly banging them on the display surface to force the tracking to correct itself. We are continuing to further develop the TViews sensing technology to address the current sensing issues.

Figure 2. Map Browser user interaction.

4.2.2. Application and Object Interactions. In general, people found the pucks intuitive to use and liked the idea of a shared tabletop interface for the home. Figure 1 shows the results of the feedback questionnaires. On average, people found the picture sorting and browsing activities (with the Picture Sorter and Map Browser applications) less intuitive than the games (Pente and Springlets). This was somewhat surprising: we had imagined that since the Picture Sorter application is based on a real-world metaphor, it would be very easy to understand. One reason for this result might be the position errors, which sometimes made it difficult to grab and hold the photos. Another reason might be that the pucks were acting only as generic controls (similar to a stylus). Since users tend to focus on the photos themselves rather than on the interaction objects or technology, direct touch on the tabletop might serve as a better means for dragging/manipulating images.

Users responded slightly better to the Map Browser than to the Picture Sorter. In the Map Browser (see Figure 2), users attached collections of photos (sorted by date) to different pucks. This metaphor of physical puck as containers for media content was well understood, and suggests that placing cameras or other personal media devices placed on the table would be a useful means for accessing collections of media content. The following two short dialogues show typical interactions with the Map Browser application. Jack is the host, and Fred and Amy are family members (names of the participants have been changed). In both examples, Amy and Fred are each browsing a different collection of photos on different parts of the map, and repeatedly switch focus between the two collections.

Map Browser Example 1

Amy: [*Dragging an image collection to a location*] Two pictures from Jill's home town... or college...

Fred: [*Switching focus from his own puck*] Oh, the college... I took these!

Amy: That's the college? [*Moving to next picture in the collection*] Oh... and there she is in her big coat... it's cold there.

Jack: Cold, rainy and wet...

Amy: Rainy and wet in Ireland...

Map Browser Example 2

Fred: [*Looking over at Amy's puck*] Ah yes, driving on the sand bar, haha...

Amy: [*Focusing back to Fred's pictures for a moment and referring to a previously mentioned paint job*] I'm sure you're proud of your work.

Jack: [*Pointing at picture from the puck Amy is holding*] Do you see this one right here?

Amy: [*Looking back to her puck to see what Jack is showing*] Yes.

Jack: This was an island off the coast and we were driving by over here [*indicating location on map*] and we saw some cars driving over and we were wondering what was going on over there. And mom said "oh, they do auto commercials on the beach." [*Amy takes another puck and drags aside the image Jack is talking about for a closer look*] So we drove closer and it turned out that when the tide is out you can actually drive... you can't really see it in this picture because it's zoomed out... [*Pointing at picture again*] but there are road signs that go all the way through.

Amy: [*Leaning over to look*] Oh weird!

Jack: And it's basically what the locals do... they drive out onto the beach but you can only do it at certain times of day. [*Stepping through pictures on puck*] The other picture might actually show it better here... [*Stopping at picture*] That one, see... there's a road sign.

Amy: Oh yeah, neat!

From these short sequences, we see how people are able to fluidly switch focus between their own puck interactions and those of the others around them. It is important to notice that the user interactions are not turn-based, but simultaneous. The nature of their interactions transitions easily from the way they used to browse physical photographs on a table, and allows casual conversation and informal storytelling to emerge around digital media content. This example shows how a traditional activity like photo-browsing can transition easily onto a novel platform like a digital tabletop, and integrate the benefits of automatic

(temporal and geographic) organization of the photos. It also demonstrates that such a platform can transition easily into existing spaces like the home living room by making use of and adapting to existing social practices and conventions within the shared environment.

After the first few interaction sessions, it became evident that different groups of users were interested in different applications based not only on personal preference, but also on their relationship to the host. For instance, of the six groups invited for interaction sessions, the three groups that included family members were far more interested in browsing photos than in playing games. Since the Map Browser application was used to navigate a collection of photos from the host's recent trip to Ireland, family members all wanted to hear him tell stories about his trip. Since the photos were from a single vacation, it was possible to browse the entire collection within 10-15 minutes. However these users typically spent 1-2 hours with the Map Browser application, and most of the time thus went to storytelling triggered by the photos and locations they were looking at. The Picture Sorter was the least frequently used application. User feedback suggested that this was because they weren't interested in sorting another person's (in this case the host's) photo collection. This suggests that a Picture Sorting application on tabletop should allow users to contribute their own collections, and might do best to focus on sharing and swapping rather than on organization.

The groups that included more casual friends or acquaintances on the other hand were least interested in the photos, and chose to play games instead. This included the Springlets application and the Pente game. Like the photo-related applications, Springlets encouraged simultaneous user interactions, while Pente followed a turn-based approach like traditional board games.

All six groups tried Springlets, which proved to be a nice background/ambient application that users could interact with off and on in a casual manner (e.g. while eating or having conversations). Three groups (one with two family members, and two groups of friends) got very engaged in the Springlets interaction for around 30 minutes. This was quite surprising since we had initially thought that the application might be too simplistic for real use, but we found that many participants became very engaged with the improvisational form of interaction, calling it "addictive" and "mesmerizing". Participants often turned the interaction into a form of game play, where they would try to capture the bouncing masses with their pucks, sometimes even using two pucks at a time (one in each hand) or trying to coordinate their movements with those of other players. During the brainstorming sessions, participants said they wanted to see more games on the table that would engage them in collaborative or competitive play where they have to coordinate their movements with one another. Along those lines, a number of participants suggested that simulation games would be particularly appropriate, such as the line of popular games produced by Maxis (SimCity, The Sims, etc.).

Figure 3. Users playing a game of Pente.

The Pente game (see Figure 3) proved to be very popular, particularly with participants who were already familiar with the board game. The puck interaction was very natural, and people did not focus on the technology at all during gameplay (aside from the times when a sensing error caused a mistake in a person's move). Three of the groups played the Pente game for 1-2 hours, becoming very competitive at times. The following short dialogue is an excerpt from a typical three player Pente session at the TViews table. Jack is the host, and Bob and Tom are close friends (names of the participants have been changed).

Pente Example

Bob: [*Pointing*] But you've gotta put it there...
Tom: [*Pointing*] Right, because he'll have... [*Indicates region of pieces on board*]
Bob: No, I guess it doesn't really matter.
Jack: [*Laughs*]
Tom: Ah, we'll put it here... [*Places piece*]
Jack: I love my friends.
Tom: [*To Bob as he prepares to place piece*] So you gotta knock that out, and then he'll have [*indicates area on board*]... and you'll get to put another piece somewhere. [*Bob places piece*]

This short sequence shows players being playfully competitive, and interacting in a similar manner to traditional board games. Even though Pente is a turn-

based game, all participants said they preferred to each have their own puck rather than to share a single puck between multiple people. Since traditional board games typically provide separate pieces for each player, this is a well-known interaction style and it provides players with a physical object that they can identify with during game-play. We observed that several people actually held the puck in their hands even when they were not using it, rather than leaving it sitting on the table. This behavior brings up an interesting design issue, which is how to map the pucks to the virtual objects within the game space. Different board games use different approaches to map the playing pieces to the space of the game board. For instance in a game of chess or Monopoly, the pieces must remain on the board at all times and they move around mostly within the space of the board (unless they are captured for instance). In contrast, in a game such as Pente the stones are picked up from a central bin at each turn and deposited onto the game board, which suggests a mapping where pucks are used to drop stones rather than act as stones themselves.

4.2.3. Assimilation into the Home. The TViews Table was quite easily assimilated into the living room, and users found the shared media interactions to be a lot of fun. It was clearly important that, in addition to being a shared media platform, the table could also act as a regular coffee table with its display turned off. When asked whether they would like to have a media table in their home, user responses ranged from neutral to a very positive "yes". Some were hesitant to add another technological device to their lives and worried that it might demand too much of their time. Several people said they would like many surfaces around their home to be media-enabled, so they could turn them on/off as desired and use them in place of their regular desktop PCs for everyday tasks such as checking calendars or managing other media devices. A few people said they wanted a table like this simply to play games.

Another important observation in terms of adoption relates to shared vs. single person use. Given that our applications were designed for multi-user interaction, the host rarely played with them by himself. Instead, he would use the table, together with an ordinary wireless mouse and keyboard, to check the weather or read the news in a web browser over his morning coffee, or to search for information, such as directions to a store. Since the computer inside the table was always running (the table would go into standby mode after 20 minutes of non-use), this was quicker and easier than starting up his laptop as he would otherwise have done (he did not have a desktop PC).

During the brainstorming sessions, participants suggested a broad range of applications for media interaction tables. These were by no means limited to interaction within the home environment, but included applications for other physical contexts, such as workplaces, classrooms and public places. Suggested applications for the home environment fit into two broad categories: personal home management and leisure or entertainment activities. Personal home management includes information retrieval (calendars, recipes, directions, etc.), management of home devices (appliances, lighting, media center, etc.), management of portable devices (cell phones, MP3 players, etc.) and messaging and remote communication. Suggested leisure activities included gaming (board games, networked games, educational games, simulations, role-playing, etc.), storytelling, virtual terrariums, audio control (mixing, playlists), and media browsing and editing. While more investigation needs to be done to assess who will use media tables in the home, how often, and for what purposes, we feel that in addition to leisure activities, the practical (and often single-user) uses will be important for adoption.

5. Summary of Findings

In this section, we provide a brief summary of our findings based on the observations and feedback discussed above. These include lessons learned about the practicality and logistics of conducting digital tabletop trials in real homes (5.1 & 5.2), and lessons learned about the design and development of digital media tables and applications for the home (5.3 & 5.4).

5.1. Novelty Factor

There is a high level of novelty associated with digital tabletops in the home, and users are likely to be impressed by this. Interaction sessions thus need to be long enough for users to get engaged in the applications and media content, and not simply be impressed by the table alone. Relevant and personal media content is important in this respect, since it focuses user attention on their own interests and lives, and engages them in natural interactions in which the novel technology can become transparent to them.

5.2. Natural Setting

To keep the interaction sessions natural (as close as possible to the home's normal social gatherings), subjects can be drawn only from people who normally socialize with and visit the host. However different people have personal preferences for different forms of entertainment. These can be influenced by many complex factors, both permanent (e.g. some don't like

board games) or temporary (e.g. are they in the mood to play a game, have they already seen those photos). Trials with a much larger subject base and in many different homes should be done to get a clearer sense of which applications have the broadest appeal.

5.3. Form and Robustness

An appliance and furniture item such as a digitally enhanced coffee table most likely replaces the existing non-digital equivalent in the home. As such, in addition to providing new functionality, it needs to support the ordinary uses of the table. The form of the table thus needs to be of an appropriate size to fit in the space, and of the correct height to be usable with the couch and chairs. Moreover, the table and technology need to be robust enough to support ordinary use. People at home are less careful with new technology than in a laboratory setting; they drop food and spill their drinks on their coffee tables all the time.

5.4. Applications and Use

The potential applications for digital media tables in the home are broad, and further exploration is needed to understand the full scope. For example, our findings suggest that single-user practical applications could be as critical as multi-user leisure-oriented applications. While some users (particularly the non-technically-oriented ones) were hesitant to add more technology into their lives, there is potential that in certain cases a digital tabletop could replace regular PCs for specific tasks, e.g. searching for information like travel directions. Also important is the ability for the table to communicate with other devices, such as cell phones and PDAs, particularly for technically-oriented users who already have many devices and for whom compatibility is a major issue. Lastly, as mentioned above, users have different preferences for leisure activities at home. Depending on the application, different means of interaction are more or less suitable (e.g. tangible objects or touch), and one must think carefully about their design in each case.

6. Conclusion

As digital applications such as media sharing and gaming increasingly permeate our everyday lives, we need think about how these activities can be integrated into our everyday physical and social settings in a way that minimizes the gap between our physical and digital world interactions. Digital tabletop platforms provide a solution to the physical/digital separation within certain contexts, such as shared spaces in the home. However the physical settings and possible uses for tabletop platforms are very different from desktop PCs, and there is much work to be done to move this emerging field forward.

Tabletop research ranges from sensing and hardware development, to the study of collaborative interactions with co-located users, and to the design and development of tabletop interfaces and applications. Important questions are whether and how real-world settings can assimilate these new platforms in practice: how does ordinary table usage successfully extend into the digital realm, and what are the applications and methods that can enrich user experiences and social interactions around digital tabletops. Our first field trial of the TViews media table has provided some initial insight into how such a device might be adopted in a real-world home. Based on our findings, we plan to further develop the TViews platform and applications in order to provide engaging experiences for users.

7. Acknowledgements

We would like to thank our collaborators at Samsung and the Media Fabrics group at the MIT Media Laboratory.

8. References

[1] Apted, T., Kay, J., Quigley, A. (2006). "Tabletop Sharing of Digital Photographs for the Elderly" in *Proceedings of CHI '06*, pp.781-790.

[2] Dietz P., Leigh D. (2001). "DiamondTouch: A Multi-User Touch Technology" in *Proceedings of UIST '01*, pp.219-226.

[3] Gaver, W. et. al. (2004). "The Drift Table: Designing for Ludic Engagement" in *Extended Abstracts of CHI '04*, pp.885-900.

[4] Hinrichs, U., Carpendale, S., Scott, S., Pattison, E. (2005). "Interface Currents: Supporting Fluent Collaboration on Tabletop Displays" in *Proceedings of Smart Graphics '05*, pp.185-197.

[5] Loenen, E. van, Bergman, T., Buil, V., Gelder, K. van, Groten, M., Hollemans, G., Hoonhout, J., Lashina, T. and Wijdeven, S. (2007). "Entertaible: A Solution for Social Gaming Experiences" in *Proceedings of the Tangible Play workshop, Intelligent User Interfaces conference*, pp.16-18.

[6] Magerkurth, C., Memisoglu, M. and Engelke, T. (2004). "Towards the Next Generation of Tabletop Gaming Experiences" in *Proceedings of Graphics Interface GI '04*, pp.73-80.

[7] Mazalek, A., Davenport, G. (2003). "A Tangible Platform for Documenting Experiences and Sharing Multimedia Stories" in *Proceedings of ACM Multimedia Workshop on Experiential Telepresence*, pp.105-109.

[8] Mazalek, A., Reynolds, M., Davenport, G. (2006). "TViews: An Extensible Architecture for Multiuser Digital Media Tables" in *IEEE Computer Graphics and Applications Journal*, 26(5), Sep/Oct 2006, pp.47-55.

[9] Microsoft Surface, http://www.microsoft.com/surface/

[10] Morris, M.R., Ryall, K., Shen, C., Forlines, C., Vernier, F. (2004). "Beyond Social Protocols: Multi-User Coordination Policies for Co-located Groupware" in *Proceedings of CSCW '04*, pp.262-265.

[11] Patten, J., Ishii, H., Hines, J., Pangaro, G. (2001). "Sensetable: A Wireless Object Tracking Platform for Tangible User Interfaces" in *Proceedings of CHI '01*, pp.253-260.

[12] Ryall K., Forlines C., Shen C., Morris M.R. (2004). "Exploring the Effects of Group Size and Table Size on Interactions with Tabletop Shared-Display Groupware" in *Proceedings of CSCW '04*, pp.284–293.

[13] Scott, S.D., Carpendale, M.S.T., Inkpen, K.M. (2004). "Territoriality in Collaborative Tabletop Workspaces" in *Proceedings of CSCW '04*, pp.294-303.

[14] Shen, C., Lesh, N.B., Vernier, F., Forlines, C., Frost, J. (2002). "Sharing and Building Digital Group Histories" in *Proceedings of CSCW '02*, pp.324-333.

[15] Shen, C., Vernier, F.D., Forlines, C., Ringel, M. (2004). "DiamondSpin: An Extensible Toolkit for Around-the-Table Interaction" in *Proceedings of CHI '04*, pp.167-174.

[16] Underkoffler, J., Ishii, H. (1999). "Urp: A Luminous-Tangible Workbench for Urban Planning and Design" in *Proceedings of CHI 1999*, pp.386-393.

Living with a Tabletop: Analysis and Observations of Long Term Office Use of a Multi-Touch Table

Daniel Wigdor[1,2], Gerald Penn[2], Kathy Ryall[1], Alan Esenther[1] Chia Shen[1]

[1]*Mitsubishi Electric*
Research Labs
{ryall | esenther | shen} @ merl.com

[2]*Department of Computer Science,*
University of Toronto
dwigdor@dgp.toronto.edu, gpenn@cs.toronto.edu

Abstract

Multi-touch tabletops have been the focus of significant recent study but, to date, few devices have moved from prototype to installed use. In this paper, we present observation and analysis of a subject who has used a direct-touch tabletop as his primary computing environment for the past 13 months, driving all manner of applications in a standard MS Windows environment. We present the results of three research instruments: a structured interview with the user, an analysis of touch and click locations when operating in desktop and tabletop modes over several days, and linguistic analysis of email composition over several months. From the product of these instruments we then report on several open avenues for research, including physical parameters, hardware limitations, touch vs. click in the WIMP, and text entry techniques.

1. Introduction

Horizontal, direct-touch tabletops, which overlay large display and input surfaces, have recently been the focus of much study. Although a great number of experiments have been conducted which examine various aspects of tabletops, the majority of these experiments are conducted in a lab or similar setting, and require participants to perform some task over the course of several minutes or hours ([4][6][7][9][10][12][14]). Although scientifically valid for answering specific research questions, these efforts have limited abilities to predict patterns and desires for *long term* users of direct-touch tabletops.

In the present work, we describe the results of the study of an executive who has been using a direct-touch tabletop in place of an office computer for the last 13 months. Because of the length, setting, and tasks performed by this user, a great deal of "in the wild" experience is reflected in his responses. In addition, we perform a pair of analyses in order to learn more about his use of the table: first, we report the locations and frequencies of touch events, and compare it to logs of his use of a traditional pointing device, in order to extend and validate previous results suggesting that touch table use differs from mouse use in this measure. Second, we report the results of a computational linguistic analysis of email messages

sent over the 13 month period, comparing those composed on the tabletop and those typed on a regular keyboard.

A touch table as a primary office system is outside its typically described use. It is our hope, however, that the insights gleaned by studying this user, who has chosen to use the table in this way for his work, will be helpful to the community. It is our aim, in conducting this research, to inform the design of general problems, rather than those encountered only in this type of use.

1.1 Participant

The participant, *AB*, is a marketing executive at a local research lab. The tasks performed on the table are every day office tasks, and are limited to common applications – very little custom software is included in his setup (Figure 1). AB's use of the tabletop is motivated primarily by his work: his role is the marketing and sale of the touch table. The system driving the table is AB's laptop, which he also uses on the road and at home, not connected to a touch table. This pairing of input devices has allowed us to perform some simple comparative statistics on table and desktop use.

Figure 1. Our participant working at the touch table in his office. The table is his primary computer for everyday office tasks.

0-7695-3013-3/07 $25.00 © 2007 IEEE
DOI 10.1109/TABLETOP.2007.33

IEEE
computer
society

1.2 Research Instruments

In order to gain insight in to AB's usage of his touch table, we employed three research instruments. We now describe each in turn.

1.2.1 Mouse vs. touch use analysis

As we have described, AB uses a touch table for everyday computing tasks while in the office. While travelling on business or working at home, he uses traditional interfaces to control the same computer. In order to compare his pointing activity, we instrumented his laptop computer with two pieces of logging software: one to log the location of mouse clicks, and one to record touches on the touch table. This software recorded all such events over a three week period.

1.2.2 Email linguistic analysis

When AB composes email on the touch table, he uses an on-screen soft keyboard, while email written away from the office is typed with a traditional keyboard. In order to examine differences in email composition, we performed a comparative linguistic analysis on all of AB's outgoing email sent during the 13 month period he used his table as his primary office computer.

1.2.3 Interview

Finally, we conducted an extensive interview with AB, in which we sought to understand how his usage of the tabletop office system has evolved over the past 13 months.

1.3 Limitations

There are several limitations to the results described in this paper, each of which must be considered before generalizing our results to other designs. Despite these limitations, however, we are confident that the results described in the present work will be of use to researchers and designers.

First, as we have described, the present work describes the observation and analysis of a single user. Although AB has been using the touch table for every day computing for an extended period of time, this paper described only his experiences. Second, because we will be examining AB's use of a touch table for every day office tasks, nearly all of the experiences we will report on will be of single user applications. And, finally, because the tabletop is setup to operate as a "normal" desktop system, most of the interaction with the system was done by mapping the tabletop input to a single point, emulating a mouse.

Despite these limitations, many of the results we will describe offer useful insights for researchers and designers of interactive tabletop systems.

2. Related work

Although in its infancy, a number of researchers have reported results in the tabletop domain which are relevant to the present work. Generally, we divide these in to two categories: those which relate to touch locations, to inform on our mouse versus touch analysis, and those which report results from observation and contextual inquiry, and therefore relate to our interview. We are unaware of any use of linguistics for the comparative analysis of text entry devices.

2.1 Touch Location

Several results describe factors which might influence touch location. Scott and various co-authors have described issues in territoriality (summarised in [12]) which suggest that individuals working in groups will establish a personal working area directly in front of them. This is confirmed in by Ryall et al. who examined the interaction of group and table size on performance of tasks around a tabletop, and found that group members tended to focus their interaction (touches) directly in front of them. Finally, Ringel Morris et al. describe the results of a comparative study, which found that, when given the choice, users prefer UI that each group member have private copies of controls close to them on the table, rather than centralised, shared controls.

Although compelling, each of these previous works does not directly inform on the present work, since each examined the use of a tabletop in a group, rather than for private use by an individual.

2.2 Observation and Contextual Inquiry

In [12], Scott reported observations of a group of individuals interacting around a traditional table, describing the portioning of the workplace for individual and group tasks. In [9], Rogers et al. describe the observed use of finger talk, whereby users would gesture for both manipulation and conversation. Ryall et al. reported on observations of tabletop users in a multitude of environments, offering several recommendations and guidelines [11]. Both Tang et al. [13] and later Kruger et al. [6] described the use of orientation and spatial positioning of on-table objects for the delimiting of personal and group working spaces.

Although informative, each of the research efforts described above has been limited in their scope due to the constraints of time and scope. In this paper, we describe the results of interview and analysis of work performed on the tabletop over more than a year, and by a user who has adopted the tabletop as his primary workspace.

3. Environment

In this section, we describe the physical environment, the tasks being routinely performed, and the software and hardware employed.

3.1 Physical Space

AB's office features a regular desk, complete with traditional computer apparatus (monitor, keyboard, and mouse), as well as a large *DiamondTouch* touch table [2], with a touch surface measuring approximately 87x 64cm. The keyboard, mouse, and monitor are attached to the same system as the tabletop, with the monitor displaying the same content. The desktop setup is arranged on a desk behind the tabletop, such that the monitor cannot be seen while working at the table.

The DiamondTouch is mounted on a sloped surface, creating a drafting table style of interaction. As shown in Figure 2, the height of this was set so as to allow AB to use it while standing (left) or seated (right).

Figure 2. The touch table is oriented as a drafting table. Its height is set for both standing and sitting.

3.2 Application software

Although special circumstances may arise, AB uses the tabletop primarily for everyday office software. The list of regularly used applications includes word processing (MS Word), spreadsheets (MS Excel), presentation software (MS PowerPoint), email (Mozilla Thunderbird), and the web (Mozilla Firefox).

3.3 Touch table software

All of the application software used by AB is unmodified for use on a tabletop. To enable direct-touch input to drive these applications, two tools are required: mouse emulation, and a soft keyboard.

3.3.1 Mouse input

Because AB's primary use of the DiamondTouch is in applications designed for the mouse, he uses a software utility, *DTMouse*, which maps multi-touch input to mouse events [3]. Although input is ultimately delivered to a single pixel when it is converted to mouse actions, a set of gestures on the tabletop is used to differentiate between mouse actions (see Table 1).

Table 1. The mapping of multi-touch gestures to single-pixel mouse events in *DT Mouse*.

Mouse Event	Touch Action
Left mouse: Depress Drag Release	**Single finger:** Touch table Slide along table Lift from table
Right mouse: Depress Drag Release	**Touch table with finger, then:** Tap second finger Slide first finger Lift first finger from table
Middle mouse: Depress Drag Release	**Touch table with finger, then:** Double-Tap second finger Slide first finger List first finger from table
Wheel Wheel up Wheel down	**Place closed-fist on table, then:** Slide fist up Slide fist down

In addition to this mapping, DTMouse can be used in a *precise selection* mode, in which the user places any two fingers on the table simultaneously. The cursor then relocates to the centre point between those fingers, without sending any button events. Touching a third finger to the table depresses the left mouse button, and removing it from the table releases the button. In effect, this mode allows for two enhancements over the simpler operation described above: first, it allows the pointer position to be set without depressing any buttons; second, it allows the user to view the position of the cursor more precisely, since the finger does not occlude the display [3].

3.3.2 Soft keyboard

To enable text entry from the DiamondTouch, AB makes use of the soft keyboard built-in to Microsoft Windows. The keyboard generates text when the system pointer is used to click soft buttons arranged in a QWERTY layout. Interaction with the keyboard is facilitated using DTMouse to simulate mouse clicks. As such, speed of text entry is limited by the need to have only one finger in contact with the keyboard at a time, similar to tapping text entry with a stylus.

In the following sections, we sought to gain insight in to AB's use of his tabletop system for every day office tasks. In order to do this, we employed three research instruments. The first two, a touch location analysis and linguistic analysis of email, relied on a comparison between his use of a laptop while away from the office and the touch table while in his office. In this section, we describe these instruments and discuss their results.

4.   Touch vs. mouse logs

As previously described, the DiamondTouch table in AB's office is driven from his laptop computer. When not in the office, he uses the same computer with its built-in keyboard and track-pad. As we have previously described, a number of researchers have reported results which suggest that, when working in groups on a tabletop, individuals tend to organize their work spaces such that their efforts are focused in an area immediately in front of them, perhaps even closer than arm's reach might require [7],[10],[12]. None of these researchers examined whether this pattern was repeated for individuals, allowing for possible confound with fatigue [14].

We note that AB's touch table is sufficiently small that all points are within arms reach while it is in use. We were interested to learn whether AB, who has had ample experience to perfect any strategies that might be employed to mitigate fatigue, would follow a usage pattern similar to that described in previous work, which attributed it to effects of working in a group.

4.1   Method

In order to perform this comparison, we instrumented AB's laptop with logging software which recorded clicks and touch locations for a three week period. In both tabletop and laptop mode, AB's screen is set to 1024 x 768 pixels. The software was not capable of detecting the target applications for input.

Although it is usually the case that AB uses laptop controls when away from the office, and the touch table while at the office, our study period included several days that the laptop controls were used in the office while the touch table was unavailable.

4.2   Results

The logs contained 7034 mouse clicks and 47,972 touch events. This asymmetry was expected, since AB uses the mouse primarily while out of the office, and because multiple touch events are required to generate many types of mouse actions.

To simplify our analysis, touch and click locations were organized in to 10 x 10 pixel bins, and the results normalised. The results are shown Figure 3.

4.3   Analysis

Initially, the data are quite striking: it is very apparent that a greater number of touch events is being generated towards the bottom of the screen when using the tabletop than when using the laptop. What became apparent upon further analysis, however, is that the large cluster of events in this region was due almost entirely to the placement of the soft keyboard. Because our logging method did not provide us with a means classifying touch targets by destinations, we are unable to separate for analysis those touches used for typing from the rest of the data. As a result, we are unable to attribute the entirety of this cluster to the keyboard. What is apparent in the data, however, is that if this region is removed entirely from both sets, the remaining areas have nearly identical frequencies.

This result appears to support the hypothesis that the workspace partitioning described in the previous work ([7],[10],[12]) is indeed due to the presence of additional group members, and refutes our suggestion that this might be equally attributable to fatigue.

Although promising to inform on these issues, two significant factors limit our ability to generalise the current result. First, as previously described, the study is limited to a single participant in an uncontrolled environment. Second, an equally reasonable explanation of the difference between our single user and the results reported a user working in a group has to do with the software executing on the table during our logging. Because it was written for use with the mouse, interface features are situated without regard for minimizing reach. A quick glance at offers some support for this explanation: dense clicks can be seen at the top (menu bar), bottom (tool bar), and right side of the screen (scroll bar). Although AB might wish to organize the desktop to better suit a tabletop, he is limited by the available software.

Despite these limitations and potential confounds, the results of the study are still compelling. They suggest the confirmation of past results, and demonstrate that a tabletop is sufficient as an input device for everyday office tasks.

Figure 3. Click locations (left) and touch locations (right), organized in to bins. Red level indicates frequency.

5. Email Linguistic Analysis

Our second research instrument is a linguistic analysis of email sent by AB over the 13 month period that the touch table was used as his primary office computer. Because AB has chosen to use a soft keyboard as his input device for text entry while working on the table, we suspected that a comparative analysis of messages composed while working on that device and those composed on the laptop keyboard would yield significant differences. Such differences might arise due to difficulties with using the table and/or soft keyboard, such as during the composition of long email messages, or due to a user such as AB's belief that touch tables are more appropriate for sending certain kinds of emails.

5.1 Method

We retrieved from AB a log of outgoing messages for the study period (13 months). Messages were separated from each other, and their headers were removed using a MIME parser. From these messages, we removed those which contained repeated, standardized text (such as might be sent in reply to a sales enquiry). We also removed from analysis quoted text from each message, to ensure that the analyzed text in each message was only that which was newly composed. We then classified each message as having been composed using either the soft keyboard on the touch table, or the laptop keyboard. This was usually possible because AB's email client is configured to attach a particular footer to messages composed using the touch table.

A large number of features were computed for each message, aided in part by the Brill Tagger [1]. These measures included rates (per 1000 tokens) of:

1) *first-person pronominals*
2) *second-person pronominals*
3) *third-person pronominals*
4) *conjunct words*
5) *present-tense verbs*
6) *past-tense verbs*
7) *"private" verbs*
8) *"public" verbs*
9) *verbs of saying*
10) *nouns*
11) *nouns that start with 'q' or 'Q'*
12) *adverbs*
13) *"that" complementizers*
14) *non-existential "there"*
15) *split infinitives, and*
16) *technical vocabulary*
17) *word-instance/sentence ratio*
18) *average word length*
19) *word type/word instance ratio*
20) *total message length in characters*
21) *total message length in whitespace-delimited strings, and*
22) *total message length in lines.*

The last three being determined by the Unix *wc* command. *Word instance* refers here to a single instance of a word, whereas *word type* refers to a particular kind of word. *The meeting takes place on the 31st*, for example has seven word instances, but six word types, since the type *the* occurs in two instances.

With the exception of the three total message length features, these features are typical in computational linguistics for detecting the genre of a text document. Genre refers to a mode of language use with conventions that native speakers of the language implicitly agree upon. Instructions on tax forms, romance novels and personal letters, for example, are all genres between which these features are known to vary considerably. It is also well-known that these features are sensitive to differences between spoken and written language. To our knowledge, no previous study of their variation across input devices or input modalities has ever been conducted.

5.2 Results

We were able to classify all but 83 of the original 2376 email messages as having been written on either the tabletop or the computer keyboard. Some mailers attach quotations in such a way that the distinguishing footer that we used for classification was ambiguously attached either to the new message or to a quote of an earlier message. This was the case for all 83 of the emails that we forced discarded. We removed all of the quoted text contained in the emails, which removed a further 16 messages from consideration (messages which were forwarded email without any additional text). This left us with 1124 messages composed on the tabletop and 1153 messages written with the keyboard.

We performed a comparison of means between the two input devices for each of the word types. Of the 22 features considered, only six were found to have significantly different values on the tabletop keyboard.

The use of second-person pronomials (eg: *you, your*) was significantly more frequent for email composed on the tabletop than for email composed on the keyboard ($F_{1,2275} = 7.38$, p = 0.007, with mean frequencies of 31.3 and 27.8 per 1000 words for tabletop and keyboard messages respectively). Similarly, the frequency of technical vocabulary was significantly higher on the tabletop ($F_{1,2275} = 4.62$, p = 0.032, with means of 23.2 vs. 20.5 for tabletop and keyboard input respectively). On the other hand, the use of *that* complementizers was more frequent in keyboard email than in touch table email ($F_{1,2275} = 4.95$, p = 0.026, 10.4 vs. 11.9 touch table and keyboard). Total message length in both characters (p = 0.008) and whitespace-delimited strings (p = 0.009) was significantly longer in email composed on the tabletop, but total message length in lines, which is simply a count of newline characters, was significantly less (p = 0.000).

5.3   Analysis

Of particular interest is that the total message length was significantly different in every dimension, but no significant difference was found in either the number of characters per word, or the number of tokens (words) per sentence. It is clear that, although it has been previously reported that soft keyboards are insufficient for text entry on a touch table [11], AB shows no sign of being incapacitated by the table in composing his messages. Quite to the contrary, his messages are longer. Also of interest is that both frequent use of second-person pronominals and infrequent use of *that* complementizers are associated with less formal genres of written language, although several other features with the same association showed no significant difference. Frequent use of technical vocabulary, while also explainable by variation in topic, is associated with more formal genres, on the other hand. Topic and genre are not the same, although not statistically independent either.

Once again, we are unable to generalise the results of this to all users. In addition to the reasons previously stated, the results here point to a similarity in genre and length statistics between tabletop and physical keyboard use, but it is possible that AB's language use might happen to fall in to a genre which is particularly robust to differences introduced by a change in input methods, where others might not be.

Despite these limitations, the results point to the reasonable conclusion that the use of a soft keyboard has not limited AB's ability to perform everyday office tasks. Indeed, in most respects, the style of his language, seems more or less completely unaffected by the input device, and the lengths of his messages are longer.

6.   Interview

In this section, we present the results of our interview with AB. As often as possible, the aim of the interview was to glean insights that are generally applicable to direct-touch tabletops, rather than the particular hardware, software, or domain applications that the participant may have chosen.

6.1   Dual use

AB's tabletop system is the only horizontal surface at that side of his office. He has reported that it is often called upon to play a dual role. In addition to its traditional use as a computing device, it is also often used as furniture, serving as both coffee table and conference table for small meetings, in extreme cases being deactivated so-as not to project imagery on to objects on the table. In fact, AB reported that the angle at which his table was placed was chosen because it was the maximum possible angle before objects would begin to slide across its surface.

Because the DiamondTouch table is debris tolerant, objects placed on the table are not processed as touches by the system [2], making it ideal for this dual use. Designers of systems based on other technologies, however, must consider this dual use. Approaches might include the occlusion of a shelf in the physical design of the table, and mechanisms to rapidly disable arbitrary portions of the touch surface.

6.2   Ergonomic considerations

Several ergonomic factors were considered in the design of the setup in AB's office for the tabletop.

First, the display was placed on a slant, making it resemble a drafting table. This was done to allow both easier reach and easier viewing of pixels at the top of the display. Interestingly, the angle of the display was set such that it was as steep as possible, while ensuring that drinks placed on the table (see "dual use", above) would not slide down its surface.

Second, the height of the table was set so that it could be operated while either sitting or standing.

Third, AB had his choice of two different DiamondTouch tables, one with a diagonal measurement of 81 cm and another measuring 107 cm. Despite its use as a single-user desk, he opted for the larger table. He explained that, although this would mean having to reach farther for targets at the top of the screen, he preferred the larger field of view provided by the larger device. This, despite that the display on the DiamondTouch table is provided by an overhead projector, and so display resolution is independent of table size.

AB reports that he does not experience arm fatigue while working with the large touch surface, in contrast to previous study results which suggest otherwise [14]. This finding suggests that the field of view / fatigue trade-off is heavily skewed towards field of view.

The final ergonomic consideration is that, because the large touch surface provides a large display area, AB reports that privacy is sometimes an issue. Therefore, on some occasions he elects to work away from the touch table so as to limit this exposure.

6.3   Space management

As has previously been reported in the domain of group work, it is essential that designers provide mechanisms for easy repositioning of screen content to allow for dynamic space management by users [7], [13]. Previously, however, this was reported as necessary to facilitate the definition of shared and private spaces and to allow the use of shared resources. AB pointed out to us, however, the need for space management tools is also required to prevent the occlusion of one object while working on another.

6.4　Transition and expertise

As might be expected, AB's transition to the touch table for everyday use was a difficult one. It was initially mired by the transition to direct-touch and familiarity with the text input device. Despite these difficulties, he has persisted, and is now what can reasonably be described as an expert user (as evidence, recall that our touch analysis data, which covered only 3 weeks of use, included nearly 50,000 touch events). As such, many of the issues described in the following sections may relate to novices, experts, or both.

6.5　Bimanual interaction

Although AB describes himself as "severely right handed," he has consciously trained himself to perform touching the table with both his right and left hands. As we have previously described, the DTMouse software employed on AB's tabletop converts multi-touch input to mouse events. As such, each input event is, in effect, unimanual. AB, therefore, uses two hands in order to perform tasks which could otherwise be performed using just one hand. These include selecting objects using the closer hand and performing faster drag operations by starting the drag with one hand and completing it with the other.

In both cases, bimanual actions are utilised to save time through spatial rather than role specialisation. This suggests that, when designing interactions for the non-dominant hand, symmetric roles should be considered along side traditional, asymmetric roles [5].

6.6　Touch precision

Previous results explain that selection of small targets using a direct-touch interface is made difficult by two factors: the occlusion of the target while pointing, and the arbitrary mapping of large touch area to a more precise election point [8]. As has also been reported, this problem is exacerbated on horizontal surfaces, since near and distant touches present different fingertip shapes to the input device [4] (mitigated somewhat in AB's case by the slanting of his table). As we have described, the DT Mouse software provides a high-precision mode to aid with selection of small targets.

Perhaps surprisingly, AB reports that, after extensive experience, he no longer finds it necessary to use the high-precision mode to select small UI components, including window borders for resizing, which are only 4 pixels wide. This suggests that the issues with precise selection described in the literature may well be overcome with additional practice. Interestingly, AB *does* persist in using the precise selection mode when selecting blocks of text.

The distinction between the UI widget and the text-selection cases is the availability of visual feedback: the effects of selecting UI elements, such as the resizable border of a window, are verifiable by viewing areas of the screen not occluded by the finger, whereas precise selection of text is not. This suggests that designers seeking to overcome the issue of precision might be well served by first addressing occlusion.

6.7　Gestures and direct-touch

As we have previously described, the DTMouse software maps multi-touch input to the tabletop to a simulated mouse device. Although the simulated device operates on a single-point, the input to DTMouse does not: right and middle buttons are simulated with the tapping of a second finger on the table, and mouse wheel scroll events are generated by dragging a closed fist on the table surface.

Of interest to designers is AB's facile and immediate adoption of this mix of the tabletop as both an input and display device, without always interpreting touches in a direct-touch way, in contradiction of the results suggested by previous work by Potter et al. [8].

For example, to send a right-click to the table, AB first selects the point for the click by touching it with a finger (direct-touch). The right-click is then generated when a second finger, usually his thumb, is tapped on the table. Interestingly, the location of this tap is not an input – even if it is directly on-to a UI component, it will not generate a direct-touch event for that location. Even more striking is the indirect mapping of scrolling from touch to display: dragging a closed fist downward causes a simulated downward scroll of the mouse wheel. The consequence of this, in most applications, is that on-screen content moves *up*, in precisely the opposite direction of the gesture.

When these inconsistencies in the input metaphor were pointed out to AB, it was clear from his reaction that he had no trouble conceiving of the tabletop simultaneously as a direct and indirect device.

6.8　Text Entry

As AB put it, "a reasonable person would not use an on-screen keyboard". He pointed out to us that a number of solutions are available for text entry to a direct-touch table, including installation of a keyboard drawer. Despite these solutions, however, AB persists in his use of the soft keyboard for text entry. He attributes this decision to his desire to maintain the use of direct-touch. And, as we have seen, AB's use of the soft keyboard has had little to no impact on the content of his email messages, suggesting he is not allowing the limitations to impact is overall performance.

7. Conclusions and Future Work

In this paper, we have presented a case study of AB, a long-term user of a direct-touch multi-point touch table. We have presented the results of three research instruments, two of which revealed few differences in behaviour between tabletop and mouse/keyboard operation of a WIMP interface. A structured interview with AB provided several insights into direct-touch interfaces.

Based on the results of these instruments, several avenues for research remain open. First, it is important to remember that, because of the limited sample size and potential confounds, none of the results reported here can be safely generalised. Rather than provide authoritative results, our aim is to present insight in to potential research directions. Therefore, validation of our statistical results through larger studies is the first clear open research question.

Next, each of the sections of the interview suggest clear open questions. AB's dual use of his tabletop is supported in part by a combination of debris tolerance and projector muting. The design of software and of physical apparatus to further support this is an open question.

The interview also pointed to several ergonomic considerations: it is clear that AB prefers to angle his table towards him. However, this may limit it serving as a dual-use surface. Additionally, optimal height, and size, and mechanisms to support private work are all open questions.

The alternative use of bimanual input to minimize work, rather than to allow for more complex manipulation, is demonstrated aptly by our participant, as is the potential for learning to overcome the limitations in precision of direct-touch interfaces. Also of interest is AB's ease of mixing direct-touch and gesture/postures on the table. This suggests the need to closely examine the tradeoffs and design of these interactions to suite a particular task.

Finally, text entry is a clear open question. As AB points out, the use of a keyboard on the tabletop is one solution, but there may well exist others. Thoughtful study is required.

Given the multitude of open questions pointed to by this work, it is clear that it represents a first step, rather than a comprehensive result. Further study in all manner of tabletops for single users is warranted.

8. Acknowledgements

We offer thanks to Clifton Forlines for assistance with statistical analyses, and great thanks to AB, our participant.

9. References

[1] Brill, Eric (1995). Transformation-Based Error-Driven Learning and Natural Language Processing: A Case Study in Part-of-Speech Tagging. Computation Linguistics, 21(4):543-565.

[2] Dietz, P. and Leigh, D. (2001). DiamondTouch: a multi-user touch technology. *Proc. UIST.* p. 219-226.

[3] Esenther, A., Ryall, K., 2006. Fluid DTMouse: Better Mouse Support for Touch-Based Interactions. *Proceedings of the Working Conference on Advanced Visual Interfaces* (AVI 2006), p. 112- 115.

[4] Forlines, C., Shen, C., Wigdor, D., Balakrishnan, R. (2007). Direct-touch vs. mouse input for tabletop displays. *Proceedings of CHI 2007.* p. 647-656

[5] Guiard, Y. (1987). Asymmetric Division of Labor in Human Skilled Bimanual Action: The Kinematic Chain as a Model. *The Journal of Motor Behavior* 19(4). p. 486-517.

[6] Kruger, R., Carpendale, S., Scott, S. and Greenberg, S. (2003): 'How people use orientation on tables: comprehension, coordination and communication', *Proceedings of the 2003 international ACM SIGGROUP conference on Supporting group work.* Sanibel Island, Florida, USA, ACM Press, 2003, pp: 369-378.

[7] Morris, M. R., Paepcke, A., Winograd, T., and Stamberger, J. (2006). TeamTag: exploring centralized versus replicated controls for co-located tabletop groupware. *Proceedings of the SIGCHI Conference on Human Factors in Computing Systems.* p. 1273 – 1282.

[8] Potter, R., Weldon, L., and Shneiderman, B., 1988. Improving the accuracy of touch screens: an experimental evaluation of three strategies. *Proceedings of the ACM CHI.* p. 27-32.

[9] Rogers, Y., Hazlewood, W., Blevis, E. and Lim, Y. (2004). Finger talk: collaborative decision-making using talk and fingertip interaction around a tabletop display. *Extended abstracts of CHI.* p. 1271-1274.

[10] Ryall, K.; Forlines, C.; Shen, C.; Ringel-Morris, M. (2004) Exploring the Effects of Group Size and Table Size on Interactions with Tabletop Shared-Display Groupware. *Proceedings of CSCW.* p. 284-293.

[11] Ryall, K., Morris, M., Everitt, K., Forlines, C., and Shen, C. (2006). Experiences with and observations of direct-touch tabletops. *Proceedings of IEEE TableTop the International Workshop on Horizontal Interactive Human Computer Systems.* pp. 89-96.

[12] Scott, Stacey D. (2005). *Territoriality in Collaborative Tabletop Workspaces.* Ph.D. Dissertation, Department of Computer Science, University of Calgary, Calgary, Alberta, Canada,

[13] Tang, J.C. (1991). Findings from observational studies of collaborative work. *International Journal of man-Machine Studies*, 34. p. 143-160.

[14] Wigdor, D., Leigh, D., Forlines, C., Shipman, S., Barnwell, J., Balakrishnan, R., Shen, C. (2006). Under the table interaction. *Proceedings of the 2006 ACM conference on User Interface Software and Technology* (UIST 2006). p. 259-268

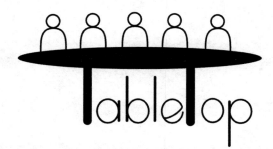

Reading, Writing & More: Tabletop-User Experiences

Applying an Aesthetic Framework of Touch for Table-Top Interactions

Thecla Schiphorst
Simon Fraser University
thecla@sfu.ca

Nima Motamedi
Simon Fraser University
nimam@sfu.ca

Norm Jaffe
Simon Fraser University
turing@shaw.ca

Abstract

In this paper, we propose a conceptual framework for understanding the aesthetic qualities of multi-touch and tactile interfaces for table-top interaction. While aesthetics has traditionally been defined as the visual appearance of an artifact, we promote a tactile aesthetics that is firmly rooted in the experience of use and interaction. Our model of tactile aesthetics comprises four distinct yet overlapping areas: 1.) Embodiment which grounds our framework within the larger philosophical context of experience. 2.) Materiality which emphasizes the importance of the physical shape, form and texture of interactive systems. 3.) Sensorial Mapping which is the creation of appropriate cross-modal relationships between touch and our other senses. 4.) Semantics of Caress which is the investigation into the meaning of touch which can then inform computational models of gesture recognition. We apply this framework to evaluate a series of tactile and multi-touch artworks and discuss how our model can benefit the design of future multi-touch systems.

1. Tactile Aesthetics

In an era where 'emotion' and 'experience' are key descriptors of interactive systems [1] [9], there is a growing recognition in HCI that considering aesthetics may be useful when designing for experience [3] [12]. But traditional aesthetic theory poses a problem for interactivity. Primarily concerned with visual appearance, these theories are incompatible with interactivity because of the large role that tactility, the body, and usability have in mediating the user experience. In response, many HCI researchers [3] [12] turned to 'pragmatist aesthetics', a theory where the emphasis is on the aesthetic experience of physical use [16]. What is missing, however, is an aesthetic framework which connects pragmatist aesthetic theory with decisions derived directly from interactive art practice. From interactive art we can learn how to apply strategies used by artists to create emotional and meaningful experiences with technology.

In this paper, we propose a model of tactile aesthetics that has resulted from identifying four recurring and entwined themes emerging from our work with multi-touch tabletop artworks. The first theme is the overarching philosophy of *embodiment* which grounds and contextualizes our work in experience design [2]. The second theme is *materiality* which stresses the importance of the physical shape, form, and texture in mediating an aesthetic experience. Our third theme is *sensorial mapping* which is the potential of combining touch with appropriate visual or audio feedback to simulate a rough haptic sensation. The final theme is *semantics of caress* which is the investigation into the different meanings encoded in touch and gestures. Since our framework emerged from our artistic practice, we explain our model by sharing a narrative on the trajectory of our work in tabletop interactive artworks. The development of our tactile aesthetics begins with the interactive artwork *BodyMaps*, and is then traced to the *Soft(n)* project. Finally, we conclude by outlining current and future work in multi-touch tabletop interfaces.

2. Experience of BodyMaps

Bodymaps is an interactive table installed in the center of a darkened gallery room with speakers distributed around the four corners and hung from the ceiling on either end of the table. As an interactive artwork *Bodymaps* was designed specifically to direct the users attention to their tactile sensations, inviting a 'purpose-free' exploration of active touch, and using the synthesis and simultaneity of the visual and auditory material to invoke an intensified and heightened sense of affect and 'connection'. As an artwork this was intended to move interaction experience more toward 'phatic' technologies [18] that emphasize the experience of connection rather than information content, thereby creating a more deeply resonant emotional space. A table was selected (rather than a bed or another furniture object) because of its metaphoric use as a familiar everyday domestic object and its flexible open-ended use in social settings such as gathering, sharing, eating, working and celebrating.

0-7695-3013-3/07 $25.00 © 2007 IEEE
DOI 10.1109/TABLETOP.2007.20

In *Bodymaps*, the gallery visitor sees an image of a body projected from above: it lays still and silent on the surface of the table. Images and sound utilized in *Bodymaps* enable an open interpretation, and its metaphorical use of visual material such as water and fire, sheets or tablecloths allow multiple meanings and emotional associations [15]. This design strategy is commonly used in artistic practice as a way of poetically evoking experience and thoughtful reflection. It is a mechanism to provoke experience utilizing the pleasure of direct sensation to bring imagination and memory into play. Contemporary artists such as Bill Viola and Paul Sermon have used similar strategies to achieve poetic and resonant experience. As someone approaches the table, they hear the sound of a single drop of water dripping from directly above the table. When the user reaches out to touch the table, proximity and electromagnetic field sensors detect the presence, proximity, and location of the hand as it hovers above the surface. This triggers the sound of water being splashed and mixed in direct correspondence to the user's hand movement. The sonic sensation is one of water running through the fingers. Once the user physically touches the table's surface, they feel the warmth and sensual texture of the silk velvet inviting them to caress and stroke the fabric. Touching the projected body causes her to move in a direct relationship to the user's gesture (Figure 1). For example: stroking her shoulders causes her turn on her side, while tickling her feet forces her to roll off the table. As the intensity of the touch increases (with greater pressure, speed and area covered), the room fills with layered and ambiguous sounds such as crying, laughing, sighing or breathing. This multi-layered reactive space immerses the user in a sensual and affective sound and image-scape. As the user steps back from the table, the imagery and sound slowly begin to fade, waiting to be touched again. When all tactile interaction stops, everything becomes quiet. All that remains is the sound of a single drop of water dripping from above.

Figure 1: Bodymaps installed in a gallery

3. Embodiment

The first theme is the philosophy of embodiment and how 'being-in-the-world' is critical for understanding experience in HCI [2]. In the context of multi-touch interfaces, we know that gestures in the physical world are rich and intricate and can be mapped to create more intuitive gesture commands [11]. Being aware of the capabilities of tactility is essential for creating interfaces which utilize the full resolution and bandwidth of touch, such as the skin's ability to detect temperature, proximity, weight, and volume [7]. With *BodyMaps*, one of the explorations was to create an interface that invoked a tactile response in people and allowed them to interact with the system with a gesture repertoire beyond the typical binary 'touch/release' input range common in interactive systems. Since people intuitively feel surfaces by moving their hands across the texture in order to gather information on the object [4], the piece was designed to respond to this temptation. As a result, the sensor hardware embedded inside the table had to be able to detect presence, location, and the proximity of hands as they hover across and touch the surface creating two levels of tactile engagement. The material used for the construction along with the appropriate visual and sonic sensory mapping played a large role in compelling people to interact with the piece.

4. Materiality

The second theme in our framework is the importance of materials in mediating an aesthetic interaction similar to the role materials have in traditional arts and crafts. The specific form of the table including its height and scale was designed with a strategy to enable ambiguity and open interpretation [15]. The height of the table is slightly lower than a dining table so that its physical correspondence to a human body could also begin to suggest alternative objects (such as a bed or a coffin). In the case of *BodyMaps,* it was critical to identify a material that had the affordance of caress [5] and encouraged users to explore the surface with their hands. After an extensive search where numerous natural fabrics were prototyped and evaluated according to these parameters, the final selection was to use white silk-velvet. This fabric possesses several properties that made it suitable for compelling a tactile response in users. First, stroking across the surface changes the direction of the knap leaving behind a shadow. This can be erased with a stroke in the opposite direction, or it can be left has a visual memory of touch. Also, silk-velvet captures and retains body heat making the table surface warmer to touch. When combined with the material's softness, this encourages gentler and slower gestures. The net result of these properties gives the textile display a high degree of tactile resolution.

The resolution of textile displays is measured using different metrics than conventional computer screens or projections. Whereas optical performance is the main criteria for conventional displays, textile displays are evaluated for their haptic quality or how the material feels. Understanding the trade-off between technical resolution and affective resolution is an aesthetic decision and one that impacts the overall experience of the system [6]. While the degree to which materials impact the experience is still not entirely known, the choice of material still has tremendous impact not just on the technical performance of the system, but on the overall feel and experience. Selecting materials primarily for their optical purposes may be critical for multi-touch projection systems, but this choice should not neglect or ignore the material's tactile attributes.

5. Sensorial Mapping

The third theme in our framework is sensorial mapping where touch is combined with appropriate visual and sonic feedback to simulate a synesthetic haptic sensation. This effect has been shown to exist even with lower level tactile inputs such as a mouse with appropriate visual changes in the graphical cursor [17]. In *Bodymaps*, the relationship between touch and audio-visual senses occur on two separate layers of the user experience (Figure 2). The first occurs when a hand penetrates the electro-magnetic field that blankets the area above the surface. This triggers the sound of water splashing and mixing which is mapped to the user's gesture, simulating the haptic sensation of running fingers through water. People can interact with the piece by feeling this virtual fluid sonically before they eventually touch the table when they feel comfortable. Touching the velvet surface is the second layer of the sensorial interface. A projected image of a body responds directly to the relationship of the user's touch. If someone touches her shoulder she will turn on her side, or if someone tickles her feet she will roll off the table. At this point another audio layer is added as sounds of natural human emotions such as sighing, breathing, and crying grows louder as the amount of contact on the body intensifies. Since the audio is ambiguous, the user is open to interpret their actions and meaning [15]. We observed that there was often a heightened affective response of users to the interface, and participants reported being very moved, or

becoming reflective as a result of the interaction. Sensorial mapping differs from haptic interfaces in that instead of creating a direct physical relationship between two sense modalities, it is implied and left to the user to make the connection and 'feel' inside their body and mind.

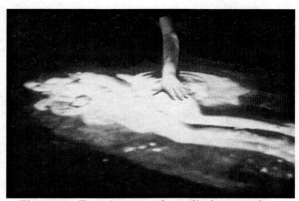

Figure 2: Two layers of tactile interaction: hovering and touching the surface

6. Semantics of Caress

The final theme in our model is the development of our work in building a taxonomy of affective 'tactile gestures' based on the semantics of caress. This resulted originally from direct observations of participants' interaction with Bodymaps, and has been developed and tested through a number of interactive art prototypes and devices. We observed and documented patterns of commonality in the tactile gestural *quality* used in the system. For example, people tended to jab the surface harder and user quicker gestures when they were impatient or they would use gentler and longer gestures during moments of strong affect. Analyzing movement quality has been used in choreography and in movement analysis[8]. We formalized observations by studying the quality of multi-touch gestures. Initially, implementation of our qualitative semantics was based on definitions from Laban-Effort-Shape Analysis [8] (Figure 3) which was computationally mapped onto the Tactex MTC Express multi-touch tablet using computer-vision signal processing for recognition [14]. Afterwards, these same heuristics were applied to custom-made multi-touch foam pads that were sewn into a family of pillow objects for the *Soft(n)* project [13]. *Soft(n)* is an interactive art installation with 12 networked pillows that communicate to one another and to their users based on touch qualities. Each pillow was able to recognize different touch qualities and respond to touch input. Our work in classifying the qualitative touch gestures compliments existing taxonomies which focus on gestures for graphical manipulation, CSCW, and other task-oriented commands [10] [17] [19].

touch-effort	Description
tap	A soft, short, small, touch, usually rendered with a single finger.
pat	A bigger version of "tap" and a soft version of "slap". Usually rendered with an open hand or palm.
hold	A lingering, soft, big, touch. A "hold" has an encompassing feel.
touch	"Touch" is a small version of "hold". It is an indication of comfort and is rendered with the fingers, hand, or palm.
stroke	A traveling touch, soft but directional, rendered with fingers, hand or palm.
glide	A traveling, meandering, touch. Soft and directionless and rendered with the fingers, hand, or palm.
jab	A hard, short, small, touch. A hard poke by a finger or blunted object. Also known as "poke".
knock	A medium-sized, fist against, rapping hard. In our scheme, it is different than "jab" and "slap" in size only.
slap	An open-handed, hard, short, touch. In our scheme, a large version of "jab" and "knock".
press	This is a long, hard, touch.
rub	This is a moving, hard, touch.
knead	Kneading involves many fingers moving hard and in a slightly wandering fashion.
other touch-efforts not attempted in this system:	
punch	This is like a "knock", but is different in intensity and slightly different in timing.
flick	This is like a "jab", but is slightly different in shape over time. A "flick" travels slightly in relation to a "jab", which is more stationary.

Figure 3: Touch efforts with corresponding metrics for computation

7. Discussion & Future Work

In this paper, we outlined the beginnings of a conceptual framework for evaluating the tactile aesthetics in table-top interactions. The main strength of our model is that it originated directly from artistic practice. However, we will need to use our model to assess other designs and artworks to gauge the validity of our framework. We also plan to expand and refine some of the ideas we presented. Currently, we are in the midst of a project where we are networking multiple multi-touch tables in remote locations. In this research, we are interested in adapting or expanding our affective gesture library to include touch efforts that connect people separated by location. This will also involve expanding our gesture library to include bimanual multi-touch interactions for larger surfaces. In addition, we want to include research into the qualitative semantics of 'feel'. Just as we encode meaning in the gestures we make and in the way we touch, we also decode meaning from objects that we

feel, and in the way we are touched. Indeed, as aesthetic theory is still in its infancy in HCI, our work on tactile aesthetics can only grow and improve.

8. References

[1] Bødker, S. 2006. When second wave HCI meets third wave challenges. NordiCHI '06, vol. 189. ACM Press, p 1-8.
[2] Dourish, P. Where the action is: the foundations of embodied interaction, MIT Press, Cambridge, MA, 2001
[3] Fiore, S., Wright, P., and Edwards, A. 2005. A pragmatist aesthetics approach to the design of a technological artefact. CC '05. ACM Press, New York, NY, 129-132
[4] Gibson, J. J. (1962). Observations on active touch. Psychological Review, 69(6), 477 - 491.
[5] Gibson, J.J. (1979). The Ecological Approach to Visual Perception, Houghton Mifflin, Boston.
[6] Hallnäs, L., Melin, L., and Redström, J. 2002. Textile displays: using textiles to investigate computational technology as design material. NordiCHI '02, vol. 31. ACM Press, New York, NY, 157-166.
[7] Krueger, Lester. Tactual Perception in historical perspective: David Katz's world of touch. Cambridge University Press, (1982)
[8] Laban, R., Lawrence, F. C., Effort: Economy of Human Movement, second edition, MacDonald and Evans, 1947, 2nd Edition, 1973
[9] McCarthy, J. Wright, P. Technology as Experience, The MIT Press, (2004)
[10] Morris, M. R., Huang, A., Paepcke, A., and Winograd, T. 2006. Cooperative gestures: multi-user gestural interactions for co-located groupware. CHI '06. ACM Press, New York, NY, 1201-1210
[11] Moscovich, T. 2006. Multi-touch interaction. In CHI '06 Extended Abstracts on Human Factors in Computing Systems CHI '06. ACM Press, New York, NY, 1775-1778.
[12] Petersen, M. G., Iversen, O. S., Krogh, P. G., and Ludvigsen, M. 2004. Aesthetic interaction: a pragmatist's aesthetics of interactive systems. DIS '04. ACM Press, New York, NY, 269-276.
[13] Schiphorst , T et al. PillowTalk: Can We Afford Intimacy? Proceedings, TEI 2007.
[14] Schiphorst, T., Lovell, R., and Jaffe, N. 2002. Using a gestural interface toolkit for tactile input to a dynamic virtual space. CHI '02. ACM Press, New York, NY, 754-755.
[15] Sengers, P, Gaver, W, Staying Open to Interpretation, Engaging Multiple Meanings in Design + Evaluation, DIS'06
[16] Shusterman, R. Pragmatist Aesthetics. Living Beauty, Rethinking Art. Blackwell, (1992)
[17] Van Mensvoort K (2002) What you see is what you feel: exploiting the dominance of the visual over the haptic domain to simulate force-feedback with cursor displacements. In: Proceedings of DIS '02. ACM Press, NY.
[18] Vetere, F., Howard, Gibbs, MR Phatic Technologies: Sustaining Sociability through Ubiquitous Computing, CHI 2005, in: Proceedings of CHI'05. ACM Press, NY.
[19] Wu M, Shen C, Ryall K, Forlines C, Balakrishnam R, Gesture, Registration, Relaxation and Reuse for Multi-Point direct-Touch Surfaces, Proc 1st IEEE Workshop on Horizontal Interactive System p 185-192 Jan 2006

Reproducing and Re-experiencing the Writing Process in Japanese Calligraphy

Kumiyo Nakakoji[1,2], Kazuhiro Jo[1], Yasuhiro Yamamoto[1]
Yoshiyuki Nishinaka[2], Mitsuhiro Asada[2]
[1]*RCAST, University of Tokyo*   [2]*SRA-KTL Inc., Japan*
{kumiyo, jo, yxy}@kid.rcast.u-tokyo.ac.jp   *{nisinaka, m-asada}@sra.co.jp*

Abstract

Japanese calligraphy is the art of brush writing where a person writes Japanese characters with a Chinese brush against a sheet of paper. We have implemented a mechanism to capture the process of producing Japanese calligraphy using MERL's DiamondTouch (DT) table. We add a very thin metal wire along the length of the brush to carry an electric signal from the writer's body through the brush tuft and ink to the table. As the brush tuft is touches a sheet of paper placed on the surface of the DT table, the ink in the tuft carries the signal from the users to DT. We capture the movement of the brush tuft to produce the visual and auditory representations of the writing process and for later replay.

1. Introduction

Japanese calligraphy (called "Shodo" in Japanese) is the form of writing Japanese characters with a Shodo brush ("Fude") and ink ("Sumi"). It uses the brush "to deliver harmonious rhythm with varying brush posture, speed, and pressure" [3].

While Japanese calligraphy might be thought of as a visual representation, it is also about the process; its rich visual expressions are the result of dynamic strokes and the rhythm of writing [7]. A stroke's formation "largely depends on the constantly changing brush footprints generated from the artist's manipulation of the brush" [3].

Most children in Japan learn calligraphy in elementary school and some adults adopt it as a hobby. The traditional manner of learning Shodo is to use examples writing as guide for the student to mimic. The example is usually placed to the left of a blank sheet of paper and the student refers to it in practicing with a brush soaked with ink. It is often difficult for the student to match the given example, because it is a static image of a dynamic process. A teacher therefore will sometimes hold the student's brush hand and guide the brush in order to teach the motion, angle, direction and force.

2. The Basic Idea

Our approach is (1) to preserve the Shodo experience in a natural setting, and (2) to unveil the temporal and rhythmic process information embedded in the produced visual representation for non-Shodo experts.

We use MERL's DiamondTouch (DT) table [4] to sense the calligraphy activity produced in the natural setting where a user writes with a traditional brush with ink, on a sheet of paper placed on the flat surface of the DT table (Figure 1(a)). Our idea is to use water, more specifically, ink loaded in a brush tuft, as the conductive material between the brush and the DT surface. So we add a very thin metal wire to the brush handle to make an electric circuit from the user's body, through the brush handle, through the ink and finally to the DT surface via the ink flowing onto the paper (Figure 1(b)). Because the brush handle is made of wood, this thin wire is the least obtrusive way to preserve all the most important aspects of the feel of media and medium to the artist.

Because the ink is conductive, we can approximate the touched area of the brush tuft put against the sheet of paper placed on the DT table. Recording a series of the sensed brush touched area allows us to re-produce a Japanese calligraphic representation with temporal information.

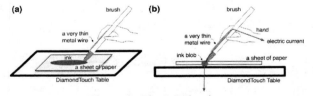

Figure 1: The Mechanism

3. The Calligramp System

We have implemented the *Calligramp* (Calligraphy Amplifier) system based on the above idea.

3.1. An Overview

The Calligramp system (Figure 2) detects the brush tuft movements through the DT table and stores them as time-stamped stroke data. It then produces visual and auditory representations from the data, and presents them to a user through means such as speakers, a visual monitor, and/or a projector.

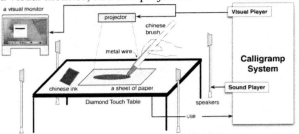

Figure 2: The Calligramp System

Figure 3 shows how a brush tuft touch via a sheet of paper is detected by the DT table. Figure 3-Left shows how our system preserves the physical setting for the user. Figure 3-Right shows how the user's action is sensed in realtime.

Figure 3: How a Brush Tuft Touch is Sensed by DT

We tested with different types of inks. We originally used black ink, which is usually used in Japanese calligraphy. This ink consists of carbon, which is conductive. The problem is that as the artist adds to the work, the entire drawing becomes conductive even when it dries out. This prevents the DT table from recognizing exactly where the current brush stroke is. We solved this problem by using Shodo red ink, which is not conductive.

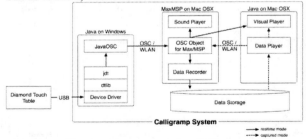

Figure 4: The Architecture of the Calligramp System

Figure 4 illustrates the architecture of the Calligramp system. The system supports two interaction modes: *realtime mode*, and *capture mode*. In the realtime mode, the brush strokes detected by DT are processed in realtime and visual and/or audio feedback is provided to the user. In the capture mode, the brush strokes detected by DT are collected for later replay. The solid line in Figure 4 represents the data

flow in the realtime mode and the dotted line represents that of the capture mode.

3.2. Data Collection

We use DT SDK2.0, dtlib and jdt to access sensory data detected by the DT table on Windows XP. We first filter the data captured by the DT table, and then use JavaOSC to convert it into the OSC protocol and transfer it via wireless network to the MaxMSP program that runs on Mac OS X. The received data is then stored for replay. The data is currently stored as a non-proprietary text file.

We use two data formats, one for the realtime mode and the other for the capture mode. For the realtime mode, in order to minimize delay, we use the minimum set of information (see Figure 5(a)). The capture mode includes all realtime data plus calculated information containing more characteristics of the brush tuft movements (see Figure 5(b)).

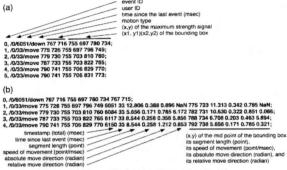

Figure 5: Data Formats Used in Calligramp

3.3. Writing Processes

To illustrate how a Shodo master and non-masters' writing processes differ, we have used the captured data to analyze the dynamics of stroke data produced by a Shodo master and non-masters.

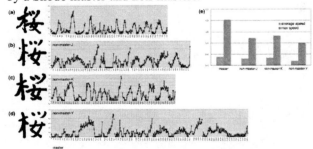

Figure 6: Process Differences between Shodo Master and Non-Masters

Figure 6(a) shows the data captured from a Shodo master and by three non-masters (Figure 6(b)-(d)), each with a graph showing how the stroke speed changes over time during the writing process. From the four graphs, one can see how rhythmical the master moves the brush by alternating high speed and low speed.

Figure 6(e) shows a graph comparing the average and maximum speed of moving a brush tuft by each of the four individuals. The master's (leftmost) graph has the highest value for speed.

3.4. Feedback Mechanisms

The Calligramp system currently supports two types of interaction with the augmented Shodo writing process: (1) *after writing* when the system reproduces visual effects and/or the theme music for the produced calligraphy, and (2) *while writing* when the system provides immediate visual and/or audio feedback or the system provides guidance for a writer by replaying the data captured from the writing of a Shodo master.

3.4.1. The Visual Data Player

The Visual Data Player component currently provides a movie player-like interface for interacting with the recorded stroke data. Figure 7 illustrates the visually reconstructed representation from the data. Figure 7(a) is a picture taken for the actual calligraphy written by a Shodo master. Figures 7(b)-(d) are screen shots of the Visual Data Player when loading the master's writing data.

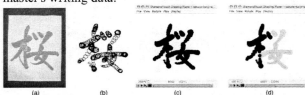

Figure 7: Real Writing (a) and Screen Shots of the Visual Player Component (b-d)

The Visual Data Player draws brush strokes as inscribed ovals along the path of the captured event data (Figure 7(b)). A series of the ovals colored in black produces the brush stroke like representation (Figure 7(c)).

In addition to a brush tuft's touches, the Visual Data Player component displays the peak lines (in green lines in Figure 7(d)) of the strokes by connecting line segments between each pair of two consecutive peaks (i.e., the max_signal_points). The yellow lines are peak lines using width as indicator of the inverse of the speed; the slower, the thicker (Figure 7(d)). A user may play back the writing process by using the movie player-like control bar located in the bottom of the window with various speeds (by changing the value in the window located in the bottom left; the default is 100%).

The Visual Data Player also provides mechanisms to view the writing from different angles as a way to augment the Shodo experience. For instance, Figure 8 shows the directed Tuft view mode, which shows the

visual representation as if one becomes the tip of the tuft. The stroke always moves upward and the character instead moves around in the canvas area.

Figure 8: Different Views in the Visual Player

3.4.2. The Sound Data Player

To represent the rhythm and dynamism of the writing process, auditory display [5] is an effective way to emphasize such properties especially as the writing process is replayed.

We have implemented the Sound Data Player component by using MaxMSP to produce different kinds of auditory feedback for the data captured by the Calligramp system (Figure 9). We have particularly paid attention to designing sound representations that stress the rhythm and dynamism of the speed and changing direction of the brush tuft movement. We have currently implemented 26 sound primitives that can be linked to some of the properties of the event data entry as described in Figure 5.

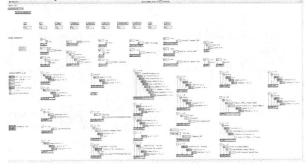

Figure 9: The Sound Data Player

For instance, one of the sound primitives we have implemented to stress the dynamism of the changing speed of the brush tuft, is the one that produces the sound of a racing car engine. It produces the engine-like sound with high or low RPM depending on how large or small the value is.

Examples of other sound primitives we have implemented include the metronome, footsteps, glass crush, piano scale, controlling music playing speed, and sinewave. We leave the description of details of each sound implementation to another paper due to the page limitation.

4. Discussions

Many of the existing system support approaches for oriental calligraphy and brush drawing (such as [2] and [3]) simulate brushwork to produce visual representations of brush strokes. Our approach, in contrast, is to use the real brush, ink and a sheet of paper, to nurture the calligraphy experience in a natural setting. The visual representation exists as a real document, and we use the captured process data to augment the experience without ruining the real, natural, experience of writing.

The Calligramp system can be viewed as a history tool for writing, which enables people to re-experience the process of creating artifacts. Our underlying belief is that knowing the process of creation makes the difference in understanding the artifact. For example, the movie, "The Mystery of Picasso" [6], shows the painter's painting process, where most of paint moves made on the canvas had been overdrawn by later painting moves and did not remain in the final drawing. In the process, a variety of objects, characters and themes emerged, and disappeared by being overdrawn, literally embedded in the final drawing. One sees very different things in the resulted paining after one watches the movie and knows the process. Another example that shares the same philosophy is the airconditionvideo project [1]. An interesting abstract picture is made by taking a series of successive snapshots of a person's body movement. One cannot tell how the picture is created without looking at the process of making the movie. Once one understands the process, one can appreciate the picture in a completely different manner.

Shodo has a similar nature in its visual representation. When a Shodo master looks at a work of calligraphy, the master is able to reinterpret and re-experience the process from the resulted visual representation; that is, the dynamics and rhythm of the brush movement. For non-masters, one can only focus on the shape and visual attributes of the calligraphy. It is difficult to "read" from the visual representation the temporal and rhythmic aspects of the calligraphy. The goal of Calligramp is to partially make such temporal and rhythmic information available for those who are not Shodo masters.

The Calligramp project is still ongoing and can be expanded in several ways. First, we are still exploring the space of visual and sound design for better representing and communicating the writing process data. Once designed, visual and sound design alternatives need to be studied in order to understand the effectiveness of them as feedback. Second, we also plan to identify richer events from the data to better understand the writing process. For instance, we can identify the moment when two strokes intersect. We can then generate visual and/or audio emphases to the user, which gives innovative ways to experience Japanese calligraphy.

The project described in this paper is a way to augment a regular tabletop interaction experience in the form of Japanese calligraphy. Our design is not to reform the writing experience by itself. A user engages in Japanese calligraphy in a very traditional form by using a brush, ink, on a sheet of paper on the horizontal, flat surface. We use the captured data to augment the process.

We believe that our approach, which differs from most of existing Tabletop computing tools [6] since users are not directly interacting with computing objects, demonstrates a new direction in expanding the horizon of the tabletop computing.

5. Acknowledgements

We are very grateful to the Shodo Master, Kousei Yamane, for letting us observe and collect data from his precious Shodo performances. We would also like to thank MERL for generously letting us use a DT, and Brent Reeves and Yoshinari Shirai for valuable discussions. This work is supported by MEXT Grant-in-Aid for Scientific Research (A) 16200008, 2004-2007.

6. References

[1] Aircondition, http://oliverlaric.com/airconditionvideo.htm

[2] W. Baxter, V. Scheib, M. Lin, and D. Manocha, DAB: Interactive Haptic Painting with 3D Virtual Brushes, Proceedings of ACM SIGGRAPH 01, pp. 461-468, 2001.

[3] N.S.H. Chu, C-L. Tai, Real-Time Painting with an Expressive Virtual Chinese Brush, IEEE Computer Graphics and Applications, pp.76-85, IEEE, September/October 2004.

[4] P.H. Dietz, D.L. Leigh, DiamondTouch: A Multi-User Touch Technology, ACM Symposium on User Interface Software and Technology (UIST), pp. 219-226, November, 2001.

[5] G. Kramer, An Introduction to Auditory Display, Auditory Display: Sonification, Audification, and Auditory Interfaces, G. Kramer (Ed.), Addison-Wesley, Reading, MA., pp.1-77, 1994.

[6] The Mystery of Picasso, http://www.imdb.com/title/tt0049531/

[7] E. Takase, Learn Japanese Calligraphy, Takase Studios Inc., 2003.

Reading Revisited:
Evaluating the Usability of Digital Display Surfaces for Active Reading Tasks

Meredith Ringel Morris, A.J. Bernheim Brush, Brian R. Meyers
Microsoft Research
{merrie, ajbrush, brianme}@microsoft.com

Abstract

A number of studies have shown that paper holds several advantages over computers for reading tasks. However, these studies were carried out several years ago, and since that time computerized reading technology has advanced in many areas. We revisit the issue of reading in the workplace, comparing paper use to state-of-the-art hardware and software. In particular, we studied how knowledge workers perform reading tasks in four conditions: (1) using paper, (2) using a dual-monitor desktop system, (3) using a pen-enabled horizontal display surface, and (4) using multiple tablet computers. We discuss our findings, noting the strengths and shortcomings of each configuration. Based on these findings, we propose design guidelines for hybrid horizontal + vertical systems that support active reading tasks.

1. Introduction

Contrary to expectations, the proliferation of the personal computer has not eliminated the use of paper for office work [20]. One common use of paper in office settings is printing digital documents for *active reading* (*i.e.*, annotating a document while reading for increased understanding and later reference).

In their 1997 study [13], O'Hara and Sellen observed knowledge workers perform an active reading task in which participants read and summarized a scientific magazine article. They found several ways that paper outshined a computer for performing this task, and provided three design recommendations for computer systems based on their observations: (1) "Recognize that annotation can be an integral part of reading and build support for these processes." (2) "The need to support quicker, more effortless navigation techniques." (3) "The need to support more flexibility and control in spatial layout."

Ten years have passed since this seminal study, and many of O'Hara and Sellens' suggestions have been

incorporated into modern personal computers. For example, word processing software typically includes several mechanisms for annotating documents, such as the "comment" and "highlighter" tools in Microsoft Office Word. Tablet PCs and other similar products support annotation through the use of a stylus, and free-form ink written with a stylus can be added to documents using several software tools. Users also have more flexibility in laying out documents on-screen, since display resolution has increased dramatically, and it is increasingly common for users to have more than one display connected to their computer [5].

We conducted a study, closely modeled on O'Hara and Sellens' original methodology, to examine whether the affordances of modern computing hardware and software have succeeded in improving the usability of digital documents for active reading tasks. In our study, we observed participants performing active reading tasks in four conditions (see Figure 1): using paper, using a traditional computer with vertical displays, using a stylus-enabled horizontal surface, and using multiple tablet computers.

We contribute detailed findings on the usability of vertical, horizontal, and tablet computing systems for active reading. Additionally, we contribute design guidelines for hybrid horizontal + vertical systems that we believe will provide improved support for this common office task scenario. Before discussing our study and findings, however, we first present related work in the areas of computer-based active reading and horizontal computing research.

1.1 Related Work

1.1.1 Reading and Annotation

In addition to O'Hara and Sellens' study [13], there have been several other studies of digital reading and annotation. Adler *et al.* conducted a diary and interview study in 1998 [1], which allowed them to develop taxonomies of the different types of reading and writ-

0-7695-3013-3/07 $25.00 © 2007 IEEE
DOI 10.1109/TABLETOP.2007.12

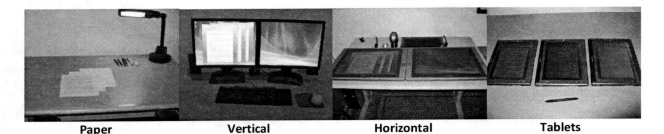

| Paper | Vertical | Horizontal | Tablets |

Figure 1: In the Paper condition, participants had a printed article, blank paper and a variety of writing tools. In the Vertical condition, participants had two monitors, a keyboard, and a mouse. In the Horizontal condition, participants had two pen-enabled displays positioned horizontally on the desk, a stylus, a mouse, and a keyboard. In the Tablets condition, participants had three tablet computers and a stylus.

ing activities performed by people with varying occupations. They found a strong preference for paper, that reading was commonly performed in conjunction with writing, and that participants often switched between multiple documents during a single reading/writing task. Marshall and Ruotolo [10] studied the use of paper and digital versions of course by university students, and reported on when and why students chose to use different versions. Obendorf [12] compared the use of special software for annotating websites with typed text to the use of pencil and paper for annotating printouts of the same content, and found that paper was superior due to the flexibility it provided over the "Webnize Highlighter" tool. Hornbaek and Frokjaer [8] compared the use of normal, fisheye, and overview + detail representations of digital documents for a reading and summarization task, and found that fisheye views reduced task time while overview + detail views resulted in higher quality summaries. Studies of the ergonomics of reading from paper versus monitors have also been reported in the literature [3].

In addition to the aforementioned studies of reading and annotation practices, some researchers have developed novel systems intended to enhance the digital reading experience. Paper Augmented Digital Documents [6] attempt to preserve the affordances of both the paper and digital worlds for active reading tasks by using a special pen and paper to enable digital capture of annotations. The XLibris system [15] was a tablet computer designed specifically to support active reading; it used a stylus for ink annotations, allowed users to use their thumb to flip pages, and provided visual feedback about a document's length and the users' position within a document. PARC's eXperiments in the Future of Reading (XFR) project [7] produced several museum exhibits demonstrating futuristic reading interfaces; however, the designs were whimsical and provocative in nature, not suitable for everyday work.

1.1.2 Horizontal Computing

Advances in sensing and display hardware (such as DiamondTouch [2] or PlayAnywhere [25]) have resulted in an increased interest in novel computing form factors, particularly horizontal computing surfaces. These horizontal systems include both *table systems* (collaborative horizontal surfaces, such as [4][11][14][17][18]) and *desk systems* (single-user horizontal surfaces, such as [22][23][26]). Some, such as ConnecTables [21] or the UbiTable [18], involve several computing surfaces that operate together as a single system, while others involve only a single surface.

In their 2003 article on design guidelines for horizontal displays [16], Scott *et al.* state that the need to "elucidate which tasks are most suitable for tabletop" is still an area for future research. Researchers have been exploring the appropriateness of horizontal systems for a variety of domains, including visualization [4], photo management [17], gaming [14], and artistic expression [11]. A few systems offer affordances that are aimed toward office productivity tasks, such as the DigitalDesk's hybrid physical/virtual calculator [22] or the ability to use a fingertip to draw ink annotations on text, image, and html documents provided by UbiTable [18] and DiamondSpin [19]. The DeskJockey system [26] projects ambient content on a desk, but does not support input-based tasks such as active reading. Wigdor and Balakrishnan [24] performed a study showing the performance impacts of reading text at varying angles on a tabletop display; however, their study focused on reading short snippets (*e.g.*, words or phrases), while we are studying active reading tasks of a scope similar to typical office work practices. We were unable to find any studies of the use of a horizontal system to perform a realistic active reading task -- therefore this paper contributes valuable information regarding the suitability of horizontal computing systems for common tasks in this domain.

2. Methodology

To evaluate and compare the active reading experience using paper and three computer-based setups, we borrowed heavily from the methodology described in O'Hara and Sellens' 1997 paper [13], which allows us to make comparisons to their findings from ten years ago. Like [13], we used a text summarization task and set up the vertical condition to emulate a conventional situation. However, we chose to use a within-subjects design with all participants using all four setups (in a counter-balanced order) rather than between participants (as in [13]) so that we could gather participants' qualitative preferences among the four conditions. In this section, we describe our experimental methodology in detail.

We recruited twelve participants (half female) from within a large technology company. Participants had a variety of job roles (*e.g.*, administrative assistant, marketing, program manager, software developer), and ranged in age between 20 and 50 years. All participants had prior experience using a stylus to operate a Tablet PC, in order to reduce the training necessary for them to complete the two ink-enabled conditions (horizontal and tablets).

Before beginning the study, all participants completed a tutorial demonstrating how to use a stylus and specific features of our chosen word processing application (Microsoft Office Word 2007); this tutorial was done using the horizontal system's equipment, since it included both a stylus and a mouse and keyboard. The features covered in the tutorial were selected because they satisfied the design recommendations put forth by O'Hara and Sellens' original study – features for highlighting a document, inserting comments, adding ink annotations, repositioning and resizing windows, changing the number of pages visible at a time, and navigating within a document. Participants were able to refer to a printed copy of this tutorial throughout the remainder of the study.

Participants were then told that their manager had asked them to provide a one-paragraph summary of a four-page article from the New York Times science section. Participants were asked to think aloud while completing the task, and were given fifteen minutes in each condition (in order to enable completion of all four conditions within a reasonable time frame).

This reading-to-summarize task was familiar to our participants, and on our post study questionnaire all but one of them indicated that they performed similar tasks as part of their daily work. Participants offered examples of analogous tasks that were part of their jobs, such as reading and evaluating specification and legal documents, reading about new technologies and providing an overview to colleagues, and summarizing long emails to convey core ideas to others.

We used four different articles of similar length (between 974 and 1039 words) and complexity (as judged by pilot testing). The combination and presentation order of articles and conditions was counter-balanced, using a Latin Square design. In the paper condition, the article was printed single-sided; in all other conditions, the article was presented in Microsoft Word 2007.

Participants were also presented with two blank Word documents (piles of paper in the paper condition). The first was a "scratch" space, provided for optional note-taking, and the second was for composing the final summary. In all conditions, participants were informed that they could annotate the original article if they wished, and that they could modify any aspect of the setup (the position of paper, displays, input devices, windows, etc.) so as to be comfortable. All four setups used were situated on identical desks, measuring 48'' by 30''.

In the "paper" condition (see Figure 1), subjects were provided with three overlapping stacks of paper – the article on top, followed by the scratch paper and then the summary paper. There was also an array of writing implements (a pencil, red, blue, and black pens, and pink, orange, and yellow highlighters).

In the "vertical" condition (see Figure 2), participants were provided with a mouse, keyboard, and dual-monitor display. Each of the LCD displays measured 21'' diagonally and had a resolution of 1600 x 1200 pixels. We chose a dual-monitor configuration to represent status-quo computing setups since increased use of such setups is reported in the literature [5]. Additionally, on our post-study questionnaire, 75% of our participants reported having two or more displays connected to their office computer. The article, scratch, and summary documents were each open in separate windows of the word processing application. The windows were positioned overlapping by a small offset on the left-hand monitor. The article was on top, followed by the scratch and then the summary documents. Each window was zoomed so that the first page of the document was entirely visible

In the "horizontal" condition (see Figure 3), participants were provided a horizontal computing surface composed of two Wacom Cintiq 21UX[1] devices, operating as a dual-monitor system. Each Cintiq device consists of a stylus-sensitive, 21.3'' diagonal LCD screen with a resolution of 1600 x 1200 pixels. A stylus, wireless mouse, and wireless keyboard were initially located on the desk behind the displays. Additionally, touch strips on the device's bezels could be

---

[1] http://www.wacom.com/cintiq/

used to scroll within documents. The documents were configured on the left-hand Cintiq in a fashion identical to the vertical condition.

In the "tablets" condition (see Figure 4), participants were initially presented with three Motion Computing LE1600 slate tablets, each in the portrait orientation and having resolution 1024 x 768. Each tablet contained a single word processing document, maximized to use the entire display, and set to have the first page entirely visible. The tablets were laid on the desk with the article on the left, then the scratch document, then the blank summary. A single stylus, which could be used to operate all three tablets, was also on the desk.

The specific display technologies used in each condition were chosen to preserve ecological validity, utilizing high-end, commercially available hardware representing the status quo for each of the three digital form-factors.

Two observers took structured notes during the study, coding several behaviors inspired by [13] and by our own pilot studies. Participants were also videotaped. After participants had read the article and written their summary in one of the conditions, they completed a questionnaire about the experience. Participants also filled out a final questionnaire asking them to make comparisons among all four setups.

3. Results

After completing the study, participants ranked each of the four conditions based on the experience of reading the article, annotating the article, taking notes, and writing the summary (with a rank of 1 indicating the most preferred condition for each subtask, and a rank of 4 indicating the least preferred). Table 1 reports the median rankings for each subtask in each condition.

The ranking differences for each subtask were statistically significant[2]: Reading, χ^2 (3, N = 12) = 12.70, $p = .005$; Annotating, χ^2 (3, N = 12) = 12.10, $p = .007$; Note-taking, χ^2 (3, N = 12) = 12.13, $p = .007$; Writing, χ^2 (3, N = 12) = 22.36, $p < .001$. Pairwise tests reveal more detailed significance trends. For the reading subtask, the paper and tablets conditions were preferred to the vertical condition ($p < .015$). For the annotation subtask, the paper, tablets, and horizontal conditions were all preferred to the vertical ($p < .025$). For the

---

[2] Because the data is not normally distributed, all of our analyses use non-parametric tests. We use the Friedman test to compare across the four conditions, and follow-up pairwise comparisons are done via Wilcoxon Signed Ranks tests. We use an alpha level of .05 for all statistical tests.

Table 1. Rankings of preferences for each condition by subtask (Median reported, scale 1-4 where 1 is the best possible ranking).

	Reading	Annotating	Notes	Writing
Paper	2	2	2	4
Vertical	4	4	4	1
Horizontal	3	3	3	2
Tablets	2	2	1.5	3

note-taking subtask, paper was preferred to vertical ($p < .04$). For the writing subtask, the vertical condition was preferred to all of the others ($p < .02$), and the horizontal condition was preferred to both the paper and the tablets ($p < .03$).

In O'Hara and Sellens' original study, they found that paper was superior to the computer for active reading; they explained these differences as due to challenges of computer tools in the areas of annotation, navigation, and spatial layout. Our preference data, however, indicate that computing tools now are comparable with, or superior to, paper in several respects. We explore the reasons for these preferences, examining annotation, navigation, and spatial layout issues, as well as issues relating to composition and ergonomics.

3.1 Annotations and Note-Taking

Ten years ago, O'Hara and Sellen found annotating on paper to be clearly superior to annotating using a traditional (*i.e.*, vertical) computer setup. The subjective ratings in Table 1 show that in our study, the vertical condition again fared poorly for annotation tasks; however, other computer form-factors (horizontal and tablets) provided an annotation experience comparable to paper. Participant comments highlight the positive experience of annotating in the tablets and horizontal conditions. For example, on the post-task questionnaire for the tablets condition, P7 commented, "The rest [reading, annotating, summarizing] feels like pen work, so I like that." Similarly, P2 commented, "Marking up the document was much more natural, as was taking notes." Referring to the horizontal condition, P2 said, "Annotating [is] fairly easy," while P11 commented, "Easy to annotate while reading." Participants did however, still experience challenges annotating in the digital conditions, such as insufficient margin space, and the overhead of entering a special inking mode in the word processor.

To evaluate any quantitative differences in how many and what type of annotations participants made in different conditions, we coded the annotations on the articles using the scheme introduced by Marshall and Brush [9]; annotations were counted and classified as *anchor-only* (*e.g.,* highlighted or underlined portions of the article's text), *content-only* (*e.g.,* a word or mark added to the page, but not explicitly connected to any portion of the article's text), or *compound* (*e.g.,* a word or mark added to the page with a line or other connection indicating a relationship to a portion of the article's text). Table 2 shows the annotation patterns for each condition, averaged across participants.

The stark difference between the vertical condition and the other three conditions supports the qualitative feedback. The total number of annotations applied to the articles differed significantly across conditions, χ^2 (3, N = 12) = 11.77, *p* = .008. Pairwise testing found that the total number of annotations applied in the paper and horizontal conditions was significantly higher than in the vertical condition (*p* < .03). Among the three conditions where participants annotated (paper, horizontal, tablets) there were no significant differences in the types of annotations (anchor, content, compound) that participants made.

One advantage the vertical condition did have over the others was the ease of using copy and paste as a method for taking notes and composing the summary. In the vertical condition, 75% of participants (8), used copy and paste while 16.7% of participants (2) used it in the horizontal condition and 25% of participants (3) attempted to copy and paste in the tablets condition although this functionality did not exist (due to using three separate tablets). P12's comments highlighted the importance of this feature, "A big part of 'active reading' for me is copying quotes and images from the source to the summary. This doesn't work on paper."

3.2 Navigation

Navigation between and within documents was another place that O'Hara and Sellen saw large differences between using paper and working digitally. In particular, they observed that using paper their participants could easily interweave navigation with reading using two-handed movements.

In our study we saw that the horizontal condition offered participants something more similar to their experience using paper for interleaving navigation with reading using two handed movements. Seven of the 16 participants (43.7%), used the touch strip on the bezel of the Cintiq displays with their non-dominant hand while pointing or using the stylus with their other hand. P10 commented: "It [touch strip] makes me feel like I'm multi-tasking and is an easy way to go through the document." In the tablets condition, 25% of participants (3) used one hand to mark a location in the article while using the other to write. This behavior was also common in the paper condition. These types of bi-

Table 2. Number of annotations applied to the original article in each condition (Mean reported).

	Anchor Only	Content Only	Compound	Total
Paper	19.8	1.6	1.5	22.9
Vertical	4.8	0.0	0.8	5.7
Horizontal	16.2	1.0	0.3	17.4
Tablets	15.2	0.4	0.5	16.1

manual interactions, for example, using one hand to mark a place in the article while operating an input device with the other hand, were not seen in the vertical condition.

3.3 Spatial Layout

O'Hara and Sellen observed many problems related to spatial layout in their vertical condition. Specifically, the limited viewing area afforded by the monitor meant participants in their study had to either shrink the documents or overlap windows, and spent time managing the position and size of windows.

We found that the multi-monitor setups we used in the digital conditions allowed participants to have several documents visible simultaneously, enabling glancing back and forth between documents to serve as a lightweight means of navigation similar to the paper condition. Several participants also viewed multiple pages within a document simultaneously. For example, in the tablets condition, 4 people (33.3%) set the article so two or more pages were visible, while 3 people (25%) viewed multiple pages at once in the horizontal condition. Watching our participants attempting to lay out multiple pages led us to conclude that there is still plenty of room for improvement to better support flexible and smooth arrangement of digital pages – for example, participants wanted but were unable to simultaneously view four pages laid out in a row, or to view non-consecutive pages of an article for side-by-side comparison.

Window management remained an issue for our participants and all participants spent time in the digital conditions tiling their windows so as to avoid overlap and avoid spanning monitors' bezels. Ironically, we may have moved from not having enough digital space in 1997 to having too much in 2007. In the horizontal condition, 4 participants (33.3%) explicitly mentioned the size of the Cintiq and being overwhelmed by it. For example, P1 commented "too much real estate - sprawled over multi-mons with no easy way to get back and forth." Five participants (41.7%) in the horizontal condition chose to use only one of the two available displays and 2 participants (16.7%) did this in the vertical condition (6 unique participants).

O'Hara and Sellen also observed that participants had problems integrating reading and writing in the vertical condition because only one window could accept input at a time. We similarly observed that digital systems' ability to have only one window in focus created confusion for our participants. An example of this occurred in the horizontal condition, and involved the use of the touch strips. Three of our participants assumed that the strip on the left of the display would scroll the leftmost document and the strip on the right of the display would scroll the rightmost document. They were confused to find that all the touch strips scrolled the single, focal document, regardless of its location. The former behavior, however, would have better supported bimanual interactions, such as scrolling through the article with one hand while writing the summary with the other.

3.4 Composition

When composing their summary, participants indicated a preference for text, rather than handwriting. In the horizontal condition, when participants had a choice of using the stylus to write their summary or the keyboard to type it, 75% (9) chose to type the summaries, despite the inconvenience of accessing the keyboard (6 participants pushed the display further away from them in order to make room for the keyboard, and 3 placed the keyboard on their laps). In the tablets condition, where no keyboard was available, 25% (3) of participants still created text summaries by using automatic handwriting-to-text conversion (a technique that we did not cover during the tutorial).

This preference for text reflects several factors. 33.3% of participants (4) mentioned that a handwritten summary seemed sloppy or unprofessional, and would not be considered acceptable by their colleagues. 41.7% (5) mentioned that their hand felt fatigued or cramped after writing the summary out on paper. 66.7% (8) also pointed out that they type more quickly than they write. Also, the ability to utilize special functionality, such as spell-checking, was considered desirable. Half of our participants (6) used spell-checking or thesaurus features, although doing so was never suggested by the experimenters.

3.5 Ergonomics

In all conditions, we told participants to feel free to adjust any aspect of their workspace in order to be more comfortable. Participants naturally repositioned the printed documents during the paper condition, and

also in the tablets condition where every participant moved the tablets from their original position and 50% (6) tilted them off the surface of the desk (by holding them in the air, leaning on their lap, or propping them against other tablets). One participant even took the tablet over to a couch to sit and read. Four participants (33.3%) adjusted the positions of the monitors in the vertical condition by angling their center edges toward the back of the desk, creating a shallow "V" shape.

In contrast to the quick and somewhat effortless ergonomic adjustment in the paper, tablets, and vertical conditions, the horizontal condition required more thought and effort for 75% (9) of our participants. Two participants raised the height of the desk and worked from a standing position. Four participants propped books underneath the back edge of the displays so that they were tilted in drafting table style. Six pushed the displays backwards to make room for a keyboard and mouse, and four even rotated the Cintiq displays to be at a more paper-like writing angle.

On their questionnaires, 41.7% of participants (5) mentioned that they found the horizontal setup uncomfortable to use, although we did not explicitly ask about this. Comments included: "touch screens not at a good angle for use as a monitor" (P1), "bad angle for reading" (P3), "it made me nauseous to look at the screens" (P6), "you start to feel a little strained in the neck" (P10), and "not a comfortable working environment" (P12).

4. Discussion

At a high level, our results show that computing support for active reading tasks has made substantial progress since the mid-nineties. Our participants' preference rankings showed that the vertical and horizontal setups were preferred for the writing sub-task, that the horizontal and tablets setups performed on par with paper for the annotation sub-task, and that the tablets were on par with paper for the reading sub-task. While these results show that computing devices can be as good as, and even better than, paper for active reading, they also indicate areas for improvement. It's noteworthy that no single computing setup emerged as a clear choice for active-reading-based office work.

The vertical setup, which is the status quo in many modern offices, was a clear win for writing-intensive portions of the task. While annotation support for mouse-and-keyboard systems has clearly improved since O'Hara and Sellens' study, there is still further room for improvement, since nearly half the subjects did not avail themselves of annotation tools in this condition, and the available tools did not support content-only annotation styles. The vertical setup also did not support common bimanual actions, such as using one hand to "bookmark" interesting content while operating an input device with the other, perhaps because the vertical orientation would have made such pointing uncomfortable by requiring participants to hold their arms in an elevated position. While multi-monitor setups enabled glanceability, the user experience of laying out windows in a non-overlapping manner could be improved.

The horizontal setup was strong in its support for annotation, and in allowing users to bridge the worlds of handwriting and text. The orientation and hardware encouraged bimanual interactions, such as pointing-to-bookmark and scrolling while writing; further bimanual interactions could be supported by using multi-touch hardware. However, the displays' large size overwhelmed some users, with window management issues again degrading the experience. Additionally, the ergonomics of the horizontal setup were troublesome, requiring customization for the majority of users, and causing several to report physical discomfort (*e.g.*, muscle strain, nausea).

The tablets showed strong performance for reading and annotation. Users liked the freedom to rearrange the tablets, pick them up, and move them around in a manner analogous to paper. However, the lack of a keyboard and the inability to easily move information between different tablets was a drawback of this approach.

Because active reading tasks are commonplace for knowledge workers (for example, all but one of our participants reported performing such tasks as part of their job), it is important for hardware and software designers to consider how they can improve the utility of computing systems for this class of tasks. Based on the findings of our study, we recommend a hybrid approach for next-generation office computing systems that combines the best features of horizontal, vertical, and repositionable surfaces in order to capitalize on the affordances each offers for active reading. Such a system should:

Include both horizontal and vertical displays: With a hybrid system, digital documents could be easily moved between the horizontal and vertical spaces depending on whether they were the focus of annotation, reading, or composition.

Be configurable: Based on the challenges we saw as participants configured their environment in the horizontal condition, it is clear that any hybrid computing system must be highly configurable. For example, the angle of tilt of the horizontal display surface should be adjustable, and could also include tablet-sized removable components that could be lifted out and positioned for optimal comfort.

Support multiple input devices: Compared to ten years ago, current technology offers annotation options that performed on par with paper, but these are not typically part of office setups. In addition to stylus input for annotations, users' preference for text during composition makes a mouse and keyboard important – positioning these in a manner compatible with the horizontal surface may be challenging.

Allow bi-manual input and focus: Displays should support multi-point touch and stylus input to enable bimanual operations. In addition to the ability of hardware to receive multiple simultaneous inputs, software should support binding different parts of the input stream to different windows, in order to enable simultaneous bimanual interaction with two documents.

Improve software support for window navigation and management: Window management is known to be a challenge for multi-monitor environments [5], and hybrid systems will only increase users' difficulties, in this respect. Software is needed so that that users can quickly navigate among documents without being overwhelmed by the positioning choices created by a large display area. Automatic facilities for creating non-overlapping, non-bezel-spanning window layouts would enable users to focus on the documents, rather than on tweaking the documents' on-screen positions. Software should also be flexible in terms of within-document page layouts, allowing users to display more than two pages side-by-side in order to better take advantage of large displays. Also, restrictions allowing only consecutive pages to be shown side-by-side should be removed.

5. Conclusion

In this paper, we have presented quantitative and qualitative results from our study of active reading. Although digital systems have improved their support for active reading in the last ten years, there is still room for improvement. Our results reveal the strengths and weaknesses of status quo "vertical" systems, horizontal systems, and multi-surface tablet-based systems for this commonplace productivity task. Our findings on the suitability of each setup for annotation, navigation, spatial management, composition, and ergonomic comfort can inform the design of next-generation hardware and software for standard, horizontal, and tablet systems. Additionally, by synthesizing users' experiences with each system type, we proposed design recommendations for a hybrid system that would combine the strengths of vertical, horizontal, and reconfigurable surfaces. In future work, we plan to explore the potential of such a hybrid system for enhancing reading-based productivity tasks.

6. References

[1] Adler, A., Gujar, A., Harrison, B., O'Hara, K., and Sellen, A. A Diary Study of Work-Related Reading: Design Implications for Digital Reading Devices. *Proc. of CHI 1998*, 241-248.

[2] Dietz, P. and Leigh, D. DiamondTouch: A Multi-User Touch Technology. *Proc. of UIST 2001*, 219-226.

[3] Dillon, A. Reading from Paper Versus Screens: A Critical Review of the Empirical Literature. *Ergonomics*, 1992.

[4] Forlines, C. and Shen, C. DTLens: Multi-User Tabletop Spatial Data Exploration. *Proc. of UIST 2005*, 119-122.

[5] Grudin, J. Partitioning Digital Worlds: Focal and Peripheral Awareness in Multiple Monitor Use. *Proc. of CHI 2001*, 458-465.

[6] Guimbretière, F. Paper Augmented Digital Documents. *Proc. of UIST 2003*, 51-60.

[7] Harrison, S., Minneman, S., Back, M., Balsamo, A., Chow, M., Gold, R., Gorbet, M., and MacDonald, D. The What of XFR: eXperiments in the Future of Reading. *Interactions Magazine*, 8(3), May/June 2001, 21-30.

[8] Hornbaek, K. and Frokjaer, E. Reading of Electronic Documents: The Usability of Linear, Fisheye, and Overview + Detail Interfaces. *Proc. of CHI 2001*, 293-300.

[9] Marshall, C. and Brush, A.J. Exploring the Relationship Between Personal and Public Annotations. *Proc. of JCDL 2004*, 349-357.

[10] Marshall, C. and Ruotolo, C. Reading-in-the-Small: A Study of Reading on Small Form Factor Devices. *Proc. of JCDL 2002*, 56-64.

[11] Morris, M.R., Huang, A., Paepcke, A., and Winograd, T. Cooperative Gestures: Multi-User Gestural Interaction for Co-located Groupware. *Proc. of CHI 2006*, 1201-1210.

[12] Obendorf, H. Simplifying Annotation Support for Real-World Settings: A Comparative Study of Active Reading. *Proc. of ACM Hypertext and Hypermedia 2003*, 120-121.

[13] O'Hara, K. and Sellen, A. A Comparison of Reading Paper and On-Line Documents. *Proc. of CHI 1997*, 335-342.

[14] Piper, A.M., O'Brien, E., Morris, M.R., and Winograd, T. SIDES: A Cooperative Tabletop Computer Game for Social Skills Development. *Proc. of CSCW 2006*, 1-10.

[15] Schilit, B., Golovchinsky, G., and Price, M. Beyond Paper: Supporting Active Reading with Free Form Digital Ink Annotations. *Proc. of CHI 1998*, 249-256.

[16] Scott, S.D., Grant, K.D., and Mandryk, R.L. System Guidelines for Co-located, Collaborative Work on a Tabletop Display. *Proc. of ECSCW 2003*, 159-178.

[17] Shen, C., Lesh, N., Forlines, C., and Vernier, F. Sharing and Building Digital Group Histories. *Proc. of CSCW 2002*, 324-333.

[18] Shen, C., Everitt, K., and Ryall, K. UbiTable: Impromptu Face-to-Face Collaboration on Horizontal Interactive Surfaces. *Proc. of UbiComp 2003*, 281-288.

[19] Shen, C., Vernier, F., Forlines, C., and Ringel, M. DiamondSpin: An Extensible Toolkit for Around-the-Table Interaction. *Proc. of CHI 2004*, 167-174.

[20] Sellen, A. and Harper, R. The Myth of the Paperless Office. *The MIT Press*, 2001.

[21] Tandler, P., Prante, T., Muller-Tomfelde, C., Streitz, N., and Steinmetz, R. ConnecTables: Dynamic Coupling of Displays for the Flexible Creation of Shared Workspaces. *Proc. of UIST 2001*, 11-19.

[22] Wellner, P. The DigitalDesk Calculator: Tangible Manipulation on a Desk Top Display. *Proc. of UIST 1991*, 27-34.

[23] Wellner, P. Interacting with Paper on the DigitalDesk. *Communications of the ACM*, July 1993, 36(7), 87-96.

[24] Wigdor, D. and Balakrishnan, R. Empirical Investigation into the Effect of Orientation on Text Readability in Tabletop Displays. *Proc. of ECSCW 2005*, 205-224.

[25] Wilson, A. PlayAnywhere: A Compact Interactive Tabletop Projection-Vision System. *Proc. of UIST 2005*, 83-92.

[26] Ziola, R., Kellar, M., and Inkpen, K. DeskJocky: Exploiting Passive Surfaces to Display Peripheral Information. *Proc. of Interact 2007*, in press.

Photohelix: Browsing, Sorting and Sharing Digital Photo Collections

Otmar Hilliges, Dominikus Baur, Andreas Butz
Media Informatics Group, University of Munich
Amalienstr. 17, 80333 Munich, Germany
otmar.hilliges@ifi.lmu.de, dominikus.baur@ei-performance.de, butz@ifi.lmu.de

Abstract

In this paper we debut Photohelix, a novel interactive system for browsing, sorting and sharing digital images. We present our design rationale for such a system and introduce Photohelix as a prototype application featuring a novel visualization and interaction technique for media browsing on interactive tabletops. We conducted a user study in order to evaluate and verify our design. We will present our findings in this paper and discuss further implications for future development of such systems derived from our experiences with Photohelix.

1. Introduction

In recent years digital media formats have had tremendous success and impact in almost all aspects of life. Digital photography, for example, has practically replaced its analog counterpart. In response to this, a variety of software for browsing, organizing and retrieving digital media, and particularly photos, has been developed.

Most digital photo tools have been designed to efficiently archive photo collections as well as to retrieve specific photographs as fast as possible. Two strategies to achieve these goals have matured over time: First, advanced grouping methods [10, 13, 23] and/or zooming interfaces [1, 14] are applied in order to maximize screen real-estate and to show as many pictures as possible at one time. Second, search engines help users to retrieve specific photos in a more goal-driven way. Since photos are perceived through the content shown, effective search relies on textual annotations or tagging with automatically derived meta data [6, 31, 26, 34]. Tagging-based approaches are very popular for online sharing of pictures (e.g., Flickr.com, Zoomr.com). However, recent studies suggest that users are reluctant to make use of annotation techniques [25] and might not even want to perform query-based searches [18] in their own personal collections.

These approaches share one property: They have been designed and optimized for single-user interaction on standard desktop computers. The PC is not well suited for co-present collaboration since the size and orientation of standard displays impede face-to-face communication. Desktop systems mostly preclude mutual eye contact and body language, as well as other properties which are important for verbal and non-verbal communication. Furthermore, PCs lack the tangibility of physical media, which is also very important for co-experiencing photo collections [8, 15].

In contrast interactive surfaces, and interactive tables in particular, offer a compelling platform for shared display collaboration, allowing multiple users to interact simultaneously with a shared information landscape. Collaboration around interactive tabletops has attracted a great deal of attention recently [7, 11, 19, 28, 27]. While digital photo browsing has served as a scenario in tabletop research [29, 21, 22], to our knowledge no system is available that takes the peculiarities of the cognitive and social processes of photo handling into account.

In this paper we introduce Photohelix, our prototypical design for the co-located browsing, organizing and sharing of digital pictures on an interactive tabletop. We present our design rationale for tabletop photoware based on literature review and empirical observations. We also describe one implementation of the aforementioned design. Then we present the results from the user study we conducted to verify our design and implementation of Photohelix. Finally, we discuss our conclusions and how they might inform the future development of similar systems.

2. Existing Tabletop Interfaces

The technology for large interactive surfaces has rapidly matured over the last years. Interactive tabletop systems, in particular, have come close to the point where we can expect them to be productized and marketed, hence impacting our daily lives more significantly. This was also strongly confirmed by the recent announcement of Microsoft's "Surface Computer".

SmartTech's DViT [32] is a vision-based, direct-touch

0-7695-3013-3/07 $25.00 © 2007 IEEE
DOI 10.1109/TABLETOP.2007.14

technology, which is commercially available and widely used in research [3, 33] as well as in commercial products such as interactive kiosks. Also commercially available is the DiamondTouch [5] tabletop, which also provides multiple simultaneous inputs with the added benefit of user identification. It is based on the capacitive sensing technology. Further research in the fields of capacitive sensing, frustrated internal reflection and optical flow analysis is driving technology even further forward [9, 24, 35] and opens up new and interesting opportunities for tabletop applications.

Several studies have been conducted to better understand the specific requirements and unique properties of interactive horizontal surfaces. Early work by Kruger et al. [16] helped to explain the role of virtual artifacts orientation for communication in tabletop groupware. Scott et al. [28] observed collaborative group work on both conventional and interactive tables and derived a set of guidelines for the development of tabletop systems supporting collaborative group work. A later study [27], which observed how people organized and managed the surface space on tables, reported the importance of separate regions for private information, public information and storage. Several other approaches have been presented to support the development of orientation aware systems [17, 30], which offer different techniques to automatically re-orient information artifacts and support explicit rotation of items to enhance communication and mutual engagement. Further research efforts have focused on visualization and interaction techniques that take these findings into account to improve collaboration and communication amongst members in a group [7, 11, 20].

Not surprisingly, the popular application field of digital photography has served as a scenario for tabletop research. Hinrichs et al. [12] have studied the effects of their "interface currents" on the collaborative use of photo collections. Morris et al. [22, 21] have explored how the orientation and distribution of control elements influence group performance on interactive tables using a photo tagging/searching scenario. An extensive body of literature about consumer behavior regarding digital (but also printed) photos has emerged in recent years [4, 8, 15, 25]. All studies confirm that users share a strong preference for browsing through their collections as opposed to explicit searching. Thus our goal was to support the *browsing* process and its associated activities.

The personal digital historian (PDH) [29] is a tabletop application that enables users to share pictures based on the four Ws of storytelling (i.e., Who, Where, What, When). However, to render this support possible the PDH requires an extensive set of meta data, which is seldom found in personal image collections (cf. [25]). With Photohelix we present our approach to support browsing, organizing (i.e., creating and maintaining long term hierarchical structures)

and co-located sharing of arbitrary sets of pictures, without requiring cumbersome annotation of image collections.

2.1. Design Goals

Throughout the body of literature [4, 8, 15, 25], a set of typical activities performed with media collections can be found. Future applications should try to support these activities, which are: *1) Filing* - The task of sorting media into folders or albums. *2) Selecting* - A repetitive activity in which users go through their collections and decide which items to keep and which to get rid of. *3) Sharing* - Often the ultimate usage of media at the end of its lifecycle. This can be performed remotely via e-mail or websites but also (and preferably [4]) co-located for communication and storytelling, such as updating friends and family about recent events. *4) Browsing* - Users look at pictures from different time periods, possibly to revive old and forgotten memories.

While these activities should be supported by any photo software, it is worthwhile to take a closer look at how certain properties of hardware and software configurations might support or hinder the photo-handling process. Frohlich et al. [8] coined the notion of "photo talk," which was later picked up and further investigated by Crabtree et al. [4]. To summarize, photo talk refers to the process of looking at (physical) photographs with friends and family while explaining what is depicted on the photographs or sharing an anecdote connected to the captured moment. This process is highly unstructured and can include several parallel actions or sub-activities, such as viewers joining or leaving the room, passing pictures around or detailed explanation of certain pictures.

These activities are well supported by physical photos, which afford the kind of flexible interactions necessary for browsing and sharing images. It is, for example, very easy to pass individual or stacks of photos around in a group seated at a table. Furthermore, physical photos impart a sense of personality and engagement that digital images fail to deliver. Frohlich et al. [8] even report that users are "turned off" by looking at pictures on a computer screen. Tabletop interfaces have promising attributes that could help overcome some of these problems by mimicking the flexibility and tangibility of physical media while coupling these qualities with the advantages of digital photography.

To support the photo handling process effectivly we identified the following design goals.

Overview at all times Refers to providing users with a visualization that represents an entire digital photo library, but also conveys information about where to find specific images when needed. This can be done by appropriately sorting photos (preferably by time [25]) and/or automatically clustering them so that many pictures can be displayed at once.

Details on demand   Means that an individual image can be quickly and easily retrieved for sharing or manipulation.

Support for temporary structures   Allows users to create temporary collections of images that are important for storytelling and especially its epistemic component. A tabletop photo application should provide the means to quickly create (and dissolve) arrangements of pictures, not necessarily from the same group or folder. For example, a user might wan to call up a set of beach shots from different vacations or several portraits of one person over the years. This should not affect the media collections' long-term organizational structure.

Flexible spatial arrangements   Help support the dynamic nature of photo handling [8] and demands that every element of the graphical user interface can be flexibly oriented and positioned. For example, such a system should not only be usable from each edge of the table, but also from each corner without problems. When handling photos, a walk-in-walk-out behavior is observed frequently. People will use the system from unusual positions and should not be hindered in doing so, nor should they disturb others.

3. Overview of PhotoHelix

Figure 1. PhotoHelix with its physical control object on our interactive table

Photohelix is a spiral-shaped, time-based visualization of photo collections. In addition to this visualization, it provides tangible, gesture-based and bi-manual interaction techniques.

The system (see also Video[1]) was developed and deployed on a custom interactive table, which contains a 42-inch LCD display with a native resolution of 1360 × 768

[1]www.mimuc.de/team/otmar.hilliges/files/ph.avi

pixels and an overlaid touch-sensitive DViT [32] panel for interactivity.

To fashion the physical control object, we disassembled an IKEA kitchen timer and equipped it with the electronics of a wireless mouse to measure rotation. Turning the upper part of the control object results in a standard mouse event that translates to the rotation of the helix. The position of the control object on the table is tracked by the DViT panel (see Figure 1).

Figure 2. A screenshot of Photohelix. The distinct functional areas (here: details above the helix, storage to the right) evolve dynamically and can be rearranged individually.

Photohelix was written in Java with a graphical presentation layer based on the University of Maryland's Piccolo framework [2]. We wrote an additional event-handling system that merges and interprets rotary encoder and touch events. These events are fed into a gesture recognizer, which enables gesture-based interaction with, and manipulation of, the photo collection and individual pictures. Metadata for individual photos, such as the capture date, is taken from the EXIF data.

3.1. Visualization

Tightly coupled to the physical control object is its virtual counterpart, a graphical visualization of the photo collection. It has the shape of a spiral and represents a timeline, on which the photos are organized, according to their capture date. Initially, photos are grouped into piles if they belong to a temporally continuous sequence (see Figure 2 on the left). This gives users an overview of their collection and supports orientation within the collection by narrowing down the search space.

The position and rotation of the spiral are controlled by the physical control object, hence it serves as a natural token to facilitate control allocation and turn taking in face-to-face communication and as a physical embodiment of the entire collection. The timeline is dynamically generated and

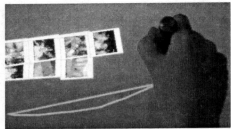

Figure 3. Grouping photos into a new event.

spans from the oldest image in the collection – placed in the center of the spiral, to the most recent image – placed at the outer end of the spiral. The inner spiral windings are shorter than the outer ones. This implies, that more space is available to place image piles in the outer, or newer, regions of the spiral. This nicely matches the observation, that people tend to take more photos with increased frequency over time. Furthermore, newer piles are depicted bigger and hence are easier to decipher. This also correlates with the observation that newer collection items are more frequently accessed than older ones [15].

Another component to Photohelix's spiral-shaped timeline is a semi-transparent lens that is overlaid on a certain section of the spiral. Pictures and piles of pictures that fall under the lens are shown in more detail thus providing "details on demand" (see Figure 2 above the helix). Photohelix works in two organizational forms: spatial arrangement and semantic grouping. Pictures are either shown individually (but arranged chronologically) or as so-called events. Events denote a stronger, more semantical coherence of the images therein and have to be created by the user (see Figure 3). Events are similar to folders in standard file managers. Each picture or event, when it falls under the lens, is called out and enlarged. It remains connected to the respective pile on the helix by an "umbilical cord". These images are again arranged chronologically along an imaginary line that runs parallel to the spiral's timeline. This leaves temporal relations intact and, in most cases, is equivalent to a semantic grouping, since temporal sorting tends to create spatial arrangements that are perceived as coherent [25].

3.2. Interaction

When the control device is set down onto the table, the spiral appears. For a few seconds, it remains semi-transparent and both the lens and the spiral rotate with the physical handle. During this time, a user can determine the initial position of the lens. Right-handers will, for example, move the lens to the upper right side of the spiral (see Figures 1, 2) so that they can conveniently turn the handle with the left hand, while using their right hand and a pen for interaction with the enlarged photos.

This mechanism also solves the general orientation problem by allowing each user around the table to adjust their Photohelix to best suit their needs (if several helices are available). It is also possible to reorient the whole interface at any time by just lifting it up, if several people share one helix or if the seating arrangement changes. To always ensure a comfortable working position, the helix can also be repositioned at any time by moving the physical handle to another spot on the table.

After the user has adjusted the initial orientation, the spiral is rendered solid and the lens remains fixed on an imaginary line running along the radius of the spiral. The spiral now turns with the handle, and the user can bring different areas of the spiral underneath the lens. The lens will travel inward and outward with the spiral windings, with every full turn applied by the user. To scroll faster, the handle can be twisted and then let run freely, to scroll back or forth several windings. The physical inertia of the handle in connection with a non-linear mapping of the time scale thus supports fast physical scrolling to cover larger time frames.

Individual images and events can be moved freely on the table surface, for example, when overriding the default chronological arrangement or organizing larger arrangements into sub-groups. To create events of closely related images, the user can simply circle the individual images with the pen. These are then automatically grouped into a new event, rendered as a slightly curved box containing semi-overlapping images (see Figure 3). New events also appear as new piles on the spiral and are connected to their pile by the umbilical cord. Cutting this cord dissolves the event again. To inspect the contents of events, the user can flip through the stack with the pen and see each individual photo in full (see Figure 4). This interaction technique resembles the handling of flip-books.

When a photo is dragged out of such a group, a full-size copy of the image is created and positioned on the table (see Figure 4, third image), which can then be moved with the pen or a finger. With the dedicated widget at one of its corners, it can be scaled and rotated (see Figure 5). This mechanism specifically supports the creation of temporary structures (e.g., several shots of the same person in

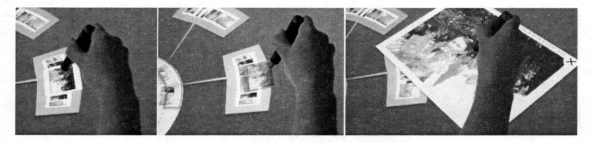

Figure 4. Flipping through an event to inspect images. Dragging images out of the event to create an enlarged copy.

one pile), without modifying the long term organization of the collection.

4. Browsing, Filing and Sharing

Browsing a photo collection can be done on different scales: Large-scale browsing indicates the act of going through a collection to identify a certain set of pictures. Small-scale browsing refers to inspecting events and images in more detail, for example, comparing several similar images to further use them for sharing or printing. Photohelix provides a convenient overview of the entire collection, structured by time. The automatic grouping of photos into piles of thumbnails serves two functions. First, the collection is presented in a space efficient way to avoid information overflow. Second, specific events or situations can be recognized on the basis of their representatives and the pile's position in time. Turning the helix brings different time intervals under closer inspection. Events and pictures displayed in the detail view (see Figure 2) convey more information to the user since all images are (at least partly) visible. This presentation is still very space-efficient, and also resembles the way in which printed photos can be spread out. Flipping through events allows a very fast inspection of large sequences. And the photos found while browsing, can easily be dragged out of the sequence in order to inspect the full-size version of individual pictures in

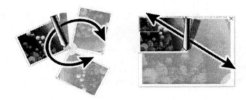

Figure 5. Rotating and resizing pictures in Photohelix.

further detail. The *filing* process is made more efficient by the automatic arrangement by time, and the ability to freely manipulate photos and events. This eliminates additional steps such as navigating folders. In many cases, the chronological sorting already meets the users' organizational intent. In addition, photos can be spatially arranged on the entire surface of the desk, which allows individual semantic mappings. For example one can create piles (e.g., left is for bad photos, right for good ones, top for funny, bottom for serious).

Photohelix particularly supports the *sharing* of photos, in this scenario, showing the photos to the people around the table. For this purpose, they can be freely moved and rotated toward others. In fact, the individual arrangement on the table can be used to convey parts or the structure of the story to the observers. For example, users can create a heap of pictures close to their edge of the table. While telling a story they can subsequently move and orient currently discussed images toward the audience. Additionally, collaborators can pick photos up and further inspect them at any time. It is also easy to hand over the entire collection since it is represented by and linked to the physical handle.

The current implementation of Photohelix does not support the *selecting* activity. In order to support this, it would be mandatory to delete "bad" pictures. We experimented with several interaction techniques to delete pictures. However, all of them where prone to in-accurate or faulty input. Furthermore, we encountered difficulties in attaining "raw" images, since many users already performed the selection process during or directly after downloading images from their camera. For these two reasons we decided not to to support selecting.

5. Evaluation

To verify our design decisions, we evaluated Photohelix in a qualitative user study. We were specifically interested in whether our interaction techniques actively support the highly dynamic and informal activities associated with photo handling (described earlier in Section "Design Goals").

Participants Twenty participants (13 male, 7 female) between the ages of 18 and 34 were recruited from amongst our students and the local community. All of them had normal or corrected-to-normal vision and were right-handed. All participants were power users who worked on a PC for four or more hours daily. In contrast, most participants had little to no exposure to interactive surfaces (including PDAs and Tablet PCs). Only one participant reported an occasional usage of interactive whiteboards. All participants own a digital camera (33% use it 3 to 5 times a year, 48% take pictures once or twice a month 19% use it weekly or daily) and image collection sizes ranged from approximately 100 to 10,000 pictures (with an average of 3340).

Study Setup and Tasks We envisioned a scenario that includes elements of storytelling and picture-sharing, which required that participants be familiar with the images. Participants were therefore asked to bring a subset of their own collection. Typical image sets included 80 to 100 pictures from a time frame of approximately two years. They were also distributed over 6 to 8 different occasions (e.g., vacation, barbecue). While the size of these sample collections were not realistic, their distribution over occasions and time seemed to resemble real configurations (cf. [15]).

The four tasks were designed so that users would gain exposure to all aspects of Photohelix's functionality, and so that we could map tasks to the different activities identified in our requirements analysis. After completing an explorative warm-up task scaffolded with instructions on using Photohelix, participants were asked in Task 1 to *file* the images of their collections into events, thus permanently archiving the pictures. In Task 2 they should *browse* the entire collection and choose one particular event. They were subsequently asked to select one representative photo, enlarge it and explain why they had chosen it. Task 3 was aimed at *sharing* and participants had to give an update about a recent vacation. During the course of this process they were asked to enlarge several images and show them to the study conductor, who played the role of a friend or acquaintance. Task 4 was to choose four possible candidates from each of the four seasons to be used as the desktop wallpaper.

5.1. Results

In our experiments we gathered quantitative data (i.e., Likert-scale responses) as well as qualitative data from a semi-structured interview with open-ended fill-in responses. We also video taped every session and analyzed these recordings afterwards.

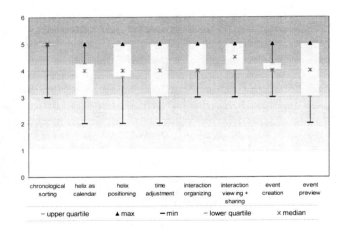

Figure 6. Appreciation of different functionalities in Photohelix. (Scale: dislike (1) – neutral (3) – appreciate (5))

We wanted to find out whether users liked our system, and which aspects were especially appreciated or needed improvement. To answer these questions we evaluated the responses to several Likert-Scale questions (Scale: disagree (1) – neutral (3) – agree (5)) as well as the free-form comments. In general people liked Photohelix (4.1/5) and thought it was "easy" and to use (3.7/5). They also liked the look and feel of the interface (4.2/5). Additionally, they thought that the visualization provides a good overview of the photo collection (3.9/5). When asked to rate specific functionalities of the system (See Figure 6), users liked the chronological sorting of pictures (4.85/5) and the visualization of time using a spiral-shaped calender (3.8/5). Furthermore, the possibility to freely position the spiral (4/5) and images (4.35/5) on the table received good ratings, as did the usage of the physical handle to adjust the time (3.85/5). Users appreciated the interaction techniques to create (4.1/5), flip through (3.7/5) and dissolve (4/5) events as well as the interaction techniques to rotate and scale images (4.3/5).

The qualitative comments we received further emphasize the above ratings. Several comments suggest that our design goals have had a positive impact. One participant said *"I like that all the pictures are already ordered by time. I like that I could see all the pictures quickly, just by turning the dial or flipping through the photos, and that I don't have to click into a folder in order to retrieve pictures."* Several other comments along these lines suggest that the *overview at all times* and *details on demand* paradigms are indeed beneficial for the browsing and filing activities. We also received many comments on the *flexibility* of the interface: *"... it was very intuitive, cumbersome copying of images becomes obsolete due to the possibility to create copies and temporal collections by simple dragging"*; and on its qualities for sharing: *"... browsing and viewing photos together is nicer with this kind of interface. It's more fun, too."*

Identified Issues   Our evaluation also uncovered several shortcomings of the Photohelix prototype. The most frequent complaint (6 out of 20 participants) was that the thumbnails on the calender were too small, which made it difficult to recognize the possible contents of the group depicted by the thumbnail pile. Many users also complained that there was no shortcut to jump directly to a certain group of pictures or that twisting the physical knob (which we hoped could serve as a quasi-shortcut) was too inexact.

Some users did run out of screen space or suffered from visual clutter, because they did not make frequent use of the possibility to rearrange the interface configuration. To find out why, we reviewed the video recordings. While there was no statistical correlation between the described problem and the overall usage time in Photohelix, we still observed that users who spent more time in the exploratory phase started to make more frequent use of the features over time (i.e., creating piles of enlarged copies, re-positioning and re-orienting the helix). Further research is necessary to find out whether more experience with this kind of flexibility in the user interface would help in reducing visual clutter.

6. Discussion and Future Work

The results from our evaluation suggest that the current design provides several benefits for browsing, organizing and sharing (as in storytelling) digital photo collections. The physical handle serves as a graspable representation of the entire collection and the helix shaped calendar functions as a possible visualization that is coherent with most users' mental model of their collection. Thus the combination of the two provides effective means to access the collection and to retrieve individual pictures for further inspection. It seems that the flexibility of the interface, which allows users to create individualized arrangements of interface elements, might help to close the gap in emotional attitude toward digital photos versus their printed counterpart by creating a pseudo-physical experience.

However, our prototype also has several limitations which must be addressed before the system could be used under realistic (or close to realistic) circumstances. First of all, the current implementation does not support the *selecting* activity. This is partly due to the difficulties we encountered with unintentional input, which led to the unwanted deletion of pictures. Also, the interaction techniques that we had planned for this activity (e.g., crossing-out, moving-of-the-table) were not robust enough against this kind of

faulty input. In the future we plan to experiment with different interaction techniques to delete information artifacts in tabletop interfaces.

Photohelix was designed and implemented in order to assess the validity of the identified requirements and our design considerations – not as a system working under realistic circumstances. Hence, scalability is an issue in the current state of implementation. We do not optically condense the information shown at any given time further than pre-grouping images into piles on the helix. Therefore, the current approach does suffer from visual clutter once these groups contain more than approximately 30 pictures each. This would be rather frequent under realistic circumstances, for example many pictures taken at a wedding (i.e., over a short period in time).

We plan to address the scalability problem in different ways, for example, by applying automatic clustering algorithms or by techniques that automatically adjust the zooming of the area where thumbnails and events are positioned. The overall size of the collection is also an issue, in order to maintain a good overview the size of the entire collection and the time difference between the oldest and the youngest events need to be balanced. Currently only a few hundred pictures, spread over approximately two years, are displayed in a satisfactory manner. A possible solution would be to render the timeline in a non-linear fashion to optimize screen real-estate while still conveying the temporal information.

Finally, we plan for the future to further support the co-located *sharing* of pictures by increasing the concurrency of the interactions. The biggest hurdle at the moment is the limitation of our hardware, which only allows two simultaneous contact points. Once more simultaneous contact points become feasible one could easily extend the current system so that it allows several users to exchange pictures from their personal collections, each represented by an individual helix.

7. Acknowledgments

This work was partially funded by the Bavarian state and the "Deutsche Forschungsgemeinschaft" (DFG). We would like to thank our participants for their valuable time and feedback. We also thank Amy Ko for copy-editing our manuscript as well as David Kim and Bettina Zech for their help with the video figure.

References

[1] B. Bederson. Photomesa: a zoomable image browser using quantum treemaps and bubblemaps. In *Proceedings of UIST '01*, pages 71–80, 2001.

[2] B. Bederson, J. Grosjean, and J. Meyer. Toolkit design for interactive structured graphics. *IEEE Trans. Softw. Eng.*, 30(8):535–546, 2004.

[3] J. Borchers, M. Ringel, J. Tyler, and A. Fox. Stanford interactive workspaces: a framework for physical and graphical user interface prototyping. *Wireless Communications, IEEE*, 9(6):64–69, 2002.

[4] A. Crabtree, T. Rodden, and J. Mariani. Collaborating around collections: informing the continued development of photoware. In *Proceedings of CSCW '04*, pages 396–405, 2004.

[5] P. Dietz and D. Leigh. Diamondtouch: a multi-user touch technology. In *Proceedings of the ACM UIST '01*, pages 219–226, 2001.

[6] S. Drucker, C. Wong, A. Roseway, S. Glenner, and S. De Mar. Mediabrowser: reclaiming the shoebox. In *Proceedings of AVI '04*, pages 433–436, 2004.

[7] C. Forlines and C. Shen. Dtlens: multi-user tabletop spatial data exploration. In *Proceedings of UIST '05*, pages 119–122, 2005.

[8] D. Frohlich, A. Kuchinsky, C. Pering, A. Don, and S. Ariss. Requirements for photoware. In *Proceedings of CSCW '02*, pages 166–175, 2002.

[9] J. Han. Low-cost multi-touch sensing through frustrated total internal reflection. In *Proceedings of UIST '05*, pages 115–118, 2005.

[10] O. Hilliges, P. Kunath, A. Pryakhin, H. Kriegel, and A. Butz. Browsing and Sorting Digital Pictures using Automatic Image Classification and Quality Analysis. In *Proceedings of HCI International '07*, July 2007.

[11] O. Hilliges, L. Terrenghi, S. Boring, D. Kim, H. Richter, and A. Butz. Designing for Collaborative Creative Problem Solving. In *Proceedings of Creativity and Cognition '07*, July 2007.

[12] U. Hinrichs, S. Carpendale, and S. Scott. Evaluating the effects of fluid interface components on tabletop collaboration. In *Proceedings of the working conference on Advanced visual interfaces*, pages 27–34, 2006.

[13] D. Huynh, S. Drucker, P. Baudisch, and C. Wong. Time quilt: scaling up zoomable photo browsers for large, unstructured photo collections. In *Proceedings of CHI '05 extended abstracts*, pages 1937–1940, 2005.

[14] H. Kang and B. Shneiderman. Visualization methods for personal photo collections: Browsing and searching in the photofinder. In *IEEE International Conference on Multimedia and Expo (III)*, pages 1539–1542, 2000.

[15] D. Kirk, A. Sellen, C. Rother, and K. Wood. Understanding photowork. In *Proceedings of CHI '06*, pages 761–770, 2006.

[16] R. Kruger, S. Carpendale, S. Scott, and S. Greenberg. How people use orientation on tables: comprehension, coordination and communication. In *Proceedings of the International ACM SIGGROUP conference on Supporting group work*, pages 369–378, 2003.

[17] M. Matsushita, M. Iida, T. Ohguro, Y. Shirai, Y. Kakehi, and T. Naemura. Lumisight table: a face-to-face collaboration support system that optimizes direction of projected information to each stakeholder. In *Proceedings of CSCW '04*, pages 274–283, 2004.

[18] T. Mills, D. Pye, D. Sinclair, and K. Wood. Shoebox: A digital photo management system. Technical report AT&T Laboratories Cambridge., 2000.

[19] M. Morris, A. Cassanego, A. Paepcke, T. Winograd, A. Piper, and A. Huang. Mediating group dynamics through tabletop interface design. *IEEE Computer Graphics and Applications*, 26(5):65–73, 2006.

[20] M. Morris, A. Huang, A. Paepcke, and T. Winograd. Cooperative gestures: multi-user gestural interactions for co-located groupware. In *Proceedings of CHI '06*, pages 1201–1210, 2006.

[21] M. Morris, A. Paepcke, and T. Winograd. Teamsearch: Comparing techniques for co-present collaborative search of digital media. In *Proceedings of TABLETOP '06*, pages 97–104, 2006.

[22] M. Morris, A. Paepcke, T. Winograd, and J. Stamberger. Teamtag: exploring centralized versus replicated controls for co-located tabletop groupware. In *Proceedings of CHI '06*, pages 1273–1282, 2006.

[23] J. Platt, M. Czerwinski, and B. Field. Phototoc: Automatic clustering for browsing personal photographs. Microsoft Research Technical Report MSR-TR-2002-17, 2002.

[24] J. Rekimoto. SmartSkin: an infrastructure for freehand manipulation on interactive surfaces. In *CHI '02: Proceedings of the SIGCHI conference on Human factors in computing systems*, pages 113–120, 2002.

[25] K. Rodden and K. Wood. How do people manage their digital photographs? In *Proceedings of CHI '03*, pages 409–416, 2003.

[26] B. Schneiderman, B. Bederson, and S. Drucker. Find that photo. *Communications of the ACM*, 49, 2006.

[27] S. Scott, M. Carpendale, and K. Inkpen. Territoriality in collaborative tabletop workspaces. In *Proceedings of CSCW '04*, pages 294–303, 2004.

[28] S. Scott, K. Grant, and R. Mandryk. System guidelines for co-located collaborative work on a tabletop display. In *Proceedings ECSCW 2003*, pages 159–178, 2003.

[29] C. Shen, N. Lesh, F. Vernier, C. Forlines, and J. Frost. Sharing and building digital group histories. In *Proceedings CSCW '02*, pages 324–333, 2002.

[30] C. Shen, F. Vernier, C. Forlines, and M. Ringel. Diamondspin: an extensible toolkit for around-the-table interaction. In *Proceedings of CHI '04*, pages 167–174, 2004.

[31] B. Shneiderman and H. Kang. Direct annotation: A drag-and-drop strategy for labeling photos. In *Proceedings of Information Visualisation (IV'00)* , page 88, 2000.

[32] SmartTech. DViT Technology. http://www.smarttech.com/DViT/.

[33] N. Streitz, J. Geiler, T. Holmer, S. Konomi, C. Müller-Tomfelde, W. Reischl, P. Rexroth, P. Seitz, and R. Steinmetz. i-land: an interactive landscape for creativity and innovation. In *Proceedings of CHI' 99*, pages 120–127, 1999.

[34] L. von Ahn and L. Dabbish. Labeling images with a computer game. In *Proceedings of CHI '04*, 2004.

[35] A. D. Wilson. Playanywhere: a compact interactive tabletop projection-vision system. In *Proceedings of the ACM UIST '05*, pages 83–92, 2005.

Information Layout and Interaction on Virtual and Real Rotary Tables

Hideki Koike,   Shintaro Kajiwara,   Kentaro Fukuchi
Graduate School of Information Systems
University of Electro-Communications
1-5-1, Chofugaoka, Chofu
Tokyo 182-8585, Japan
koike@acm.org, {kaji, fukuchi}@vogue.is.uec.ac.jp

Yoichi Sato
Institute of Industrial Science
University of Tokyo
4-6-1, Komaba, Meguro-ku
Tokyo 153-8505, Japan
ysato@iis.u-tokyo.ac.jp

Abstract

Many tabletop systems have been developed, but few of them deal with the problems of visualizing and manipulating a large amount of information such as files on a tabletop that is physically limited in size. In order to address this issue, we developed a rotary table system. The system recognizes users' hand gestures, and the users can rotate the table virtually. The table acts as a scroll wheel, and users can see a great deal of information by scrolling the table. We investigated three layout methods: sequential, classification, and spiral. We investigated these on the system and conducted user studies. Moreover, we also developed a real rotary table by using a roller bearing and a round tabletop. Then, we conducted comparative experiments on the usability and intuitiveness of the two rotary tables.

1 Introduction

Recently, many tabletop systems have been developed. There are various implementations for such tabletop systems. Some systems use LCD projectors to display images onto the tabletop. Other systems use LCD displays as a tabletop by placing them horizontally.

One of the advantages of such tabletop systems is that they are suitable for collaborative work where people surround the table and discuss each other's views. In a small meeting, vertical screens are often used to display information that can be shared by attendees. However, since the attendees have to look at the screen and cannot see others' faces, it is relatively difficult to establish good communication. Second, when someone wants to point at the information on the screen, he or she often needs to point remotely with a laser. Third, the displayed information can be manipulated by only one person, and other people cannot control the screen.

On the other hand, in a meeting with a tabletop system, since the people can discuss the topic displayed on the table while seeing other people's faces, it is easier to communicate with each other. Each attendee can point at the information on the table, for example, with his or her finger. Moreover, each attendee can manipulate the information on the table and control the display.

However, there are some issues in connection with tabletop systems. The first is display direction of the information. Since users surround the table and see from different directions, some people cannot see the information from the right direction. Another issue in the tabletop systems is how to display and manipulate more information than can be displayed on the table at one time.

This paper describes a design and implementation of tabletop systems that display information in a circular area that can be rotated by users. By rotating the table, users surrounding the table can see the information from the right direction as needed. The table also provides a virtual scroll capability that is designed for a round-top table. We developed two variations of such a round-top table. One is a virtual rotary table and the other is a real rotary table. We conducted comparative experiments to evaluate the usability and intuitiveness of these tables.

2 Related Work

There are a number of works on tabletop systems such as [6, 14, 15]. Some of these are intended to be used for collaborative work. In this paper, we also focus on systems that are intended to be used for collaboration.

Augmented Surfaces [12] is an augmented tabletop system for collaboration. It enables users to exchange their digital files seamlessly via tabletop. It also demonstrates the relationship of the tabletop to room design. However, the article does not discuss how to visualize a large number of files using the tabletop.

0-7695-3013-3/07 $25.00 © 2007 IEEE
DOI 10.1109/TABLETOP.2007.31

MediaTable [9] is a round tabletop system with a touch panel. Although it can detect only one touch point at a time, people can communicate by seeing and manipulating information displayed on the table. Each piece of information can be placed freely on the table. When the user executes a command, the displayed information comes close to the user and is aligned in one direction. However, the article does not discuss how to display and navigate through a large amount of information.

PDH (Personal Digital Historian) [13] is a round tabletop system using DiamondTouch [2] as an input device. The information is laid out according to annotation of time, place, and other features. PDH also tries to display a large amount of information, particularly a hierarchical structure, by using HyperbolicTree [7]. It shows that the round-top table is adequate for displaying HyperbolicTree. However, the interaction with HyperbolicTree is the same as that in a GUI environment and is not optimized to the round tabletop. The article also does not discuss issues in visualizing and navigating through a large amount of linear data such as sorted files.

EnhancedTable [5] is a tabletop system for a face-to-face small meeting. EnhancedTable utilizes computer vision technology as an input device. EnhancedTable provides two kinds of workspace (WS): personal WS and shared WS. When the user puts a mobile phone on the desk, his or her personal WS is automatically shown on the table. The shared WS is displayed at the center of the table. This shared WS can be rotated virtually by recognizing a user's hand gesture. The users can exchange their personal data in their personal WS via the shared WS. However, the issue of displaying a large number of files is not discussed. Our work is a successor to this EnhancedTable.

Interface Currents [3] provides virtual belt conveyors whose shape and speed can be changed by the user. It gives more flexibility in using such a rotational interface. However, the interaction is done by a touch pen. Also, the issues of visualizing and navigating through a large number of files are not discussed.

Lumisight Table [4] tried to address the view-direction issue in tabletop systems by using special screen material. It provides different views for different users. However, the number of users is limited to four. Also, the article does not discuss the small screen problem in tabletop systems.

3 Visualizing and Navigating through a Large Amount of Information

Based on observation of the related work, we decided to focus on designing an interface for a round-top table when visualizing and navigating through a large amount of information. This section describes our approach.

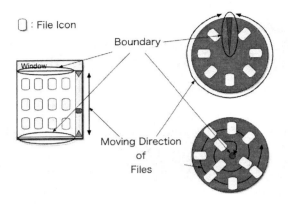

Figure 1. Traditional scroll in window system (left) and scroll in the rotary table (right). Two variations for the scroll in the rotary table are desplayed: sequential layout and its scroll (top right) and spiral layout and its scroll (bottom right).

In the traditional GUI environment, files are displayed as icons in each window. In order to display a large number of files in a window that is physically limited in size, a method called "virtual scroll" (or just "scroll") is generally used. The virtual scroll is a way to look at a part of a large 2-D plane, where many files are laid out, through a window that can be moved horizontally or vertically (Figure 1(left)).

We extended this metaphor of virtual scroll to the round-top table. Figure 1(right) illustrates its conceptual idea. In traditional scrolling, there are boundaries on the top and bottom of the window (and/or left and right). When the user moves a scroll bar vertically, files appear at one boundary and disappear at another boundary.

Our first design is illustrated at the top right of Figure 1. There is a boundary line in the circle that starts from its center and ends at its circumference. To scroll, the user rotates the circle. Files appear at one side of the boundary and disappear at the other side of the boundary.

The second design is illustrated at the bottom right of Figure 1. Files are laid out as a spiral from the center to the circumference. When the user rotates the circle, the files appear from the center and disappear at the circumference.

4 Virtual Rotary Table

We first developed a rotary table that can be rotated virtually by recognizing users' hand gestures. This section describes the system in detail.

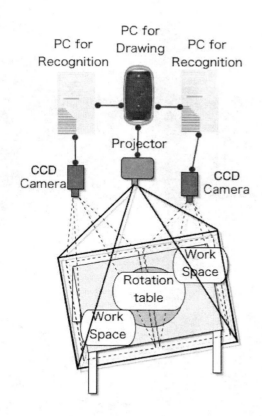

Figure 2. Hardware setup of a virtual rotary table.

4.1 Overview

Figure 2 shows an overview of the system. The system is composed of a table, an LCD projector, two CCD cameras (SONY DFW-VF500), two PCs (Pentium 4 2.8GHz, 512MB memory, Linux) for image processing, and one PC (Pentium 4 2.8GHz, 512MB memory, Windows) for image generation. The CCD cameras capture the images on the table, and these images are processed by the two image processing PCs. To recognize users' hands and fingers, we used a real-time finger tracking method we previously developed [10]. As image processing software, we used Intel's OpenCV library. Each PC can recognize up to two hands in about 10 frame/sec. Then the computer-generated images are projected on the table.

4.2 Information layout

We explored three types of layout methods on the rotary table, that is, sequential, classification, and spiral layout. Before displaying the files on the table, the files are sorted by the features the user specified. For example, the files can be sorted by filename, date of creation, or size. In addition,

image files can be sorted by their values of hue, saturation, and brightness.

- Sequential layout

  In sequential layout, the sorted files are laid out sequentially on the table as shown in Figure 3(left). There is a boundary in the circle. When the user rotates the table, files appear at one side of the boundary and disappear at the other side of the boundary.

- Classification layout

  In classification layout, files are also laid out sequentially, but they are classified based on a feature that the user selects (Figure 3(middle)). When the user selects one of the features from the menu which is described later, files are automatically classified and laid out on the table.

- Spiral layout

  In spiral layout, the files are laid out to make a spiral from the center to the circumference of the circle. The size of the files increases as they go to the circumference.

4.3 Interaction

In a GUI environment, the primitive operations are selecting, executing, and moving the file. For example, in the case of a Macintosh computer with a one-button mouse, these are assigned to single-click, double-click, and mouse-drag, respectively. Other additional or complex operations are done by using menus.

We implemented these primitive operations by using our hand/finger recognition as follows:

Selection and Drag: When users pinch a file with their thumb and index finger, the file is in selection mode, and they can drag it by moving their hand with two fingers closed (Figure 4(a)).

Execution: If the user points at the file with his or her finger, the file is automatically magnified as shown in Figure 4(b).

Rotation: When the user shows five fingers and moves his or her hand inside the circular area, all the images are virtually rotated (Figure 4(c)).

Displaying menus: When the user points at the background in the circular area with his or her left hand, the structured menu appears (Figure 4(d)). The user can select each menu item using his or her right hand. This two-handed interaction of menu is derived from [1].

The user first selects the feature used to sort files. Then, the second menu appears where the user selects the layout method.

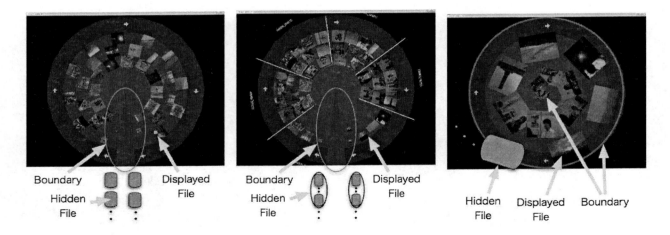

Figure 3. Three layout methods. Sequential (left), classification (middle), and spiral (right).

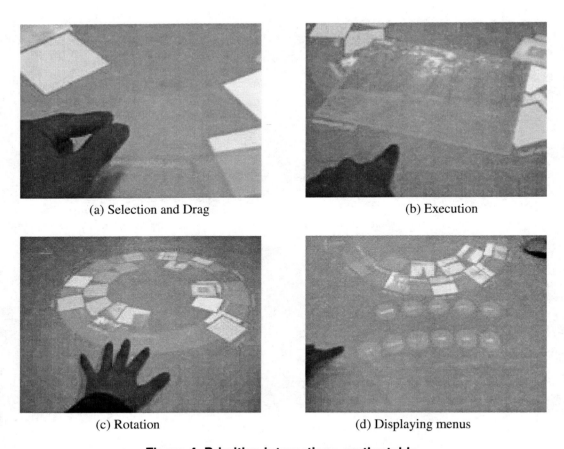

(a) Selection and Drag   (b) Execution

(c) Rotation   (d) Displaying menus

Figure 4. Primitive interactions on the table.

4.4 Evaluation

We conducted informal user studies on the usability of the three layout methods. We asked users to use the system and comment on it.

All of them were interested in using the system and they preferred to use sequential (or classification) layout rather than spiral layout. Since the size of images continuously changes in spiral layout, the users sometimes failed to find or failed to track the image. On the other hand, in sequential and classification layouts, it is easier to find the image by browsing the entire table even if the user missed the image when it first appeared from the boundary.

Our hand/finger recognition is robust[10], but sometimes it failed to track hands due to hand shapes. Since rotating the table is essential interaction in the rotary table, it should be more reliable. Thus, we decided to develop the next version of the rotary table: the real rotary table.

5 Real Rotary Table

5.1 Overview

We developed a real rotary table by using an acrylic round-top and a roller bearing. Figure 5 shows the setup of the system, and Figure 6 shows an overview of the system. The cameras and the projector are the same as in the virtual rotary table. An optical mouse is used to detect the angle of rotation of the round-top.

5.2 Interaction

Interactions provided for the user are almost same as those in the virtual rotary table. The major difference is rotation of the table. Instead of rotating the table virtually by using a hand gesture, the user actually rotates the table.

6 Experiments

In order to evaluate the usability and intuitiveness of the table, we conducted the following comparative experiment. Although the main focus of the experiment was on comparing the virtual rotary table and the real rotary table, we decided to compare them also with pen-based interfaces that are often used in other tabletop systems. We modified the virtual rotary table so that it could be rotated by touch pen. As the touch pen, Mimio [8] was used, as seen in Figure 7(b).

Tasks Six graduate students were asked to find three target images out of 500 images by using three table setups. Images were displayed randomly. The subjects could see

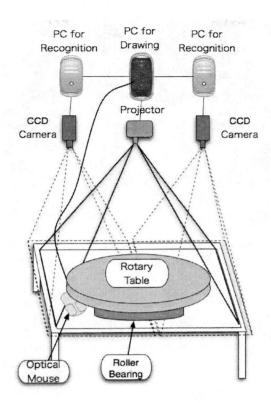

Figure 5. Hardware setup of a real rotary table.

30 images at a time. Thus, in order to browse all the images, the table had to be rotated at least 16 turns. The subjects were asked to find images in 10 minutes. If the subject could not complete the task in 10 minutes, the experiment was aborted.

Result Figure 8 shows the times spent to complete the task. This graph shows that most of the subjects finished the task faster with the real rotary table than with the other two setups. Only one subject (Subject 2) could not complete the task within 10 minutes with the real rotary table. This was because he turned the table so fast that he missed the target image.

Using the virtual rotary table, another subject (Subject 3) could not finish the task in 10 minutes. This was because the target image was projected just on his hand when he turned the virtual table and he could not recognize the target image.

After the experiment, we asked each subject to score the three systems between 1 and 5, and we also interviewed them to ask how they felt about the systems. The real rotary table obtained the highest score. Then, pen-input was the second and the virtual rotary table was the third. They told

Figure 6. An overview of a real rotary table.

(a) Rotating the virtual table by hand gesture.

(b) Rotating the virtual table by pen interface.

Figure 7. Experiments

us that turning the real table was more intuitive than turning the virtual table. They also told us that turning the virtual table with the pen or their hands required larger movements of their hands. On the other hand, they could turn the table with smaller hand movements in the case of the real rotary table.

7 Discussion

Implementation issues As we described in the previous sections, the real rotary table was more reliable than the virtual rotary table. Although we used an optical mouse in our current implementation, more reliable sensors, such as a rotary encoder or a potentiometer, could be used.

As pointing devices, a touch pen or a touch panel might be more reliable than computer vision-based approaches. However, CV allows simultaneous inputs and it also allows gesture interaction. Moreover, it can recognize real objects on the table. Therefore, we think the CV approaches are still useful.

Like other tabletop systems, a projector was used in our system. In order to get bright images on the table, the room should be dark. Practical meetings, however, are not always held in such dark rooms. Rear projection provides more bright images than front projection. However, such rear projection requires relatively bigger, heavier, and more expensive hardware. On the other hand, large LCD displays and plasma displays are getting less and less expensive. We are currently developing a tabletop system with large LCD displays.

Multimedia controller In the previous sections, the design and implementation of rotational scrolling were mainly described. We also designed and implemented other intuitive interactions using rotation. Figure 9 illustrates a multi-

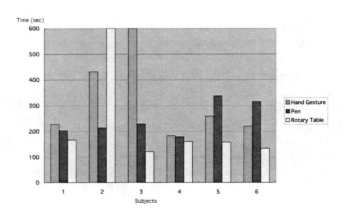

Figure 8. Experimental result.

media controller interface which was also implemented on our rotary table. When the user selects and executes an audio file on our rotary table, the CD jacket is displayed at the center of the table and the music is played. Likewise, when the selected file is a movie file, the movie clip is played in the center of the table. As seen in Figure 9, a circular gauge that indicates the current played position is shown around the file. The user can play forward or backward by rotating the table. This kind of audio interface can be found in the jog shuttle in video editor or the turntable of disc/video jockey. The rotary table can also be applied to such multimedia controllers.

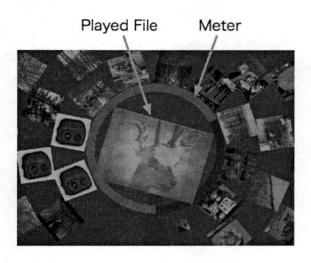

Figure 9. A multimedia controller. When the user selects the audio or movie file, the CD jacket or the movie clip is displayed and played at the center of the table. The user can play forward or backward by rotating the table.

Rotational scrolling The rotational scrolling described in this paper is similar to that in Apple's iPod and that in Panasonic's note PC [11]. One of the advantages of such rotational scrolling is that users can keep scrolling without releasing their finger from the touch pad. On the other hand, in the window systems with a scroll wheel mouse, the user needs to turn the wheel many times. Thus, the rotational scrolling is much faster in browsing a large number of files than traditional scrolling.

There are two differences between our rotational scrolling and that in an iPod. The first is a relation between finger/hand movement and scrolling direction. In an iPod, the rotational movement at the touch pad is mapped to the horizontal movement of the list on the display. On the other

hand, in our table, the rotational movement of the table is mapped to the rotational movement of the files on the display. The second is an integration of input device and output device. In an iPod, the input device (i.e., the touch wheel) and the output device (i.e., the LCD screen) are different. On the other hand, the input device and the output device are the same in our table. This is more intuitive to the user.

8 Conclusions

This paper described designs and implementations of virtual and real rotary tables. We proposed methods for visualizing and navigating through a large number of files on the rotary table. The comparative experiment showed that the real rotary table is more usable and intuitive than the virtual one. We also showed an application of a rotational interface to the multimedia controller.

In future work, we are going to develop the real rotary table where the real objects and digital information are highly integrated. In practical collaborative work, people often discuss a project by seeing the real object such as an architectural model, and so on. The tabletop system needs to support such capability in the real world.

References

[1] X. Chen, H. Koike, Y. Nakanishi, K. Oka, and Y. Sato. Two-handed drawing on augmented desk system. In *Proc. 2002 Int'l Conf. on advanced visual interfaces (AVI 2002)*, pages 219–222. ACM, 2002.

[2] P. Dietz and D. Leigh. Diamondtouch: A multi-user touch technology. In *Proc. of ACM Symposium on User Interface Software and Technology (UIST 2001)*, pages 219–226. ACM, 2001.

[3] U. Hinrichs, S. Carpendale, S. Scott, and E. Pattison. Interface currents: Supporting fluent collaboration on tabletop displays. In *Proc. of the 5th Symposium on Smart Graphics*, pages 185–197, 2005.

[4] Y. Kakehi, M. Iida, T. Naemura, Y. Shirai, M. Matsushita, and T. Ohguro. Lumisight table: Interactive view-dependent tabletop display. *IEEE Computer Graphics and Applications*, 25(1):48–53, 2005.

[5] H. Koike, S. Nagashima, Y. Nakanishi, and Y. Sato. Enhancedtable: Supporting a small meeting in ubiquitous and augmented environment. In *Advances in Multimedia Information Processing - PCM 2004*, number 3333 in LNCS, pages 97–104. Springer, 2004. 5th Pacific Rim Conference on Multimedia.

[6] H. Koike, Y. Sato, Y. Kobayashi, H. Tobita, and M. Kobayashi. Interactive textbook and interactive venn diagram: Natural and intuitive interface on augmented desk system. In *Proc. of Human Factors in Computing Systems (CHI2000)*, pages 121–128. ACM, 2000.

[7] J. Lamping, R. Rao, and P. Pirolli. A focus+context technique based on hyperbolic geometry for visualizing large

hierarchies. In *Proc. of the SIGCHI conference on Human Factors in computing systems (CHI '95)*, pages 401–408. ACM, 1994.

[8] Mimio. http://mimio.com.

[9] J. Misawa, K. Tsuchiya, and K. Yoshikawa. Mediatable: A computer screen system with nonspecific direction in presenting information. In *Proc. of The 9th Workshop on Interactive Systems and Software (WISS2001)*, pages 173–178, 2001. in Japanese.

[10] K. Oka, Y. Sato, and H. Koike. Real-time tracking of multiple fingertips and gesture recognition for augmented desk interface systems. *IEEE Computer Graphics and Applications*, 22(6):64–71, November/December 2002.

[11] Panasonic. Let's Note, http://panasonic.jp/pc/.

[12] J. Rekimoto and M. Saitoh. Augmented surfaces: A spatially continuous workspace for hybrid computing environments. In *Proc. of ACM Conference on Human Factors in Computing Systems (CHI'99)*, pages 378–385. ACM, 1999.

[13] C. Shen, N. Lesh, and F. Vernier. Personal digital historian: Story sharing around the table. *ACM Interactions*, 10(2):15–22, March/April 2003.

[14] B. Ullmer and H. Ishii. The metadesk: Models and prototypes for tangible user interfaces. In *Proc. of ACM Symposium on User Interface Software and Technology (UIST'97)*, pages 223–232. ACM, 1997.

[15] P. Wellner. Interacting with paper on the digitaldesk. *Communications of the ACM*, 36(7):87–96, 1993.

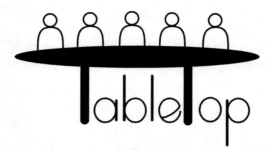

WIMP!: Bringing Traditional Interactions to the Tabletop

Examination of Text-Entry Methods for Tabletop Displays

Uta Hinrichs,[1]   Mark Hancock,[1]   Christopher Collins,[2]   Sheelagh Carpendale[1]

[1]University of Calgary, Canada   [2]University of Toronto, Canada

{hinrichu | msh | sheelagh}@cpsc.ucalgary.ca   ccollins@cs.utoronto.ca

Abstract

Although text entry is a vital part of day-to-day computing familiar to most people, not much research has been done to enable text entry on large interactive tables. One might assume that a good approach would be to choose an existing technique known to be fast, ergonomic, and currently preferred by the general population, but there are many additional factors to consider in this specific domain. We consider a variety of existing text-entry methods and examine their viability for use on tabletop displays. We discuss these techniques not only in terms of their general characteristics, performance, and adoption, but introduce other evaluative criteria, including: environmental factors unique to large digital tables and the support for multi-user simultaneous interaction. Based on our analysis we illustrate by example how to choose appropriate text-entry methods for tabletop applications with differing requirements, whether by selection from existing methods, or through a combination of desirable elements from a variety of methods. Our criteria can also be used as heuristics during the iterative design of a completely new text-entry technique.

1. Introduction

Text entry is one of the most frequent actions we undertake when working on desktop computers. Entering text is necessary for activities that require elaborate text compositions such as coding programs, authoring articles, or writing emails, as well as in situations that demand taking notes, typing in commands, or annotating content.

Text-entry methods are equally important for digital tables. Although a large variety of tabletop applications have been developed in the last decade [4, 5, 31, 32, 36], not much attention has been paid to the development of text-entry methods for tabletop displays. However, the unique characteristics and affordances of large digital tables, such as the support for multiple people and the large horizontal workspace, demand unique text-entry methods that differ from traditional physical keyboards. Enabling tabletop text entry in a way that suits the overall characteristics and affordances of large digital tables will make them more viable for everyday work and entertainment applications.

In this paper, we analyze existing text-entry methods that have been developed for desktop computers, touch sensitive tablet PCs, mobile phones, or personal digital assistants (PDAs) and examine their potential for use on tabletop displays. With this analysis we hope to seed a research agenda within the tabletop community to develop and evaluate novel text-entry methods for tabletop displays. While the research effort for tables has thus far typically focused on information manipulation and display, our reliance on the ability to enter text with most other computing technologies suggests that this research direction should be at least equally important. Our research is intended to help designers and developers of tabletop systems to invent or choose an appropriate text-entry method depending on the tabletop application's purpose and character.

We first define our evaluative criteria for text entry on digital tables. We then describe and discuss different categories of existing text-entry methods. After this we discuss the potential of the examined methods for a variety of tabletop applications and provide guidelines for the development and evaluation of future tabletop text-entry methods.

2. Evaluative Criteria

Our examination of text-entry methods is based on criteria specifically important in tabletop display environments. These criteria include visual appearance, performance, environmental factors, and simultaneous interaction.

2.1. Visual Appearance

For text-entry methods that have a visual representation of characters, the visual appearance is defined by the overall *character arrangement* (shape) and the *character layout*.

The arrangement of characters determines the overall shape of the typing device (rectangular, circular, star-shaped, etc.), while the character layout determines where specific character keys are located within the general arrangement (Q next to W, W next to E, etc.) [20]. The most common character arrangement in western culture follows a rectangular shape with a QWERTY character layout [19]. As we will later describe, the character arrangement and layout can influence the performance of a text-entry method.

While most text-entry methods have a visual appearance, for some (e. g. speech recognition and handwriting), these criteria do not apply.

2.2. Performance

The performance of text-entry methods is defined by two factors: *efficiency* and *ease of learning*. An ideal text-entry method would combine these factors to their mutual benefit.

2.2.1. Efficiency.
Efficiency is most often defined as the effective text-entry speed that a person can reach using a certain text-entry method [40]. This speed is usually measured in words per minute (wpm). For text-entry methods with a visual representation the efficiency is a function of the visual search time to find a certain character and movement time from one character to the next [18, 19]. The character layout, therefore, has an important impact on the efficiency since by minimizing distances between consecutive characters (digraphs) the movement time can be minimized as well [7, 17, 18, 19]. However, typing speed depends on several other variables that are hard to control in empirical studies. For example, the amount of training time on a given method or the level of familiarity with related typing methods can bias the outcome of typing speed measurements. In addition, to be meaningful, efficiency measures must be viewed alongside data about typing accuracy.

Often, costly long-term studies are required to make confident statements about the speed of a certain text-entry technique [40]. In order to save these costs, several predictive models have been developed, mostly based on Fitts' law, that can estimate the performance of a text-entry method [8, 18, 39]. However, the accuracy and validity of such predictive models is problematic because certain parameters within Fitts' law need to be estimated.

Another factor that determines the efficiency of a text-entry method is the visual and cognitive attention it requires [40]. The lower the attention demand, the more efficient the text-entry method [40]. As we will describe later, some methods allow for blind typing after training while other methods always require some visual attention.

2.2.2. Ease of Learning.
The success of a text-entry method not only depends on its efficiency but also on its learnability. If it takes a long time to learn a method people will not adopt it. A new text-entry method will first have a lower performance than an established method [19, 40], but potentially can, after training, exceed the existing one. This "crossover point" is an important indicator for ease of learning [19].

Efficiency and ease of learning often conflict with each other [35]. Very few text-entry methods have a high initial performance and require little learning to achieve a high general performance. Therefore, it can be crucial to rate the importance of efficiency and learnability depending on the application area the text-entry method is intended for.

2.3. Environmental Factors

While text-entry methods have been studied extensively for the domain of desktop computers [6, 7, 22, 38] or small portable devices such as cell phones or PDAs [2, 11, 15, 17, 20, 23, 34] not much research has been done for the domain of tabletop displays. For tabletop text-entry methods the unique characteristics and affordances of tabletop displays play an important role. We describe some of the table-specific factors relevant for text entry, such as size, orientation, and the support of direct-touch interaction.

2.3.1. Space Requirements.
Large digital tables have a large virtual workspace. This allows for tasks that involve large amounts of information and co-located collaboration between multiple people [26, 24]. The workspace size needs to be considered for the design of text-entry methods. Two different approaches are possible: external text-entry methods involving physical devices separate from the workspace and on-screen methods where the interaction space and the display space are superimposed. Both approaches have been developed for small displays, but the affordances of large digital workspaces are quite different.

Tabletop displays have more screen real estate available, and so an on-screen text-entry method can use more space and can involve the use of multiple fingers or two-handed interaction. However, an on-screen method that is too large may clutter the display and interfere with the space left available for information items. External methods do not interfere directly with the display space, but can require people to be slightly more removed from the display when entering text. This separation can make it difficult to maintain an overview of the entire space and an awareness of others in the environment.

With regard to space requirements of a text-entry method an important criterion to consider is its ability to be collapsed (*collapsibility*). Collapsing the keyboard can be a way of dealing with the added external or on-screen space required by a text-entry method. Collapsing can be done for physical keyboards by, e. g., providing a drawer to hide it or using a foldable keyboard. For on-screen keyboards, the visual keyboard representation can be collapsed at the request of the person using it, or automatically after a time delay. Typically, collapsing of physical devices requires more time and effort than collapsing a virtual on-screen device.

2.3.2. Rotatability.
The horizontal orientation of tabletop displays can also influence text entry. Text input is orientation-dependent on tables, since the display can be approached from different directions. It may be desirable to provide a mechanism (if one does not naturally exist) to

alter the orientation required for entering text. This rotation can be done for physical devices by rotating the device itself. For on-screen methods, rotation must be supported programmatically. However, we do not yet know how this orientation influences performance. Previous studies have investigated the impact of the display angle on touch-tapping as an input method for text entry [1, 27] but more refined studies have to be conducted for tabletop displays in particular.

2.3.3. Direct-Touch Interaction.

Most tabletop systems support direct-touch interaction using styli or hands [5, 21, 30]. Direct-touch is especially beneficial on tabletop displays because it provides awareness cues to others at the table. Ideally, a text-entry method would interfere as minimally as possible with these cues, allowing fluid transitions between text-entry and direct-touch interaction. Some existing methods could be disruptive in a tabletop environment, since they require people to switch input methods or devices, preventing a continuous awareness of their actions and the effects they have on the environment.

2.3.4. Mobility.

Digital tables afford walking around the display to obtain an alternative viewpoint, e. g., when looking at virtual maps. It may also be desirable to enter text at any of these possible viewpoints. Ideally, a text-entry method would support entering text from any location, without interfering with a person's physical ability to move around the table. For example, a wired physical keyboard may not be appropriate, since the wire would prevent circling the table several times. Carrying a physical device may also introduce fatigue.

2.4. Simultaneous Interaction

Studies have found that tabletop displays provide a space where many people can work closely together [24]. In order to support smooth and fluid co-located collaboration, tabletop displays need to support simultaneous multi-person interaction [26]. This need also must be taken into account when developing text-entry methods on tabletop displays. To support simultaneous interaction, the following criteria are important to consider: *shareability* and *duplicability*.

For applications that require very few and infrequent annotations, it might be suitable to only provide a single text-entry device that can be easily shared between multiple people. For other applications, every person interacting with the digital table may need a text-entry device. Methods that support the fast duplication of text-entry devices might be one solution for such applications.

In the following section, we examine existing text-entry methods based on the described criteria: their general characteristics, their performance, how they can be integrated in a tabletop environment considering its unique factors, and how they can support simultaneous multi-person interaction.

Table 1 shows an overview of the methods we are examining in terms of the tabletop-related criteria described above.

3. Investigating Existing Text-Entry Methods

Existing text-entry methods generally fall into two categories: *external methods* require an external physical device and *on-screen methods* are controlled in the same display space as the information being displayed (see Table 1).

3.1. External Text-Entry Methods

External text-entry methods include physical keyboards that traditionally belong to a common desktop computer environment, mobile physical keyboards that can be found on cell phones or PDAs, and speech recognition techniques.

3.1.1. Physical Keyboards.

The majority of desktop computers provide physical keyboards to enable text entry. A physical keyboard benefits from tactile feedback, improving the touch-typing performance. Physical keyboards can vary slightly in shape and character layout, but they are mostly based on the QWERTY layout described by Sholes in 1867 [38, 40]. While this layout was initially designed to avoid jamming on mechanical typewriters, its design supports alternating between both hands while typing.

Due to the visual representation of characters, novice users can apply the "hunt-and-peck" strategy using one or two fingers. With training, however, people can learn two-handed typing using ten fingers. Experts can even type without paying any visual attention to the physical keyboard. According to predictive models, the expert typing speed on a physical QWERTY keyboard is 56 wpm [22]. Various attempts to replace the QWERTY layout on physical keyboards (e. g. the Dvorak keyboard [7] or alphabetical layouts [22]) have remained unsuccessful. Due to the large majority of people familiar with the QWERTY layout this trend is not very likely to change.

As an external and somewhat large physical device, a physical keyboard does not lend itself well to a digital tabletop environment. Switching back and forth between touch-typing on an external keyboard and direct-touch interaction within the virtual workspace can be disruptive. Also, a physical keyboard can be hard to move around, rotate, or share between multiple people. Multiple keyboards can be provided for multiple people interacting on a tabletop display but the number of keyboards is limited due to their size and the available space. Another drawback of a physical keyboard is that it always requires a physical surface on which it can be placed. One could imagine drawers to store physical keyboards, installed around a tabletop display. However, this is difficult to integrate into current tabletop setups, especially when the display is projected from below. Storing and retrieving a physical keyboard would be clumsy, in particular for tabletop tasks that require quick annotations from

Table 1. Environmental criteria applied to different existing text-entry methods.

	Physical Keyboards	Mobile Keyboards	Speech Recognition	Handwriting	Gestural Alphabets	Stylus Keyboards
Space Requirements	high	low	none	none	none	variable
Collapsibility	possible	possible	not applicable	not applicable	not applicable	supported
Rotatability	limited support	possible	not applicable	not applicable	not applicable	supported
Direct-Touch Interaction	limited support	supported	supported	supported	supported	supported
Mobility	limited support	supported	supported	supported	supported	supported
Shareability	limited support	supported	supported	supported	supported	supported
Duplicability	not possible	not possible	not applicable	not applicable	not applicable	supported
Simult. Text Entry	limited (space)	supported	limited	supported	supported	supported

time to time. Permanent keyboard ledges would also create a barrier between people and the interaction space.

3.1.2. Mobile Physical Keyboards. We define mobile physical keyboards as mobile devices that have some sort of physical text-entry method. Examples for this are mobile phones or PDAs that use physical buttons for text entry. Similar to traditional ones, small physical keyboards allow touch-typing using fingers, since tactile feedback is provided. However, on small mobile devices people usually type with one finger, either while holding the device in the same hand they are typing with or in their other hand [29]. The visual appearance of mobile physical keyboards varies from device to device. Small QWERTY keyboards can be found on some PDAs. Some mobile devices have miniature alphabetical keyboards, often used with two thumbs. The most common typing interface on mobile phones is based on a physical 12-key pad [29]. Studies show that text can be entered using the T9 extension for text entry [10] at approximately 45.7 wpm for expert users [29].

In digital tabletop environments, mobile physical keyboards may be a suitable text-entry method. People can hold the mobile typing device in one hand while interacting with the tabletop workspace using the other hand. Physical keyboards with the size of a mobile phone can easily be shared between people, placed in a pocket or on the physical edge of the digital table without taking up much space. Many people are also familiar with the T9 input method from sending SMS messages [18]. However, since SMS messages are typically short, it still needs to be determined if the T9 method is suitable for typing larger amounts of text.

3.1.3. Speech Recognition. An alternative to manual text-entry is the use of automatic speech recognition. We include this method in the category of external methods, since it usually requires people to wear microphones. Speech recognition as a text-entry method is compelling because it does not require any learning on the part of the user. The quality of speech recognition is not dependent people's skills but on the technology translating human speech into machine-readable text. Although technology has improved over the recent years, studies have found that speech recognition is significantly slower than keyboard typing [13]. Studies have also revealed that people have more difficulties composing text by talking out loud than by typing [40].

Speech recognition as a text-entry method on tabletop displays has the advantage that people can move around and have both hands free to directly interact within the tabletop workspace. However, when multiple people are collaborating around a digital table they often divide up a task in order to work on different aspects individually [25]. With speech recognition, several people might need to talk out loud at the same time in order to enter text into the system. Collaborators at a tabletop display are likely to be within earshot, so such simultaneous talking is likely to be highly disruptive.

3.2. On-Screen Methods

On-screen text-entry methods are controlled directly within the display space (typically through touch). Within the group of on-screen methods, we distinguish between handwriting, gestural alphabets, and stylus keyboards.

3.2.1. Handwriting. Text-entry methods that support natural handwriting by moving a stylus or finger continuously over the touch-sensitive workspace are similar to speech recognition in their intuitiveness. Instead of having to learn a new technique, people can just apply familiar writing skills. In recent years handwriting recognition algorithms have been improved to closely match people's expectations [14]. The performance bottleneck of handwriting, however, is not due to computational but human limitations. With approximately 15 wpm, the speed of human hand printing is quite low compared to the performance of other text-entry methods [15]. Thus, handwriting is not a suitable entry method for long text passages but might be sufficient for short annotations.

Handwriting as a text-entry method fulfills and complements the unique characteristics and affordances of tabletop displays. It supports the mobility of people working around a tabletop display, it only requires hands or a stylus, and it complements existing direct-touch interaction methods for manipulating virtual artifacts. It also supports interaction by multiple people without leading to interferences, as with speech recognition. Handwriting is, thus, a highly lightweight text-entry method for tabletop displays. However, as described above the performance limitations are a drawback that make it unsuitable for certain tabletop applications. In addition, the relatively low input resolution on current large digital tables [12] can negatively impact the accuracy and speed of handwriting recognition. Also, current input solutions on tabletop displays can cause problems when resting the hand on the tabletop surface while writing because the hand could block cameras.

3.2.2. Gestural Alphabets.
Gestural alphabets were developed to increase the speed and the accuracy of handwriting on touch-sensitive surfaces [9]. Instead of allowing for individual handwriting, they provide a gestural representation for each character. Different gestural alphabets have been developed such as Unistrokes [9] and Graffiti [3]. Most of the effort in developing these alphabets has been put into making the representations of characters easy to learn and easy to computationally distinguish from other characters [9]. Unistrokes' performance was found to be 34 wpm [9, 15]. Although much faster than handwriting, this speed comes at the cost of learnability. Unistrokes was also found to be harder to learn than Graffiti, which may explain its low adoption rate [16].

Gestural alphabets were developed for small mobile devices that have touch-sensitive displays. With regard to environmental factors unique for tabletop displays, they have similar advantages as handwriting. Because gestural alphabets use fluid gestures with a stylus or finger, they are compatible with other direct-touch interaction techniques. As with handwriting recognition, no visual representation is required, thus issues such as collapsibility, rotatability, mobility, shareability, and duplicability do not apply. However, using gestural alphabets on a large display may be problematic due to the lack of physical boundaries present on small mobile devices. This lack of constraints may lead to "sloppiness" when writing, which has been shown to result in more recognition errors [9]. Introducing small physical frames as suggested by Wobbrock et al. [37] may prevent such errors, but requires an additional physical device (a plastic frame) and might be hard to install on a large display.

3.2.3. Stylus Keyboards.
In contrast to handwriting and gestural alphabets, stylus keyboards have a visual representation within the virtual workspace. This visual representation can help to guide the novice user. A keyboard in the virtual workspace also has the advantage that it can be flexibly tailored toward the application it is used for or the environment it is installed in. For digital tables this means that a stylus keyboard can be easily developed to be collapsible, rotatable, mobile, shareable, and dublicatable. Further-

more, direct-touch interaction stylus keyboards are compatible with other touch interactions for manipulating virtual artifacts on a table. Therefore, one might conclude that stylus keyboards have the most potential on tabletop displays. However, the performance of stylus keyboards is highly design dependent. Another drawback is that the visual attention required for stylus keyboards is relatively high compared to physical keyboards or gestural alphabets.

Among stylus keyboards we distinguish between soft keyboards that are direct visual mappings of physical keyboards with some variations and gesture-based keyboards that differ in shape to support continuous gesture strokes.

Soft Keyboards. The input method for soft keyboards is touch-tapping, directly mapped from touch-typing on physical keyboards. Although soft keyboards can in theory support text entry using multiple fingers or hands, most existing systems are for single-finger or stylus input because they were designed for mobile devices. Soft keyboards typically have a rectangular or squared shape [19].

The character layout of a soft keyboard directly influences its performance. Many alternatives for the QWERTY layout have been developed for soft keyboards including alphabetical layouts, optimized arrangements based on frequently used letters and digraphs or arrangements based on physical models [17, 19, 39]. Prediction models for soft keyboards estimate an expert typing speed between approximately 43.3 wpm (for the QWERTY layout) and 55.9 wpm (for the FITALY layout [33]) and a novice typing speed of around 9 wpm (QWERTY, FITALY, alphabetical order, and others) [19]. These values differ largely based on the prediction model used and often do not conform with empirical studies [19, 39]. Also the optimal size of character keys has been studied for soft keyboards, partly with contradictory results. Sears et al. [28] state that the smaller the soft keyboard the more the typing speed decreases while MacKenzie et al. [18] found that the error rate on smaller soft keyboards increases but that there is no significant difference in text-entry speed between small and large soft keyboards. Since all these studies have been conducted on small mobile devices using one-handed input, they must still be tested in a tabletop setting to know if their findings generalize. In particular, we expect these values to vary greatly when people are allowed to use two hands.

Gesture-based Keyboards. In contrast to soft keyboards, gesture-based keyboards allow for continuous gestures to connect different visually presented letters without lifting the stylus or finger from the tabletop surface while entering a word. This continuity of gestures can improve text-entry speed [20, 23, 35]. Several gesture-based keyboards have been developed [11, 20, 23, 34, 35] following different approaches. Some systems show all characters, e. g. in a circular layout [20, 23]. One of the problems with this approach is that the space for each character decreases which leads to an either very large keyboard or to very small character keys that are, as a consequence, hard to select. In order to save character space, some systems try to divide up characters in groups and show only the parts of the character set that are needed [11, 34]. Other systems make use of predictive language models to visually emphasize characters likely to follow the previous one and minimize the rest in order to save space [35].

Gesture-based keyboards, in particular those with hidden characters and predictive language models, require some learning. Since touch-tapping seems to be a natural mapping from touch-typing, and because our everyday workstations still mostly rely on the point-and-click metaphor, a gesture-based keyboard will first appear unfamiliar to most people. This lack of familiarity needs to be considered for certain applications that require immediate efficiency.

4. Discussion

The above survey of existing text-entry methods and their potential usage on tabletop displays shows that there is no *perfect* method that can be applied without drawbacks. Although according to our analysis physical keyboards seem to be fairly unsuitable as a text-entry method for large tabletop displays, they might be appropriate for applications on small tables where a limited number of people interact and rarely change their working positions. In this case, the performance benefits of physical keyboards may outweigh the environmental factors and the need to support simultaneous interaction. In a multi-person co-located environment, text entry via speech recognition can be awkward when simultaneous text entry is desired (since people would need to speak over one another). However, in situations where text would typically not be entered in parallel, its intuitiveness and the lack of space constraints may be desirable. For tabletop applications that only require small annotations from time to time, handwriting or mobile text-entry devices might be suitable, despite the performance costs.

Our survey shows different strengths and weaknesses of existing text-entry methods in terms of their usage on tabletop displays. The character of the tabletop application and the target user group are important factors to consider when choosing an appropriate text-entry method or developing a new one. Therefore, standard user-centred design guidelines can be customized, focusing on questions such as:

- *What* is the purpose of the tabletop application? Is it a work application where efficiency is highly important or a walk-up interface where intuitive usage and visual adjustability become more important than efficiency? Does it require small annotations or the input of large amounts of text?
- *Who* are the people that are going to interact with the

tabletop display? Are they frequent keyboard users, novices, elderly people, children, etc.?
- *How* are people going to interact with each other on the digital table? Does the task require mobility or simultaneous text entry?
- *How often* will people interact with the system? Will it be worthwhile for them to learn a new text-entry method or will their use of the table be too infrequent?

Although our examination based on our evaluative criteria does not give clear answers, it shows tendencies and provides guidelines for evaluating existing and new text-entry methods for tabletop displays. The guiding questions above can help to weigh the criteria depending on the application area and targeted user group. This weighting can provide important design constraints, informing innovative text-entry methods specifically tailored toward tabletop displays.

4.1. Application Scenarios

The following two scenarios give an example of how some of the examined text-entry methods can be applied for certain tabletop applications. We describe one workplace scenario and one public walk-up-and-use scenario.

4.1.1. Work Scenario. A tabletop work scenario could involve a team of people working on a museum's catalogue. This task involves digital information in the form of text passages and photos spread out on a tabletop display. Often, such teams will divide up the work. For example, the graphics designer in the team might start to arrange the photos within a page layout while the content managers work on the creation of textual content that is still missing, or edit text passages to fit better into the design. Working together on the same large display is beneficial because upcoming questions can be quickly clarified and changes can be done immediately with the whole team involved. For the graphics designer's task, short annotation within the page layout is required. Certain parts of the layout may need short comments or marks for later refinement. For this task, *handwriting* is a suitable text-entry method, since it allows a person to quickly annotate while moving around freely to look at the page layout from different perspectives. Since the annotations can be done by hand or with a stylus, it is easy to switch back and forth between annotating and manipulating content in the tabletop workspace. For the content managers who create additional textual content, a *physical keyboard* that is installed in the tabletop system is a good way to enter text. For them, it is most important to be able to efficiently enter large amounts of text into the system. Mobility or shareability of the text-entry system is not important. For editing text passages already embedded in the page layout on the tabletop display, a *gesture-based keyboard* or *gestural alphabet* might be most appropriate. They are more efficient and accurate than handwriting but the text passages can still be edited in place. Both techniques also support a high amount of mobility and shareability.

4.1.2. Walk-up-and-use Scenario.

For a company that designs and develops public tabletop installations for museums or trade shows, intuitiveness and immersiveness of the tabletop interface have highest priority. Their clients expect tabletop systems that look visually appealing and that are tailored toward the theme of the particular exhibition. The tabletop interface needs to invite people to interact with it. In this scenario, text-entry functionality can be provided through *soft keyboards*. Because they exist in the virtual space, soft keyboards can be visually tailored toward a certain look-and-feel that matches the overall tabletop interface. A QWERTY character layout and touch-tapping input method can be used to capitalize on the familiarity of most people with QWERTY keyboards. Additionally, language models that highlight characters with a high probability to follow the previously typed character can be applied. This helps those not familiar with QWERTY keyboards to enter text. Mechanisms to collapse soft keyboards can save work space. In general, soft keyboards can be designed to be rotatable and translatable across the tabletop workspace making them easy to share between multiple people. Although soft keyboards using a QWERTY layout are not the most efficient text-entry method, they are highly suitable for supporting an intuitive and immersive multi-user experience. In contrast to our work scenario, it is acceptable to sacrifice efficiency for our other evaluative criteria. Namely, the visual appearance should be aesthetically pleasing, the method should not interfere with the space required for the main attraction, the entry method should be collapsible, rotatable, minimally interfere with direct-touch interaction, allow people to remain mobile and support many people using the display simultaneously. An appropriately designed soft keyboard can achieve a balance between these criteria.

4.2. Evaluation of Text Entry Methods

Our examination of existing text-entry methods for their potential use on tabletop displays is the first step toward enabling text entry on tables. As a next step, both their efficiency and their suitability for specific tabletop display environments need to be empirically evaluated. For efficiency testing, predictive models should be developed that also take two-handed typing into account. These models are also important for developing new text-entry methods for tabletop displays since they are less costly than empirical studies. Additionally, observational user studies can provide insights into people's subjective preferences regarding text-entry methods for tabletop displays. People's satisfaction is crucial for the adoption of a text-entry method.

Long-term studies need to be conducted that provide insights into the learning curves of text-entry methods. Although some learning-curve studies have been reported for small mobile devices, their results are not directly applicable for tabletop displays due to the different environmental factors, nor are they directly comparable to each other because they used different study parameters [40].

Since the tabletop research community is just starting to investigate text-entry methods, we should learn from the problems encountered studying text-entry methods for mobile devices [40]. We as a community need to come up with consistent methods to empirically study text-entry methods on tabletop displays for gaining comparable results throughout different research laboratories.

In-depth studies of text-entry methods on tabletop displays can lead to the development of new innovative methods specifically tailored toward tabletop displays.

5. Conclusion

In this paper we have examined existing text-entry methods for their potential use on tabletop displays. Our examination is based on a collection of evaluative criteria that directly follow from the environmental characteristics of tabletop displays. We analyzed text-entry methods for their space requirements, collapsibility, rotatability, their compatibility with other direct-touch interaction techniques, and their support of mobility, shareability, duplicability, and simultaneous multi-person interaction.

Although our examination cannot provide a clear answer about which particular text-entry method is the best for tabletop displays, it reveals tendencies that help to choose text-entry methods depending on the tabletop application and targeted user group. While not much research has been done so far regarding text-entry methods on tabletop displays, our analysis provides first insights into this important topic. Text entry is an essential activity for all sorts of applications and more research needs to be done regarding how to support this activity on tabletop displays. The evaluative criteria we applied for our examination can be understood as guidelines for the empirical evaluation of existing text-entry methods on tabletop displays and the development of new techniques specifically tailored toward large digital tables.

Acknowledgements

We would like to thank all iLab members for their insightful comments and suggestions and our funding agencies SMART Technologies Inc., Alberta Ingenuity, iCORE, CFI, and NSERC.

References

[1] B. Ahlström, S. Lenman, and T. Marmolin. Overcoming touchscreen user fatigue by workplace design. In *Proc. CHI Posters and Short Talks*, pp. 101–102. ACM Press, 1992.

[2] T. Bellman and I. S. MacKenzie. A probabilistic character layout strategy for mobile text entry. In *Proc. GI*, pp. 168–176. Canadian Information Processing Scoiety, 1998.

[3] C. H. Blickenstorfer. Graffiti: Wow! Pen Computing Magazine, pp. 30–31, January 1995.

[4] O. de Bruijn and R. Spence. Serendipity within a ubiquitous computing environment: A case for opportunistic browsing. In *Proc. Ubicomp*, pp. 362–370. Springer-Verlag, 2001.

[5] P. Dietz and D. Leigh. DiamondTouch: A multi-user touch technology. In *Proc. UIST*, pp. 219–226. ACM Press, 2001.

[6] C. G. Drury and E. R. Hoffman. A model for movement time on data-entry keyboards. *Erognomics*, 35(2):129–147, 1992.

[7] A. Dvorak, N. L. Merrick, W. L. Dealey, and G. C. Ford. *Typewriting Behaviour*. American Book Company, 1936.

[8] P. M. Fitts and J. Peterson. Information capacity of discrete motor responses. *Journal of Experimental Psychology*, 67(2):103–112, 1964.

[9] D. Goldberg and C. Richardson. Touch-typing with a stylus. In *Proc. INTERCHI*, pp. 80–87. ACM Press, 1993.

[10] D. L. Grover, M. T. King, and C. A. Kuschler. Patent No. US5818437: Reduced keyboard disambiguating computer. Tegic Communications, Inc., http://www.tegic.com, 1998. Visited June 9, 2007.

[11] F. Guimbretière and T. Winograd. FlowMenu: Combining command, text, and data entry. In *Proc. UIST*, pp. 213–216. ACM Press, 2000.

[12] T. Isenberg, P. Neumann, S. Carpendale, S. Nix, and S. Greenberg. Interactive annotation on large, high-resolution information displays. In *Conf. Comp. VIS/Info-Vis/VAST*, pp. 124–125. IEEE Computer Society, 2006.

[13] C.-M. Karat, C. Halverson, D. Horn, and J. Karat. Patterns of entry and correction in large vocabulary continuous speech recognition systems. In *Proc. CHI*, pp. 568–575. ACM Press, 1999.

[14] I. S. MacKenzie and L. Chang. A performance comparison of two handwriting recognizers. *Interacting with Computers*, 11(3):283–297, 1999.

[15] I. S. MacKenzie and R. W. Soukoreff. Text entry for mobile computing: Models and methods, theory and practice. *Human-Computer Interaction*, 17(2):147–198, 2002.

[16] I. S. MacKenzie and S. X. Zhang. The immediate usability of Graffiti. In *Proc. GI*, pp. 129–137. Canadian Human-Computer Communications Society, 1997.

[17] I. S. MacKenzie and S. X. Zhang. The design and evaluation of a high-performance soft keyboard. In *Proc. CHI*, pp. 25–31. ACM Press, 1999.

[18] I. S. MacKenzie and S. X. Zhang. An empirical investigation on the novice experience with soft keyboards. *Behaviour & Information Technology*, 20(6):411–418, 2001.

[19] I. S. MacKenzie, S. X. Zhang, and R. W. Soukoreff. Text entry using soft keyboards. *Behaviour and Information Technology*, 18(4):235–244, 1999.

[20] J. Mankoff and G. D. Abowd. Cirrin: A word-level unistroke keyboard for pen input. In *Proc. UIST*, pp. 213–214. ACM Press, 1998.

[21] Microsoft. Microsoft Surface. http://www.microsoft.com/surface/, 2007. Visited June 14, 2007.

[22] D. A. Norman and D. Fisher. Why alphabetic keyboards are not easy to use: Keyboard layout doesn't much matter. *Human Factors*, 24(5):509–519, 1982.

[23] K. Perlin. Quikwriting: Continuous stylus-based text entry. In *Proc. UIST*, pp. 215–216. ACM Press, 1998.

[24] Y. Rogers and S. Lindley. Collaborating around vertical and horizontal large interactive displays: Which way is best? *Interacting with Computers*, 16(6):1133–1152, 2004.

[25] S. D. Scott, M. S. T. Carpendale, and K. M. Inkpen. Territoriality in collaborative tabletop workspaces. In *Proc. CSCW*, pp. 294–303. ACM Press, 2004.

[26] S. D. Scott, K. D. Grant, and R. L. Mandryk. System guidelines for co-located collaborative work on a tabletop display. In *Proc. ECSCW*, pp. 159–178. Kluwer Academic Publishers, 2003.

[27] A. Sears. Improving touchscreen keyboards: Design issues and a comparison with other devices. *Interacting with Computers*, 3(3):253–269, 1991.

[28] A. Sears, D. Revis, J. Swatski, R. Crittenden, and B. Shneiderman. Investigating touchscreen typing: The effect of keyboard size on typing speed. *Behaviour and Information Technology*, 12(1):17–22, 1993.

[29] M. Silfverberg, I. S. MacKenzie, and P. Korhonen. Predicting text entry speed on mobile phones. In *Proc. CHI*, pp. 9–16. ACM Press, 2000.

[30] Smart Technologies Inc. Dvit digital vision touch technology. February 2003.

[31] O. Ståhl, A. Wallberg, J. Söderberg, J. Humble, L. E. Fahlén, A. Bullock, and J. Lundberg. Information exploration using The Pond. In *Proc. CVE*, pp. 72–79. ACM Press, 2002.

[32] N. Streitz, P. Tandler, C. M'uller-Tomfelde, and S. Konomi. i-Land: An interactive landscape for creativity and innovation. In *Proc. CHI*, pp. 120–127. ACM Press, 1999.

[33] TextwareSolutions. The FITALY one-finger keyboard, 1998.

[34] D. Venolia and F. Neiberg. T-Cube: A fast, self-disclosing pen-based alphabet. In *Proc. CHI*, pp. 265–270. ACM Press, 1994.

[35] D. J. Ward, A. F. Blackwell, and D. J. C. MacKay. Dasher—A data entry interface using continuous gestures and language models. In *Proc. UIST*, pp. 129–137. ACM Press, 2000.

[36] P. Wellner. Interacting with paper on the DigitalDesk. *Communications of the ACM*, 36(7):87–96, 1993.

[37] J. O. Wobbrock, B. A. Myers, and J. A. Kembel. EdgeWrite: A stylus-based text entry method designed for high accuracy and stability of motion. In *Proc. UIST*, pp. 61–70. ACM Press, 2003.

[38] H. Yamada. A historical study of typewriters and typing methods: from the position of planning japanese parallels. *Journal of Information Processing*, 2(4):175–202, 1980.

[39] S. Zhai, M. Hunter, and B. A. Smith. The Metropolis Keyboard—An exploration of quantitative techniques for virtual keyboard design. In *Proc. UIST*, pp. 119–128. ACM Press, 2000.

[40] S. Zhai, P.-O. Kristensson, and B. A. Smith. In search of effective text input interfaces for off the desktop computing. *Interacting with Computers*, 17(3):229–250, 2005.

Tabletop File System Access: Associative and Hierarchical Approaches

Anthony Collins, Trent Apted, Judy Kay

School of Information Technologies, University of Sydney, Australia
{anthony,tapted,judy}@it.usyd.edu.au

Abstract

This paper presents the design of two tabletop file system interfaces: OnTop, a novel associative access approach to file system interaction, where users navigate multiple file systems by selecting focus files; and the Browser, a hierarchical interface that is based upon the same mental model as conventional desktop file system access. We report a qualitative study with ten users to explore both approaches. OnTop was found to better facilitate collaboration on file access and use, while the more familiar hierarchical model of the Browser was found to be more natural on very early use and has a clear role—particularly in cases where the associative approach fails.

1. Introduction

The collaborative possibilities afforded by tabletop interfaces make them appealing for sharing digital files and personal information between group members. Although users may not perceive a tabletop interface as a conventional personal computer [17], a form of file system interface seems important: A file system, and its interface, constitute a core facility of an operating system [13]. This paper explores tabletop file system access, taking particular care with those aspects that distinguish tabletop interaction, notably their role for collaborative interaction. The following scenario illustrates requirements on tabletop file access:

> *James and Alice have an assignment to design a Greek history museum exhibit. James is discussing the project requirements with the exhibition co-ordinator via e-mail, and collecting photographs of Greek artefacts. Alice is doing research to write descriptions of these artefacts, and associated aspects of ancient Greece. James and Alice now need to combine their work, making decisions about which artefacts to use in the exhibition. They choose the tabletop to support this collaborative activity.*

Tabletop interfaces are appealing for tasks like this, involving *sharing* of digital files and personal information. Notably, this scenario involves multiple file systems because James would naturally have used his own computer for work, while Alice would have used hers. Now, they need their files to be available at the tabletop. Although the e-mail, images and text may happen to be in arbitrary hierarchies on those computers, we want to facilitate easy and natural access to all the relevant files and to exploit each user's own knowledge of their own file system, while supporting collaboration with the combined file-set at the tabletop.

Hierarchical organisation and navigation of file systems has become the standard in conventional personal computers. However, the properties and constraints of multi-user tabletop interaction call for rethinking this standard approach to file system interaction. First, there are limitations of physical interaction that affect how information can be presented, and how user input can be accepted. These limitations are the result of a low resolution on the tabletop, which is needed to make targets sufficiently large for direct-touch interaction. A keyboard and mouse is typically not present in a multi-user tabletop setting. Even a projected keyboard on the tabletop surface is problematical—there is no tactile feedback on pressing keys, and it lacks a fixed reference for users to place their hands (a serious problem when the projected keys would be occluded by a user's hand). Collaborative tabletop interfaces must also be orientation independent (as people could be sitting anywhere around the table). This poses problems for text presentation, such as file and directory names.

Finally, the collaborative nature of the tabletop interface encourages users to share their files with each other, meaning that the files presented on a tabletop often need to come from multiple collections. Required documents may be in various folders across the separate file systems, and retrieving a particular document may only be possible for the user who owns that file system. While users may have a hierarchical mental model of file system interaction, we need to explore alternative approaches, as a core requirement of a tabletop file system interface is the ability to interact with multiple (and potentially unfamiliar) large collections of files.

This paper presents our exploration of *natural* file system interaction with tabletop interfaces, based on two radically different approaches: associative and hierarchical. We first review previous work on tabletop file access and file system visualisation, then present an overview of our two approaches and their qualitative evaluation.

2. Related Work

2.1. Tabletop File Access

Tabletop and pen-based interface research has explored interaction with small collections of information, such as digital photographs [3], or a desktop of files [1]. Research on importing files to tabletops has been limited. *MultiSpace* [6] uses *micro-mobility* for explicit and visible portal-based transfer of files between devices, which is similar to earlier work in creating continuous workspaces for hybrid computing environments [12]. As such, the focus of this past work is not on interacting directly with file systems from the tabletop, but interacting with specific files that have been explicitly and visibly transferred to the tabletop first. *UbiTable* [18], and an approach using tangible drawers [8], require users to move their files from a laptop computer or personal storage device into a shared region of the tabletop display (and so, the user is privately copying files onto the tabletop). Furthermore, files are presented on the table in a *flat* unstructured collection.

Techniques for collaborative searching of large collections on tabletops have been explored in *Team-Search* [10], although these require manual Boolean query formation. However, the benefits of collaborative searching are highlighted, such as facilitating stronger collaboration and awareness among group members. Providing a search interface alone is not sufficient for supporting natural browsing of multiple file systems on a tabletop.

Pure hierarchical interaction has been explored in the *Personal Digital Historian* project [21], as a way of increasing the scalability of a tabletop interface. However, hierarchical presentation tends to quickly fill the tabletop display, which makes navigation of multiple file system hierarchies problematic. Interaction with large hierarchies through passive and active associations has also been explored [19], although results obtained suggest that participants highlighted "clutter" and "over crowding" within groups of information as major problems in the interface. This crowding issue is noted as an important factor to address in tabletop interfaces [17].

2.2. User Interfaces to File Systems

The limits of hierarchies for managing files have been recognised as a problem in modern personal computers. Various novel interfaces have been explored in an effort to improve the flexibility and efficiency of file system retrieval [9, 11]. Research on associative file systems, such as the *Semantic file system* [7] and *Presto* [5], has explored dynamic file system interaction based on file meta-data attributes. Content-based search, such as with *Google Desktop Search*[1], *Apple Spotlight*[2], and *Windows Vista Instant Search*[3], allows interaction with a single information-space that merges relevant content regardless of its type and where it is stored. However, these associative and content-based access mechanisms provide a targeted search interface that would be difficult to adapt to a collaborative tabletop.

File system visualisations, such as *Cone Trees* [16] and *Tree-Maps* [20], present information in a novel way to aid cognition, but are also susceptible to the problems inherent in hierarchical file systems, and are based on the assumption that the user is familiar with the file system organisation. Visualising multiple intersecting hierarchies has been explored in *Polyarchy* [14], although this is dependent on the hierarchical structure, rather than content (thus, it would be difficult to visualise related information from different documents across multiple file systems). Other document visualisation approaches, such as *Data Mountain* [15], favour spatial layout rather than hierarchical structure to allow more natural information retrieval.

3. Drivers for Design

When designing for the tabletop, one needs to take account of the constraints described in the introduction: limited resolution; orientation independence; restricted modes of input; and problems with clutter. In addition, we have a key goal to support collaboration based on files from multiple file systems. We have identified two approaches to designing tabletop file system interfaces.

The *OnTop* interface provides *associative* file access where a user focuses on one file of interest, with the system automatically retrieving all "related" files across multiple remote file systems, and showing only those deemed to be relevant. The associative approach has the potential to address the constraints imposed by tabletop and hierarchical file system interaction.

---

[1]http://desktop.google.com/
[2]http://developer.apple.com/macosx/spotlight.html
[3]http://www.microsoft.com/vista/

The *Browser* interface enables collaborative navigation of multiple *hierarchical* file systems at a tabletop. As hierarchical file system interfaces are standard in current operating systems, many users have a strong existing mental model of them. Consequently, the main driver behind the design of the Browser was to embrace the existing hierarchical model, and provide an interface similar to a conventional file browser that is designed for tabletop interaction.

4. User View

We build upon the *Cruiser* tabletop platform [2], a multi-user, gestural, collaborative tabletop interface. It uses the *Mimio Capture* whiteboard pen system, but is independent of the hardware (a version called *SharePic* [3], used the *DiamondTouch*). As both OnTop and the Browser are based on Cruiser, they share some common gestures.

The image representations of files appear to be placed on top of the tabletop surface. A file or other interface object can be *moved* by selecting the object in the main area inside the dotted lines (see Figure 1) and dragging it. When moving files, they have a realistic momentum so they can be *flicked* around the tabletop. Files can be rotated and resized (in a combined *rosize* action) by selecting the object at one of its corners and dragging the corner. Files can be *flipped* by selecting an image from within a stippled triangle along one of the its edges and dragging it across to the opposite edge. This action is presented gradually in simulated 3D to keep the original point under the pen tip. Once flipped, the user sees the file name written on the back.

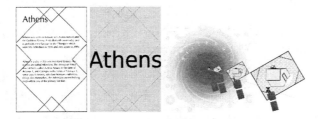

Figure 1. A selected file (left), a flipped-over file (centre), and the Black Hole (right).

To reduce clutter on the tabletop, users can move unwanted items into the *Black Hole* (see Figure 1). A file reduces in size as it is dragged closer to the centre of the Black Hole until it is completely hidden. The hole can be moved, rotated, and resized just as any other object. Files placed in the Black Hole may be retrieved by reducing the hole's size and flicking it with sufficient momentum, causing the contained files to "fall out".

4.1. File Access with OnTop

Figure 2 shows two users interacting with OnTop. When OnTop is first launched, a broad *start view* shows the first file (alphabetically) in each exported directory of each remote file system in a radial layout. This assumes users have a reasonable organisation of their files, and that the first file in a directory will be moderately representative of the folder's contents. Exploring alternative approaches to this start view is an area for future work.

Figure 2. People using the OnTop interface to share and discuss their personal files.

File navigation is based on the notion of a *focus* file. Once a user selects a focus file, all other *related* files are displayed (regardless of where they are stored or which file system they belong to). A user may navigate the file systems by re-selecting focus files. The focus file approach allows content-based file access without any user text entry. To select a focus file, a user dwells (depresses the pen for one second) on an image representation of the document. A 'click' sound gives feedback that it has been selected. After each focus selection the initial size of a file is used to indicate its relevance to the focus, and irrelevant files are automatically hidden in order to reduce clutter on the tabletop. Figure 3 shows a collection of documents after two successive focus selections from the initial start view.

A query is sent to each connected machine to find documents related to the newly selected focus item. This query request contains meta-data associated with the focus file, so that similar files can be found in separate file systems. Matching results are returned and displayed immediately. If a file was previously displayed on the tabletop, it is presented in its last location to provide spatial consistency between focus selections, and to allow users to create arbitrary spatial groupings of documents (as in [15]).

The *History Browser*, shown at the top of Figure 3, supports 'back' and 'forward' operations for file system navigation. It shows a thumbnail representation of

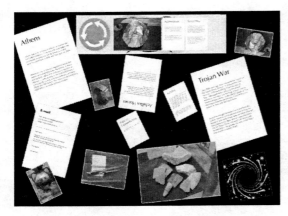

Figure 3. The OnTop interface showing files from multiple file systems.

Files have been rearranged by users, and are sized according to their relevance to the focus (a document about the Trojan War). Most relevant files appear large and prominent, while less relevant files appear small and unobtrusive.

Figure 4. Two folder objects (left) that have been opened to retrieve an image file (right).

The circled sub-folder (top left) has been dragged-off, resulting in a new folder object being created that shows the sub-folder's content (bottom left), which is a collection of image files. The circled file has been dragged to right to view it at original size.

each past focus item (typically the last five, depending on thumbnail width). A user dwells on a past focus item to go 'back' to the display of the documents associated with it. A special circular icon on the far left of the History Browser represents the start view of the file systems, which can be recalled by dwelling on the icon.

4.2. File Access with the Browser

In the Browser, a file system directory is displayed as a special *folder object* on the tabletop, which contains thumbnail representations of its contents. Each file system has its own *root* folder object. A folder object is indicated by solid triangular corners, and it can be moved, rotated and resized like any file.

A user drags thumbnails off a folder object to display the original file on the table (shown in Figure 4). If a thumbnail represents a sub-directory, the first file in the sub-directory is used as an icon to represent it. The sub-folder can be opened by dragging it off the parent folder object, resulting in another folder object being created at the drag-off co-ordinates. When a file is dragged off a folder object, the original thumbnail in the folder object remains in-place and unmodified. As such, multiple copies of a file's image representation can be made by repeating the drag gesture.

The Browser closely resembles a conventional *spatial* file browser (such as GNOME Nautilus), rather than a *navigational* file browser (such as Windows Explorer). This approach leverages the physicality of the tabletop, as each folder is represented as a realistic object on the table, and multiple folders can be present on the tabletop at once—this is critical for supporting concurrent access to multiple file systems. Clicking to open

files and folders was replaced with drag—a smooth operation that is more robust to accidental touches—and thumbnails are favoured over text due to clutter, rotation and legibility problems on large dot-pitch tabletop displays.

5. Exporting Files

To make files accessible by the OnTop interface, users run the *OnTop File Exporter* on their personal computer (typically connected to the same Local Area Network). Users are given explicit control over the files accessible by tabletops, and which tabletops can connect to the computer. Users can also configure which directory should be the base of the start view for their file system.

A critical element of OnTop is calculating file relevance. For the associative access to operate effectively, it is essential that this will correctly retrieve the relevant files. Given the personal nature of file system organisation and content, we have created a mechanism for users to customise (with the File Exporter) how their files are determined relevant to a given focus. This is based on assigning weightings to 11 supported meta-data attributes (including the full text document content) in a simple user interface. OnTop does not require users to manually attach meta-data to their documents, although keywords can be used to influence the relevance calculation. Since this paper concerns the interaction at the tabletop, we do not deal with the relevance calculation details, which are described elsewhere [4].

OnTop File Exporter uses Apple *Spotlight* (an existing content-based search framework), which scales well to large file systems. The difference in search time between a small collection and an entire file system is unnoticeable. Files are loaded on the table while the computer is retrieving further results in the background, so that users immediately see the effect of their focus selections. Accessing multiple file systems, rather than a single file system, has no effect on the overall time taken for relevant files to be presented on the table, as the retrieval process is parallel and asynchronous.

The Browser currently provides an interface to multiple local file systems residing on the computer powering the tabletop display. Portable USB drives can be plugged into the table, and their content automatically appears on the tabletop, where each file system is represented by its own root folder object.

6. Evaluation

The goal of the evaluation was to gain a qualitative understanding of both the associative approach of On-Top and the hierarchical approach of the Browser. The sub-goals were to assess *success* in task completion, number of *errors* made, and *affective aspects* of user preferences.

Ten participants (4 female and 6 male) between the ages of 22 and 50 were recruited for the evaluation. Six were students (5 with IT backgrounds, another with a cognitive science background), while the others used computers for work. Three participants had used a tabletop interface before (for less than 20 minutes each). All participants used a conventional hierarchical file system on a daily basis—five participants used their computer for 30–49 hours each week, four for 50–69 hours per week, and one for over 70. Consequently, participants had a strong mental model of file systems. The evaluation was conducted in pairs, and participants had a prior social background with their partner.

6.1. Collaborative Tasks

Participants worked in pairs on five collaborative tasks. The tasks related to the scenario outlined in the introduction, and involved working together to create a set of information about ancient Greek history. One participant was allocated text documents related to the project, while their partner had photographs and e-mails. The tasks were designed to be authentic for collocated collaboration, representative of typical interactions with a file system, and to involve retrieving files from a diverse range of locations (multiple personal file systems, as well as multiple categories of documents and images).

Participants were asked to complete the following:

1. Locate an e-mail listing the artefacts required for the exhibition (from the exhibition co-ordinator).

2. Locate a fact sheet about the Trojan Horse for the exhibition (as specified in the previous e-mail).
3. Locate the images of Trojan Horses, and decide with your partner which to use in the exhibition.
4. Locate a fact sheet for an exhibit about the city of Athens.
5. Locate the images of Athens landmarks, and decide with your partner which to use in the exhibition.

A key feature of the task design was the location of required files. Each task related to information stored in one set of personal files—this meant that in a task one user would find files from their personal files, and their partner would add related information retrieved from their personal files (such as in Tasks 2, 3, and 5). Consequently, each task involved locating files stored in very different locations, which required users to navigate through their file system. Some tasks involved locating a document that was not immediately related to those already on the tabletop (such as in Tasks 1 and 4) to ensure that the tasks were not biased towards the associative file access condition.

6.2. Experiment Procedure

To gain insight into the impact of file system size for each of the interfaces, two sets of test data were used: one having 59 files, the second having 114 files with more, and deeper, sub-directories. The number of files used in each case was enough to potentially clutter the table, and it was a plausible number of files for the scenario given to participants. A sheet with a personal file list, showing the hierarchical organisation scheme for the files they had been assigned, was given to each participant. Participants were free to refer to this at any stage during the experiment.

The files were grouped by type at the root directory level, and then further grouped by topic, with no more than 10 files in each directory. In the larger test data set, a deeper level of sub-directories was achieved by increasing the granularity of the topic classification scheme. Keywords were assigned to images in order to enhance the relevance calculation performed by OnTop, as the content-based search could not be fully utilised. For example, a Trojan Horse image was assigned the keyword "Troy" to relate the image to Troy documents. The keywords were used as directory names in the hierarchical file system, so that the keyword information was available to participants in both file access interfaces. The meta-data weightings for relevance calculation were fixed between experiments, with a high weighting given to textual document content, keywords, and filenames.

The ordering of both the conditions used, and file

Table 1. Browser performance observations.

Observation	Participants
Clutter caused difficulty in navigating files. Degree increased when file system larger.	1A*, 1B*, 2A, 3B
Regularly moved unwanted files and folders into the Black Hole or corners to reduce clutter.	2A, 2B, 3B, 4A*, 5A*, 5B*
Carefully reduced size of each folder while exploring hierarchy to reduce clutter.	3A, 4A*, 4B*, 5A*, 5B*
Needed reminding about file system organisation when performing tasks for the first time with the Browser.	1A*, 1B*, 2A, 2B, 3B, 4A*, 5A*, 5B*
Difficulty distinguishing which file system directory a folder object represented.	1A*, 1B*, 3A, 3B, 5B*
Demonstrated sense of ownership of personal file system (folder objects oriented only towards themselves, and would not touch their partner's folder objects).	All Pairs
Key: * = Browser used first (before OnTop)	

Table 2. OnTop performance observations.

Observation	Participants
Focused on a document in their partner's file system to find a required document in their own.	All Pairs
Helped their partner by suggesting potential focus files from their own set of files.	1A*, 2A, 2B, 3A, 4A*, 4B*, 5A* 5B*
Focused on a document purely because of its type (to find other files of the same type).	1A*, 2A, 3B, 4A*, 5A*
Used the History Browser to return to a past focus file relevant to the task.	All Pairs
Used the History Browser to return to the start view even though a highly relevant document was already visible.	1A*, 2A, 3A
Made additional focus selections (even though the required file was show on the tabletop) to reduce the number of files displayed.	2A, 2B, 4A*, 4B*
Key: * = Browser used first (before OnTop)	

system size varied between experiments[4] to ensure that the evaluations were comparable. Participants were asked to complete the same list of tasks for each interface and file system size.

In the first step of the experiment, participants were given a brief tutorial on the Cruiser interface, introducing core functionality. After the tutorial, participants were given five minutes to practice manipulating ten images, followed by using each of the two file access conditions: OnTop and the Browser. Before using either of the interfaces, participants were told the scenario of the tasks they were going to perform, and the experimenter was responsible for reading out the tasks.

After completing the tasks, participants were asked to complete a short questionnaire about computer use and feedback on each of the experimental conditions. The evaluation was captured on video, and the experimenter later analysed this to identify interesting features of interaction and to code these for each condition.

7. Results

Observations made while participants were completing tasks with the Browser are summarised in Table 1. A significant issue for the Browser was clutter, with participants adopting strategies to manage it (such as using corners of the tabletop for storing files and folders, or placing them in the Black Hole). Pairs 2–5 informally adopted a clean-up protocol, where a participant would resize and move their files and folder objects out of the way (or place them in the Black Hole) before their partner would begin the next task.

Five participants had difficulty distinguishing which file system directory a folder object represented, due to

---

[4]The order of conditions and file system sizes was assigned randomly to pair 5, as the ordering was already balanced with 4 pairs.

limited familiarity with the file systems. However, after referring to the file system layout sheet, participants were able to proceed with the task without any trouble. Furthermore, eight participants needed reminding of the file system layout when performing tasks for the first time with the Browser, but did not need reminding for the second time.

Notably, participants were private with their file system interactions due to a high sense of ownership, and they never interacted with their partner's folder objects. In contrast, participants were more social and co-operative when completing tasks using OnTop—participants often helped their partner to complete the tasks by suggesting possible focus files in their own file system. The performance observations made with OnTop are summarised in Table 2.

Participants embraced the unfamiliar idea of associative access, employing different ways to navigate the file systems. In some tasks, where the required files were related to something from the previous task, participants only needed to make one focus selection in order to complete a task. However, additional focus selections were made by some participants to further refine the relevant files displayed.

In the Browser interface, errors arose due to participants opening directories that did not contain the files they were searching for. Participants made a total of nine errors during the experiment using the Browser. In contrast, only one error was made by participants using OnTop (caused by selecting an incorrect focus document).

Questionnaires indicate that participants found OnTop consistently easier to use, and eight participants considered OnTop to be more efficient, as summarised in Table 3. No participants found OnTop harder or

Table 3. Summary of questionnaire responses.

Participant	1A	1B	2A	2B	3A	3B	4A	4B	5A	5B
Condition	B	B	O	O	O	O	B	B	B	B
Order	s	s	s	s	L	L	L	L	s	s
Ease of use ratings (1…6, 1 = Poor, 6 = Excellent)										
Browser	2	2	2	2	2	4	3	3	3	4
OnTop	5	5	5	6	5	6	5	6	6	4
Efficiency ratings (1…6, 1 = Poor, 6 = Excellent)										
Browser	3	2	2	3	3	3	4	5	3	3
OnTop	5	5	4	5	3	6	5	3	5	5
Tasks harder/slower to complete when file system was larger										
Browser	Y	N	Y	Y	Y	Y	Y	Y	N	N
OnTop	N	N	N	N	N	N	N	N	N	N
Key: B s - Browser with small file system used first; O L - OnTop with large file system used first										

slower when the file system size was doubled, compared to seven who thought this was true of the Browser.

The feedback for both file access interfaces was positive—notably, participants considered the tabletop to be an important collaborative medium, and the seamless access of personal file systems on a tabletop was considered to be an exciting feature.

All participants said the Browser interface had a familiar mental model, which initially made it easier for them to understand. Three participants expressed concerns about not being able to locate files due to the associative search failing. Two (3A, 4B) stated that they would like to see the inclusion of some features common to hierarchical file browsers in OnTop, such as the ability to quickly navigate to specific files or directories, which is why they did not rate the efficiency of OnTop highly (shown in Table 3). For this reason, they commended the Browser interface because they can always access specific files.

All participants found the OnTop interface highly efficient at finding documents related to something that they were already working on, particularly when each file was in a completely different file hierarchy. This was highlighted by participants as an important feature for collaborating with team members over shared documents. One participant reported finding OnTop very efficient to locate files because "it skipped through the hierarchy". Four participants commended the OnTop start view as a way to restore the state of the tabletop when searching for documents unrelated to the currently viewed files, or recalling frequently accessed documents important to their task.

The Browser was received positively when compared with a conventional desktop computer file system browser due to its spatial nature. Three participants liked the fact that they could place as many folders as necessary on the table (and leave important ones open

at all times), and it was easy to see the contents of a folder through the use of thumbnails rather than text. No participant suggested that the Browser should operate more like the *navigational* file system browser they use on their personal computer.

8. Discussion and Conclusions

The most striking outcomes of the evaluation relate to the issues of collaboration and management of clutter. Beginning with collaboration (a key goal for tabletop interaction), we observed that OnTop appeared to give better support for users to collaborate on the access process when working to complete a joint task. This seems to follow from the fact that OnTop presents an amalgam of the files from both users' file-spaces. By contrast, the hierarchical Browser has the tendency to make each user take charge of accessing their own files. This suggests that the associative access afforded by OnTop is particularly promising and valuable for tabletop interaction.

With the Browser, the majority of participants were initially unsure about the file system organisation when completing tasks for the first time, although these participants had no trouble when completing the tasks for a second time. This highlights an important property of the Browser—it potentially makes it difficult to navigate unfamiliar file systems, as file access is dependent on a knowledge of the file system layout.

The issue of clutter management, noted as a recurring concern in tabletop interfaces [10, 17, 19], was also affected by the differing file access mechanisms we explored. With the Browser, clutter posed a problem for users and they needed to systematically clean-up. OnTop's automatic 'pruning' proved helpful for reducing clutter. It is more difficult to achieve this with the Browser: it seems natural to provide at least one Browser folder object per file system and if the user needs to explore various parts of it, it seems natural to allow several sub-folder objects to be available at once. Tabletop file system interfaces need to provide facilities to manage clutter with minimal distraction from (or limiting of) the user's task.

A caveat to our conclusions is that participants were asked to complete these tasks with a set of files that we provided, rather than files that they had created, to make our results more comparable. Even so, the results show that novel file access interfaces, such as the associative approach taken with OnTop, can effectively support natural collaborative file system access at tabletops. However, it is clear that an associative approach may not always be sufficient, and there must be ways to access files explicitly (in the case of a file system, one approach is conventional hierarchical navigation).

We have presented two radically different interfaces for file system interaction on tabletops: OnTop, a novel associative access approach to file system interaction; and the Browser, a hierarchical interface based on the folder metaphor. The evaluation highlights the strengths of each approach. OnTop makes efficient use of limited display area, and seamlessly merges related content from multiple remote file systems. However, facilities for explicit file access (such as hierarchical navigation) must also be provided depending on the task, as the associative access may fail, or users may prefer to access specific files and folders. This paper makes a contribution to the interface challenges of support for the key system functionality of file access. The work has demonstrated two interfaces that operate effectively within the constraints of a tabletop environment to support collaboration—one of the core goals of the tabletop interface.

9. Acknowledgements

We are grateful to the participants in our evaluation. This work is partially funded by the Smart Internet Technology CRC.

References

[1] A. Agarawala and R. Balakrishnan. Keepin' it real: Pushing the desktop metaphor with physics, piles and the pen. In *Proceedings of CHI '06*, pages 1283–1292. ACM Press, 2006.

[2] T. Apted, J. Kay, and M. Assad. Sharing digital media on collaborative tables and displays. In *Online Proceedings of The Spaces In-between: Seamful vs. Seamless Interactions (in conjunction with UbiComp 2005)*, 2005.

[3] T. Apted, J. Kay, and A. Quigley. Tabletop sharing of digital photographs for the elderly. In *Proceedings of CHI '06*, pages 781–790. ACM Press, 2006.

[4] A. Collins. Exploring tabletop file system interaction. Undergraduate Thesis, University of Sydney, http://www.it.usyd.edu.au/ anthony/thesis.pdf, 2006.

[5] P. Dourish, W. K. Edwards, A. LaMarca, and M. Salisbury. Presto: an experimental architecture for fluid interactive document spaces. *ACM Trans. Comput.-Hum. Interact.*, 6(2):133–161, 1999.

[6] K. Everitt, C. Shen, K. Ryall, and C. Forlines. Multi-Space: Enabling electronic document micro-mobility in table-centric, multi-device environments. In *Proceedings of TABLETOP '06*, pages 27–34. IEEE Computer Society, 2006.

[7] D. K. Gifford, P. Jouvelot, M. A. Sheldon, and J. W. O. Jr. Semantic file systems. In *Proceedings of the 13th ACM Symposium on Operating Systems Principles*, pages 16–25. ACM Press, 1991.

[8] B. Hartmann, M. R. Morris, and A. Cassanego. Reducing clutter on tabletop groupware systems with tangible drawers. In *Adjunct Proceedings of UbiComp 2006*, 2006.

[9] G. Marsden and D. E. Cairns. Improving the usability of the hierarchical file system. In *Proceedings of SAICSIT '03*, pages 122–129. South African Institute for Computer Scientists and Information Technologists, 2003.

[10] M. R. Morris, A. Paepcke, and T. Winograd. TeamSearch: Comparing techniques for co-present collaborative search of digital media. In *Proceedings of TABLETOP '06*, pages 97–104. IEEE Computer Society, 2006.

[11] D. Quan, K. Bakshi, D. Huynh, and D. R. Karger. User interfaces for supporting multiple categorization. In *Proceedings of INTERACT 2003*, pages 228–235. IOS Press, 2003.

[12] J. Rekimoto and M. Saitoh. Augmented surfaces: A spatially continuous work space for hybrid computing environments. In *Proceedings of CHI '99*, pages 378–385. ACM Press, 1999.

[13] D. M. Ritchie and K. Thompson. The UNIX time-sharing system. *Commun. ACM*, 17(7):365–375, 1974.

[14] G. Robertson, K. Cameron, M. Czerwinski, and D. Robbins. Polyarchy visualization: visualizing multiple intersecting hierarchies. In *Proceedings of CHI '02*, pages 423–430. ACM Press, 2002.

[15] G. Robertson, M. Czerwinski, K. Larson, D. C. Robbins, D. Thiel, and M. van Dantzich. Data Mountain: Using spatial memory for document management. In *Proceedings of UIST '98*, pages 153–162. ACM Press, 1998.

[16] G. G. Robertson, J. D. Mackinlay, and S. K. Card. Cone trees: Animated 3D visualizations of hierarchical information. In *Proceedings of CHI '91*, pages 189–194. ACM Press, 1991.

[17] K. Ryall, M. R. Morris, K. Everitt, C. Forlines, and C. Shen. Experiences with and observations of direct-touch tabletops. In *Proceedings of TABLETOP '06*, pages 89–96. IEEE Computer Society, 2006.

[18] C. Shen, K. Everitt, and K. Ryall. UbiTable: Impromptu face-to-face collaboration on horizontal interactive surfaces. In *Proceedings of UbiComp 2003*, volume 2864 of *Lecture Notes in Computer Science*, pages 281–288. Springer, 2003.

[19] C. Shen, N. B. Lesh, F. Vernier, C. Forlines, and J. Frost. Sharing and building digital group histories. In *Proceedings of CSCW '02*, pages 324–333. ACM Press, 2002.

[20] B. Shneiderman. Tree visualization with tree-maps: 2-d space-filling approach. *ACM Trans. Graph.*, 11(1):92–99, 1992.

[21] F. Vernier, N. Lesh, and C. Shen. Visualization techniques for circular tabletop interfaces. Technical Report TR2002-001, Mitsubishi Electric Research Laboratories, March 2002.

Improving Menu Interaction for Cluttered Tabletop Setups with User-Drawn Path Menus

Daniel Leithinger, Michael Haller
Upper Austria University of Applied Sciences
Softwarepark 11, 4232 Hagenberg, Austria
{daniel.leithinger, michael.haller}@fh-hagenberg.at

Abstract

Many digital tabletop systems have a graphical user interface (GUI) that features context (or pop-up) menus. While linear and pie menus are commonly used for direct pen and touch interaction, their appearance can be problematic on a digital tabletop display, where physical objects might occlude menu items. We propose a user-drawn path menu, that appears along a custom path to avoid such occlusions. This paper introduces four different metaphors for user-drawn context menus: the Fan Out Menu, the Card Deck Menu, the Pearl String Menu, and the Trail Menu. It also presents the results we acquired from a user study, where participants were able to work faster when using our user-drawn menus, on cluttered tabletop setups.

1. Introduction

Since the introduction of Wellner's DigitalDesk in 1991 [18] numerous PC interfaces based on digital tabletop setups have emerged [16]. Several metaphors have been proposed to deal with the problem of direct interaction with information on large surfaces [1]. These metaphors, however, have been developed for displays only obscured by the user's hand, which means applying them to digital tabletops would require an empty desk. Figure 1 depicts a table in a meeting room to illustrate the problem. Assuming this table is equipped with a digital tabletop and with a standard GUI, the work area would have to be emptied prior to each use. However, in a number of scenarios, meeting participants might need to use the physical objects and the digital tabletop simultaneously. When the user works on the tabletop next to a physical object and opens a context menu, its size, layout and position might cause it to overlap with objects nearby. In such a case, either the object or the menu has to be moved. Either one of these options disrupts the workflow and possibly leads to a suboptimal workspace arrangement.

Figure 1: A meeting room with typical objects like notebooks, pens, fruits, coffee cups and mobile phones on the table.

Figure 2 depicts a scenario where both a rectangular drop-down menu and a pie menu fail on a table setup, due to visual overlapping with physical objects. We propose a *user-drawn* path menu which allows a customizable arrangement of the menu items and is thus easily adaptable to the available tabletop display space.

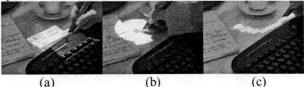

(a)　　　　(b)　　　　(c)

Figure 2: (a) drop-down menus and (b) pie menus become hard to see or even unusable when overlapping with physical objects. (c) We propose a user-drawn path menu, which allows an optimal placement of the menu.

In the next section, we present related research, followed by a closer description of our four user-drawn menus. Then we present a user study followed by a detailed discussion of the results. Finally, we conclude with an outlook of further research.

0-7695-3013-3/07 $25.00 © 2007 IEEE
DOI 10.1109/TABLETOP.2007.24

2. Related Work

2.1. Digital Tabletops

Wellner introduces the approach of augmenting a tabletop for an intuitive computer interface [18]. DigitalDesk is designed to provide a seamless link between real paper and the PC through the augmented tabletop. Ishii and Ulmer's metaDESK [17] integrates physical objects on a digital tabletop as part of a tangible user interface. Rekimoto and Saitoh introduce Augmented Surfaces [14], which allow users to exchange data with their laptop computers on an interactive table. Objects on the tabletop are tracked with optical markers and that way part of the user interface. DiamondTouch [5] is a digital tabletop surface supporting multiple users. In contrast to other input devices, the tracking technology is not disturbed by physical objects on the table. Interactive Environment-Aware Display Bubbles [4] are designed to map rectangular content onto freeform shapes for a space efficient arrangement of content on the table surface. Physical objects on the table are tracked with a top-mounted camera to avoid collisions with interface bubbles. To select bubble operations, a pie menu is used.

2.2. Pen Input

In our test setup, users interact directly on the tabletop display with a digital pen as a stylus. The following research has investigated the problems raised by direct touch or pen input and proposed a number of solutions.

Accot and Zhai investigate user performance of pointing at a target with a pen based input device versus crossing it and propose an interface based on crossing instead of point-and-click [1]. Apitz and Guimbretière propose an alternative to the standard WIMP-interface for tablet PCs entirely based on crossing [3]. Examples of context menus developed especially for pen input include FlowMenu [8] and Tracking Menus [7]. Tracking Menus were designed to prevent round trips to tool palettes with the pen.

Since the occlusion shadow of a user's hands on a direct input display can obstruct context menu options, several strategies have been proposed to improve the placement of such menus [9]. These strategies determine the user's handedness to predict a possible occlusion and adapt the menu position accordingly. Li et al. investigate various mode switching techniques in pen-based user interfaces [12]. Their findings can be applied to context menu activation on the tabletop, which is not investigated in this paper.

Most menus for direct pen or touch input have been designed for either small displays (e.g. PDAs, tablet PCs) or for large non-cluttered surfaces. In contrast to the related work, user-drawn path menus are designed especially for avoiding occlusions by physical objects.

3. User-Drawn Path Menus

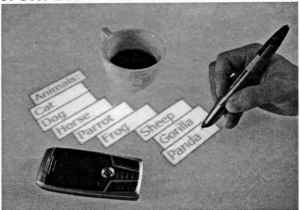

Figure 3: A user-drawn path menu.

Previous research to avoid menu occlusions produces very good results when dealing only with the user's hand [9]. But possible occlusion shadows created by other physical objects are substantially harder to determine. These occlusions can be even more problematic, since items like full coffee cups are more cumbersome to move than the user's hand.

To avoid possible menu occlusions, the system could try to determine the size and position of all physical objects on the tabletop with a camera. It could then adapt the context menu position and appearance accordingly. A disadvantage of this approach is the added technical overhead. Another problem is the lack of comprehensible consistency in the automated menu placement decision. If a menu is lacking space at the desired location, the system has to decide to either change its size and shape or to render it at another position altogether. Since these decisions are made by the system, the user never really knows where the menu will be displayed next.

Our approach is different, since our system does not predict possible occlusions, but lets the user decide the menu size and shape. Instead of the context menu popping up after a user input, it appears along a user-drawn path (see Figure 3). This metaphor derives from the layers-as-a-stack-of-cards analogy [13], which is based on the idea of representing information layers as individual cards of a card deck. Each menu item is represented as a card and placed along the user-drawn path in different ways. This metaphor has the following advantages. Firstly, the user can easily create a menu not occluded by physical items by simply drawing a path around them. Secondly, since the menu placement and shape is created by the user, it poses less confusion than an automated placement. We propose four different metaphors to position the menu items along the path which we derive from natural ways of spreading information. In each of these metaphors, only the menus' root element appears when the input device first touches the surface. The menu items are placed along a path, created by the pen tip and stay on their last placed position, when the pen is lifted. The user can then select an item by tapping on it with the pen tip or close the menu by tapping on the root item.

3.1. Fan Out Menu

This metaphor is similar to the approach described by Agarawala and Balakrishnan [2] to display information by fanning it out along a custom path. All of the menu items are positioned on the path between the start and current end point, with an even path distance between the center point of each item. While the path is drawn, the path distance between the items grows so they appear to fan out (see Figure 4).

The advantage of this metaphor is that since all menu items are spread out along the path simultaneously, the number of items is easy to determine while the stroke is drawn. Therefore the path length needed to display all menu items can be predicted by the user. The disadvantage to the other user-drawn menus is that it is always necessary to spread all items before selecting one.

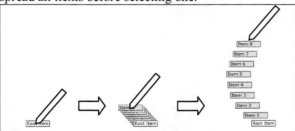

Figure 4: Fan Out Menu. The root item appears first then all menu items are spread along the path simultaneously.

3.2. Card Deck Menu

The Card Deck Menu behaves similar to a deck of playing cards with individual cards taken from the deck and placed behind each other on the table. When the pen tip touches the surface, the menus root element is displayed. While the pen moves on the surface, the distance between each new pen point and the previous menu item is evaluated. A new menu item is placed with its center at the pen tip, if it does not occlude the previous menu item. In contrast to the fan out menu, each menu item stays at the position it is placed. After

all items are placed, moving the pen has no further visible effect on the menu (see Figure 5).

The advantage of the card deck menu is the possibility to place menu items on top of items other then the immediate predecessor to save space. It also allows the selection of an item immediately after placing it without finishing the path for the remaining menu.

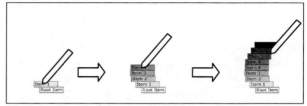

Figure 5: Card Deck Menu. Darker items appear later.

3.3. Pearl String Menu

The behavior of the Pearl String Menu is very similar to the Card Deck Menu, but the order in which the menu items appear is reversed. When the pen tip touches the surface, the menus root element is displayed. While the pen moves, the first menu item follows the position of the pen tip. Each subsequent menu item is placed along the path from the pen tip to the root item. Each item is placed to not occlude its predecessor. As soon as all menu items are visible, moving the pen has no further effect on the menu (see Figure 6).

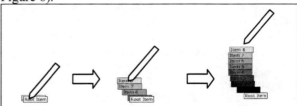

Figure 6: Pearl String Menu. Darker items appear later.

3.4. Trail Menu

The behavior of the Trail Menu is similar to the Pearl String Menu. But after all menu items are visible, they follow the pen tip like a tail instead of staying at their position (see Figure 7).

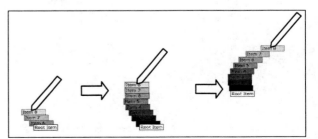

Figure 7: Placement of menu items in the Trail Menu. Darker items appear later.

3.5. Implementation

All prototype menus were created using C# with Windows Presentation Foundation (WPF) for rendering. The test system either required Windows XP or Windows Vista.

4. Hypotheses

According to the Hick-Hyman Law [10][11] and to Fitts' Law [6], our proposed menus should be less efficient than traditional menus. One reason is the time required by users to draw the path for the user-menu, which takes longer than a simple click, needed for the pie/pop-up menu[1]. The second reason is the varying distance from target to the root-item, according to the free space available on the display. Both Hick-Hyman and Fitts' Laws are developed for menus that are visible immediately. Thus, no cluttering object is occluding the menu. Summarizing, we formulated the following hypotheses:

- *Hypothesis 1: We expected better performance (in time and errors) for the pie menu and the pop-up menu compared to our proposed menus, while working on an empty table.*

- *Hypothesis 2: We expected better performance (in time and errors) for our proposed menus while working on a cluttered table. We also expected that participants will subjectively prefer our menus under this condition.*

Based on these hypotheses, we measured the performance, the error rate provided by the task outcome, and the subjective measures (user opinions).

5. Experiment

5.1. Apparatus

We conducted a laboratory user study where users stand in front of a horizontal, rear-projected table (112 x 85 cm). The resolution of the projected display was 1024 x 768 pixels (cf. Figure 8).

The tracking of the stylus is realized by using a large Anoto pattern printed on a rear-projection foil in conjunction with digital pens (we used the Bluetooth digital pen from Maxell at 50 Hz). The pattern is clamped in-between two acryl panels to provide a stable and robust surface while protecting the pattern from scratches. The advantage of the Anoto tracking technology is a high tracking resolution, which is unaffected by physical objects on the tabletop. The tabletop was accompanied by a 19" LCD screen.

---

[1] In the following, we use the term pop-up menu for all rectangular context menus and pie menu for a circular context menu.

Figure 8: The rear-projection table and the LCD display used in our experiment.

5.2. Participants

12 volunteers (8 males and 4 females), aged between 23 and 38 participated in the experiment. 11 participants were right handed and controlled the pen with their right hand. All participants were frequent computer users and had experience with Windows. Eight participants had previously worked with digital tabletop systems.

Eleven of them had already pen- and/or touch-based interface experience (e.g. Tablet PC).

5.3. Task

For our experiment, users were presented with an item name on the LCD display next to the table. The users were instructed to open a menu on the tabletop and select the displayed item name as quickly and accurately as possible. The menu could be opened by either tapping the empty table surface for traditional menus, or drawing a path for user-drawn menus. Participants were asked to complete a series of five menu selections under three different conditions using six different menu layouts. Each item of the menu was 80 x 20 pixels, with the same size being used throughout the study. The Pie Menu had a diameter of 200 pixels.

Our software logged all pen events and measured the time to complete the task from the initial display on the LCD display until the final selection. Whenever the participant missed a menu item, an error was logged in our software.

5.4. Conditions

We used three different conditions for our experiment:

1. *Empty table:* users performed the task on an empty table (cf. Figure 8).

2. *Obscured table with movable content:* under this condition the tabletop was cluttered with digital content to simulate physical objects. 36 randomly placed and rotated white rectangles where used to simulate paper, which occluded more than 50% of the display. The participant had the possibility to move the content with the digital pen if it occluded an underlying menu, which always appeared on the bottom layer of the table (cf. Figure 9).

3. *Obscured table with non-movable content:* in contrast to condition 2, the digital content could not be moved (cf. Figure 9).

Figure 9: The rear-projection table and the LCD display used in our experiment.

5.5. Procedure and Design

A repeated measure within-participant design was used in our user study. The order of presentation of the six different menus was counterbalanced among participants. All users were presented with the same content. We also changed the order of the items appearing in the different menu categories to avoid a learning effect. The presentation (position) of additional content for both conditions two and three was randomized.

All participants had a short block of practice trials before each test session. Each condition lasted about 7 minutes. Participants took short breaks after every condition – an experimental session lasted about 30 minutes. Finally, users completed a post-experiment user preference questionnaire. Summarizing, the total number of trials can be computed as follows:

12 participants x 5 trials x 6 menu types x 3 conditions = 1,890 trials in total.

The dependent variables measured were the time the users took for the overall trial (sometimes, users had to

click the menu to different places to see all menu items), the selection time and the errors.

5.6. Results

5.6.1. Performance Analysis

Figure 10 depicts the overall time participants used for the six menus under the three conditions[2]. The overall time is the duration from displaying the task word on the LCD screen until the final selection of an item in a menu (this includes the time it takes to find the adequate menu position). An ANOVA of the collected data did not show a significant difference under the first two conditions. We also didn't find any difference between the user-drawn menus and pie menus (although users had to draw the path menu which usually should take longer than just a single pen click).

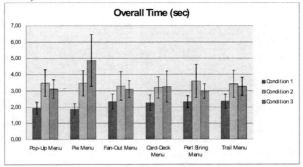

Figure 10: Overall time for each menu under the three different conditions.

We were surprised about the performance under condition 2, where the participants had the possibility to move the content. Although users had to move the digital content before getting the "traditional" menus under optimal conditions, they were not slower than sketching the path for the user-drawn menu. Under real conditions, however, users would have to move real printouts and obstacles, which is very depending on the type of object. Thus it can require more time than to move digital projected content.

The overall time for the different menus under condition three was different: The Pearl String Menu was the fastest (mean 2.98, SD 0.45), followed by the Fan Out Menu (mean 3.11, SD 0.51), the Pop-Up Menu (mean 3.12, SD 0.57), the Card Deck Menu (mean 3.26, SD 0.95), Trail Menu (mean 3.27, SD 0.55), and the Pie Menu (mean 4.87, SD 1.59). Users took longer using the Trail Menu, because most of them still moved the menu although all items of the menu were already displayed. Often, participants also wanted to place the menu somewhere else – again this

---
[2] All spreadsheets are available at www.officeoftomorrow.org

cost time. Participants had most problems with the Pie Menu under the third condition. The maximum time was 15.88 seconds using the Pie Menu for selecting one item. A repeated measures analysis of variance showed a high significant difference between the overall time under the third condition ($F_{11,60} = 12.316$, $p < 0.0001$).

Finding an adequate menu position was easier for condition 1 and 2 (cf. Figure 11). We found no significant difference between the time for finding the position for the six menus. In condition 3, however, it was sometimes impossible (especially for the Pie Menu) to find an adequate free position. We found a significant difference between the six menus under condition 3 ($F_{11,60} = 5.83$, $p < 0.001$).

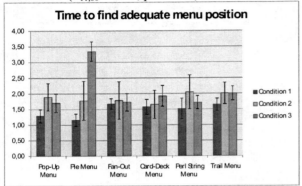

Figure 11: Time required to find an adequate position for the menu.

The most extreme time difference was measured using the Pie Menu under the three different conditions. Due to the large radius of the Pie Menu, users could not find an adequate position on the table, which resulted an average time of approximately 3.5 sec.

Figure 12 shows the average of moved objects under the second condition. Not surprisingly, participants had to move more objects using the Pie Menu and the Pop-Up Menu. There was a significant difference between the Pop-Up/Pie Menu and the other menus ($F_{11,60} = 6.62$, $p < 0.001$), but no difference between the Fan Out Menu, the Card Deck Menu, the Pearl String Menu, and the Trail Menu. Only one person never moved any objects - even in the scenario, where he/she could do it.

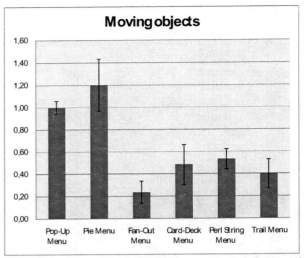

Figure 12: Participants often moved obstructing objects using the Pie Menu (under condition 2).

Figure 13 depicts how often participants had to open the menu to get the adequate position for selecting the target item.

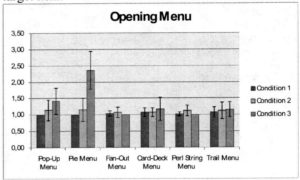

Figure 13: How often did participants open the menu to find an adequate position for an optimal item selection?

Analysis of variance of counting the opened menus showed a high significant main effect for all menu-types ($F_{11,60} = 10.864$, $p < 0.0001$) under condition 3, where participants had no possibility to move the cluttering digital content. A post-hoc Tukey HSD test indicated that this was the only significant difference. No differences could be found for all menu types under condition 1 and 2. One person had to open the Pie Menu 12 times before getting able to select the correct item.

The time for selecting the menu item after having found an adequate menu position was, of course shorter (cf. Figure 14). A repeated measured ANOVA showed that there were significant differences between the menus under the three conditions (Condition 1:

$F_{11,60} = 11.69$, $p < 0.001$; Condition 2: $F_{11,60} = 13.099$, $p < 0.001$; Condition 3: $F_{11,60} = 7.5$, $p < 0.001$).

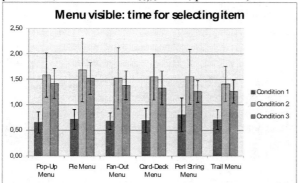

Figure 14: Selecting an item after having positioned the menu takes less time than finding an adequate menu position.

These lend support to hypothesis *H1* – hence, both the conventional Pop-Up Menu and the Pie Menu demonstrated a better performance under condition 1. Moreover our results also support hypothesis *H2*, where our proposed user-drawn path menus were faster on a cluttered table.

5.6.2. Error Detection Analysis

Overall, there were little differences between the menus in terms of selecting the wrong item ($F_{11,60} = 1.16$, $p = 0.32$) with a mean error rate of 5% for the Pie Menu and 0 - 1.7% for the user-drawn menu (all under condition 2 and 3). The Trail Menu was the worst with a mean error rate of 3.3% once the table was empty. One reason for this was that users still moved the trail menu while selecting the item.

5.6.3. Subjective Preference Analysis

In the post-study questionnaire we asked the participants to assign an overall rank to each of the six different menus and a preferred menu type for each of the three table conditions. In the 12 following questions, the participants rated the ease of use of each menu type for empty and cluttered tables, using a 5-point Likert-scale (1 = totally disagree, 5 = totally agree).

We asked all participants which menu style they preferred for the empty table. 6 users chose the rectangular Pop-Up Menu as their favorite, 5 users chose the Pie Menu as their favorite, and 1 participant preferred the user-drawn menu on the empty table. On the obscured table with movable elements, none of the users reported the Pie Menu as a favorite. 2 users still preferred the Pop-Up Menu under this condition, but noted that they would prefer the user-drawn menu for more than 8 menu items. All participants chose the user-drawn menu as their favorites under the 3rd condition, where they had no possibility to move the occluding elements.

Table 1 shows the results of the question about how easy the users felt it was to use the menu under two different conditions (empty table, cluttered table).

Menu	Empty Table	Cluttered Table
Pop-Up Menu	4.92 (SD 0.29)	2.29 (SD 1.24)
Pie Menu	4.75 (SD 0.45)	1.75 (SD 1.22)
Fan Out Menu	4.00 (SD 0.74)	3.83 (SD 0.94)
Card Deck Menu	4.25 (SD 0.87)	3.83 (SD 0.72)
Pearl String Menu	4.25 (SD 0.67)	4.25 (SD 0.75)
Trail Menu	4.50 (SD 0.67)	4.33 (SD 0.98)

Table 1: Subjective Survey Responses.

The overall ranking showed strong preferences for the trail menu. Participants, who ranked this metaphor highest, claimed the main reason was the possibility to move it around on a cluttered table until the optimal position and appearance was reached. All of the other menus had to be re-drawn or re-opened if they were not placed right the first time. One participant reported that the user-drawn menu seems to be "handy" for cluttered table and he/she liked the possibility to move the whole menu (even once the items are already open). From the user study, we also noticed that none of the participants had troubles to adapt to the new interface.

One drawback users didn't like was the fact that they didn't see the menu length of the drawn menus immediately, which makes the decision of where to start drawing the menu more difficult. They suggested "visualizing" the menu length. Some users noted no fundamental differences between the different types of user-drawn path menus, but recognized them to be advantageous when used on the cluttered table. And finally, one user suggested visualizing the link between the items of the Fan Out Menu.

6. Discussion

The results show that users do feel that user-drawn menus make a strong sense while working on a cluttered table. Even on an empty table, we could only find a short time lag while using our approach. In our experiment, we used digital content instead of real printouts to simulate a counterbalanced setup. Consequently, users could move the content with the digital pen. In a real environment, however, users would have to move the keyboard, the coffee mug etc. which can require more time, although it allows two handed interaction.

7. Conclusion and Future Work

In this paper, we have presented a user-drawn interface for tabletop interaction. Our work builds on previous research (e.g. Pie Menus, Tabletop Setups) and introduces a novel context menu. Our main observation was that current graphical user interface metaphors were perceived to be too inflexible for a tabletop cluttered with objects. In this paper, we presented four different user-drawn menus. The results we achieved in our first user study present a significant reduction of time using these menus on an obscured tabletop display. Moreover, users also postulated the user-drawn menus as their favorites. Our ongoing work will continue to add and analyze cascading user-drawn menus.

Acknowledgement

This project is sponsored by the Austrian Science Fund FFG (FHplus, contract no. 811407) and voestalpine Informationstechnologie GmbH. The authors would like to express their gratitude to the anonymous reviewers and to Sean Castle for their useful comments, and to all the participants of the user study.

References

[1]   Accot, J. and Zhai, S. 2002. More than dotting the i's --- foundations for crossing-based interfaces. In *Proceedings of the SIGCHI Conference on Human Factors in Computing Systems: Changing Our World, Changing Ourselves* (Minneapolis, Minnesota, USA, April 20 - 25, 2002). CHI '02. ACM Press, New York, NY, 73-80.

[2]   Agarawala, A. and Balakrishnan, R. 2006. Keepin' it real: pushing the desktop metaphor with physics, piles and the pen. In *Proceedings of the SIGCHI Conference on Human Factors in Computing Systems* (Montréal, Québec, Canada, April 22 - 27, 2006). R. Grinter, T. Rodden, P. Aoki, E. Cutrell, R. Jeffries, and G. Olson, Eds. CHI '06. ACM Press, New York, NY, 1283-1292.

[3]   Apitz, G. and Guimbretière, F. 2004. CrossY: a crossing-based drawing application. In *Proceedings of the 17th Annual ACM Symposium on User interface Software and Technology* (Santa Fe, NM, USA, October 24 - 27, 2004). UIST '04. ACM Press, New York, NY, 3-12. Canada, 2005.

[4]   Cotting, D. and Gross, M. 2006. Interactive environment-aware display bubbles. In *Proceedings of the 19th Annual ACM Symposium on User interface Software and Technology* (Montreux, Switzerland, October 15 - 18, 2006). UIST '06. ACM Press, New York, NY, 245-254.

[5]   Dietz, P. and Leigh, D. 2001. DiamondTouch: a multi-user touch technology. In *Proceedings of the 14th Annual ACM Symposium on User interface Software and Technology* (Orlando, Florida, November 11 - 14,

2001). UIST '01. ACM Press, New York, NY, 219-226.

[6]   Fitts, P. The Information Capacity of the Human Motor System in Controlling the Amplitude of Movement. J. Experimental Psych., 47. 1954. 381-391.

[7]   Fitzmaurice, G., Khan, A., Pieké, R., Buxton, B., and Kurtenbach, G. 2003. Tracking menus. In *Proceedings of the 16th Annual ACM Symposium on User interface Software and Technology* (Vancouver, Canada, November 02 - 05, 2003). UIST '03. ACM Press, New York, NY, 71-79.

[8]   Guimbretiére, F. and Winograd, T. 2000. FlowMenu: combining command, text, and data entry. In *Proceedings of the 13th Annual ACM Symposium on User interface Software and Technology* (San Diego, California, United States, November 06 - 08, 2000). UIST '00. ACM Press, New York, NY, 213-216.

[9]   Hancock, M. S. and Booth, K. S.: Improving Menu Placement Strategies for Pen Input. In *Proceedings of the Graphics Interface 2004 Conference* (May 17-19, 2004, London, Ontario, Canada). Heidrich W. and Balakrishnan R., Canadian Human-Computer Communications Society, 221-230

[10] Hick, W. On the rate of gain of information. J. Experimental Psychology, 4. 1952. 11-36.

[11] Hyman, R. Stimulus information as a determinant of reaction time. J. Experimental Psych., 45. 1953. 188-196.

[12] Li, Y., Hinckley, K., Guan, Z., and Landay, J. A. 2005. Experimental analysis of mode switching techniques in pen-based user interfaces. In *Proceedings of the SIGCHI Conference on Human Factors in Computing Systems* (Portland, Oregon, USA, April 02 - 07, 2005). CHI '05. ACM Press, New York, NY, 461-470.

[13] McGuffin, M. J., Tancau, L., and Balakrishnan, R. 2003. Using Deformations for Browsing Volumetric Data. In *Proceedings of the 14th IEEE Visualization 2003* (Vis'03) (October 22 - 24, 2003). IEEE Visualization. IEEE Computer Society, Washington, DC, 53.

[14] Rekimoto, J., and Saitoh, M. Augmented surfaces: a spatially continuous work space for hybrid computing environments. In *CHI '99: Proceedings of the SIGCHI conference on Human factors in computing systems*, pages 378–385, New York, NY, USA, 1999. ACM Press.

[15] Robertson, G., Czerwinski, M., Baudisch, P., Meyers, B., Robbins, D., Smith, G., and Tan, D. The large-display user experience. *IEEE Comput. Graph. Appl.*, 25(4):44–51, 2005.

[16] Scott, S. D. Territoriality in collaborative tabletop workspaces. PhD thesis, Calgary, Alta., Canada,

[17] Ullmer, B. and Ishii, H. 1997. The metaDESK: models and prototypes for tangible user interfaces. In *Proceedings of the 10th Annual ACM Symposium on User interface Software and Technology* (Banff, Alberta, Canada, October 14 - 17, 1997). UIST '97. ACM Press, New York, NY, 223-232.

[18] Wellner, P. 1993. Interacting with paper on the DigitalDesk. *Commun. ACM* 36, 7 (Jul. 1993), 87-96.

Multimodal Split View Tabletop Interaction Over Existing Applications

Edward Tse[1,2], Saul Greenberg[2], Chia Shen[1], John Barnwell[1], Sam Shipman[1], Darren Leigh[1]

[1]*Mitsubishi Electric Research Laboratories,* [2]*University of Calgary, Canada*

[tsee, saul]@cpsc.ucalgary.ca, [shen, barnwell, shipman, leigh]@merl.com

Abstract

While digital tables can be used with existing applications, they are typically limited by the one user per computer assumption of current operating systems. In this paper, we explore multimodal split view interaction – a tabletop whose surface is split into two adjacent projected views – that leverages how people can interact with three types of existing applications in this setting. Independent applications let people see and work on separate systems. Shared screens let people see a twinned view of a single user application. True groupware lets people work in parallel over large digital workspaces. Atop these, we add multimodal speech and gesture interaction capability to enhance interpersonal awareness during loosely coupled work.

1. Introduction

In everyday physical collaboration over a shared visual surface, people fluidly transition between working closely together (tightly coupled) and working in parallel (loosely coupled). The situation is somewhat different in the digital domain.

When people are geographically distributed, they routinely work together while viewing *independent applications* (Figure 1 left; A and B are different applications). Because they cannot see each other's screens and bodies, they use other channels (voice, instant messaging) to explicitly state what is visible on the screen. To improve this unwieldy situation, *shared screen systems* duplicated the output of one person's application so that it was also visible on distant screens (Figure 1 middle; A' is a duplicated view of A). Joint action was allowed by a wrapper that gathered and serializing people's input through a turn-taking mechanism, and then passed it onto the application [3]. This is essentially a what-you-see-is-what-I-see (WYSIWIS) view, where each person sees exactly the same visuals and fine-grained changes on their display [14]. Because of the strong linkage between views, shared screen views work well for tightly coupled work. Alternately, *true groupware systems* understood that multiple people were working in the space (Figure 1 right; A$_1$ and A$_2$ are instances of the same groupware

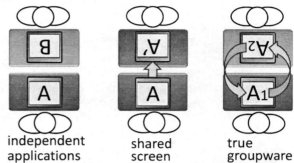

Figure 1. Software configurations for two people working face to face on a split view tabletop

application that are linked with one another). True groupware systems facilitate loosely-coupled work by allowing simultaneous input, and by relaxing WYSIWIS to allow people to navigate and work independently on different parts of a large digital workspace [14]. Generally, the transition between loosely and tightly coupled work in distributed applications is enabled by the *mechanics of collaboration* [6]. People's awareness of each other's speech, gestures, and gaze actions produce consequential communication around the work surface that facilitates how they engage, interact, coordinate, and transition between loosely-coupled and tightly-coupled work. Common groupware awareness methods supporting these mechanics include telepointers for gesturing [5], and radar overviews to give people a sense of what others are doing if they are working on different parts of scene [6].

Within the context of co-located groupware, things are somewhat analogous. The *independent applications* configuration of Figure 1 (left) happens when people seated next to each other are working on separate computers; their talk can draw attention to each other's display. As they turn to look at one of the screens, they have just transitioned to a simple shared screen system. The limitation is that there is only one input device, so only one person actually interacts with the system, or they manually share that device through turn-taking.

To mitigate this, early single display groupware (SDG) systems provided multiple input devices so people could work in parallel [15]. There are two primary approaches to SDG.

1. *Basic SDG* exploits how most operating systems merge the input from multiple mice into the single input stream seen by the standard single user application. The result is akin to screen-sharing (Figure 1, middle). While each person has a mouse, they still have to negotiate whose turn it is. That is, basic SDG favors very tightly coupled work through strict WYSIWIS turn-taking.

2. *True SDG* uses custom-built groupware applications that recognize and take advantage of multiple mice. Typically, all people have their own cursor and can work in parallel [15] akin to true groupware (Figure 1 right). However, the constraints of the small display usually mean that people are limited to a strict-WYSIWIS view, which in turn favours tightly coupled work. More recently, the development of high-resolution digital walls and tables provide a large enough surface so that people can work somewhat more loosely-coupled when using true SDG: while they all still share the same view, they can work on their corner or side of the surface.

Obviously, true SDG is more flexible than basic SDG in supporting the spectrum of loosely- to tightly-coupled work. The problem is that very few existing real world applications are built as true SDG, thus limiting what people can do. On the other hand, basic SDG can immediately leverage existing applications, but is really amenable only to tightly-coupled work. The question is: can we exploit basic SDG in a way that allows people to work in a loosely-coupled fashion, while still giving them the ability to move towards tightly-coupled interaction by providing strong awareness cues of what the other is doing?

Our answer is *multimodal split view interaction*: a split-screen tabletop configuration that supports both loosely and tightly-coupled joint work over conventional applications projected on a digital table, where the table also promotes awareness through multimodal interaction. The remainder of this paper introduces this concept. We begin with split view interaction, and define three software configurations that constrain how it can be achieved. We continue by adding multimodal speech and gesture interaction capabilities to these split views, which enhance awareness during loosely-coupled work.

2. The Split View Tabletop

The first half of our system is the *split view tabletop (SVT)*. It is defined as a digital tabletop, where its surface is split into two adjacent projected views, and a person is seated in front of each view. SVT size expectations are that each person can easily see and reach into any part of their view. Seeing and reaching into the other view is slightly more difficult, but can be done by looking up, or by standing and leaning over the table. The basic idea is that people can work in a loosely coupled manner over their own individual views, and can also work in a tightly coupled manner either by shifting their attention to the other view or by linking their views together through software. Several key factors influence SVT: the actual software being projected, seating, size, and input devices used.

2.1 Projected Software

One of our goals is to work with existing 'conventional' applications rather than re-write applications from the ground up. If successful, our SVT can be repurposed for myriads of available applications in co-located work. In this section, we describe three configurations that leverage existing software over SVT. Each is analogous to the distributed configurations described previously, so we reuse Figure 1 to illustrate each software view configuration in SVT. We show how each configuration offers different application sharing abilities, and how each supports different levels of collaborative work.

Individual applications allow people to work on their own separate application, each displayed on one side of the split view surface (Figure 1, left). For example, one person can use a web browser while the other person uses a digital map. The advantage is that people can work over separate applications in parallel yet still have some peripheral awareness of the actions of others simply by glancing up. The disadvantage is that both applications are not aware of each other, so that people have to resort to shifting attention and reaching over to one of the views if they wish to work in a tightly-coupled manner.

Screen sharing takes the screen displaying an unaltered single user application and projects it onto both views (Figure 1, middle) [3]. This can be implemented trivially using variants of the Virtual Network Computing (VNC) protocol [11]. As in the distributed setting, this forces a strict WYSIWIS view and sequential interaction through a turn-taking policy, making it also somewhat equivalent to *basic SDG*. Within SVT, screen sharing means that people can work very closely together over a single application, even though only a single person can interact at a time. unlike individual applications, rich awareness cues arising from gaze and gestures are available.

True groupware uses applications designed for distance-separated people, where it instead displays an application instance in each view on the digital table (Figure 1, right). This means we can exploit real-time distributed groupware within the co-located setting, which is akin to true SDG. This includes many PC games, as these are actually groupware designed to run over the Internet. This configuration naturally affords relaxed WYSIWIS, where people can work on their own part of the system without affecting others.

2.2 Seating Arrangements

Seating arrangements give different affordances to the SVT setting, where they can profoundly influence collaborative practice. Consider the following three common seating configurations.

Face to face seating provides people with easy visibility of each other's gestures and gaze actions on the work surface, as well as easy viewing of one another during conversation [13][12] (Figure 2 left). This is done simply by glancing up. This arrangement is commonly preferred for co-acting and conversation [7]. The cost is orientation, where studies have shown that displays that are text-heavy are significantly more difficult to read when upside down [20]. As well, a person can directly interact in the other view only by standing up and leaning over the table, or by actually moving to the other side of the table.

Side by side seating also affords visibility of each other and their work by side glances (Figure 2 middle). One can also reach into the other's view simply by sidling over. Orientation is not an issue, as text is usually upright to both viewers. This arrangement is commonly preferred for cooperative tasks [13], as it easier to read text on a collaborator's display [20]. The disadvantage is that side glances are more effortful than glancing up, and thus happen less frequently. As well, simultaneously viewing another person and the workspace at the same time is somewhat harder as the viewing angles are different. Finally, pairs are in very close proximity, and this could be discomforting if they do not know each other well [7].

Catty-cornered seating is a compromise (Figure 2 right). As with face to face, a glance up provides easy viewing of the other's work and their body. Its 90^0 viewing angle offers slightly better text readability of their partner's screen [20]. However, eye contact is harder to maintain when people are working over the surface. This seating arrangement is commonly preferred for tasks involving extended conversations as it supports the viewing of other's gestures while not requiring continual eye contact [13].

2.3 Size, Working Area, Reach, and Gaze

The physical size of each person's view can have

Face to Face   Side by Side   Catty Corner

Figure 2. Seating arrangements for two people.

considerable effect on interaction [7][13].

Small views mean that people can easily reach into both spaces and that they can engage in each other's activity at a glance. The trade-off is limited working area, which is important for parallel work [12].

Arms length views are sized so that a person can just reach all parts of their own view while seated, yet still reach into parts of the other person's view if they stand up or lean over. This is a size where collaborators can still engage in each other's activity at a glance [13].

Large views afford even more space to work in parallel. The cost is that people cannot easily reach all parts of their view while seated, let alone the other person's space. Awareness is also harder to maintain as the other person's display is further away and details become difficult to see [13].

2.4 Input Devices for Pointing / Selection

Input devices for pointing and selecting have a large effect not only on a person's individual work, but on how others can maintain awareness of the gestures of others. Rather than catalog the myriad of tabletop pointing devices and techniques that are under active development, we consider them as broad categories.

Decoupled devices such as a mouse or trackball are physically independent from the display surface. While efficient for individual work, other people may have a hard time noticing small device movements and button presses. A person will likely find it difficult or impossible to interpret what another person's activities mean unless he is looking directly at the telepointer [5] or the artifacts being affected.

Distant freehand devices are directed at the surface but do not directly touch the spot that it is manipulating. Examples are systems that use ray casting or laser pointers on a large display. While the actions of others tend to be more visible, it may still be difficult to interpret one's activities.

Direct touch devices correspond directly with the part of the surface being manipulated. Examples include touch tables such as Smart Boards and DiamondTouch [2]. Within a split view setting, the direct engagement of these absolute devices maximizes one person's awareness of the other's activities and their meaning.

3. Multimodal Interaction for Awareness

The second half of our system is its ***multimodal speech and gesture*** interaction capabilities, provided both to facilitate a person's fluid interaction with applications on the table, and to promote awareness between working partners.

Existing applications displayed by our SVT system are almost always designed for a mouse, which is a decoupled device. That is, if people are working in a loosely-coupled manner, these small device movements will be hard for others to notice. For example, observational studies [12] of people working over a wall and table display using single user applications revealed that people maintain awareness [6] by "physically moving back to the table to be in close proximity" to other collaborators and using "outlouds to get the attention of others" and attract the attention of people on distant displays by "shouting out and giving directives to him/her as to what to do next."

For this reason we advocate multimodal speech and gesture commands that serve as both commands to the computer and as awareness for other collaborators [19]. Gestures create consequential communication of each other's bodies and activities, while speech serves as verbal communication to others. While single user applications do not understand gestures or speech, we can create gesture and speech wrappers (macros) that activate keyboard and mouse sequences that in turn invoke application functionality [17]. No changes of the underlying application code are required.

Previous work by Tse, et. al. [19] used multimodal speech and gesture commands to enhance how people interacted over a digital table using single user applications. Their studies revealed that people exploited this for communicative purposes such as answering questions, validating understanding and agreement, and affirming statements made in prior conversations [18]. They also used this awareness to coordinate near-simultaneous activity by gracefully interleaving speech and gestures commands across people in the construction of commands.

4. Case Studies

We developed hardware and software to illustrate the multimodal SVT concept. Descriptions of the final systems are provided here, with implementation details deferred to §5.

The physical arrangement of our multimodal SVT implementation is illustrated in Figures 3-5. We decided upon the face to face seating arrangement (§2.2) as we were most interested in situations where

Figure 3. Split View over Independent Applications

people moved from loosely-coupled to tightly-coupled work involving co-acting and conversation. We chose an arms-length physical size (§2.3) to balance reach and availability. For input devices (§2.4), we refactored a multimodal speech and gesture recognition system [17]. Gestures were recognized through a DiamondTouch multi-user touch surface [2] as a direct touch device (§2.4), while speech was recognized through headset microphones (§3).

The case studies below show example implementations of all three software configurations (§2.1).

4.1 Independent Applications

Our independent applications configuration is appropriate when multiple people need to work independently over separate applications while still being aware of the actions of collaborators. Figure 3 shows two people planning a trip together by simultaneously browsing the web. Each runs a completely independent instance of the Mozilla Firefox web browser in their view. On the left (and in fuller view in the left inset), the woman is searching for Hotels using Google Maps. On the right the man is finding nearby attractions using an online Lonely Planet Guide.

We created a wrapper around Firefox that allows people to interact with it through gestures and speech. Gesture commands include one finger select, five finger pan/scroll, a two finger gesture to move back/forward or to open/close a tab, and two-handed region selection for highlighting a large region. Speech commands include "bookmark this page", "go to [bookmark name]", "back", "forward", "home", and "search". The "open keyboard" command opens an onscreen keyboard for typing in URLs or searches. Gestures across the seam are allowed: if the man drags

Figure 4. Screen Sharing using VNC and The Sims

Figure 5. True Groupware using Warcraft III.

a web link from his browser across to hers, that page is automatically loaded in her browser.

In Figure 3, the woman uses a voice command to bookmark the current page and a one-finger gesture to select the detailed information box of a hotel. She is simultaneously conversing, where she tells the man that the hotel could be a good one. The man responds by glancing over at her selection, and then referring to an attraction in his view that is close by that hotel.

As shown by this example, this configuration is good for loosely-coupled work during a joint task, where people can occasionally bring attention to some of their activities, e.g., by having the other person view it. While joint viewing is easy, joint interaction is difficult as one person would have to reach over the table to access the other view.

4.2   Screen Sharing

The screen sharing configuration is appropriate when people need to work tightly coupled over the same view. Figure 4 shows two people interacting with a shared view of The Sims by Maxis, a single user simulation game that allows a player to create a virtual home and to control the actions of its inhabitants. As seen in Figure 4, the views of both people are identical.

We created a wrapper around The Sims specifically for a furniture layout task. Speech commands include "create [object]", "<1st/2nd> floor" while gesture commands include one finger placement, five finger movement and one fist object stamping. There are also multimodal commands that require both speech and gesture, such as "create [object] [one finger point]", which creates an object at the location being pointed to. This interaction is powerful, for statements like "create a table [one finger point]" not only commands the system, but provides awareness to other collaborators about their actions. This is necessary for people to interleave their actions through turn-taking.

Figure 4 illustrates how this works in practice. The man is indicating through speech that he wants to create a TV while using a gesture to point at the spot, while the woman is 'simultaneously' moving a fridge.

Of course, this shared view could have been implemented by having a single instance of the Sims appear across the entire surface. Yet the split view could be advantageous if multiple people want to work together without concern of one's body occluding the other person's work area [13]. As well, the split view means that each person can reach the entire space.

A concern with screen sharing is that true simultaneous interaction cannot be guaranteed. However, awareness minimizes conflict: when people know what the other is doing, they mediate their actions accordingly. Still, global actions can cause interference, e.g., if one person pans the map as another person is creating an object on a particular spot.

4.3   True Groupware

True groupware is appropriate when people need to work both in a loosely- and tightly-coupled manner, and when their combined activities reflect changes in the common workspace. Figure 5 shows two people interacting with Warcraft III, a groupware game originally designed for distributed Internet players. As seen in Figure 5, the views of both people into the game's map surface can differ. Yet both views share the same common game environment, so actions by either person occurs in both places.

Akin to other configurations, we map speech and gestures to keyboard / mouse actions. Gestures include one finger unit selection, one hand panning and two hand side bimanual selection [19]. Speech commands, some combined with gestures, include "[selection] label as unit #", "<move/attack> here [point]", "build [building]", and "stop". Players can also move troops across the seam by saying "move here [point]" and touching in their partner's view.

Figure 5 illustrates how this works as each person is pursuing duties on different parts of the scene. The woman is directing worker construction in one area through a speech/gesture action ('build a farm here [point]'), while the man is directing troop actions in a region in a different area ('label as unit one [select region]). An overview map on the bottom left of each view shows the entire map surface, and immediately reflects each other's actions.

Leveraging distributed groupware to the split view setting is obviously powerful, for it allows simultaneous action in a relaxed-WYSIWIS setting. Of course, people can also align their views to achieve WYSIWIS, although this has to be readjusted during panning (as scrolling is not synchronized). Awareness support within the distributed groupware system, such as radar views and feedthrough of other's actions in the scene [6], is enhanced by seeing the speech and gestural acts of others. People can leverage gestures over the seam, e.g., the man selects units in his view, and moves them to the woman's view by saying "move here", and pointing to the woman's view.

4.4   Moving between Configurations

SVT can be configured so that people can switch to a more conventional tabletop mode that presents a single view onto the surface. Ideally, they should be able to switch between variations of the configurations above: this part of our software remains to be implemented, but is straightforward. For example, the travel planners in Figure 3 could move into tightly-coupled work over Google Maps by switching from the independent application mode to a shared screen mode. If they want to work even more closely together, they can switch it again so only a single view of Google Maps is shown across the entire table. Similarly, the Warcraft players in Figure 5 can move from a true groupware view into a shared screen or the single view configuration if they wish to move into tightly-coupled strict-WYSIWIS interaction. Alternately, one player can bring up a different view as an independent application, e.g., to look up a cheat sheet for Warcraft III on the Internet.

5. Implementation

Multimodal SVT interaction over existing single user applications is a new concept. Yet we were able to build our environment by repurposing various hardware / software systems at our disposal (Figure 6).

5.1   Hardware
Hardware comprises 2 touch-sensitive tables, 2

projectors, 2 computers, and speech input.

The split view digital table. The digital table seen in Figures 3, 4 and 5 is called the Double DiamondTouch (Figure 6, row 1). We designed as a face to face (§2.2) and arms-length (§2.3) surface. The table's total size is 148 x 116 cm, comprising an active area of 98 x 65 cm and a 25 cm wide solid oak bezel. This active area is made of two smaller DiamondTouch surfaces [2] laser cut to produce almost no seam (or break) between the two surfaces. The oak bezel and its beveled edges provide a comfortable resting area for people's arms that would not unexpectedly perform an action on the display surface. The beveled corners were designed to prevent arm strain over extended use.

Projecting multiple views. We used two projectors (Figure 6, row 5) and two computers (Figure 6, left and right half) to top-project two views onto the table, one in each half. Our two 1024x768 LCD projectors give a total resolution of 1536x1024.

Switching. As described in §4.4, one can switch between a single large shared display from one computer to two separate views from two computers. To do this, we used a KVM (Keyboard, Video, Monitor) switch (Figure 6, row 5). Projector A is connected to the primary display for Computer 1, while Projector B is connected to the KVM switch. The KVM switch is connected to both Computer 1's secondary display and Computer 2's primary display. Thus toggling the switch either displays Computer 1's contiguous view across the entire table, or Computer 1 and 2's view in the corresponding split views. The orientation of the projected image is adjusted so that it is the right way up for the seated viewer. This manual switching process is automated, where we use Phidgets [4] to programmatically control the KVM switch. A person uses simple voice commands "split view mode" or "shared view mode" to transition between the two.

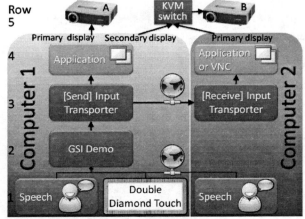

Figure 6. The SVT Infrastructure

Detecting touch input from multiple people. The DiamondTouch provides the necessary multi-user simultaneous touch input [2], as well as a reliable way to uniquely identify which person belongs to each touch. This is necessary to disambiguate who is doing what in our SVT environment. Both DiamondTouch surfaces are connected to a single DiamondTouch hardware controller board that has modified firmware to handle the larger board size. To the end programmer, the Double DiamondTouch appears as a single large DiamondTouch surface. All its input is sent to a single computer (Computer 1 in Figure 6), where a driver on that computer receives that input so that it can be used in application development.

Detecting speech input from multiple people. We used the technique described in [17][18] to gather simultaneous speech input. Two Labtec LVA 7330 noise cancelling microphones are each connected to off the shelf speech recognition software. Recognized speech is then sent to a single computer for further processing (Computer 1 in Figure 6).

5.2   Software

Software is built atop GSI Demo [17], a system originally developed for a single display multimodal tabletop surface (Figure 6, row 2. With GSI Demo, people program by demonstration to map speech and gesture actions onto keyboard and mouse events for multiple people. After training, GSI Demo listens for people's speech and gesture commands, and invokes the appropriate mouse/keyboard counterpart.

Processing input. We consolidate the speech and gesture input of multiple people to a single computer so that we can process it more easily. This makes some tasks, such as turn taking management, much easier. Figure 6 shows the SVT software infrastructure behind this. Input from multiple microphones and the Double DiamondTouch (Row 1) are eventually received by the single computer using GSI Demo (Row 2). GSI Demo then plays back the appropriate keyboard/mouse actions as if the user had entered them [17] (Row 4).

As an aside, the original GSI Demo was developed for adding multimodal input atop a single display. In multimodal SVT, GSI Demo now mediates input and output from multiple computers. To do this, it uses the distributed shared dictionary data structure provided by the GroupLab Collabrary [1] to send and received speech and gesture input to the appropriate computer (Figure 3, Row 3). Events sent include: speech volume /recognition/hypothesis; gesture down/move/up events.

Mapping input to screen coordinates. The raw input coordinates of a gesture cannot be used directly, as input is provided in table coordinates. This differs

from the screen coordinates for either computer. For example, the top left of Computer 1's display does not correspond to the top left of the table. To solve this, we created input mapping rules that convert gesture coordinates into screen coordinates. These rules consider the orientation, resolution and size of each display. In particular, the input transporter (Figure 6, Row 3) uses a configuration file to set the seating arrangement, display and software configuration. Using this information, all transported input is converted to screen coordinates for each computer using a simple linear transformation.

Mapping speech / gesture to keyboard / mouse events. To implement screen sharing, the input transporter creates a VNC-like system [11], where it sends screen snapshots captured by the GroupLab Collabrary [1] every 100 milliseconds to all client computers (Figure 6, Row 4). All input is serialized by the input transporter, and this is passed on as keyboard / mouse events to the computer running the single application. GSI Demo also includes several turn-taking protocols that mitigates interference when people try two work simultaneously [3][17][19].

For both true groupware and independent applications configurations, the appropriate speech / gesture map is loaded onto each machine. Input for each computer is then managed as if it originates from each of the DiamondTouch surfaces that correspond to a particular computer, i.e., input from a particular view is passed onto the appropriate computer running the groupware instance or independent application.

In all cases, the single user applications shown in Figure 6, Row 4 receive simulated keyboard and mouse events and are completely oblivious to the use of speech, gestures and transported input.

Handling input across the seam. The Input Transporter API lets a programmer map custom actions onto drag or touch actions across boundaries. For example, if two desktop systems are running, the programmer can create a mapping that detects if a file is dragged across the boundary, and then invoke a 'copy file' onto the desktop of the other computer.

6. Related Work

There is a long history of research in distributed groupware [5][6], shared screen systems [3][9], single display groupware [15], large digital tables and displays [2][12][16][20] and multimodal interaction [19]. However, several works stand out in regards to multimodal split view tabletops.

Within screen sharing context, turn-taking protocols in distributed shared screen applications [3] and more recently in the large display SDG setting [16][19] regulate and limit how one person can interfere with another's activity. Simultaneous interaction with existing applications can be simulated if commands are combined into unitary chunks and then interleaved with others. This has been done in various SDG systems using PDAs [10] and multiple mice [15].

There are other systems related to split screen tables [12]. Within the gaming world, there are a plethora of multi user console and arcade games that split a single screen, where each person works in their own view. Unlike our generalized solution, these games are typically implemented as special-purpose true groupware. Within office productivity world, many applications let its user split a document into two independently scrollable views. Almost all are limited to a single point of input, although Li et al. [9] produced an application that could leverage a split view for multi user simultaneous input. Sing, Gupta and Toyama (of Microsoft Research India, research.microsoft.com/research/tem/) split a single computer display vertically: each person independently works on their half using their own keyboard and mouse (equivalent to independent applications).

Finally, two separate personal devices can be connected into a single display. With Connectables [16], two people move their small tablet displays into close proximity: sensors notice this and combine them into a shared workspace [16]. Alternately, force sensors detect what sides of two tablets bump against each other, and use that information to combine and adjust the orientation of the view automatically [8].

7. Conclusion

We explored the design space of multimodal split view tabletop interaction over existing single user applications. We also offered a generalized approach to leveraging three types of existing software in SVT: independent views, shared screens and true groupware. We also added multimodal input as a way to promote awareness between collaborators. Three proof-of-concept systems illustrate how this works in practice.

We do not expect multimodal SVT to replace conventional single view digital tables. Rather, it offers alternate configuration that could be used as particular situations warrant it. In the future we plan to explore the Split View tabletop concept for groups of three or more and examine its use in a practical setting.

8. References

[1] Boyle, M. and Greenberg, S. (2005) Rapidly Prototyping Multimedia Groupware. *Proc. Distributed Multimedia Systems '05*, Knowledge Systems Institute.

[2] Dietz, P.H.; Leigh, D.L., (2001) DiamondTouch: A Multi-User Touch Technology, *Proc ACM UIST'01*.

[3] Greenberg, S. (1990). Sharing views and interactions with single-user applications. *Proc ACM/IEEE Conference on Office Information Systems*, 227-237.

[4] Greenberg, S., Fitchett, C. (2001) Phidgets: Easy Development of Physical Interfaces through Physical Widgets. *Proc. UIST '01*, ACM Press, 209-218.

[5] Greenberg, S., Gutwin, C., and Roseman, M. (1996). Semantic Telepointers for Groupware. *Proc OzCHI '96*, IEEE Computer Society Press. 54-61.

[6] Gutwin, C., and Greenberg, S. (2004) The importance of awareness for team cognition in distributed collaboration. In E. Salas, S. Fiore (Eds) *Team Cognition: Understanding the Factors that Drive Process and Performance*, APA Press, 177-201.

[7] Hall, E. (1966) *The Hidden Dimension.* Anchor Books

[8] Hinckley, K. (2003) Synchronous Gestures for Multiple Users and Computers, *Proc. ACM UIST '03*.

[9] Li, D. and Lu, J. (2006) A lightweight approach to transparent sharing of familiar single-user editors. *Proc. CSCW '06*. ACM Press, 139-148.

[10] Myers, B., Stiel, H., and Gargiulo, R. (1998): Collaborations using multiple PDAs connected to a PC. *Proc ACM CSCW'98*, ACM Press. 285-294.

[11] Richardson, T., Stafford-Frasser, Q., Wood, K. and Hopper, A. (1998) Virtual network Computing. *IEEE Internet Computing*, 2(1), 33-38.

[12] Rogers, Y. and Lindley, S. (2004) Collaborating around vertical and horizontal large interactive displays: which way is best? Interacting with Computers (16), 1133-1152. Elsevier.

[13] Somer, R., (1969) *Personal Space: The Behavioural Basis of Design, Spectrum*, ISBN 0-13-657577-3.

[14] Stefik, M., Bobrow, D., Foster, G., Lanning, S., Tatar, D. (1987) WYSIWIS revisited: early experiences with multiuser interfaces. *ACM TOIS*, 5(2), 147–167.

[15] Stewart, J., Bederson, B., Druin, A. (1999) Single display groupware: A model for co-present collaboration. *ACM CHI'99*, 286-293.

[16] Tandler, P., Prante, T., Müller-Tomfelde, C., Streitz, N., Steinmetz, R. (2001) Connectables: dynamic coupling of displays for the flexible creation of shared workspaces. *Proc. UIST '01*, ACM Press, 11-20.

[17] Tse, E., Greenberg, S. and Shen, C. (2006) GSI DEMO: Multiuser Gesture / Speech Interaction over Digital Tables by Wrapping Single User Applications. *Proc. ICMI'06*, ACM Press. 76-83.

[18] Tse, E., Shen, C., Greenberg, S. and Forlines, C. (2007) How Pairs Interact Over a Multi*modal Digital Table. Proc. ACM CHI '07, ACM Pre*ss.

[19] Tse, E., Shen, C., Greenberg, S. and Forlines, C. (2006) Enabling Interaction with Single User Applications through Speech and Gestures on a Multi-User Tabletop. *Proc. AVI'06*, ACM Press. 336-343.

[20] Wigdor, D., Balakrishnan, R. (2005). Empirical investigation into the effect of orientation on text readability in tabletop displays. *Proc. ECSCW '05*.

Going Deeper: a Taxonomy of 3D on the Tabletop

Tovi Grossman, Daniel Wigdor

Department of Computer Science, University of Toronto

{ tovi | dwigdor } @ dgp.toronto.edu

Abstract

Extending the tabletop to the third dimension has the potential to improve the quality of applications involving 3D data and tasks. Recognizing this, a number of researchers have proposed a myriad of display and input metaphors. However a standardized and cohesive approach has yet to evolve. Furthermore, the majority of these applications and the related research results are scattered across various research areas and communities, and lack a common framework.

In this paper, we survey previous 3D tabletops systems, and classify this work within a newly defined taxonomy. We then discuss the design guidelines which should be applied to the various areas of the taxonomy. Our contribution is the synthesis of numerous research results into a cohesive framework, and the discussion of interaction issues and design guidelines which apply. Furthermore, our work provides a clear understanding of what approaches have been taken, and exposes new routes for potential research, within the realm of interactive 3D tabletops.

1. Introduction

Horizontal, direct touch tabletops, which overlay large display and input surfaces, have recently been the focus of numerous studies. As the display and interaction surface of the typical tabletop display is 2D, the majority of this increasingly large body of work has focused on 2D applications and 2D interactions. However, the tasks which we carry out on physical tables are commonly three-dimensional in nature. It is thus desirable to consider how such tasks could be carried out and supported by interactive tabletop systems.

Example applications are numerous: A team of doctors could plan a surgery with a 3D virtual representation of a patient's body; an architect could inspect a virtual 3D model of a new building and its surrounding area before creating a physical model; a new car model could be displayed and annotated in a design studio before a 1-to-1 scale physical clay model is built. Given the inherent 3D nature of such applications, it would seem appropriate that designers consider 3D display, input, and interaction technologies.

A number of projects have extended the tabletop to the third dimension, using a wide variety of techniques and technologies. However, the majority of these applications and the related research results are scattered across various research areas and communities, such as interactive 3D graphics, virtual reality, augmented reality, and tangible user interfaces. An interface designer creating a 3D tabletop application is thus left with the challenging endeavour of sorting through the previous work to help make appropriate design decisions. In an effort to alleviate this problem, it is our goal to review and classify the previous work in interaction with 3D tabletops, in an attempt to provide insights for future applications and research.

In this paper, we provide an extensive review of the previous work done with interactive 3D tabletops and present a taxonomy which unifies this research into a single cohesive framework. We then discuss interesting areas of the taxonomy which have yet to be explored, along with a set of general interaction issues and design guidelines which are applicable within this framework.

1.1 Interactive 3D tabletops

While interactive tabletop research tends to focus on 2D applications and interactions, significant research has also examined 3D tabletop systems. Often such systems diverge from the typical tabletop setting, and thus may not be referred to as tabletop systems.

For the purpose of our work, we consider an interactive 3D tabletop system as any system which presents a 3D virtual environment on or above a horizontal surface. Furthermore, we do not limit our considerations to any specific interaction metaphors. While the majority of tabletop systems provide direct-touch interaction, systems using indirect touch and supplementary input devices have also been explored, so we consider similar systems for 3D tabletops.

It is our goal to review and categorize such systems to provide future researchers with a clear understanding of what has been done and what can be done in the realm of interactive 3D tabletops. In the following section we review the 3D tabletop platforms and applications which have been developed. Following this literature review we will categorize the previous systems into a taxonomy of interactive 3D tabletops.

0-7695-3013-3/07 $25.00 © 2007 IEEE
DOI 10.1109/TABLETOP.2007.18

2. Existing technologies

In this section we review the existing technologies used to implement 3D tabletops.

2.1 Two-dimensional tabletop technologies

The most basic implementation of a 3D tabletop system uses a 2D tabletop display. Such systems typically display two-dimensional imagery atop a multi-touch input device. Although the underpinnings of such surfaces stem from the early 1980's [33], there has been a recent slew of technologies employed for multi-touch input on a tabletop [12],[23],[42],[48],[58],[57]. While most commonly such systems are used for 2D applications, they can be used for interacting with 3D data. Roomplanner allows users to interact with floor plans, using an orthographic top-view projection [59]. The ActiveDesk is a large scale drafting table which designers can work in a similar method to a traditional drafting table [7]. More recently, Hancock et al. explored "shallow depth" interactions for 3D using a 2D tabletop [24].

2.2 Stereoscopic technologies

With the use of stereoscopic technologies, the imagery presented by a 2D tabletop displays can be perceived as "popping out" of the table, potentially providing the user with a more realistic 3D experience. For example, the ImmersaDesk [11] is a large scale drafting table which provides stereoscopic images. Users wear shutter glasses, and their viewing location is tracked so that the imagery is coupled with the user's viewpoint, providing a depth cue known as motion parallax. The user interacts with the imagery using a wand tracked in 3D. A similar platform is the responsive workbench, a virtual working environment that provides virtual objects and control tools on a physical "workbench" [1],[30]. Users collaborate around the workbench, with shutter glasses and head tracking providing a non-immersive virtual environment. The virtual workbench is a smaller implementation, which also presents 3D imagery using shutter glasses [39]. However with the virtual workbench, the display is actually above the perceived location of the tabletop and facing down. The user looks through and interacts behind a half-mirror.

2.3 Augmented and virtual reality

In virtual reality systems, head mounted displays are commonly used to immerse the user in a 3D environment [8]. While head mounted virtual reality environments tend to be large areas which the user can explore, some systems use head mounted displays for table centric spaces, such as in surgical procedures [18].

A less immersive alternative, which allows the user to maintain the context of their surrounding environment, is to use a head mounted augmented reality display [15]. Such displays have been used for tabletop interactions, such as in VITA, a system supporting offsite visualization of an archaeological dig [6], which displays 3D imagery above a direct-touch tabletop. Another method of augmenting a physical workspace is to place a transparent projection screen between the viewer and the table, as in ASTOR, where virtual labels appeared alongside physical objects [35].

2.4 Tabletop spatially augmented reality

The augmented reality systems described in the previous subsection augment the physical world by placing virtual imagery on a viewing plane. In this section we described systems which augment the physical world by projecting imagery directly on to physical objects. Such systems have been termed "Tabletop spatially augmented reality" [40]. An advantage of such systems is that supplementary hardware devices, such as glasses and head mounted displays, are not required. A disadvantage is that the display space is constrained to the surface of objects.

Illuminating Clay [38] and Sandscape [52] are two examples of tabletop spatially augmented reality systems. In these systems, users interact with physical clay and sand, with the deformations being sensed in real time, and virtual imagery being projected on to the surface. In URP, [50] physical architectural placed on a workbench are augmented with dynamic virtual imagry projected on to the scence. With tablescape plus [28], animated objects are projected on to small, vertical planes which can be moved around the table.

2.5 Three-dimensional volumetric displays

Volumetric displays present imagery in true 3D space, by illuminating "voxels" (volumetric pixels) in midair. Favalora provides a thorough survey of the various technological implementations of volumetric displays [14]. The true 3D imagery in volumetric displays has been shown to improve depth perception [19] and shape recognition [43].

Besides providing true 3D images, the main difference from the other 3D tabletops displays is that volumetric display are generally enclosed by a surface. This means that users cannot directly interact with the 3D imagery. Balakrishnan et al. explored the implications of this unique difference to interaction design by using physical mockups [4]. More recent working implementations have allowed users to interact with the display by using hand and finger gestures on and above the display surface [21], and by using a hand-held six degree-of-freedom input device [20].

3. Taxonomy

We have provided an overview of the existing 3D tabletop display technologies. As discussed, a number of implementations have been explored, each with their own benefits and drawbacks. However many of these research results are scattered across various research areas, without any overall organization. Complicating the matter is that while all of the work fits our description of a 3D tabletop research, many of the results were not intended to be considered tabletop research. In some cases the interactive tabletop research area had yet to be recognized. Such work may be overlooked when tabletop researchers start considering approaches for 3D applications.

With the outlined previous work in mind, we now define a taxonomy of the various implementations of interactive 3D tabletops. Our hope is to help future researchers understand the possible design space of interactive 3D tabletops, clarify which aspects of the design space have been explored, and expose possible implementations which have yet to be considered. This taxonomy will also serve as a basis for a discussion of specific interaction issues and design guidelines applicable to the various areas of the taxonomy, which we will provide in Section 4. Our taxonomy is organized into 3 main areas: display properties, input properties, and physical properties (Figure 1).

3.1 Display properties

The first main area of the taxonomy is the display properties. We consider the perceived and actual display spaces, along with the correlation between the user's viewpoint and the provided viewpoint of the imagery.

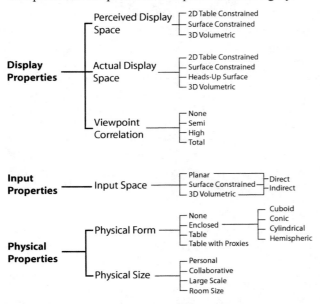

Figure 1. Taxonomy of interactive 3D tabletops.

3.1.1 Perceived display space.
The perceived display space is defined as the possible spatial locations for which displayed imagery can exist based on stereoscopic depth cues.

2D Table Constrained: In a traditional 2D tabletop display, the display space is 2D. Even when 3D imagery is displayed using a perspective projection on the table [24], we still consider the display space to be 2D if no stereoscopic depth cues are provided.

Surface Constrained: In tabletop spatially augmented displays, imagery is projected onto the table surface *and* physical proxies. We term the resulting display space as surface constrained. While the displayed imagery exists in 3D space, the imagery itself is 2D.

3D Volumetric: When stereo cues are provided, via a head mounted display, shutter glasses, or a volumetric display, the perceived display space is truly 3D.

3.1.2 Actual display space.
The actual display space considers where the actual displayed imagery exists. While this property is not meant to impact the user's perception of the imagery, it has been shown to affect the user's depth perception [19] and performance in three-dimensional tasks [53]. It is also an important property to consider as it will affect overall experiences and interaction affordances [8].

2D Table Constrained: In a tradition tabletop setup, the actual display space is also the 2D table itself. In systems where users wear stereo shutter glasses, the actual display space is also constrained to the table, even through the user perceives 3D imagery.

Surface Constrained: In the spatially augmented reality applications, which project imagery onto physical proxies, the actual display space is constrained to surfaces on and above the table. Although the actual display space exists in 3D, we do not consider it to be truly 3D or volumetric, since imagery cannot exist anywhere in the working volume.

Heads-Up Surface: When the actual display space is on a surface between the user and table, we term the display space as Heads-up-Surface. This is the case when using a head mounted display, or when virtual imagery is projected on a see-through display plane.

3D Volumetric: When imagery can appear anywhere on or above the display, the display space is *3D volumetric*. Currently, volumetric displays are the only technology with this capability.

3.1.3 Viewpoint correlation.
When we move our heads in the physical world our viewpoints change, which affects the visual images which we receive. The last property of the display which we consider is the range of viewpoints which can be obtained of the imagery by physically moving around the display. For this property, there are no discrete values; we categorize the technologies based on 4 magnitudes.

None: In a traditional tabletop set up, the user's viewpoint is independent of the displayed imagery. The displayed image is static, regardless of the users viewing location.

Semi: In some systems, such as spatially multiplexed autostereoscopic displays [13], a limited number of viewpoints are provided. With such systems, the transitions from one viewpoint to the next can be choppy, but the basic motion parallax effect is provided.

High: High viewpoint correlation means that the viewpoint of the virtual imagery continuously changes with the user's viewing location, with limited exceptions. This can be achieved with a standard 2D display and tracking the user's head, or by using a volumetric display. The expectation with such technologies is when the user moves below the horizontal plane of the table. In this case, the user will see the bottom of the table, not the bottom of the imagery on top of the table. This is also the case when working with a physical table.

Total: When using a head mounted display to create a virtual reality tabletop experience, total correlation between the user's viewpoint and the displayed imagery can be achieved. Without the presence of a physical table, users could potentially view imagery from below the horizontal plane of the virtual table.

3.2 Input Properties

An important consideration for 3D tabletop displays is how the user interacts with the displayed imagery. A full categorization of input technologies and techniques is beyond the scope of the paper, and we refer the reader to relevant previous literature [26]. For the purpose of our taxonomy, we only consider the input space.

3.2.1 Input space. The input space is defined as the physical location where the user can provide input. This property is important because it will impact the type of interaction techniques and usage metaphors which must be made available.

As we have seen, in the 2D realm, tabletops typically overlay input and display devices for direct-touch input. When working in 3D, this may no longer be feasible for three reasons: first, virtual objects may be perceived above the display plane, and thus cannot be "touched" by touching the display surface; second, display technologies may impair the ability to reach within the volume; and third, objects may simply not be within reach of the user. Clearly, the adaptation of the direct-touch input paradigm to the third dimension is not a simple one. The following lists input spaces which have been considered:

Direct 2D: The most common form of input with tabletop displays is direct 2D input, where the user can directly touch and interact with the displayed imagery.

Indirect 2D: Indirect 2D input is useful when the display space is larger than the user's reach. Implementations include mapping a small local area of the display as the input space to the entire display surface [41], or by using a mouse or similar supplementary device [17],[37].

Direct Surface Constrained: In the spatially augmented reality systems where the virtual imagery is constrained to the surface of physical objects, interaction could also be constrained to those surfaces. For example, a user could add virtual paint to a physical object by using a physical brush tracked in 3D space.

Indirect Surface Constrained: Interaction can be surface constrained and indirect if an intermediate interaction surface is present. Such is the case with a volumetric display, where the display enclosure can act as a touch sensitive surface [21].

Direct 3D: When the user can directly reach into the virtual imagery and grab objects in 3D space, the interaction is direct 3D. This is a common input metaphor in virtual reality environments, and is also possible in systems using stereo glasses.

Indirect 3D: In some virtual environments, the input is 3D, but indirect interaction techniques are provided. This is necessary when objects are out of the users reach [34]. Indirect 3D interaction can also be used in volumetric displays, to overcome the physical surface between the user and displayed imagery [20].

3.3 Physical properties

The last area of our taxonomy is the physical properties of the display. This is an important factor as it will affect how the user will interact with the display. Most relevant to the interactions is the physical properties of the actual work area, or perceived display space, and not the display hardware.

3.3.1 Physical form. The physical form refers to the physical shape of the system. This property may affect possible input spaces, and required input mappings.

None: In head-mounted VR displays, the entire environment is virtual, so the work area has no physical form at all.

Enclosed: Most volumetric displays have an enclosed physical form, to protect the user form the mechanics of the display. Various shapes of this enclosure have been proposed, including cuboid, conic, cylindrical, and hemispheric.

Table: In a typical tabletop setting, or a tabletop using stereo shutter-glasses, the physical form consists of the planar table surface.

Table with Proxies: In spatially augmented tabletops, the physical form is defined by the table and the location and shape of the addition physical proxies.

3.3.2 Physical size. The other important factor relevant to physical properties is the size of the display. The affect of size has been discussed in the 2D tabletop literature [44], and we expect that similar issues will be present in 3D tabletop displays. We categorize sizes by what users can reach and what they can see, as these will be critical factors in the design of interfaces. While the definitions consider the areas within the reach of the user, it does not necessarily imply that the technology actually allows the user to reach into the display.

Personal: A personal sized 3D Tabletop display is small enough that the user can easily reach the entire display area.

Collaborative: With a collaborative sized display, a user can easily reach the *center* of the display. Such display sizes, for 2D tabletops, are generally meant for multiple users, so that between each user, the entire display space is accessible [44].

Large Scale: We define a large scale 3D tabletop display as being too big for a user to reach the center of the display. This means that even with multiple users, there will be areas inaccessible via direct touch interaction. However the display is small enough that users can easily see and interpret all areas of the displayed imagery.

Room Size: A room sized display would take up the entire space of a room. This means that there will be areas that the user cannot reach, and also areas that the user cannot easily see.

3.4 Taxonomy application

One of the contributions of the taxonomy which we have presented is that it classifies the work which has been done into a cohesive framework. By examining where the existing technologies fall within this taxonomy, we can provide insights on what areas of research have been thoroughly explored, and what areas have been given less attention. Furthermore, by combining the various properties of the taxonomy in different ways, we can propose new and interesting 3D tabletop system implementations which have yet to be explored. Table 1 shows one such combination.

This particular arrangement of parameters allows us to focus on combinations of technologies, so that we might examine platforms for past and future development. As is immediately evident, some technologies have received more focus than others, while others have received almost no attention. A discussion of all areas is not within the scope of this paper: we will now review a few of the more compelling cells of this view of our taxonomy.

3.4.1 Planar input to 2D display (cells 1,2). Cell 1 represents the large collection of 2D tabletop research which has been described previously [7],[24],[59],

while cell 2 includes the multitude of 2D tabletop displays which were augmented with stereo viewing [1],[11],[29],[39]. This has defined the baseline for research in 3D tabletops, though we hope to expand that focus.

Table 1. Three parameters of our taxonomy: *Perceived Display Space, Input Space,* **and** *Actual Display Space.* **Light grey cells are unexplored. Dark grey cells are impractical.**

Perceived Display Space		Actual Display Space			
	Input Space	2D Table	2D Heads Up	3D Surface Const.	3D Volume
2D	2D Planar	#1	#3		
	Surface-Const.				
	Volumetric				
3D Surface	2D Planar			#4	
	Surface Const.			#5	
	Volumetric			#6	
3D Volume	2D Planar	[11]	[6]	#7	#10
	Surface Const.			#8	[21]
	Volumetric	#2	[6] [35]	#9	[20]

3.4.2 Heads-up display of 2D (cell 3). Without a tabletop, this cell might describe various augmented reality projects. We are not aware, however, of any use of heads-up displays to augment a tabletop with 2D imagery. Although perhaps not as compelling as some of the 3D uses of this technology (from cell 2), heads-up displays for 2D tabletops might allow for interesting mixes of public and private information [59], and differentiate the view of each user [1], advantageous for reasons described by Matsuda et al. [32].

3.4.3 Surface constrained 3D (cells 4-6). Cells 5 and 6 include a number of projects which project imagery onto 3D surfaces. These projects include methods which limit input to moving objects around on the surface of the table [28] (cell 4), those which constrain it to the surfaces of 3D objects [38],[52] (cell 5), and those that allow unconstrained input [40],[50] (cell 6). The taxonomy allows for a quick distinction between these works, while also identifying an unexplored area (cell 4): the use of planar input to surface-constrained display areas. Such systems could provide interesting mappings between input and display spaces, such as manipulating objects by interacting with their shadows [25].

3.4.4 Stereo spatial augmentation (cells 7-9). These cells represent an as-of-yet unexplored use of 3D for tabletops. It describes a concept similar to both Sandscape [52] and Illuminating Clay [38], in that it would involve projecting onto the surface of 3D objects. However, with the addition of shutter glasses the system could present imagery which diverges from the structure of the physical proxies. With the current tabletop spatially augmented systems this is not possible. Such systems could be useful for scenarios where users view 3D models, and also want the ability to make minor adjustments to the structure.

3.4.5 Planar input with volumetric displays (cell 10). This currently unexplored cell represents interacting with volumetric displays using traditional 2D input methods. This could be interesting to explore, since the input configuration could support standard desktop interactions which users are already familiar with.

4. Interaction issues and design guidelines

Due to the lack of a unified framework, previously interaction issues related to 3D tabletop systems have been discussed based on specific point designs and implementations. Similarly, the design decisions gone into the development 3D tabletops system, have been made on a one-by-one basis for each technological implementation. An intended contribution of our work is to be able to discuss interaction issues, and design guidelines for 3D tabletop systems at a higher level, independent of the specific implementation, based solely on where systems exist within the taxonomy. In this section, we present some of these generalized interaction issues and design guidelines.

4.1 Caveats in increasing perceived display space

In our taxonomy we discuss 3 possible perceived display spaces, with 3D volumetric being at highest level. The motivation to diverge from a 2D perceived display space is to improve the user's perception of the 3D environment, and in some cases to provide a more realistic simulation. While research has shown that introducing stereoscopic cues can improve a user's ability to carry out 3D tasks [53], designers should be careful before deciding upon the display configuration.

First, with the exception of autostereoscopic displays, providing a perceived 3D scene means introducing supplementary hardware, such as shutter glasses or head mounted displays. Such devices can be uncomfortable, reduce the ubiquity of the system (as they will no longer be walk-up-and-use), and can cause the user to lose the context of their surrounding environment or collaborators [8],[19].

Furthermore, when the perceived display space is inconsistent with the actual display space, the depth cues which the human brain receives become inconsistent. Most critical is the discrepancy between the accommodation and convergence cues, as this has been known to cause asthenopia in some users [36]. Symptoms associated with this condition include dizziness, headaches, nauseas, and eye fatigue.

A more subtle issue is that when the actual display space is 2D table constrained and the perceived display space is 3D volumetric, there is actually a constraint on the perceived display space. Because the user is seeing pixels on the surface of the display, it would be impossible to perceive imagery that is above the user's line of sight to the back of the display. This means that the perceivable display space is actually triangular in shape – the further away the imagery is to the user, to less height it can have. As a result, such a configuration would not be very appropriate for applications where tall objects will appear, such as the architectural design of a high rise building.

The display configurations unaffected by these limitations are 2D tabletop systems, spatially augmented reality tabletop systems, and volumetric displays. These configurations should be considered if the designer foresees the discussed limitations as being problematic.

4.2 Losing discrete input and tactile feedback

Increasing the input space to 3D, whether it is direct or indirect, allows users to directly specify and manipulate objects in 3D space. However, there are a number of drawbacks of this input paradigm.

One problem is that discrete contact-to-surface events, which are typically used to trigger events in 2D tabletop interfaces, do not occur. As such, designers must provide interactions to execute discrete events. One possibility is to use free-hand gestures [5], such as a gun gesture to perform selections [21]. The alternative is to have the user hold an input device which has buttons that can be used to execute the discrete events.

Second, when interacting in midair, the user loses the tactile feedback present when interacting on 2D surfaces. This is problematic as sensory feedback is considered to be essential when interacting in 3D spaces [27]. Some explored solutions include bimanual input, physical proxies, and force feedback devices [27].

We refer the reader to Hinckley's survey paper on "spatial input" for a thorough discussion of other associated difficulties and possible solutions [27]. Due to these difficulties, designers should consider planar or surface constrained input, even if the technological implementation can support a 3D input space.

4.3 Mapping 2D input to 3D space

If planar or surface constrained input is being used, then the system needs a way to map two degrees-of-freedom interactions into 3D space. An exception is if no three degrees-of-freedom tasks are required in the application, such as the case for shallow depth interactions [24]. Otherwise, with only two degrees-of-freedom input, tasks such as moving an object to a point in 3D space must be carried out sequentially. A number of interactions have been developed to support 3D interactions with 2D input, such as three dimensional widgets [10]. Other possible approaches are to use supplementary input streams for added degrees-of-freedom, such as using a mouse scroll wheel [51], mouse tilt [2], or pressure [9] to define depth during interactions. Another way to increase the degrees-of-freedom is to use bimanual interactions [3].

4.4 Indirect interactions may be required

While there are tradeoffs to using direct and indirect interactions in 3D tabletop applications, there are some cases where we would strongly suggest that indirect interactions be provided. Obviously if the input space is indirect, then indirect interaction techniques must be provided. Furthermore, when the physical form of the system is enclosed, then the interaction space must be indirect. Lastly, when the physical size is large scale or room size, then indirect interactions are required to make all areas of the display accessible.

One possible indirect interaction technique is to use a virtual cursor, which has a positional offset form the user's hand or handheld input device [34]. Another technique commonly used in VR applications is a ray cursor, which acts like a virtual laser pointer being emitted from the users hand [31]. This approach has also been used in 2D tabletop systems [37], and studied within volumetric displays [20]. The use of physically "flicking" objects to move them to inaccessible areas has also been investigated [41].

4.5 Providing navigation and visual aids

The transition from 2D to 3D necessitates a series of changes in the way navigation is handled and visualized. For example, in systems which lack viewpoint correlation of 3D imagery, a mechanism will be required to allow for the viewpoint to be changed. Conversely, in those systems which do provide some correlation of viewpoint to head position, visualization of the automatic change of viewpoint may be required to overcome orientation effects.

This is equally true as the perceived or actual space grows beyond the tabletop: in room sized displays, mechanisms to allow the user to see distant imagery may be required.

4.6 Lessons from 2D

Each of the above guidelines were derived through categorization and examination of efforts already expended in 3D tabletop systems. Here we describe lessons already learned by researchers of traditional tabletops, which may need to be re-examined when moving to 3D.

4.6.1 Common, shared display and input area. Various research efforts have uncovered behaviours of both individuals and groups using tables and interacting with either physical or virtual objects. These include user territoriality [45], effects of group and table size [44], closeness [32], and the use of orientation for communication [29]. As tables move to 3D, several of these issues may increase in prominence, and new issues may arise.

4.6.2 Varied point of view. With users seated around all sides of a tabletop, each participant receives a distinctly different view of information on the display. As such, traditional desktop interfaces, which assume a particular orientation, are clearly inappropriate for these displays. A great deal of research has gone into the effects of orientation on group interaction [30],[45],[49] and perception [16],[54],[56], and interfaces to help overcome or exploit these issues [16],[47]. Naturally, with 3D tabletops, this problem is much more severe, since the rotation of objects can be in any of three orientations, and in fact faces of 3D objects may be completely invisible to some users. Early work describing this issue with text readability found interesting results [22], but further is required.

5. Conclusions

In this paper, we have introduced a taxonomy of 3D tabletop systems. This taxonomy categorizes 3D tabletops based on their display, input and physical properties. A contribution of this taxonomy is that it allows us to organize previous research into a single high-level framework. Furthermore, it allows us to identify combinations of the discussed properties which have yet to be explored.

Evident from the large body of work in 3D tabletops is that they are a compelling platform for future development. It is our hope that, through the creation of the taxonomy, we will inspire and aid further development in this domain.

6. Acknowledgements

We thank Andy Wilson, members of the Dynamic Graphics Project at University of Toronto, and members of the Mitsubishi Electronic Research Laboratories.

7. References

[1] Agrawala, M. et al. (1997). The two-user Responsive Workbench: support for collaboration through individual views of a shared space. *Comp. Graphics and Interactive techniques*. p. 327-332.

[2] Balakrishnan, R. et al. (1997). The Rockin'Mouse: Integral 3D manipulation on a plane. *CHI*. p. 311-318.

[3] Balakrishnan, R. and Kurtenbach, G. (1999). Exploring bimanual camera control and object manipulation in 3D graphics interfaces. *CHI*. p. 56-62.

[4] Balakrishnan, R. et al. (2001). User Interfaces for Volumetric Displays. *IEEE Computer*, 34(3). p. 37-45.

[5] Baudel, T. and Beaudouin-Lafon, M. (1993). Charade: remote control of objects using free-hand gestures. *Communications of the ACM*, 36(7). p. 28-35.

[6] Benko, H. et al. (2004). Collaborative Mixed Reality Visualization of an Archaeological Excavation. *The International Symposium on Mixed and Augmented Reality*. p. 132–140.

[7] Buxton, W. (1997). Living in augmented reality: Ubiquitous Media and Reactive Environments. *Video Mediated Communication*. p. 363-384.

[8] Buxton, W. and Fitzmaurice, G. (1998). HMD's, Caves, & Chameleon: A human centric analysis of interaction in virtual space. *Computer Graphics, The SIGGRAPH Quarterly*. p. 64-68.

[9] Cechanowicz, J. et al. (2007). Augmenting the Mouse with Pressure Based Input. *CHI*. p. 1385-1394.

[10] Conner, B.D. et al. (1992). Three-dimensional widgets. *Symposium on Interactive 3D graphics*. p. 183-188.

[11] Czernuszenko, M. et al (1997). The ImmersaDesk and infinity wall projection based virtual reality displays. *Computer Graphics*, 31(2). p. 46-49.

[12] Dietz, P. and Leigh, D. (2001). DiamondTouch: a multi-user touch technology. *UIST*. p. 219-226.

[13] Dodgson, N. (2005). Autostereoscopic 3D Displays. *IEEE Computer*, 38(8). p. 31-36.

[14] Favalora, G.E. (2005). Volumetric 3D Displays and Application Infrastructure. *IEEE Computer*, 38 (8). p. 37-44.

[15] Feiner, S. et al. (1993). Knowledge-based augmented reality. *Communications of the ACM*, 36(7). p. 53-62.

[16] Forlines, C. et al. (2006). Exploring the Effects of Group Size and Display Configuration on Visual Search. *CSCW*. p. 11-20.

[17] Forlines, C. et al. (2007). Direct-Touch vs. Mouse Input for Tabletop Displays. *CHI*. p. 647-656.

[18] Geis, W.P. (1996). Head-mounted video monitor for global visual access in mini-invasive surgery: an initial report. *Surgical Endoscopy*, 10(7). p. 768–770.

[19] Grossman, T. and Balakrishnan, R. (2006). An evaluation of depth perception on volumetric displays. *AVI*. p. 193-200.

[20] Grossman, T. and Balakrishnan, R. (2006). The design and evaluation of selection techniques for 3D volumetric displays. *UIST*. p. 3-12.

[21] Grossman, T. et al. (2004). Multi-finger gestural interaction with 3D volumetric displays. *UIST*. p. 61-70.

[22] Grossman, T. et al. (2007). Exploring and reducing the effects of orientation on text readability in volumetric displays. *CHI*. p. 483 - 492.

[23] Han, J. Y. (2005). Low-cost multi-touch sensing through frustrated total internal reflection. *UIST*. p. 115-118.

[24] Hancock., M. et al. (2007). Shallow-Depth 3D Interaction: Design and Evaluation of One-, Two- and Three-Touch Techniques. *CHI*. p. 1147-1156.

[25] Herndon, K, et al. (1992). Interactive shadows. *UIST*. p. 1-6.

[26] Hinckley, K. (2002). Input technologies and techniques. *The human-computer interaction handbook: fundamentals, evolving technologies and emerging applications*. p. 151-168.

[27] Hinckley, K. et al. (1994). A survey of design issues in spatial input. *UIST*. p. 213-222.

[28] Kakehi, Y. et al. (2006) Tablescape Plus: Upstanding Tiny Displays on Tabletop Display. *SIGGRAPH 2006*, Emerging Tech.

[29] Krueger, W. and Froehlich, B. (1994). The Responsive Workbench. *IEEE Comp. Graphics and Apps.*, 14(3). p. 12-15.

[30] Kruger, R. et al. (2003). How people use orientation on tables: comprehension, coordination and communication. *SIGGROUP*. p. 369-378.

[31] Liang, J. and Green, M. (1994). JDCAD: A highly interactive 3D modeling system. *Computers and Graphics*, 18(4). p. 499-506

[32] Matsuda, M. et al. (2006). Behavioral analysis of asymmetric information sharing on Lumisight table. *TableTop 2006*. p. 7-14.

[33] Mehta, N. (1982). *A Flexible Machine Interface*. M.A.Sc. Thesis, Electrical Engineering, University of Toronto.

[34] Mine, M. (1995). *Virtual environment interaction techniques*. UNC Chapel Hill Technical Report. TR95-018.

[35] Olwal, A. et al. (2005). ASTOR: An Autostereoscopic Optical See-through Augmented Reality System. *ISMAR*. p. 24-27.

[36] McCauley, M. and Sharkey, T. (1992). Cybersickness: perception of self-motion in virtual environments. *Presence: Teleoperators and Virtual Environments*, 1(3). p. 311-318.

[37] Parker, J. et al. (2005). TractorBeam: Seamless integration of remote and local pointing for tabletop displays. *Graphics Interface*. p. 33-40.

[38] Piper, B. et al. (2002). Illuminating clay: a 3-D tangible interface for landscape analysis. *CHI*. p. 355-362.

[39] Poston, T. and Serra, L. (1994). The virtual workbench: dextrous VR. *Virtual reality software and technology*. p.111-121.

[40] Raskar, R. et al. (1999). Table-Top Spatially-Augmented Reality: Bringing Physical Models to Life with Projected Imagery. *Augmented Reality*. p.64.

[41] Reetz, A. et al. (2006). Superflick: a natural and efficient technique for long-distance object placement on digital tables. *Graphics Interface*. p. 163-170.

[42] Rekimoto, J. (2002). SmartSkin: an infrastructure for freehand manipulation on interactive surfaces. *CHI*. p. 113-120.

[43] Rosen, P. et al. (2004). Perception of 3D spatial relations for 3D displays. *Stereoscopic Displays XI*. p. 9-16.

[44] Ryall, K. et al. (2004). Exploring the effects of group size and table size on interactions with tabletop shared-display groupware. *CSCW*. p. 284-293.

[45] Scott, S.D. et al. (2004). Territoriality in Collaborative Tabletop Workspaces. *CSCW 2004*. p. 294-303.

[46] Shen, C. et al. (2004). DiamondSpin: an extensible toolkit for around-the-table interaction. *CHI*. p. 167-174.

[47] Shen, C. (2006). Informing the design of direct-touch tabletops. *IEEE Computer Graphics and Applications*, (26)5. p. 36-46.

[48] Smart Technologies Inc. Digital Vision Touch Technology. http://www.smarttech.com/dvit/.

[49] Tang, J. (1991). Findings from observational studies of collaborative work. *Int. J. of Man-Machine Studies*, 34(2). p. 143-160.

[50] Underkoffler, J. and Ishii, H. (1999). Urp: a luminous-tangible workbench for urban planning and design. *CHI*. p. 386-393.

[51] Venolia, D. (1993). Facile 3D direct manipulation. *INTERCHI*. p. 31-36.

[52] Wang, Y. et al. Sandscape. 2002. http://tangible.media.mit.edu/projects/sandscape/

[53] Ware, C. and Franck, G. (1996). Evaluating stereo and motion cues for visualizing information nets in three dimensions, *ACM Transactions on Graphics*, 15 (2). p. 121-140.

[54] Wigdor, D. and Balakrishnan, R. (2005). Empirical Investigation into the Effect of Orientation on Text Readability in Tabletop Displays. *ECSCW*. p. 205-224.

[55] Wigdor, D. et al. (2006). Under the table interaction. *UIST*. p. 259-268.

[56] Wigdor, D. et al. (2007). Perception of Elementary Graphical Elements in Tabletop and Multi-Surface Environments. *CHI*. p. 473-482.

[57] Wilson, A. D. (2005). PlayAnywhere: a compact interactive tabletop projection-vision system. *UIST 2005*. p. 83-92.

[58] Wilson, A. D. (2004). TouchLight: an imaging touch screen and display for gesture-based interaction. *International Conference on Multimodal Interfaces*. p. 69-76.

[59] Wu, M. and Balakrishnan, R. (2003). Multi-finger and whole hand gestural interaction techniques for multi-user tabletop displays. *UIST 2003*. p. 193-202.

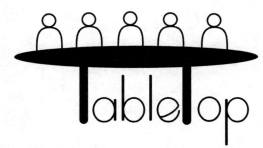

Inside & Out: Novel Tabletop Interactions and Infrastructure

Augmenting Mood Boards: Flexible and Intuitive Interaction in the Context of the Design Studio

Andrés Lucero, Dima Aliakseyeu, Jean-Bernard Martens
Department of Industrial Design, Eindhoven University of Technology, the Netherlands
{a.a.lucero, d.aliakseyeu, j.b.o.s.martens}@tue.nl

Figure 1: Browsing images on a coffee table using hand movements in the design studio.

Abstract

In our studies aimed at understanding design practice we have identified the creation of mood boards as a relevant task for designers. In this paper we introduce an interactive table that supports one part of the mood-board making process (i.e. image browsing) by providing flexible and intuitive interaction for designers in the context of their design studios. We propose an image browser that: 1) merges with the real context allowing designers to work in the comfort of their existing design studio environment, 2) captures the current flexibility of interaction with physical images by allowing designers to work using hand movements, and 3) provides an alternative solution to a cluttered desk and messy design studio by using the space above the table for interaction. Exploratory evaluations show that designers were able to use the system with no prior training, and to see a practical use of the proposed image browser in their design studios.

1. Introduction

The use of mood boards in the early stages of the design process is common practice for designers [6, 11]. Designers use mood boards to explore, communicate, and discuss ideas together with their clients. These boards can be created with different types of media although designers usually use images to say something about the target audience, product, and/or company they are designing for. Designers spend a great deal of time looking for such images in magazines.

Browsing magazines in search for images is one of the first steps of the mood-board making process. Designers prefer going through their large collections of magazines in a comfortable place where they can freely start creating ad-hoc piles of magazines and pictures, making a 'soft' pre-selection of images.

Designers end up with a large number of images taking up all available usable space in their design studios including tables, walls and floor (Figure 2). Space is not only limited to spreading images in the studio but also for storing magazines. Designers must throw away magazines in order to grow their collections with new material.

Desktop and digital systems provide solutions for displaying and storing large amounts of images, however they do not provide the conditions to browse and select images in a flexible way and in comfortable spaces for designers in their design studios.

In this paper we present an image browser (Figure 1) for designers that: 1) merges with the real context allowing designers to work in the comfort of their existing design studio environment, 2) captures the current flexibility of interaction with physical images by allowing designers to work using hand movements, and 3) provides an alternative solution to a cluttered desk and messy design studio by using the space above the table for interaction.

0-7695-3013-3/07 $25.00 © 2007 IEEE
DOI 10.1109/TABLETOP.2007.17

Figure 2. A designer's studio with images all over the place including the wall behind her.

2. Background

The field of human-computer interaction (HCI) has been investigating how people interact with computer systems at work (and more recently at home), trying to help them achieve their goals. Within HCI, researchers have started to see the potential behind tables as a more natural and familiar setting to design (collaborative) interactions around them. Some notable examples of interactive tables include the DigitalDesk [22], DiamondTouch [4], Sensetable [16], Lumisight [14], and more recently the Entertaible [9], and Microsoft's Surface [21]. Although initially research in this area was mostly driven by technology, we have slowly started to witness a user-perspective approach to tabletop, studying the needs and aspirations of users [2, 13], as well as their limitations [18].

The ID-MIX project [13] tries to assess the relevance and impact of augmented reality systems in work practice. The question the project tries to answer is if professional users (i.e. industrial designers) would change their current work practice favoring the use of an augmented reality system that supports their work.

Figure 3. A designer in her studio browsing images, seating on a couch by a coffee table.

We aimed at understanding design practice by systematically involving designers in user studies using different methods. In the first user study with ten industrial designers we used cultural probes [7] that allowed us to identify a relevant task: making mood boards. Since the probe study, we have conducted two further studies to get a better understanding of why designers use mood boards and how they create them. We did contextual inquiries [10] with Dutch industrial designers (n=4), and 'mood board interviews' with Finnish fashion and textile designers (n=10).

3. Augmenting mood boards

In these studies we identified several opportunities for 'augmenting' mood boards. The process of making mood boards can be divided into these five stages: 1) 'image collecting', 2) 'image browsing', 3) 'image piling', 4) 'building mood boards', and 5) 'expanding mood boards'.

3.1. Image collecting

Designers who use mood boards for their work are constantly collecting images. If they see something interesting, they collect it. They mostly use images from large-sized magazines printed on glossy paper that they find in magazine shops and bookstores, and from the Internet. Occasionally they will also use pictures from their private/personal collection or they will especially make pictures for a mood board at hand.

Adding images from the Internet to a digital table can be solved through different available options (i.e. network drive, USB stick). The same holds for pictures made with a digital camera that can be sent wirelessly to the system. The Cabinet system [11] has addressed the issue of adding images from physical magazines onto a digital table, thus breaking the divide between physical and digital. It photographs objects placed on the workspace and replaces them with a digital footprint in the same place.

3.2. Image browsing

Designers start looking for images that will help them build a story or say something about the target audience, product, or company they are designing for. Designers browse magazines, cutting out pictures from them and ending up with a large number of images, in a process that can take a considerable amount of time. Designers prefer going through their large collections of magazines in a comfortable place (Figure 3) where they can freely start creating ad-hoc piles of magazines and pictures, making a 'soft' pre-selection of images.

Figure 4. After making a soft-selection, designers end up with one large pile of images that they carry around with them.

Figure 5. Creating piles of images on a table. Labels are also created at this stage. The final selection of images is created.

Designers end up with a large pile of pre-selected images that they carry with them if they want to share its contents with colleagues for discussion (Figure 4).

3.3. Image piling

Once designers have collected enough images, they will 'categorize' their collections of images. For some of them it is a very structured personal process keeping images in boxes under labels (i.e. human, modern, kitchen, etc.). For others, the categories are looser, keeping the complete magazines arranged in a bookshelf according to brand, topic or theme, ready for later retrieval. In any case, be it a loose or structured categorization, these categories are very personal and make sense most of the time to the designer only.

Designers will start sorting their collection (Figure 5) by throwing images in categories (usually up to 30 images per concept). They will sometimes label the piles with notes. They also like the easiness of piling and arranging images within the pile. Growing piles create smaller piles and sub-piles can be mixed together in a simple way. Retrieving an image that they have seen before is as simple as going to the pile and getting the image. Once the piles are ready, they have an overview where they can see what they have and they can start thinking what they want to do (layout).

The creation as well as the handling of piles on digital tables has already been explored in recent systems such as Cabinet [11] where designers load images into the system and maintain workbooks of related images, with each workbook acting as a digital pile. We have also explored interaction with digital piles [1] identifying three basic tasks that must be supported by a digital pile (navigation, reorganization, and repositioning), and have proposed three interaction techniques that meet these requirements (DragDeck, HoverDeck, and ExpandPile).

3.4. Building mood boards

Once designers have found the right images, they like cutting the images with scissors and dragging the images to try different layouts.

Designers use different techniques to control the overall expression of the mood board. For example, they will add subtle effects such as blurring by adding semi-transparent colored sheets of paper to give a more uniform feel about the color of the mood board. They may also include the logo and name of the company to create a greater sense of identity with the company. Color tablets can also be included on the mood board to show the color schemes that are being used and to make sure that the right Pantone colors are used in the new designs that emerge from the mood boards. Text with keywords can also be part of the mood board. Placing the keywords is the last thing they do.

3.5. Expanding mood boards

In our interviews with designers participants shared with us scenarios for possible future expansions of mood boards. In some companies they already present mood boards as part of PowerPoint presentations, sometimes including music to help create the atmosphere. Other designers encouraged us to explore creating mood boards with moving images.

4. Designing the 'image browser'

In the previous section, we have identified and described the five main parts of the mood-board making process that we aim to provide support for with augmented reality. As was previously mentioned, out of these five parts, we have already conducted some exploratory studies in relation to 'image piling' [1]. Based on the requirements we gathered from designers, we have decided to now focus our work on supporting the second part of this process, image browsing, by designing an 'image browser' that: 1) merges with the real context allowing designers to work in the comfort of their existing design studio environment, 2) captures the current flexibility and intuitiveness of interaction with physical images, and 3) provides an alternative solution to a cluttered desk and messy design studio by using the space above the table to interact.

4.1. Merging with the real context: coffee table

From our contextual inquiries, we discovered that the context of use is an essential part of supporting the work of designers. We aim to design a space for creativity where designers feel comfortable and keep a good attitude. This space would create a positive effect [15] that facilitates creative thinking in designers.

We envision a space that encourages designers to move around their design studio pretty much as they do now. Designers have their desks with their computers on them but they prefer to look for images away from large desks or computers. They will usually prefer browsing for images while comfortably seated on a couch, in a coffee corner or at the coffee table in a living room (i.e. when working at home). As such, our system should encourage breaking the rhythm and doing activities away from their desks [11].

In this context, we have decided to design the interaction using a coffee table to encourage image search in a more relaxed environment within a design studio. Designers can sit around the coffee table and sit back comfortably on a couch. Designing interaction around a coffee table (120x40x40 cm.) has its own implications and challenges from an ergonomic point of view. Looking at the Dreyfuss charts [5], we realize there are aspects related to appropriate viewing angle, posture, reach, and the time people would be sitting around the table that need to be taken into account when designing interactions around such elements.

4.2. Flexibility of interaction: hand movements

From our studies we have learned that for activities involving creation designers prefer working with their hands with tools that allow flexibility and intuitive interaction (i.e. pencil and paper). Their current way to browse, select (cut out), and create soft-piles of images is a good example of flexible and intuitive interaction. Inspired by this example, we decided to encourage interaction through hand movements, allowing designers to work with both hands towards achieving the goal of pre-selecting images. Designers use their hands collaboratively; each hand with a different function, as when one is using a knife and fork.

4.3. Avoiding the mess: space above the table

When designers are looking for images in magazines, they start cutting out pictures from them and end up with a large number of images. Designers will create soft-piles of images and thus create a great amount of mess around their design studios. Piles of images and magazines will create cluttered desks and take up all available usable space in their design studios including tables, walls and floor.

To provide a solution for this problem, we have decided to extend the available space for interacting and displaying information by using the space above the table [20]. The active area above the work-surface is divided into multiple layers extending the design space. In our case, this space can be used to interact with soft-piles of images.

5. Interaction techniques

We now describe how the 'image browser' provides support for navigating images and interacting with soft-piles.

5.1. Browsing by flipping pages

We propose two ways to browse images. The first one is similar to flipping pages of a magazine in the sense that users must mimic with their dominant hand the movement anywhere above the table to switch to the next page (Figure 6). Three large-sized images are displayed simultaneously to allow designers to be captured by the atmosphere and contents of the image, hence the 1:3 ratio of the chosen table. The next or previous three images will be displayed depending on the direction of the movement. The change of pages is accompanied with a page-flipping sound.

5.2. Browsing by flicking

Augmenting the process of making mood boards implies extending the current practices by providing relevant support using the advantages of new technologies. As such we extend image browsing by introducing techniques that pertain to the digital world.

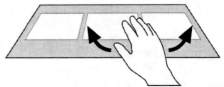

Figure 6. Browsing by mimicking a 'flipping-page' movement anywhere above the table.

Figure 7. Browsing by doing a 'flicking' movement on the table.

We use a flicking movement to initiate continuous scrolling. The flicking movement is similar to the flipping movement only that it is longer (Figure 7) and triggers a distinctive longer flipping-page sound. We map the direction of flicking to the scrolling direction, and the flicking speed to the rate at which the pictures scroll. The approach is similar to the one used for scrolling on the iPhone and on the 'Cover Flow' view of iTunes (with a difference that we do not use inertia or friction, so once scrolling starts it continues with constant speed until the stop movement is performed). Users can stop the scrolling by tapping on the table.

5.3. Soft piling

We propose the use of layers above the digital table in order to create more space to store images and create soft-piles. Once designers find an image that captures their attention, they can place the image in a soft-pile. Placing their dominant hand over an image at the table-level, and then quickly moving the hand upwards orthogonally with respect to the horizontal table surface achieve piling (Figure 8). The image will be placed into one of two locations at 30-50 cm. (soft-pile 'A') and 50-70 cm. (soft-pile 'B') above the table surface, depending on the highest point reached by the hand movement before it starts going down again to a resting position. Based on our observations of designers working with images at this stage of the mood-board making process, we have deliberately limited the number of soft-piles supported by the 'image browser' (n=2) to meet the needs of designers.

5.4. Reviewing and arranging soft piles

Placing the non-dominant hand above the table surface and changing height accordingly allows navigating within layers of soft-piles. Placing the non-dominant hand at the location of the previous placement (Figure 9a), and then placing the dominant hand at the desired new location (Figure 9b) achieve removal of an image from a soft-pile or positioning an image to another soft-pile. In this way, we are making the interaction simpler by having designers use both hands collaboratively where one hand has a different function from the other.

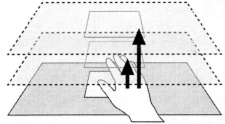

Figure 8. Creating soft piles by orthogonally moving a selected image.

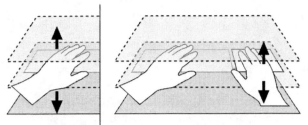

Figure 9. (a) Reviewing piles (left); (b) Placing an image on another layer (right).

6. Evaluation

The usability and usefulness of the Image Browser prototype was tested in a short exploratory user study. One of the main questions that we wanted to answer was: will practicing designers see the prototype as a relevant tool for creating mood boards? Moreover we wanted to test the interaction techniques (hand movements) in terms of naturalness, ease of learning and use. The evaluation was conducted with 5 practicing designers with at least 8 years of experience. The participants varied in gender (2 female, 3 male), age (between 30 and 40), and hand choice (4 right, 1 left). The evaluations were conducted individually.

Figure 10. Experiment setup with the coffee table, gloves and couch.

6.1. Implementation

A tabletop system was set up using a desktop PC, which controlled a top-down projector projecting an image of size 120x40 cm (1272x424 pixels) on a white IKEA table (120x40x40cm) (Figure 10), as well as an ultrasonic tracking system – InterSense IS-600 used to track hands. During the sessions participants wore custom-designed interactive gloves that contained the sensors. The gloves were made in Lycra to allow a comfortable fit for different sizes of hands and were hand sewn. Participants sat on a couch next to the table. The application was written in C# and OpenGL was used for visualization purposes.

6.2. Setup

Users were asked to focus on both the relevance of the application for the creation of mood boards, and on the interaction techniques. Following a description of the interaction (approx. 5 minutes), participants were allowed to freely explore the functionality and get acquainted with the application (approx. 5 minutes).

Participants were later asked to perform simple tasks (i.e. change pages, start and stop scrolling, create piles, re-arrange a pile), starting with 30 different images at the table-level. Finally, a short post interview was conducted. All sessions were recorded in video. The average time per participant was 25 minutes.

6.3. Findings

In the first part of our exploratory evaluations, designers started trying out the interaction techniques and as a general observation we can say that they were all able to use the system with little or no prior training. They especially liked the naturalness and simplicity of the interaction and of the overall system as can be observed from the following reactions:

- *"I think the movements that you have to make in order to browse are very natural. It really looks like you are actually browsing a magazine."* [P1]

- *"It's beautiful! It's very nice; it's a very nice interaction. (It is) what I intuitively do when I am just organizing stuff, I have piles around me, I put some things here and some things there."* [P2]

- *"It's so nice, I love it! (Reviewing layer contents with your non-dominant hand) is so nice!"* [P4]

- *"I like the flipping movement a lot, it is very quick and clear in combination with the sound."* [P5]

Regarding the interaction techniques, we observed that flicking initially caused most difficulty to our participants, followed by piling. It took two tries to get flicking going for three participants while one participant needed three tries to get piling working. In the first case, the attempt to do a flicking movement would result instead in flipping a page due to the fact that only the length of the movement differentiates both movements. After these initial difficulties participants were able to continue with the interaction.

There was one conceptual interaction problem for three participants who were trying to rearrange a pile by moving an image from the middle layer to another layer. All three participants were able to access the middle layer with their non-dominant hand but upon displaying the layer on the table, they tried to interact with the elements using their dominant hand at a table-level instead of at a middle layer-level. They all overcame the problem upon further exploration indicating it works fine once you know what to do.

Two participants expressed concern on fatigue:

- *"I am a bit concerned about how much time I have to hold my [left] hand in the air, however, the principle behind it is quite logical..."* [P1]

- *"(Doing the flicking movement repetitively) can be quite tiring for me..."* [P5]

Regarding the relevance of the proposed application, all participants saw a practical use of the image browser in their design studios. They liked the fact that they could dynamically browse images (flicking) to make connections with images:

- *"This kind of browsing gives you more opportunities to select images."* [P1]

Regarding future applications of this table, some participants speculated over possible uses of the table:

- *"It looks very promising. You could create an application in combination with the Microsoft table (Surface)."* [P1]

- *"I think that for the household, you have a digital camera with photographs from your family, children and then you can select the pictures to print out."* [P3]

7. Related work

A considerable amount of related work has influenced the design of this system. Most of this work is connected to image browsing, tabletop systems, and hand gesture/movement based interaction.

A number of tabletop systems have been designed to support image browsing and sharing. The Personal Digital Historian [19] is a tabletop, pen-based system that helps people construct, organize, navigate and share digital collections in an interactive multi-person conversational setting.

Another example of a tabletop-based system for picture sharing and browsing is SharePic [3], which was specifically developed for the elderly population. The main distinctive property of the system is that it is strongly influenced by the way physical photographs are handled and placed on physical tables.

Cabinet [11] was developed to support image collection in the context of a design studio. It has specifically addressed the issue of adding images from physical magazines onto a digital table, thus breaking the divide between physical and digital.

There is also a considerable amount of work that addresses gesture-based interaction on tables, in open spaces, or in 3D virtual environments. Tabletop systems like Diamond Touch [4], Lumisight [14], and Entertaible [9] use different hand gestures and movements to interact on the table. [17, 12, 23] have studied the general application of hand gestures and movements to support human-computer interaction.

The use of layers above the table for pen-based systems was first explored in [8] using a single layer, and later in [20] using multiple layers of interaction.

8. Discussion

8.1. Appropriateness of the (coffee) table

We believe that the choice of the IKEA table (and couch) has affected how designers perceived the prototype in a positive way. Designers realized that this was not a "standard" coffee table, but a modern and sleek one that they could perfectly see in their own design studios. As such, the chosen coffee table helped greatly in addressing the context of use issue.

Regarding how the interaction is affected by the seating position around the coffee table, the system currently allows browsing and piling images while designers are sitting comfortably and resting their back. However, for re-arranging piles, designers must lean forward to view the images (due to their smaller size), and to interact with them. We predict that designers will spend a considerably larger amount of time browsing images than re-arranging them so our main concern at this point is what would happen with the perception of the system over prolonged use.

8.2. Interaction based on hand movements

In our prototype we have used one-point ultrasonic tracking (ISense). Alternative solutions such as vision-based tracking can potentially support a richer set of movements and can also add hand gestures, however, as was pointed out above, the main motivation for choosing hand movements to interact was to keep interaction as light and simple as possible. In this respect the tracking capabilities of the ISense were enough for recognizing a small set of movements implemented in the prototype. In relation to a design-

studio context, video-based recognition will probably be more appropriate due to smaller size and price.

Designers favored not having additional interaction devices (i.e. holding tangible objects). The gloves were comfortable and unobtrusive and were perceived as a mean to track hands and not as an interaction device.

8.3. Virtual space above vs. around the table

Some participants suggested a few gestures that could be implemented in the prototype to also support interaction around the table (i.e. at a table-height level, adjacent to the table). We initially considered this option for our prototype especially because it fits the selection process (*"I choose this image, so I bring it towards me"*), however we believe this type of interaction mimics what happens on a normal desk but does not support the ergonomics of seating on a couch. On a normal desk, people sit (or stand) at a different height with respect to the table, and can rest their elbows on the table. Their reaching possibilities are fundamentally different than when seated on a couch. Reaching the vertical space above the table becomes then easier to reach than the space around it.

8.4. Interaction on vs. above the table

During the evaluation we observed that users had no problems with staying in one layer or moving between layers, however they all had some difficulties with arranging piles. While the movement itself was well understood most users needed a few tries to perform it.

All hand movements including page flipping could be performed in midair (it was not necessary to touch the table surface), however all participants used the table surface to start a hand movement and generally had less errors performing this hand movement than when performed in the air. This indicates that interaction in mid air should be kept for simple actions while interaction on the surface can be more complex (this also is inline with findings reported in [20]).

8.5. Number of piles

We defined the number of piles (n=2) for two reasons. First, our studies showed that when designers start searching images for mood boards, they create a few soft-piles (1-3) containing around 20 images each. Second, to keep the interaction above the table comfortable, we set the distance between the first layer (table surface) and the second layer at 30 cm, and the distance between the second and the third at 20 cm. Adding more layers would imply either placing layers on top in an area that is difficult to reach while sitting on a couch, or reducing the distance between layers, adding extra restrictions to the set of hand movements.

9. Conclusions

In this paper we present an interactive tabletop system that supports image browsing as one part of the process of making mood boards. The system provides flexible and intuitive interaction around a coffee table for designers in the context of their design studios. Through a user study we explored the limitations of the system in terms of placing the interaction above the table, the proposed hand movements, and the image browser itself. The evaluations showed that designers were able to use the system with little or no prior training, and to see a practical use of the proposed image browser in their design studios. We have additionally identified a number of issues related to our system such as the importance of addressing the context of use, reach, and using hand movements for interaction, which could have an effect on future interactive tabletop systems set around coffee tables.

10. References

[1] D. Aliakseyeu, S. Subramanian, A. Lucero, and C. Gutwin, "Interacting with piles of artifacts on digital tables", Proceedings of AVI '06, ACM Press, pp. 159-162.

[2] T. H. Andersen, R. Huber, A. Kretz, and M. Fjeld, "Feel the Beat: Direct Manipulation of Sound during Playback", Proceedings of Tabletop 2006, IEEE, pp. 123-124.

[3] T. Apted, J. Kay, and A. Quigley, "Tabletop Sharing of Digital Photographs for the Elderly", Proceedings of CHI'06, ACM Press, pp. 781-790.

[4] P. Dietz, and D. Leigh, "DiamondTouch: a multi-user touch technology", Proceedings of UIST '01, ACM, 219-226.

[5] H. Dreyfuss, Designing for People, Allworth Press, New York, 1967.

[6] S. Garner, and D. McDonagh-Philp, "Problem Interpretation and Resolution via Visual Stimuli: The Use of 'Mood Boards' in Design Education", International Journal of Art & Design Education, 20(1), 2001, pp. 57–64.

[7] W. Gaver, T. Dunne, and E. Pacenti, "Cultural probes", In Interactions, 6(1), January 1999, ACM Press, pp. 21-29.

[8] T. Grossman, K. Hinckley, P. Baudisch, M. Agrawala, and R. Balakrishnan, "Hover Widgets: Using the Tracking State to Extend the Capabilities of Pen-Operated Devices", In Proceedings of CHI '06, ACM Press, pp. 861-870.

[9] G. Hollemans, T. Bergman, V. Buil, K. Gelder, M. Groten, J. Hoonhout, T. Lashina, E. Loenen, and S.

Wijdeven, "Entertaible: Multi-user multi-object concurrent input", Adjunct Proceedings of UIST '06, ACM, pp. 55-56.

[10] K. Holtzblatt, J. Burns Wendell, and S. Wood, Rapid Contextual Design. Morgan Kaufmann, 2004.

[11] I. Keller, For Inspiration Only: Designer interaction with informal collections of visual material, PhD thesis, Delft University of Technology, 2005.

[12] S. Lenman, L. Bretzner, and B. Thuresson, "Using marking menus to develop command sets for computer vision based hand gesture interfaces", Proceedings of NordiCHI '02, vol. 31, ACM Press, pp. 239-242.

[13] A. Lucero, and J.-B. Martens, "Supporting the creation of Mood Boards: Industrial Design in Mixed Reality", Proceedings of TableTop 2006, IEEE, pp. 127-128.

[14] M. Matsushita, M. Iida, T. Ohguro, Y. Shirai, Y. Kakehi, and T. Naemura, "Lumisight table: a face-to-face collaboration support system that optimizes direction of projected information to each stakeholder", Proceedings of CSCW '04, ACM Press, pp. 274-283.

[15] D. Norman, Emotional Design. Why we love (or hate) everyday things, Basic Books, 2004.

[16] J. Patten, H. Ishii, J. Hines, and G. Pangaro, "Sensetable: a wireless object tracking platform for tangible user interfaces", Proceedings of CHI '01, ACM, pp. 253-260.

[17] F. Quek, D. McNeill, R. Bryll, S. Duncan, X. Ma, C. Kirbas, K.E. McCullough, and R. Ansari, "Multimodal human discourse: gesture and speech", In TOCHI, 9(3), September 2002, ACM Press, pp. 171-193.

[18] S.D. Scott, M. Sheelagh, T. Carpendale, and K.M. Inkpen, "Territoriality in collaborative tabletop workspaces", Proceedings of CSCW '04, ACM Press, pp. 294-303.

[19] C. Shen, N. Lesh, F. Vernier, C. Frolines, and J. Frost, "Sharing and Building Digital Group Histories", Proceedings of CSCW'02, ACM Press, pp. 324-333.

[20] S. Subramanian, D. Aliakseyeu, and A. Lucero, "Multi-layer interaction for digital tables", Proceedings of UIST '06, ACM Press, pp. 269-272.

[21] Surface (2007): http://www.microsoft.com/surface/ accessed 31.05.2007.

[22] P.Wellner, "Interacting with paper on the DigitalDesk", In Communications, 36(7), July 1993, ACM Press, pp. 87-96.

[23] A. Wexelblat, "An approach to natural gesture in virtual environments", In TOCHI, 2(3), Sept. 1995, ACM Press, pp. 179-200.

Tablescape Plus:
Interactive Small-sized Vertical Displays on a Horizontal Tabletop Display

Yasuaki Kakehi
Presto, Japan Science and Technology Agency
kakehi@hc.ic.i.u-tokyo.ac.jp

Takeshi Naemura
The University of Tokyo
naemura@hc.ic.i.u-tokyo.ac.jp

Mitsunori Matsushita
NTT Communication Science Labs, NTT Corp.
mat@cslab.kecl.ntt.co.jp

Abstract

This paper proposes a novel paradigm: human-centered tabletop computing, which enhances the role of an ordinary table by projecting interactive images onto tabletop objects and the table surface at the same time. The advantage of this approach is that it utilizes tabletop objects as projection screens as well as input tools. As a result, we can change the appearance and role of each tabletop object easily and fulfill two important requirements of tabletop tangible interfaces, identifiability and versatility, which have proven difficult to satisfy simultaneously in previous systems. Our prototype, Tablescape Plus, achieves these functions by using two projectors and a special tabletop screen system that diffuses or transmits images selectively according to the projection orientation. This paper presents the design principle, optical design, and implementation of Tablescape Plus. Furthermore, we introduce several interactive applications.

1. Introduction

The rapid advance of information technology allows computers to support and enhance the daily activities of our lives in various ways. One system with the potential to enhance deskwork is the tabletop display. This environment consists of an electronic display embedded into the surface of the table. On tabletop displays, user interaction must not be limited to existing interfaces such as a mouse or a keyboard because users want more real-world oriented tangible interactions.

A table is a versatile tool with a unique characteristic: it provides a surface where people can place physical objects. To offer intuitive and fluid interaction, tabletop displays must support this familiar practice. Since many in-

Figure 1. Tablescape Plus.

teractive systems use the placement of physical objects on a tabletop as input tools, there are several methods for sensing their positions. For the purpose of human-centered tabletop computing, however, we should pay more attention to the objects themselves.

When we utilize a tabletop physical object as an interface device, there are at least two requirements to meet: identifiability and versatility. Identifiability means that we can easily distinguish the object's form and function. To meet this requirement, the appearance of the object should have a concrete meaning. On the other hand, versatility requires that the object should be applicable for different situations. To meet this requirement, the design of the object needs to be flexible and convey for several meanings. Therefore, it is difficult to satisfy these two requirements simultaneously.

To solve this problem, we consider using the tabletop objects as an input tool while incorporating a projected image on it for displaying information. The projected images have concrete meanings, which make it easy to see and under-

0-7695-3013-3/07 $25.00 © 2007 IEEE
DOI 10.1109/TABLETOP.2007.25

stand the object's current purpose. In addition, by changing the projection image, we can use the same object as a tool in multiple different situations. We may use small electronic equipment as this kind of object. However, we believe that for human-centered tabletop computing the object should be as simple as possible, just like a small-sized screen without electronic structure.

This paper introduces the system, Tablescape Plus[1] (see Figure 1), which we implemented based on the considerations described above. Tablescape Plus can project different images both onto a table surface and onto upright objects. We also achieve interactivity on Tablescape Plus by using computer vision methods to recognize objects placed on the tabletop. Below we describe the optical design of the Tablescape Plus, input method that uses marker recognition and projector image calibration. Moreover, we introduce several applications for our system.

2. Related Works

In the field of Augmented Reality, several head mounted display (HMD) based systems that can overlap virtual images onto real tabletop space have been developed (e.g. "Tiles" [7], "MagicCup"[4]). However, wearing special equipments might obstruct users' natural manipulation of and interaction with objects on the table. We have adopted a projector-based approach, which does not require the user to wear any electronic equipment.

On the other hand, there are several approaches to displaying images directly onto tabletop objects. "DigitalDesk"[12] and "Urps"[11] are representative systems, resulting from prior research into how to arrange the physical objects on the desktop and how to display images on the physical objects. "Shader Lamps"[8] is another precursor of our project in regard to projecting images not only onto horizontal surfaces but also onto vertical planes of the tabletop object. These systems use a projector mounted at the ceiling to project images directly onto both the tabletop itself and the objects placed on it. However, this method has the following problems: shadows from the users' hands and other objects obstruct the images, and the amount of equipment required is large including ceilings. Some systems such as "BlockJam"[5] display information on small electronic displays embedded in the physical objects. These systems are reliable, but because they require special devices, it is difficult for users to create or modify the objects. Tablescape Plus requires no electronic devices in the objects themselves, and only employs equipment within the table to create an interactive display.

As for the tabletop interaction technology that determines the objects with which the user is interacting, there have been also various methods developed. "metaDESK"[10] and "Sensetable"[6] are the pioneering researches of tangible interface with specialized sensing technologies. Our Tablescape Plus employs cameras to capture the objects on the tabletop and recognizes physical markers attached to the underside of the objects using ARtoolkit library[3]. In comparison with other approaches, this camera-based approach allows much more versatile interaction. What is important here is that the camera can be also equipped below the tabletop surface, so users are unconscious of the physical markers.

As for the special optical system adopted in Tablescape Plus, we have introduced it previously in our Lumisight Table[2] that supports multi-user communication around a square table. Tablescape Plus focuses on the interaction with tabletop objects by a single user.

3. System Configuration of Tablescape Plus

3.1. Optics Design

We designed the system so that we can install all the devices inside a table (Figure 2). Because of this feature, we can make the system size compact and reduce occlusion by the users' hands. For this purpose, we have developed a tabletop screen system that filters out images selectively according to the projection orientation.

As for the screen material that can satisfy this requirement, we adopted Lumisty (Sumitomo Chemical) as the tabletop projection screen. Figure 3 shows the relevant optical property of the Lumisty film used in Tablescape Plus. On this material, the light from one privileged direction is diffusive, while it passes through the incoming light from other directions with a high transmission factor. We exploit this feature for Tablescape Plus' special screen system and utilize the diffusive direction for the tabletop screen. As shown in Figure 2(a), an image from projector A diffuses onto this screen, and consequently, the user can see the image on the tabletop. Furthermore, by projecting images from the transparent direction, this system can also show images on the surface of objects placed vertically (see Projector B in Figure 2(b)).

In addition, we embedded a Fresnel lens underneath the Lumisty film. To make the tabletop screen image clear, the Fresnel lens aligns the projected light uniformly before it reaches the tabletop screen.

3.2. Camera System and Marker Recognition

In order to capture the users' interaction with physical objects, we installed two cameras inside the system. Since Lumisty film is transparent from a vertical direction (see Figure 3), cameras inside the system can capture the images

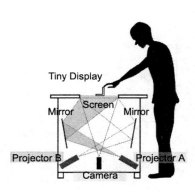

(a) Image projection onto tabletop screen.

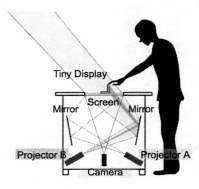

(b) Image projection onto tabletop objects.

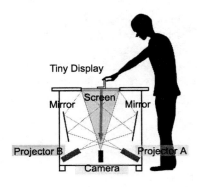

(c) Sensing by camera.

Figure 2. Hardware Design of Tablescape Plus.

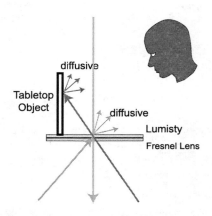

Figure 3. An Optical Property of Lumisty.

on the tabletop at the same time as the projectors display images on the table's surface as shown in Figure 2(c).

Figure 4 shows the basic structure of a tabletop object, which consists of a vertical screen and a paper marker attached on the bottom surface. To detect markers efficiently, we installed an infrared light at the bottom of the table oriented toward the tabletop and put a filter around it that shuts out the visual light on each camera. Furthermore, we utilized a retro reflective material for the paper marker in order to reflect the infrared light. Consequently, for the cameras, the marker region appears brighter than the other regions.

Figure 4. Overview of a Tabletop Object.

The reason we use two cameras is to solve the problem of undesirable reflection at the Fresnel lens. When infrared light is projected upward, some portion of the light reflects on the Fresnel lens. As a result, the camera cannot capture a portion of the tabletop scene. The location of this undetectable area depends on the positional relationship between the camera and the infrared light. To solve this problem, we installed two cameras at slightly different locations as shown in Figure 5. Based on this camera setup, there is always at least one camera that can see the physical markers beneath any of the tabletop objects. Figure 5 shows the captured image of each camera. In addition, we utilize the ARToolKit Library[3] to recognize the position, orientation and ID of each marker. In the current implementation, the system works at 30fps by using a PC with Intel Xeon 2.8GHz.

3.3. Projection Controls

We needed a way to align the projected images correctly on the tabletop objects, so in Tablescape Plus, we use two projectors and two cameras. In the initialization phase, several procedures are necessary to determine the coordinate transform matrices between each camera and each projector.

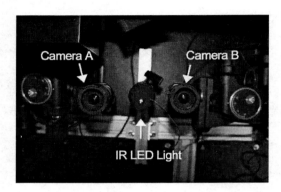

(a) Two cameras and an infrared light are installed in the table.

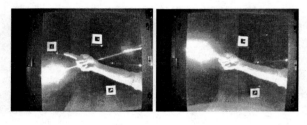

(b) View from Camera A   (c) View from Camera B

Figure 5. Views from each camera inside the Tablescape Plus.

First, we describe the calibration of projector A (see Figure 2), which is used for tabletop screen images. We can derive the coordinate transform matrices for the camera and projector coordinate spaces on the tabletop surface by taking several points on the surface and following the procedure listed below for each camera:

1. Put a screen that consists of diffusive material on the tabletop Lumisty film.

2. Project multiple (at least four) points onto the screen.

Note that the positions of the points are represented in the coordinate system of projector A.

3. Capture the scene of the tabletop screen and determine the positions of projected points in the camera coordinate system.

4. Derive the coordinate transform matrix between the camera and the projector A by using the method [9] of Sukthankar et al.

Second, we describe the calibration of projector B (see Figure 2), which is used for projection onto object surfaces. For simplicity, we assume the object screens are rectangular, of known size, and perpendicular to the table surface. In this case, the calibration procedure is as follows:

1. Derive the coordinate transform matrix between the camera and the projector B at both Plane 1 (table surface) and Plane 2 (which is parallel to the table surface and includes the tops of the objects) in Figure 6 using the same method mentioned above.

2. Determine the positions of V_A and V_B on the screen (Figure 6) in the camera coordinate system.

3. Derive the positions of the four corners of the object screen (V_A, V_B, V_C and V_D) in the coordinate system of projector B by using the two matrices derived earlier.

Figure 7 shows the results of projecting a square with a border at the computed positions of the physical objects. By using this method, this system can also project images on the appropriate position of the upright object when the user rotates it on tabletop as long as the projection light can reach the object surface (see Figure 8). However, the more the rotation angle increases, the lower the image quality becomes because of the image resolution and projection focus. In the future, we plan to include projection onto different shaped objects.

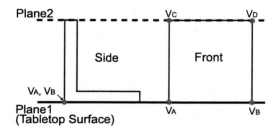

Figure 6. Planes and Points Used for Calibration.

(a) Screen-capture Image.　　(b) A Projected Image.

Figure 7. Calibration of Projected Images onto Tabletop Objects.

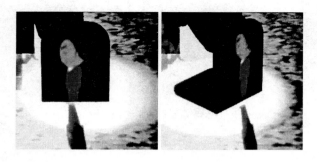

Figure 8. Appearance of Projected Image in Rotation.

4. Discussion of System Configuration

Since our system employs oblique projection, focus and resolution of the image on tabletop object change according to its position. The focus accuracy depends on the projection length. It becomes shorter as the object gets closer to the user, which means that when the image on a far away object is in focus, the images on closer objects will be blurred.

On the other hand, the resolution decreases as the object gets farther from the user. This is because the size of each pixel is designed to be uniform on a plane perpendicular to the surface on which the projector is located. Figure 9 illustrates this principle. For the farther object, the projected image on the perpendicular plane A shrinks, and consequently has fewer pixels.

As an experiment, we placed three identical objects at near, middle and far positions and projected the same image onto each object. Figure 10 (right) shows the appearance of the projected images on each object on three different focus settings (near, middle and far). As shown in Figure 10 (left), the resolution of the projected images changes according to

placement. Based on the comparison of each setting, we decided to adjust the focal length of projector B, so that the projector would focus on a point between the middle and the far focus points, increasing the quality of the images projected onto the farthest objects.

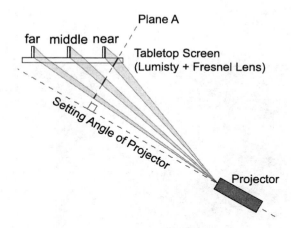

Figure 9. Projection according to the object postion.

5. Applications

Tablescape Plus holds a lot of potentials to open up new types of tabletop interaction. As we mentioned in the previous section, this system can capture the marker information from underneath small-sized object in real time. Giving image and/or sound feedback toward these inputs, we can design various interaction on this system. Below, we introduce three examples of interactive applications implemented on Tablescape Plus.

5.1. Digital Kiosk Application

A tabletop upright object is useful for displaying supplemental information on the horizontal tabletop image. In this application, the initial tabletop screen display is a map of a city. By placing upright objects on it, the users can see additional photographs or weather forecast related to the mapped region as shown in Figure 11.

5.2. Multi Aspect Viewer Application

Tabletop objects can also be useful for intuitive viewing of different aspects of complex data displayed on the horizontal tabletop display. In this application, the user can see various cross-sections of solid objects such as fruits when he/she slides a tabletop object over the plane view initially

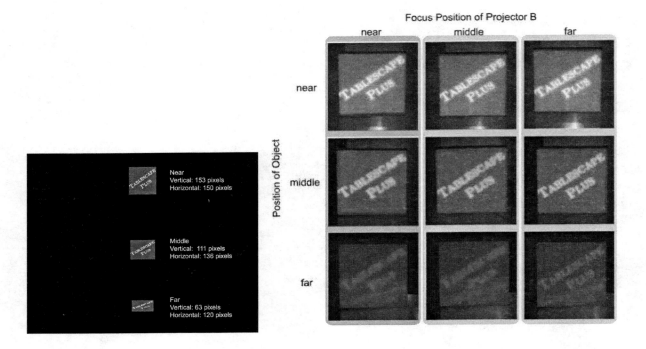

Figure 10. Appearance of projected images according to object position.

Figure 11. Digital Kiosk Application.

displayed on the tabletop screen. As shown in Figure 12, the cross section images change according to the position of the tabletop object.

5.3. Tabletop Theater Application

Everyone has played with dolls or figurines in his/her childhood. Ordinarily these dolls are static; they are not able to move and speak by themselves. However, we can create various stories or fantasy worlds dynamically by manipulating them physically (e.g. shaking their hands/moving two dolls close to each other), and complement their physical limitations with our imagination (e.g.

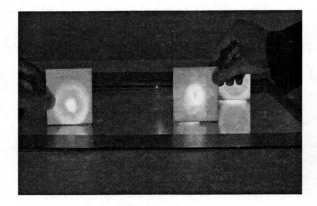

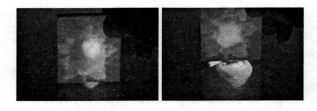

Figure 12. Multi Aspect Viewer Application.

giving a situation and roles or speaking their lines).

The tabletop theater application is designed for entertainment and the goal is to realize a novel new miniature world by blending physical objects, imagination of users and digital images. When a user visit this world, he/she can experience a miniature park with its park visitors, trees, benches and birds (see Figure 13 (top)). Green grasses are projected on the horizontal plane; trees and a bench are projected vertically perpendicular to the grass.

When the user put a square-shaped tiny screen onto the tabletop, a human character appears on it. At the same time, the shadow of the character is projected under its feet. The user could see that the character is standing on the tabletop park. Moreover, he/she can control the projected images tangibly and intuitively. When he/she moves the character object, the projected character image also moves with it. The appearance of the character changes according to the direction that the object moves (e.g. the character faces forward when the object moves forward and it faces right when the object moves right). The characters display other behaviors according to the manipulation performed by the user. For examples, when the user put one character close to other characters, they start chattering (see Figure 13 (middle)). Furthermore, the interplay between characters changes according to character combinations and situations.

Position of image is not limited to the character object. When the user put a character close to the bench, the character goes out of the character object and sits on the bench (see Figure 13 (bottom)). In other case, when the user moves a character behind the trees, the character can walk among the trees and silhouette of birds appear on the grass and fly away from the trees. Thus, on the tabletop's horizontal and vertical screens, various interactive dramas are played lively and freely.

By changing scenes, characters and stories, Tablescape Plus can show various miniature worlds on the identical screens and objects. In addition to the miniature park version, we've also implemented a different version, in which users can play with penguins and seals on ice world (see Figure 14). In this version, we used the motion speed of the object as one of the interaction keys (For example, when the user moves the penguin object faster than the threshold speed, the penguin, which normally stands or walks, begins crawling on the ice).

6. Conclusion and Future Works

The tabletop display is a human-centered computing paradigm that has the potential to enhance a user's deskwork. We have proposed to utilize tabletop objects as an input tool while incorporating projection screens onto them for displaying information. This multi-faceted application increases the identifiability and the versatility of

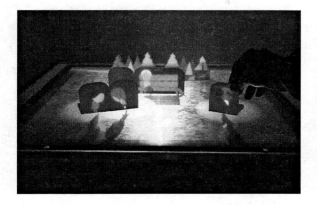

Figure 13. Tabletop Theater (Miniature Park Version).

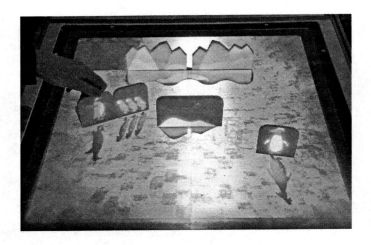

Figure 14. Ice World Version.

tabletop objects. In the future, we have following plans:

First, we will implement a series of new tabletop applications including games, simulations, educational tools, and scientific visualizations.

Secondly, we will extend the variety of tabletop objects so that they vary in shape, size, and material. For example, we can utilize ordinary daily commodities (e.g. mug, penholder, and desk calendar) just by attaching physical markers beneath them. This feature could add various new computer interaction experiences to many people's daily lives.

Thirdly, we will investigate other interaction methods such as touch sensors and camera-based hand gesture recognition.

Finally, we will connect multiple systems over a network. This feature would enable new types of teleconference and computer supported cooperative projects.

Acknowledgement Special thanks go to Prof. Hiroshi Harashima for his helpful advices.

References

[1] Y. Kakehi, M. Iida, T. Naemura, and M. Matsushita. Tablescape Plus: Upstanding Tiny Displays on Tabletop Display. In *SIGGRAPH2006 Emerging Technologies*, 2006.

[2] Y. Kakehi, M. Iida, T. Naemura, Y. Shirai, M. Matsushita, and T. Ohguro. Lumisight Table: An Interactive View-Dependent Tabletop Display. *IEEE Computer Graphics and Applications*, 25(1):48–53, January 2005.

[3] H. Kato and M. Billinghurst. Marker Tracking and HMD Calibration for a Video-based Augmented Reality Conferencing System. In *Proceedings of the 2nd International Workshop on Augmented Reality (IWAR 99)*, pages 85–94, 1999.

[4] H. Kato, K. Tachibana, M. Tanabe, T. Nakajima, and Y. Fukuda. A City-Planning System Based on Augmented Reality with a Tangible Interface. In *The Second Intern. Symp. on Mixed and Augmented Reality (ISMAR 2003) MR Technology Expo*, pages 340–341, 2003.

[5] H. Newton-Dunn, H. Nakano, and J. Gibson. Blockjam: A Tangible Interface for Interactive Music. In *Proceedings of NIME2003*, pages 170–177, 2003.

[6] J. Patten, H. Ishii, J. Hines, and G. Pangaro. Sensetable: A Wireless Object Tracking Platform for Tangible User Interfaces. In *Proceedings of the ACM Conference on Human Factors in Computing Systems (CHI'01)*, pages 253–260, 2001.

[7] I. Poupyrev, D. Tan, M. Billinghurst, H. Kato, H. Regenbrecht, and N. Tetsutani. Tiles: A Mixed Reality Authoring Interface. In *INTERACT 2001 Conference on Human Computer Interaction*, 2001.

[8] R. Raskar, G. Welch, K. Low, and D. Bandyopadhyay. Shader Lamps: Animating Real Objects with Image-Based Illumination. In *Eurographics Workshop on Rendering (EGWR 2001)*, pages 89–102, 2001.

[9] R. Sukthankar, R. Stockton, and M. Mullin. Smarter Presentations: Exploiting Homography in Camera-Projector Systems. In *Proceedings of the International Conference on Computer Vision (ICCV2001)*, 2001.

[10] B. Ullmer and H. Ishii. The metaDESK: Models and Prototypes for Tangible User Interfaces. In *Symposium on User Interface Software and Technology (UIST'97)*, pages 223–232, 1997.

[11] J. Underkoffler and H. Ishii. Illuminating Light: An Optical Design Tool with a Luminous-Tangible Interface. In *Proceedings of the ACM Conference on Human Factors in Computing Systems (CHI'98)*, pages 542–549, 1998.

[12] P. Wellner. The DigitalDesk calculator: Tangible manipulation on a desk top display. In *Proceedings of UIST'91, ACM Symposium on User Interface Software and Technology*, pages 27–34, 1991.

Spilling: Expanding Hand held Interaction to Touch Table Displays

Dan R. Olsen Jr., Jeffrey Clement, Aaron Pace
Computer Science Department, Brigham Young University
olsen@cs.byu.edu

Abstract

We envision a nomadic model of interaction where the personal computer fits in your pocket. Such a computer is extremely limited in screen space. A technique is described for "spilling" the display of a hand held computer onto a much larger table top display surface. Because our model of nomadic computing frequently involves the use of untrusted display services we restrict interactive input to the hand held. Navigation techniques such as scrolling or turning the display can be expressed through the table top. The orientation and position of the hand held on the table top is detected using three conductive feet that appear to the touch table like three finger touches. An algorithm is given for detecting the three touch positions from the table's sensing mechanism.

1. Introduction

There is a great attraction to carrying a personal computer in your pocket. It enables a nomadic style of computing that is not feasible with desktop machines or even with laptops. There are now many hand held devices that are less than one cubic inch in volume and yet have much more storage and processor power than the original Macintosh. However, the user interface to such devices is unacceptable for many applications because of display size.

The XICE project (eXtending Interactive Computing Everywhere) seeks to address the problem of very small personal computers by annexing screens where we find them in the world. XICE shares many of the goals of the Personal Server [13, 7] project as well as our own Join and Capture [6] system. Our approach stands in contrast to Pebbles [5] which uses hand held devices as controllers for applications running on other machines. In the XICE world the hand held computer is the personal computer and other devices are simply interaction servers. The advantage of this approach is that compatibility issues are sharply diminished. X-Windows [10], Virtual Network Computing (VNC) [8] and the web have all shown the compatibility advantages of standardizing interaction services.

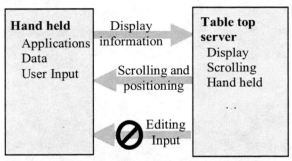

Fig 1. Hand held / Table top relationship

There are two specific challenges in this vision that we will address in this paper. The first is the integration of the hand held computer with the display services that it has annexed. We will show how the display of a hand held can be "spilled" onto a table top display to create a Focus-Plus-Context [1] expansion of any hand held application. The second issue is the security of the hand held computer. In a nomadic model of computing that uses devices encountered "in the wild" it is not safe to assume that such devices can be trusted. In this work we resolve this problem by performing most interaction locally within the hand held personal computer. We only accept navigation inputs, such as scrolling, from foreign devices. Accepting full user input from a foreign device essentially cedes control to that device with all of the accompanying dangers. Figure 1 shows the relative relationships between hand held personal computers and table top servers.

Figure 2 shows our Spilling prototype with the hand held laid on the surface of a Diamond Touch table. In this figure the application is a spreadsheet that the user is scrolling by dragging their finger across the surface. The entire application is displayed on the table surface with the interactive focus of the application displayed on the hand held. In terms of usability we compare Spilling to what is possible on a hand held alone as opposed to what might be possible on a desktop computer. The table top context of Spilling greatly enhances the ability of a user to interact with the hand held.

Fig 2. Hand held on table top display

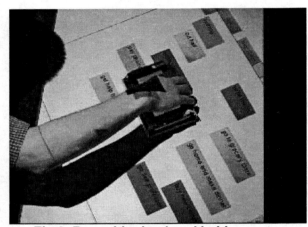

Fig 3. Repositioning hand held

Spilling draws its inspiration from Focus-Plus-Context displays [1]. The focus is on the hand held where the user can safely interact using the same interactive techniques normally used on the hand held. The context is provided by the table top display with a touch sensitive surface providing a mechanism to scroll information into the focus region. The idea is that this is a hand held computer that behaves as it always did, but it has been supplemented by this large table top display. Unlike Focus-Plus-Context which has a rather rigid configuration, the user can move the hand held around the surface and position it in whatever place is comfortable to work. Figure 3 shows the user rotating the hand held to work more comfortably on a "sticky note" application for organizing ideas. This would be

similar to tipping a sheet of paper in order to write more comfortably.

When the hand held moves, the work moves with it. When the user scrolls with their finger the work moves beneath the hand held. This is different from Ubiquitous Graphics [9] where the wall display is fixed with the smaller device moving relative to it. This fixed-world approach is also found in Peepholes [15] where the hand held device is moved relative to a large fixed display that is only shown through the hand held device providing no peripheral context. The problem with fixed-world display models is that the user can be forced to work in awkward physical positions, such as the extreme top of the display. In Spilling the user can move the work to where it is most comfortable regardless of the physical size of the contextual display. This hand held centric approach also allows the user to rotate the hand held so that the display can be seen by someone across the table as in DiamondSpin [11].

In the remainder of this paper we will address Spilling's architectural and security issues. First issue is distributing the display from the hand held to the table top. This is mostly handled by the XICE architecture. The second issue is the geometry synchronization between the hand held and the table top. Third there is the problem of sensing the location and orientation of the hand held personal computer. Lastly the UI security threats are addressed.

2. XICE Architecture

The full XICE architecture is beyond the scope of this paper. What are presented here are the essentials for implementing Spilling. The goal of XICE is to explore the software architectures that can make highly nomadic computing possible without sacrificing display or interactive capabilities. Because we wanted to rethink mobile interaction architectures we have abandoned any support for legacy software. We feel that nomadic computing is compelling enough to warrant rewriting applications to a new platform. Using XICE we have implemented a text editor, a "sticky notes" idea organizer, a presentation tool (like PowerPoint), a drawing application, and a spreadsheet as well as the games of checkers, tic-tac-toe and Risk. These give us a rich application base for exploring architecture ideas.

XICE applications are organized around *sheets*, which are similar to traditional windows. A sheet is either *local* or *remote*. A local sheet is drawn on the screen of the same computer where the application is running. A remote sheet is drawn on some machine that is accessed over the Internet.

Associated with each sheet is a *presentation tree* that represents everything to be drawn on that sheet. These presentation trees are like the scene graphs in 3D systems and the drawing architecture of Piccolo [2]. Rather than implementing the damage/redraw technique of most interactive graphics, XICE applications interact by modifying the presentation tree. Tree modifications propagate up the tree to the sheet. If the sheet is local then XICE handles the necessary damage/redraw activity to get the screen redrawn. If the sheet is remote then presentation tree changes are serialized to the remote machine where they are used to update a copy of the presentation tree. That copy is then redrawn on the remote display In Spilling all Internet access is via a wireless 802.11g connection from the hand held. The change propagation and serialization algorithms are beyond the scope of this paper. The key feature is that modifications to a transformation require just a few bytes of network traffic to modify the corresponding remote transformation node rather than the traffic for the complete redraw required in X or VNC. Since most of Spilling is transformation modification this makes the whole technique very network-friendly. The distribution of presentation trees is hidden from and irrelevant to XICE applications.

There are two points in the XICE drawing model that are key to the Spilling implementation. As in 3D scene graphs some interior nodes in a presentation tree can be geometric transformations (scale, rotate, translate or any combination). A transformation node modifies the way in which all of its children are drawn. A second feature is that all drawing is defined in View Independent Coordinates (VICs). VICs are defined to deal both with differing screen resolutions and with differing viewing distances. The informal definition is that readable text should be at least 10 VICs high. The scaling of VICs to actual pixels is handled deep in XICE where the actual display configuration is known. For each display XICE is configured with the parameters *pixels per inch* and *viewing distance* in inches. From this the VICs-to-pixels scaling is computed. This will be important in coordinating table geometry with hand held geometry.

Figure 4 shows how Spilling is implemented in the XICE architecture. At the heart of the implementation is the application's presentation tree. This embodies everything that is to be drawn in the application as well as its input event processing. Directly above the application's tree is the scrolling transformation node

S. This node positions the application work in response to the user's dragging with their fingers. Above the **S** node is a special *multi-parent* node that is responsible for synchronizing the hand held display with the table top display.

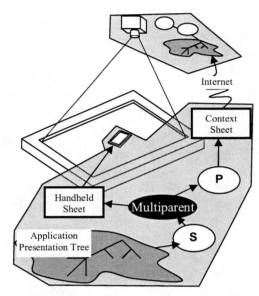

Fig 4: Spilling's XICE implementation

Also above the multi-parent node is the transformation node **P** that manages the position and orientation of the hand held. The node **P** is connected to the remote sheet for the table top context. This remote context sheet synchronizes over the Internet with the table top display's version of the presentation tree. The entire application is presented to the hand held, where most is clipped away, and also to the table top, where a more global view of the application appears. As figure 4 shows, almost everything about the application and its relationship to Spilling is contained in the hand held. The only part that is controlled by the foreign table top server is a copy of the presentation tree and the scrolling/positioning inputs.

When a change is made to the presentation tree by the application it is propagated up the tree to the multi-parent node. The multi-parent node sends the change notification both to the hand held's sheet and to node **P** where it is propagated to the context sheet and serialized to the table top display service. Both the hand held and the table top have presentation trees that reflect the current visual state of the application.

When the hand held needs to redraw its sheet for whatever reason it recursively traverses the tree down through the multi-parent node, bypassing node **P** but passing through node **S**. The position of the hand held on the table top has no effect on what should be drawn on the hand held. When the context-sheet is serializing it does pass through transformation **P** so that the hand held's position is taken into account when drawing on the table top.

The multi-parent node makes the whole display structure technically a directed-acyclic graph. However, the multi-parent node localizes the non-tree behavior that is required to get different displays drawn in different places without the application knowing about the duplication. The application is oblivious to the existence of the Spilling implementation above it in the tree. When the user interacts with the application itself through the hand held, all input events are distributed downward and transformed by S^{-1} before being sent to the application for processing. The scrolling of the display performed by Spilling is thus invisible to the application.

3. Table top interaction

When the user moves the hand held, as shown in figures 3 and 5, its location and orientation must be sensed by the table top server. This location and orientation is sent back across the Internet to the context sheet and transformation node **P** is modified appropriately as shown in figure 5. This change to **P** is serialized and returned to the table top display server which causes the table top display to update.

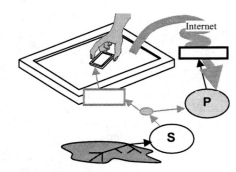

Fig 5. Changing hand held position

When the user scrolls the work under the hand held as shown in figure 2 a translation is sensed by the table top server. The change between the start and end points of the scroll is sent to the hand held and is propagated from the context sheet down through P^{-1} and used to modify transformation **S** as shown in figure 6. This change to transformation **S** is below the multi-parent node. Thus its modification is propagated to both the hand held sheet for redrawing and to the context sheet for serialization to the table top. XICE's

parsimonious network usage makes these changes much more efficient than VNC or X. In neither of these table top interactions has the presentation of the application been sent over the network. That would only happen if the application itself changed its presentation tree and then only the relevant changes would be sent. This allows spilling to move both displays at interactive speeds.

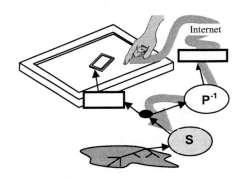

Fig 6. Finger scrolling

4. Table top technology

The table top server needs to support three tasks: display, scroll sensing and hand held position sensing. Display can either come from below or above. Display from below has many advantages in terms of installation, occlusion and elimination of shadows. Spilling is largely agnostic about the display choice except that dragging a hand held across a transparent screen may lead to excessive scratching. Projection from above would not have the scratching problem, but does create shadows.

Users might express scrolling using either a finger or a stylus. For a stylus-based technique a tablet is perfectly adequate. However, for scrolling we do not need the precision of a stylus and we would prefer not to incur the usability burden of finding and manipulating a stylus. Fingers rarely get lost.

The key sensing requirement is the location and orientation of the hand held computer. For this there are several competing technologies: cameras, structured light, pen tablets and the Diamond Touch. It would be possible to place fiducial marks on the back of the hand held computer so that a camera from below could sense the location and position. Two unique marks would clearly identify the location and orientation of the device. Camera from below poses the same surface wear problems as projection from below. However, fiducial marks can readily be painted or stuck on the bottom of the hand held to provide the necessary two points. PlayAnywhere [14] describes a set of such fiducial marks. Camera-from-below is a strong candidate for Spilling.

It is possible to place fiducial marks on the top of the hand held and put a camera above to sense the necessary three points. PlayAnywhere demonstrated that an oblique camera angle can be effective with little interference. However a quick glance at figure 3 shows that most fiducial marks would be obscured by the user's hand at exactly the time when we want to sense the hand held position. Camera from above would not be a good choice.

A structured light solution is also possible such as that proposed by Lee, et. al. [4]. This would require light sensors at the corners of the hand held device that could sense the position from the projected light signature. There are several problems here. The sensors must be manufactured into the hand held device which would make it more expensive and require a lot of cooperation between table top and hand held manufacturers. Structured light would interfere with the table top projection unless infra-red was used. Lastly the hand would obscure the sensors just as with top-side fiducial marks.

Ubiquitous Graphics [9] uses acoustic pen technology to sense the location of the focus display. Again this requires the manufacturers of hand held devices to include special hardware. The ultrasonic emitters are also large enough to add significant bulk to the hand held.

It would also be possible to use Wacom [12] tablet technology for sensing location and orientation. Embedding Wacom stylus hardware in the hand held would provide the necessary input. The passive stylus hardware could also be constructed as a "stick on" that could be attached to any hand held. This would provide an effective and accurate mechanism that would work on any of Wacom's tablet displays.

Our Spilling prototype uses the Diamond Touch table [3] as its sensing device. It has a wear resistant surface coupled with very simple user devices (fingers). Scrolling is easy by sensing the movement of a finger on the touch surface. The sensing of the hand held is more problematic. The Diamond Touch functions by sensing capacitance changes from users sitting on a conductive pad. If the chair pad causes installation difficulties we have placed it at the edge of the Diamond Touch table where it can be touched with the non-dominant hand.

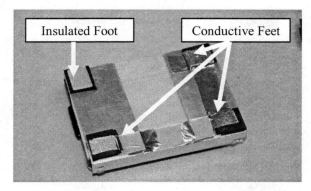

Fig 7. VAIO prototype with conductive feet

In figure 7 we show a conductive frame which we have attached to a Sony VAIO-UX hand held computer. When the user grasps the frame it becomes part of the Diamond Touch sensing circuit for that user. The result is that the three conductive feet appear to the Diamond Touch as if three of the user's fingers were touching the surface. In a real product the hand held's case would be conductive with one nonconductive and three conductive feet on the back. This would be inexpensive to manufacture into a hand held device. The VAIO is larger than we envision for most hand helds, but it was much simpler to program for this prototype.

5. Detecting hand held position/orientation

The remaining challenge is to locate the three conductive feet from the VAIO and convert their locations into the translation and rotation transformation **P**. The Diamond Touch is a projective sensing device. The locations of the touches are not sensed directly, rather a histogram of touch strength is produced for the individual X and Y coordinates. For a single touch the high points in the X and Y histograms are detected and the touch location is known. Projective sensing is not unique to the Diamond Touch. Most tablets are projection sensed through vertical and horizontal wires. Many IR-based optical tablets are also projection sensed. Projection sensing is economical because its cost grows with the perimeter length rather than the area of a sensing surface.

Projective sensing works great for single points, but it leads to ambiguity when sensing multiple points. For sensing the hand held's size, location and orientation we need to sense three unique points. However, the X, Y projections of those points are not unique. We resolve this using three techniques: 1) a known starting orientation, 2) the rigid configuration of the hand held's three conductive points and 3) continuity of motion.

Figure 8 shows the 4 possible sensing cases that must be considered in resolving the X, Y projections into the positions of 3 points on the handheld. Each case is identified by the number of peaks in each of X and Y. There are several variations of each of these cases. The numbered points for Case 1 indicate the identity of the three conductive feet on the bottom of the handheld device.

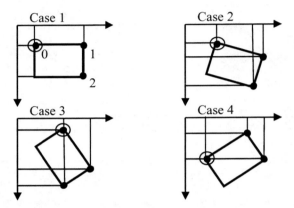

Fig 8. Cases for projection of 3 points

There is underlying software that examines the histograms from the Diamond Touch hardware and identifies the peaks that correspond to touches on the surface of the table. This histogram analysis layer returns the positions of 1, 2 or 3 peaks in each of X and Y. For the handheld device there are always 2 or 3 peaks in each of X and Y.

5.1. Case 1

Case 1 shows as 2 peaks in X and 2 in Y. Case 1 is the most ambiguous alignment and also the position for the hand held when the system is initialized. In the initial position the locations of feet 0, 1 and 2 are easily derived from the histogram information. From this position the width and height of the handheld can also be measured. It is essential that the device not be square. Having a distinct difference between width and height is critical in resolving the point positions in the other cases.

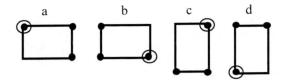

Fig 9. Variations on Case 1

Case 1 not only applies to the initial position, but also four other variations as shown in figure 9. Each of these shows as 2 peaks in each of X and Y and might occur in the course of the user moving the handheld around. Variations a and b can be distinguished from c and d by the known width and height of the handheld. Further ambiguity (a vs. b, or c vs. d) can be resolved by storing the previous position of foot 0 and the previous orientation angle. Knowing the previous position of foot 0 and the orientation angle we can pick the closest alignment to the previous position.

5.2. Resolving ambiguity

The rigid dimensions of the hand held resolve most of the ambiguity problems. The remaining problems we handle by continuity of motion. As the user drags the hand held around the surface as well as rotates it, the position and orientation at time t is very similar to time t-1. In general we find orientation a stronger predictor than position, but we use both for more robust performance.

For a single user scenario there are only a few orientations that make sense. It is unlikely that a user will frequently want to turn the work upside down. In the single user case continuity of orientation works quite well. In a multi-user scenario more drastic rotations occur when sharing the work with someone seated at a different position. Continuity of motion still works in this scenario, but there are cases where it breaks. In a multi-user scenario, the Diamond Touch can sense each user individually. A default orientation range could be associated with each user. The active user would grasp the frame and ambiguity would be resolved using the identity of that user.

In our usage, continuity of motion has worked well. There are two failure cases. The first is if the user moves very fast so that the orientation between time t and time t-1 is very different. This problem is readily resolved by processing of the points so that the sampling rate exceeds human hand speed. A more fundamental problem is when the user picks up the hand held (eliminating sensory contact) and then puts it down in a very different location and orientation. This is resolved through user instruction.

"If you pick it up rather than slide it, it may get confused."

"If it gets confused, pick it up, put it down in alignment with the image and then slide from there."

In our experience users had no difficulty in understanding the correct way to use the device and the work flow was not impeded.

5.3. Cases 2, 3 and 4

Cases 2, 3 and 4 all have a similar treatment. A discussion of case 4 will illustrate what is necessary. Given the 3 peaks in X and the two peaks in Y, in case 4, there are six possible locations for a conductive foot, as shown in figure 11. There are 120 possible assignments of the possible points to the three conductive feet. However, only a few of these possibilities will explain all of the data. Each foot must be assigned to a different X peak or one of the X peaks will be unexplained. Similarly both Y peaks must be used. For example, the combination a, b and d would leave the third X peak unexplained and therefore is not a valid combination.

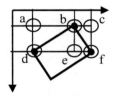

Fig 11. Points derived from X, Y peaks

For case 4 there are 6 possible point/foot assignments that use all of the histogram peaks. Given one of these possible assignments, we can test to see if the assignment is consistent with the known width and height of the handheld device. The distance between foot 0 and foot 1 must be equal to the handheld width. The distance between foot 1 and foot 2 must be equal to the height. This check will eliminate all but one possible configuration in cases 3 and 4. In some situations case 2 can have multiple configurations that are consistent with the data. The final ambiguity of case 2 is resolved using continuity of motion.

6. Display alignment

The handheld display and the context display on the touch table need to correspond in size and location. In XICE all coordinates are specified in *view independent coordinates* (VIC). When a display device

is configured its pixels per inch are specified as well as the preferred viewing distance. This configuration information is sufficient to convert VICs into pixels. If the handheld and the touch table projector have their pixels per inch set correctly and have the same viewing distance then their coordinate systems are automatically consistent when application information is drawn in VICs. There are other systems besides XICE that account for variations in pixels per inch, but the viewing distance is also critical in this focus plus context technique. The resolution of the Diamond Touch for sensing the conductive feet can lead to some misalignment between the hand held and the table top. However, the hand held bezel provides enough of a break in visual continuity that this is not noticeable.

7. User experience

We have not done formal usability studies on Spilling. We have, however, learned some things by watching people try to use the system.

Our first observation was that fixed location widgets are problematic when interacting with a Spilling table. Using the non-dominant hand users freely scroll around their workspace. However, items like menus and tool bars that are at fixed locations require that the user scroll away from their work context to bring such widgets into the focus region of the hand held. The user must then scroll back to the original work area. This is very awkward. Similar problems have been noted with very large displays where substantial effort is required to move from a work location to some distant widget group. We have dealt with this problem by providing access to all widget actions through pop-ups at the work site.

A second issue is interactions that require dragging across a distance larger than the hand held's display size. At first we believed that this was something that just could not be done. That did not concern us because such techniques are very difficult with hand helds anyway. However, users quickly learned to hold the dragged item in the hand held view and then simultaneously scroll the work with the non-dominant hand. Once a user has seen the technique it works very well and is much better than trying to do the same thing on the hand held alone. The fact that the hand held, with larger mass and sliding friction, holds still while the work is moved is also more effective than dragging by moving the hand held as in Ubiquitous Graphics or Peepholes.

8. User interface security threats

We do not presume to deal with all possible security threats to network-connected computers. However, we have tried to avoid introducing any new threats when distributing the user interface to foreign machines. In Spilling there are three security threats in the user interface. The first and most dangerous is the acceptance of input from untrusted machines. Spilling resolves this by only accepting scrolling information and by isolating that input from the application, as shown in figure 1. The second is that a table top display server has access to all of the information being presented on the table. This threat is fundamental to distributed UI architectures and cannot be removed. Any information displayed by a computer for humans to see can be stolen by the display computer.

There is one more subtle UI attack that is possible. A rogue table could lie about scrolling information and about the context while scrolling a different part of the application under the hand held and thus deceiving the user about where their input is going. The table top cannot introduce any new interaction to the hand held, it can only scroll existing elements around. For such a threat to succeed there would need to be a deep understanding of the application by the table top and an application so designed that the user could be deceived by the context. This is a very obscure threat that is easily thwarted by appropriate application design.

9. Summary

We have created an architecture where users can bring hand held devices with small screens to a table top display and "spill" their user interface onto the table. The table provides a large context to the normal interactions of the hand held device. We have also shown how the hand held and the table can be visually synchronized. Lastly we have presented an algorithm for sensing hand held position and orientation through a projective sensing devices such as the Diamond Touch.

10. References

[1] Baudisch, P., Good., N., Stewart, P., "Focus Plus Context Screens: Combining Display Technology with Visualization Techniques", *User Interface Software and Technology (UIST '01)*, ACM (2001), pp. 31-40.

[2] Bederson, B. B., Grosjean, J., Meyer, J., "Toolkit De-sign for Interactive Structured Graphics." *Software En-gineering*, IEEE (2004), pp. 535-546.

[3] Dietz, P.H.; Leigh, D.L., "DiamondTouch: A Multi-User Touch Technology." *ACM Symposium on User Interface Software and Technology (UIST '01)*, ACM (2001), pp 219-226.

[4] Lee, J. C., Hudson, S. E., Summet, J. S., and Dietz, P. H., "Moveable Interactive Projected Displays using Projector-based Tracking," *User Interface Software and Technology (UIST '05)*, ACM (2005), pp 63-72.

[5] Myers, B. A., "Using Handhelds and PCs Together", *CACM*, 44(11), ACM (Nov 2001), pp 34-41.

[6] Olsen, D. R., Nielsen, S. T., and Parslow, D., "Join and Capture: a Model for Nomadic Interaction," *User Interface Software and Technology (UIST '01)*, ACM (2001), pp 131-140.

[7] Pering, T., Ballagas, R., and Want, R. "Spontaneous Marriages of Mobile Devices and Interactive Spaces," *CACM*, 40 (9), (Sept 2005), pp 53-59.

[8] Richardson, T., Stafford-Fraser, Q., Wood, K. R., Hopper, A., "Virtual Network Computing", *IEEE Internet Computing*, 2(1), 1998.

[9] Sanneblad, J. and Holmquist L. "Ubiquitous graphics: combining hand held and wall-size displays to interact with large images." *In Proceedings of AVI 2006*, ACM, (2006), pp 373-377.

[10] Scheifler, R. W. and Gettys, J. "The X Window System" *ACM Transactions on Graphics*, 5(2), (April 1986), pp 79-109.

[11] Shen, C., Vernier, F. D., Forlines, C., and Ringel, M. "DiamondSpin: an Extensible Toolkit for Around-the-table Interaction," *Human Factors in Computing Systems (CHI '04)*, ACM, (2004), pp 167-174.

[12] http://wacom.com/

[13] Want, R., Perins, T., Danneels, G., Kumar, M., Sundar, M., and J. Light. "The Personal Server: Changing the way we think about Ubiquitous Computing." *Ubiquitous Computing* (UbiComp '02), Springer Verlag, (2002).

[14] Wilson, A. D., "PlayAnywhere: a Compact Interactive Tabletop Projection-vision System," *User Interface Software and Technology (UIST '05)*, ACM (2005), pp 83-92.

[15] Yee, K.-P. "Peephole Displays: Pen Interaction on Spatially Aware Handheld Computers." *Human Factors in Computing Systems (CHI '03)*, ACM, (2003), pp 1-8.

Supporting Multiple Off-Axis Viewpoints at a Tabletop Display

Mark Hancock, Sheelagh Carpendale
University of Calgary
Calgary, AB, Canada
{msh,sheelagh}@cs.ucalgary.ca

Abstract

A growing body of research is investigating the use of tabletop displays, in particular to support collaborative work. People often interact directly with these displays, typically with a stylus or touch. The current common focus of limiting interaction to 2D prevents people from performing actions familiar to them in the 3D world, including piling, flipping and stacking. However, a problem arises when viewing 3D on large displays that are intended for proximal use; the view angle can be extremely oblique and lead to distortion in the perception of the 3D projection. We present a simplified model that compensates for off-axis viewing for a single user and extend this technique for multiple viewers interacting with the same large display. We describe several implications of our approach to collaborative activities. We also describe other display configurations for which our technique may prove useful, including proximal use of a wall or multiple-display configurations.

1. Introduction

Interest in supporting co-located collaboration via tabletop displays has been growing rapidly. Interaction with these large displays is often provided through direct-touch or stylus input. When people use this form of interaction, we necessarily expect that they will use these displays from a very close distance. This close distance implies that the viewing angle is likely to be severely off-axis. For example, with a tabletop display the traditional viewpoint is centred directly above the screen. For normal viewing from any side of the table, one's viewpoint is extremely *off-axis* or *skewed*. This skew has already been shown to be problematic for perception of lengths in 2D interfaces on tabletop displays [19]. In 3D interfaces, the problem of off-axis viewing is exacerbated. The use of standard projection techniques (perspective and orthographic) may result in significant distortion when objects are viewed from off-axis (see Figure 1).

Despite the potential difficulties, there are several reasons to think that incorporating 3D into large-display interfaces would be beneficial. We all make good use of the third dimension in the physical world: we make stacks,

Figure 1. (left) Standard perspective projection, (right) compensated for the appropriate off-axis viewpoint. Both photographs are taken from the viewpoint of a person at one side of the table[1].

piles and looser groupings, and turn items over and use their other side. The need to support these types of information-handling functionalities has been well discussed [1, 9, 17].

We present a simplified model to compensate for off-axis viewing of 3D objects and generalize this technique for use by many people around the display. After describing both fixed and customizable alternatives for multiple viewers, we discuss the implications of each for collaboration. Our technique can also be used to compensate for distortion for large displays in general and for multiple-display configurations.

2. Related Work

There are several areas of research that are relevant to our work. There are techniques to correct projector-displayed images onto a surface that is not perpendicular to the projector, thus *correcting off-axis projection* (of primarily 2D images) in a different way. There has been work on producing images with *alternate perspective rendering* techniques. *Fish-tank virtual reality* techniques have also been used to correct off-axis distortion using head tracking. Lastly, there are existing *3D tabletop display interfaces* that resolve the multiple-viewing-angle problem.

---

[1]Note that photographs and videos taken of displays containing 3D graphics from off-axis angles have the added complexity of the camera angle. We have worked with the camera to give the most realistic depiction of what one would see with the naked eye.

2.1. Correcting for Off-Axis Projection

Dorsey et al. [7] present a system that allows images to be projected onto a (possibly curved) display from an off-axis position. Lee et al. [12] extend this idea with a system that can adaptively calibrate as either the projector or display surface moves so that the image is displayed correctly, despite the angle of projection. PlayAnywhere [20] allows for off-axis projection from very close to a surface. While these systems correct distortion caused by varying the point of projection, our model compensates for varying points of view. Theoretically, these two types of corrections could work effectively in unison.

2.2. Alternate Perspective Rendering

Agarawala et al. [3] present a way of providing multiple camera viewpoints for each object in a scene. Ryan [5] allows a static image to be created by stitching together multiple viewpoints so even single objects can be distorted and viewed at multiple angles. While these works effectively demonstrate the expressive impact of integrating multiple camera scenes, our model focuses on adjusting 3D scenes to preserve perceived shapes and sizes of 3D objects and considers both interaction and the effects on multiple people collaborating.

Zorin and Barr [21] describe many of the limitations of the use of standard perspective projection in the creation of static 3D images. Specifically, they argue that a picture of a 3D scene cannot simultaneously satisfy both properties (1) that straight lines should appear straight and (2) that objects should appear as if viewed directly. They present a formalism to manually balance these two properties. In our case, this problem is exacerbated due to (a) the desire to have a 3D image appear correct for *multiple* people viewing the image and (b) to have the "images" being viewed be interactive, and thus dynamically changing perspective.

Our work differs significantly from research dealing with the correction of viewpoint for a single person viewing a static image. In the multi-user case, we do not attempt to provide an image viewable by all users, but provide a mechanism to distort the interface in a way that better supports each user in a portion of the display. We also discuss methods to smoothly transition objects between workspaces of multiple people. Our technique relies on a much simpler technique to provide perspective correction for one user, so that extending to the multiple user case becomes easier and allows us to explore a variety of approaches to this case.

2.3. Fish Tank Virtual Reality

Previous research also explores the correction of a 3D projection based on viewing angle [6, 13] and has been dubbed "Fish Tank Virtual Reality" [18]. These systems typically use one of two approaches: they either use stereoscopic (headtracked) goggles that project an image onto two surfaces that move with the user's head motion, or they track the user's head position and correct the view for the measured eyepoint. In the former case, no off-axis correction is necessary, since the viewplane is kept perpendicular to both eyes. In the latter case, the projection must account for a potentially off-axis viewing angle, and thus these systems also provide a solution to the off-axis distortion problem for a single user. These systems have considered many variables beyond the scope of our work (including refraction and the effect of curvature of CRTs), and could be substituted for our simpler single-user solution and extended in the same way for multiple viewers.

2.4. 3D Tabletop Display Interfaces

Tabletop display interfaces have typically been designed to use only two dimensions. However, much of the interaction that takes place on traditional tables makes use of the third dimension: piling, sorting, stacking, and using orientation to communicate intention to others. There have been some interfaces and interaction techniques developed that attempt to leverage these real-world counterparts [1, 9]. These techniques focus primarily on the interaction with artifacts in a 3D world, but do not consider how those artifacts are perceived by the viewers.

The two-user responsive workbench [2] addresses the problem of different viewpoints at a table by providing correct stereoscopic 3D images to two different people. The IllusionHole can be used to integrate 2D and 3D [14] on a table by limiting the portion of the display presented at each viewing angle via a hole in the table's centre. These systems both provide stereoscopic cues via headgear and a tracking system. Our solution differs from these systems in that we focus on correcting perspective cues and we require no headgear or tracking, and thus is more suited for casual large display use. The lack of headgear also allows for more seamless collaboration, due to the possibility for eye contact.

3. Correcting Off-Axis Distortion

We present a general method to compensate for distortion caused by off-axis viewing of 3D objects projected onto a 2D surface. We first describe how to adjust this distortion for a single person's perspective and then describe several techniques for extending this method for multiple viewing angles. Note that our model for correcting distortion for a single user can be accomplished using existing techniques [3, 13]. We present a simpler model with minimal changes to the current 3D projection methods, which allows us to more easily extend the technique to multiple users and to explore a large variety of alternative projections.

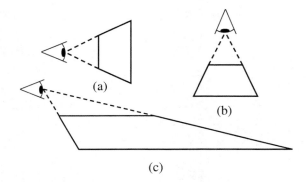

(a)

(b)

(c)

Figure 2. (a) Standard viewpoint works well for small vertical displays. (b) Standard viewpoint directly above the tabletop display. (c) Typical viewpoint for a tabletop display is close to the screen and to one side.

3.1. Correcting for One User

The standard method for projecting 3D graphics onto a 2D surface assumes that the viewpoint is at the centre and directly in front of the display (see Figure 2). A common method to achieve this projection is by transforming points in a 3D model to a canonical viewing volume [10]. For a perspective projection, the near plane is assumed to be perpendicular to the eye and so has the equation $z = -N$, where N is the distance from the eye to the near plane. Thus, all points in the model are projected by intersecting the line from the eye to the point with this near plane. Such a line would have parametric equations:

$$x = P_x t, y = P_y t, z = P_z t$$

Thus, this intersection would result in a projected point (x', y') with pseudodepth z' as follows:

$$x' = N\frac{P_x}{-P_z}, \quad y' = N\frac{P_y}{-P_z}, \quad z' = \frac{aP_z + b}{-P_z}$$

The corresponding transformation matrix is:

$$\begin{bmatrix} N & 0 & 0 & 0 \\ 0 & N & 0 & 0 \\ 0 & 0 & a & b \\ 0 & 0 & -1 & 0 \end{bmatrix}$$

When viewing a display from off-axis, the assumption that the viewer is directly in front of the display is invalid. The degree to which the viewer is off the centre axis is particularly high when viewing a large display from one side. We introduce a method for rendering 3D objects that, instead of using a perpendicular near plane, uses an arbitrary near plane with the equation:

$$Ax + By + Cz = D$$

In order to preserve the property that the z-axis intersects the plane at a distance of N from the eye, we set $C = -1$ and $D = N$. Thus, A and B represent the slope of the plane in the x and y directions, respectively. Points in the model are again projected by intersecting the line from the eye to the point with this arbitrary near plane. This intersection results in the projected point (x', y', z'):

$$x' = N\frac{P_x}{AP_x + BP_y - P_z}, \quad y' = N\frac{P_y}{AP_x + BP_y - P_z}$$

$$z' = \frac{aP_z + b}{AP_x + BP_y - P_z}$$

The transformation matrix is thus only slightly modified:

$$\begin{bmatrix} N & 0 & 0 & 0 \\ 0 & N & 0 & 0 \\ 0 & 0 & a & b \\ A & B & -1 & 0 \end{bmatrix}$$

With this simple modification to the projection matrix, 3D objects can be rendered to compensate for off-axis viewing. This method introduces no added complexity and does not interfere with the response time of interaction.

3.2. Correcting for Multiple Users

The above method allows 3D objects to be rendered correctly for a single off-axis viewpoint, but tabletop displays lend themselves to many people gathering around them, each with their own viewing angle. Thus, a single viewpoint rendering may not be sufficient. Objects can each be rendered with a different perspective transformation, depending on the position of the object. By altering the perspective matrix in proportion to the object's position, this method essentially provides an arbitrarily-shaped near surface. We present alternative methods of projecting 3D objects for multiple users at a table.

3.2.1. Partitioning Viewpoints. One method of altering the perspective for many users is to provide several dedicated areas that each optimize the viewing angle for a particular portion of the display. For example, an obvious partition for a rectangular table is to divide the table in four parts and optimize the view for the closest side to each part. Essentially, each partition provides a different "window" through which to look at the underlying 3D model. Thus, the eye position of each partition can be chosen in three different ways.

The partitions can be aligned so that the near planes of each provide the boundaries (see Figure 3 and Figure 6c). This method results in view volumes that intersect one another. When an object is within the bounds of an intersection, the objects can either be displayed at all viewpoints, or some decision must be made as to which viewpoint to use.

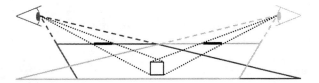

Figure 3. Partitions aligned with touching near planes result in intersecting view volumes.

Alternatively, the partitions can be aligned so that the separate view volumes do not intersect (see Figure 4 and Figure 6d). This model has the advantage that objects cannot be within two views at the same time. However, when crossing the boundary of two views, the change in projected position can be both large and discontinuous, which may make interaction confusing. Also, this method creates a volume in the model between the partitions where an object can exist without being visible.

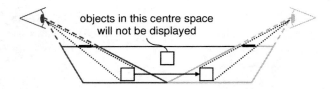

Figure 4. Partitions aligned with touching far planes result in disjoint view volumes. Objects moving between between view volumes may appear to jump.

A third method of providing correct perspective for multiple partitions is to keep the eye position above the centre of the table, but to slope the near plane differently in each partition (see Figure 5 and Figure 6e). Essentially this provides a view in each partition that is set for the correct viewing angle, while avoiding intersection of view volumes and discontinuities when objects move across boundaries. This method still compensates for off-axis distortion, but provides smoother interaction. However, because the near plane is distorted, applications requiring realism may prefer a partition with a "correct" eye position for each side.

A side effect of not moving the eye position as the slope changes is that objects become further from the near plane as they are moved closer to the table's edge. This effect can be corrected by adjusting the near plane distance so that the centre of the object is always projected to the original near plane. This new near plane distance, N', can be calculated by substituting the centre's projected point in standard perspective $(x', y', -N)$ into the equation for the plane:

$$N' = Ax' + By' + N$$

All three partitioning methods can be achieved by setting either A or B to the desired slope of the near plane.

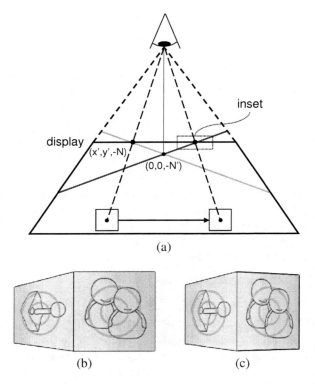

(a)

(b)   (c)

Figure 5. (a) The slope of the near plane can be adjusted to be appropriate for the adjacent table edge. Objects moving across the partition boundary do not jump and are not replicated. Insets show how the object would appear using (b) standard perspective and (c) when projected to the sloped plane.

3.2.2. Continuous Viewpoints. Instead of dividing the table into discrete parts, objects can be projected so that the viewing direction changes continuously. That is, objects can be projected so that the viewpoint is determined by the rotation (θ) about the z-axis. This method prevents objects from having to cross partition boundaries and suddenly switch viewpoints; instead, the transition is smooth across the entire display. The transition can also be made smooth at the centre of the display by adjusting the plane's slope (m) according to the distance (r) of the object from the centre of the display. This method essentially provides a hemispherical near plane (see Figure 7 and Figure 6f) and can be achieved by setting $A = mr \cdot \cos\theta$ and $B = mr \cdot \sin\theta$.

3.2.3. Customizable Viewpoints. We provide customizable views to allow users to manipulate the slope of the near plane and resize the area of influence of this near plane (see Figure 8 and Figure 6b). This slope can be controlled with a virtual handle that can be adjusted to provide the appropriate view. Again, it is possible to implement customizable views so that the eye position moves as the slope changes. However, it can be advantageous to not move the eye loca-

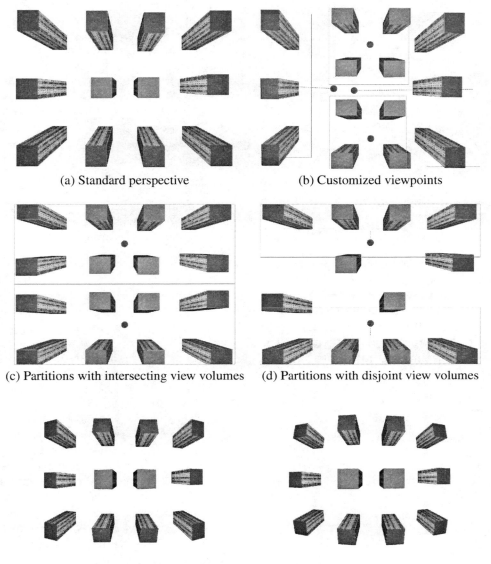

(a) Standard perspective

(b) Customized viewpoints

(c) Partitions with intersecting view volumes

(d) Partitions with disjoint view volumes

(e) Partitions with sloped planes only

(f) Continuous (spherical) viewpoint

Figure 6. (a) shows a series of 9 buildings using a standard perspective projection, which works well for someone standing directly above the table, but no one else. (b) shows four areas, each with its own customized viewpoint. The top and bottom areas are best viewed from the top and bottom respectively. The left area is best viewed from near the centre of the display and the right area is best viewed from the left side. (c) shows a partitioning of these same building into two parts. The top partition is best viewed from the top side, and the bottom is best viewed from the bottom. Note that in this correction, the view volumes intersect and so the middle buildings are replicated in both views. (d) shows two partitions with the same optimal viewing angles, but with non-intersecting view volumes. (e) shows a partitioning into four parts (left is best viewed from left, top from top, etc.), but only the planes are sloped; the eye position is kept at the centre and above the display. (f) shows a continuously changing viewpoint as objects move across the display. Objects are projected so they are best viewed along the axis from the centre of the display to the object.

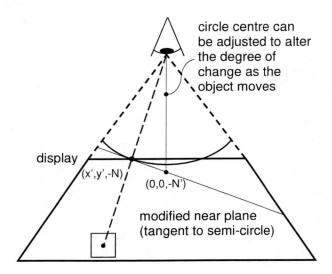

Figure 7. In continuous spherical perspective projection, as objects are moved toward the edges of the display, the near plane they are projected to increases in slope. As they move toward the centre, the near plane becomes a standard perspective. Objects will appear more correct the closer they are to the viewer's edge.

tion so that the objects do not change their projected positions as the handle is dragged.

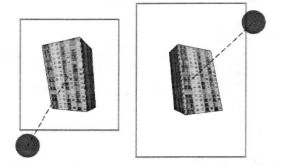

Figure 8. The left area is a custom view corrected for a viewpoint at the bottom-left and the right custom area is for a viewpoint at the top-right.

3.3. Effect on Collaboration

Choices made between off-axis projections influence the environment and how people coordinate and communicate within that environment. We discuss some of the implications and limitations of the corrections we suggest for multiple viewers.

3.3.1. Viewpoint Relativity. In all of the suggested multiple-viewer corrections, at any point in time, each object appears "correct" for only one viewpoint around the table. In order to make it appear correct for another, a person must either move the object along the surface or move a handle to adjust that viewpoint. Thus, our solution solves the multiple-viewer problem in a very different way than providing different views for each person (as in [2, 11]). The effect of our approach is that an object in "someone else's" space would still appear distorted (in fact, more so than in a standard perspective projection). This increased distortion may be a disadvantage, but on the other hand, may actually provide an added hint to a collaborator not to expect the object to appear correct. For example, a person watching the actions of another across the table would see a highly distorted image, and therefore not expect to see (say) the opposite side of a virtual cube, as they would with a real object.

3.3.2. Sensitivity to Frames. If a 3D scene is projected inside a framed box, people tend to compensate for off-axis inconsistencies. This effect may be due to the tendency to achieve shape constancy under object rotations [16]. Since the tabletop display is itself a frame, this could lead to an expectation different from the correction that we provide. Because the frame is a fixed physical entity, viewing the frame from different viewpoints (i.e. by different people) cannot be corrected for. However, because of the size of the tabletop display and the proximity of the people to the display, the frame may be too far separated from the objects being rendered to have any effect.

Framing can also be an issue in our customizable viewpoint correction, since we use a rectangular box (parallel to the edges of the display) to indicate the affected areas. It may be preferrable to use a frame that matches the correction to provide a better visual cue to the people at the display. Matching the frame to the correction may also improve a person's ability to parse objects in "someone else's" area, despite the increased distortion.

3.3.3. Fixed vs. Customizable Corrections. Both partitioned and continuous views provide a fixed correction for the entire display. These fixed corrections can be chosen based on an expected scenario of use. With these solutions, users will not have to learn additional controls and may be mostly unaware that the distortion has been corrected. Thus, this correction may become invisible to the user.

It can also be beneficial to allow people to control what areas of the screen are best viewed from what side. By providing this freedom, natural communication gestures may become available. For example, with this solution, it is possible for people to set up personal areas within which artifacts look correct as they work independently, and then can share their work by adjusting the viewpoint to be correct for another person. In general, providing this ability supports many of the mechanics of collaboration [15], including gestural messages ("this is what mine looks like"), visual evidence ("this is how they were looking at it"), and obtaining and reserving resources ("I'll look at this area from my viewpoint"). However, providing this added freedom can also add cognitive load, in that portions of the display can be set for different viewpoints, and users are assigned the added task of adjusting to the correct viewpoint.

3.4. Other Uses of Perspective Correction

Many wall-sized displays allow for interaction at close distances [4, 8]. Our technique could be used to adjust a 3D scene on such a wall to compensate for this proximity for either a single viewpoint or for multiple viewpoints as with the tabletop display. This setup would differ from the table in that the correction would likely only be necessary along one axis (horizontal adjustments, but not vertical). The view could also be coupled with such technologies as motion detection or gaze awareness to make it possible for a person's perspective view to stay correct as they explored 3D models.

It is also possible to use our technique to display a 3D scene on multiple displays configured at different angles. For example, several screens could be placed facing one another to create a long column with an adjacent column at the base (Figure 9). Two people could stand at each end of the display, and one of our multiple-user corrections could be used. Other display combinations are also possible, such as a tabletop display with an adjacent wall display or a cube with projections on each side.

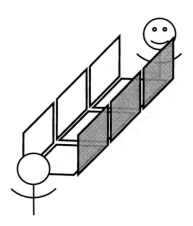

Figure 9. Our off-axis distortion correction can be applied to 3D scenes viewed across many displays, each at a different angle with respect to the viewers.

4. Conclusion

Our simplified model for correcting perspective projections for varying viewpoint positions provides support for proximal interaction with 3D interfaces on tabletop displays, and allows us to extend these ideas into a collaborative setting. Providing corrected views is a step toward making interactive 3D more viable and generalizes to many display configurations, including walls, tables and multiple configurable displays. We provide both continuous and discrete options for fixed corrections that allow interactions with perspective views automatically corrected to the closest side of the display, and customizable options that provide collaborators with many possibilities for adjusting viewpoints and the affected display regions, supporting both shared and personal views.

We would like to encourage further exploration into physical advantages of 3D interaction and enable empirical and observational studies that will further our understanding of proximal use of 3D on large displays.

5. Acknowledgments

We would like to thank Natural Science and Engineering Research Council of Canada, Alberta's Informatics Circle of Research Excellence, Alberta Ingenuity, the Canadian Foundation of Innovation, and SMART Technologies for research support. We also thank members of the iLab for their valuable input.

References

[1] A. Agarawala and R. Balakrishnan. Keepin' it real: Pushing the desktop metaphor with physics, piles and the pen. In *Proc. CHI*. ACM Press, 2006.

[2] M. Agrawala, A. C. Beers, I. McDowall, B. Fröhlich, M. Bolas, and P. Hanrahan. The two-user responsive workbench: Support for collaboration through individual views of a shared space. In *Proc. SIGGRAPH*, pages 327–332, New York, NY, USA, 1997. ACM Press.

[3] M. Agrawala, D. Zorin, and T. Munzner. Artistic multiprojection rendering. In *Proc. Eurographics Workshop on Rendering Techniques*, pages 125–136, London, UK, 2000. Springer-Verlag.

[4] A. Bezerianos and R. Balakrishnan. View and space management on large displays. *IEEE CG & A*, 25(4):34–43, 2005.

[5] P. Coleman and K. Singh. Ryan: Rendering your animation nonlinearly projected. In *Proc. NPAR*, pages 129–156, New York, NY, USA, 2004. ACM Press.

[6] M. Deering. High resolution virtual reality. In *Proc. SIGGRAPH*, pages 195–202, New York, NY, USA, 1992. ACM Press.

[7] J. O. Dorsey, F. X. Sillion, and D. P. Greenberg. Design and simulation of opera lighting and projection effects. In *Proc. SIGGRAPH*, pages 41–50, New York, NY, USA, 1991. ACM Press.

[8] F. Guimbretière, M. Stone, and T. Winograd. Fluid interaction with high-resolution wall-size displays. In *Proc. UIST*, pages 21–30, New York, NY, USA, 2001. ACM Press.

[9] M. Hancock, S. Carpendale, and A. Cockburn. Shallow-depth 3D interaction: Design and evaluation of one-, two- and three-touch techniques. In *Proc. CHI*, pages 1147–1156, New York, NY, USA, 2007. ACM Press.

[10] F. S. Hill, jr. *Computer Graphics Using Open GL*. Prentice Hall, 2nd edition, 2001.

[11] Y. Kitamura, T. Konishi, S. Yamamoto, and F. Kishino. Interactive stereoscopic display for three or more users. In *Proc. SIGGRAPH*, pages 231–240, New York, NY, USA, 2001. ACM Press.

[12] J. C. Lee, S. E. Hudson, J. W. Summet, and P. H. Dietz. Moveable interactive projected displays using projector based tracking. In *Proc. UIST*, pages 63–72. ACM Press, 2005.

[13] M. McKenna. Interactive viewpoint control and three-dimensional operations. In *Proc. SI3D*, pages 53–56, New York, NY, USA, 1992. ACM Press.

[14] K. Nakashima, T. Machida, K. Kiyokawa, and H. Takemura. A 2D-3D integrated environment for cooperative work. In *Proc. VRST*, pages 16–22, New York, NY, USA, 2005. ACM Press.

[15] D. Pinelle, C. Gutwin, and S. Greenberg. Task analysis for groupware usability evaluation: Modeling shared-workspace tasks with the mechanics of collaboration. *ToCHI*, 10(4):281–311, 2003.

[16] Z. Pizlo. A theory of shape constancy based on perspective invariants. *Vision Research*, 34(12):1637–1658, June 1994.

[17] L. Terrenghi, D. Kirk, A. Sellen, and S. Izadi. Affordances for manipulation of physical versus digital media on interactive surfaces. In *Proc. CHI*, pages 1157–1166, New York, NY, USA, 2007. ACM Press.

[18] C. Ware, K. Arthur, and K. S. Booth. Fish tank virtual reality. In *CHI '93: Proceedings of the SIGCHI conference on Human factors in computing systems*, pages 37–42, New York, NY, USA, 1993. ACM Press.

[19] D. Wigdor, C. Shen, C. Forlines, and R. Balakrishnan. Perception of elementary graphical elements in tabletop and multi-surface environments. In *Proc. CHI*. ACM Press, 2007. To Appear.

[20] A. D. Wilson. PlayAnywhere: a compact interactive tabletop projection-vision system. In *Proc. UIST*, pages 83–92. ACM Press, 2005.

[21] D. Zorin and A. H. Barr. Correction of geometric perceptual distortions in pictures. In *Proc. SIGGRAPH*, pages 257–264, New York, NY, USA, 1995. ACM Press.

Multiple input support in a model-based interaction framework

Stéphane Chatty[1,2]   Alexandre Lemort[2]   Stéphane Valès[2]

[1]ENAC   [2]IntuiLab
7 avenue Edouard Belin   Les Triades A, rue Galilée
31055 Toulouse Cedex, France   31672 Labège Cedex, France
{surname}@intuilab.com

Abstract

Developing for tabletops puts special requirements on interface programming frameworks: managing parallel input, device discovery, device equivalence, and describing combined interactions. We analyse these issues and describe the solutions that were used in IntuiKit, a model-based framework aimed at making the design and development of post-WIMP user interfaces more accessible. Some solutions are simple consequences of the support of multimodality, while others are more specific to multiple touch. We illustrate these features through examples developed in several tabletop projects, including one application aimed at improving collaboration between air traffic controllers.

Keywords: interaction framework, tabletop, multiple input, model-based architecture, event model, data-flow

1   Introduction

Developing user interfaces for tabletops is close enough to developing for desktop computers or touchscreens that one may wish to use the same programming frameworks, and reuse existing interaction components. However, there are differences that must be accounted for, in graphics as well as in input management. We will focus here on the extensions that must be brought to the input management of frameworks designed for more traditional user interfaces.

The most obvious necessary extension is the ability to handle multiple flows of input, though it is not much different from handling animation in parallel with interaction. More unusual is the ability to handle a variable number of touch points, or the implied hierarchical structure of those devices that have both multi-touch and multi-user detection. The differences between devices must also be accounted for: some do user identification but lack correlation between X and Y coordinates of touch points, others are limited to two pointers, etc. Then the connection between the graphics

system and the input system (often called "picking") must be made extensible. Then, because tabletops are still costly and developers often need to simulate them during development and unit tests, a framework for adapting, filtering and simulating input devices must be provided. Finally, support must be provided for programmers to design interaction styles that combine several input flows.

In this article, we analyse the above issues and solutions for addressing them. We present our solutions using the IntuiKit framework, that implements results on interactive software modelling carried out by a joint ENAC-IntuiLab research group and is used by IntuiLab's design teams and their partners. As IntuiKit strongly relies on abstract models of interactive software, some solutions rely on existing models and others consist of new models for new aspects of interactive software. We first describe the basic concepts of IntuiKit. We then describe the proposed solutions for supporting device addressing, input configuration and parallel interaction. We finally describe an application implemented using those mechanisms, before reviewing related works.

2   IntuiKit principles

IntuiKit is a framework for prototyping and developing post-WIMP user interfaces (that is user interfaces that do not rely on the Windows-Icon-Mouse-Pointing paradigm) as well as multimodal user interfaces. Its purpose is not only to make the programming of such interfaces feasible, but to make their design, development and deployment cost-effective enough for non specialised industries to afford it. In particular, in order to allow the reuse of design elements when switching from prototyping to final development, IntuiKit relies on a model-based architecture: as much as possible of the user interface is made of data obtained by instantiating models [6]. The resulting interface models can be "rendered" by different implementations of the framework: one aimed at prototyping (which currently offers a Perl programming interface), and the other aimed at

Figure 1. An interface with SVG graphics

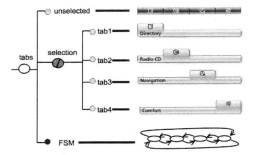

Figure 2. A part of the tree from Figure 1

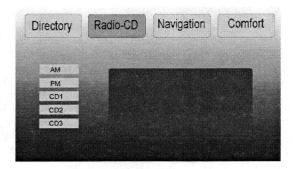

Figure 3. The same tree with another SVG file

industrial deployment (which currently offers a C++ interface). The modelling concerns graphical objects, but also elements of architecture, behaviour and control, animation trajectories, speech grammars, etc.

2.1 The application tree

The first modelling choice used in IntuiKit is to consider an interactive application as a tree of elements. The management of the tree, its traversals and the communication between elements are managed by the IntuiKit core. Terminal elements in the tree are brought by models of interaction modalities or models of behaviour description. Specialised IntuiKit modules each provide a set of terminal elements. For instance, the GUI module manages graphical elements from the SVG standard; the Speech module manages elements that represent grammar rules; the Animation module manages trajectories and collision detection; the Base module provides behaviour description elements, such as clocks and finite state machines. More complex elements named components can be built by assembling other elements. For instance, a simple button component can be obtained by combining a finite state machine (FSM), a special element that only renders one of its subtrees depending on the state of the FSM, and a series of rectangles and texts that represent the different states of the button.

The role of IntuiKit is to help programmers to build the application tree, then to manage its rendering. Programmers can assemble elements. Or they can code their own components, for instance to create functional core objects that communicate with the rest of the application using the architecture patterns supported by the core model. Parts of the tree can also be loaded at run time from XML files. For instance, the tabs from an in-car comfort and navigation system in Figure 1 are obtained by loading a given SVG file into the tree presented in Figure 2, and Figure 3 is obtained by loading another SVG file. The same type of customisation based on element loading can be used to adapt to touchscreens an application made for desktops: for a given button, one can choose to load either a FSM that implements a "take-off" or one that implements a "land-on" strategy [16].

2.2 Event model

Because user interface programmers deal with interaction and behaviour, and not only rendering, a very central part of the core models is the communication between elements. It has since long been established that event-based communication and control is well adapted to managing user input. Event communication is a pattern of control flow alternative to function call, that can be implemented on top of classical function calls. This is used by most interaction frameworks to juxtapose event communication and function calls in applications. However, a characteristic of user interaction, and especially post-WIMP interaction, is that the same actions can be triggered from very different contexts: user input, animation, or computations from the functional core. Being able to reuse components thus requires that one provide a unique model of communication for all these contexts: fragments of code that use different communication mechanisms cannot be connected easily. Furthermore, because a user interface has a parallel execution semantics [5], the overall semantics may become unclear if several control transfer mechanisms are used. That is why we use event communication as the only mechanism for transferring control from components to others: in the same way as functional programming splits all code into functions that communicate through function calls, we split all code into elements that communicate through events.

For that purpose, we use the concept of event source.

Each source has two features: its event specification format, and its event contents. For instance, the `'clock'` source has a specification format that distinguishes between one-shot timeouts and periodic timers, and accepts one argument in the first case and two in the second case. The event contents is a timestamp, with an additional repetition number in the second case. Some event sources like the clock are global to the application and brought by IntuiKit modules. Elements are also sources; this includes graphical objects or FSMs, but also any component built by programmers. In the latter case, the event specification format and the event contents depend on the structure of the component, and can be customised by the programmer. For instance, one can build a dialog box and make it emit empty "OK" and "CANCEL" events, or a wallclock component that emits "SECOND", "MINUTE" and "HOUR" events that contain the time of the day. Finally, element properties, such as the width of a rectangle, are also event sources. This serves as the basis for data-flow communication which is therefore a special case of event communication.

Event subscription is obtained by adding special elements to the application tree. All use the same pattern: a reference to an event source, an event specification, and an action. The simplest is the Binding, which links an event specification to an action. FSMs add state to this: their transitions are Bindings that are only active in given states. A Connector has an implicit event specification and action: its event source is an element property, whose value is used to update another element property when it changes. A Watcher is used inside components; it accepts several properties as event sources, and triggers an action when one or more of them changes. Watchers are used to implement rendering; Watchers and Connectors are used to produce data-flow communication: data-flow filters modify their output properties in the actions triggered by their watchers. Figure 4 shows a FSM used to control a stick-button.

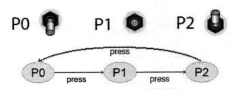

Figure 4. Behaviour of a 3-state button

3 Managing multiple devices

In most user interfaces, input devices can remain implicit in the code. In WIMP user interfaces, for instance, programmers usually subscribe to event types that are related to the mouse or to the keyboard: no need to introduce any explicit reference to the keyboard or the mouse themselves. If one is missing, the programs does not run; if there are other devices, either they can safely be ignored or the operating system manages to mix them so as to emulate one mouse and one keyboard. On a tabletop, multiplicity is the rule and one to distinguish among devices: "I want to subscribe to touches from this user", or "I want to subscribe to touches from any user, then to moves from the user that has just touched the table", etc. The event model used in IntuiKit offers a framework for this: one just needs to have different event sources representing the different input among which one wants to select, or a source with an appropriate event specification format. By adapting the sources and event specification used in a given component, one can easily adapt it from single-touch to multi-touch interaction. However, some questions still remain: how to reference a given input source? how to check if a given device is present? how to handle the fact that the number of input flows, for instance the number of users or the number of fingers, is not known in advance? how to manage complex sources such as a multi-user multi-pointer table?

3.1 Devices as external elements

The model chosen as the basis for answering the above questions is partially an extension of the semantics of the application tree. It consists of stating that input devices are elements, but elements that are located *outside* of the application tree. By stating that devices are elements, we go a long way towards allowing the programmer to reference them and towards handling new input flows. By stating that they are outside of the application tree, we give account of the fact that the programmer does not control their existence: they are context elements that may or may not be there, and it is up to the programmer to query them. This model actually applies to many resources that are external to applications: operating system resources, other applications, context capture, etc. Users interact with a system represented by a large tree, part of which represents the application being developed. This is consistent with, for instance, the way the Unix file system is extended in the Linux kernel to make various information about the kernel or programs accessible to other programs.

3.2 Referencing and fiding devices

Since devices are elements, they are event sources and can be used in event subscriptions. This can be done by using an extension to the referencing scheme in the application tree. The referencing scheme, in a similar way to the source/specification couples used for events, uses namespaces and names. Precedently, all namespaces referenced elements in the application tree. The `'input'` namespace is used to reference devices. For instance, one can use

```
new Binding(-source => 'input:diamondtouch', ...);
```

in Perl or

```
<binding source="input:diamondtouch" ... />
```

in XML to subscribe to a DiamondTouch device plugged on the computer. Device names are dependent on the configuration of the computer. Therefore one may wish to use an element property instead of a literal for the device name so as to set the device name in a configuration file, in CSS format for instance.

The above referencing scheme leads to an error if the device requested is not present. If a programmer wishes to handle this situation, it is possible to use references from the programming language as an intermediate. In Perl, for instance:

```
$d = get Element(-uri => 'input:diamondtouch', ...);
if (defined $d) {
  new Binding(-source => $d, ...);
} else {
  ...
}
```

It is possible to express typing constraints on the device:

```
$d = get DiamondTouch(-uri => 'input:diamondtouch', ...);
```

Richer constraints, such as "any pointing device", will require namespaces that handle more complex queries than a name, such as XPath-like or SQL-like requests.

3.3 Dynamicity

A feature of multi-touch or multi-user systems is the dynamicity of input. The number of touch points or pointers usually starts at zero when starting the system. It then increases as soon as a new user starts interacting, a new finger lands on the surface or a new pointer is used. When this happens, the programmer usually wishes a new feedback and possibly new behaviours to be added to the user interface. This situation is very similar to the addition of a new device, for instance a new mouse, to the computer. Actually, plugging mice successively onto the computer is a simple way of simulating a tabletop during unit tests. The dynamicity of users and touch points is very similar to hot-plugging.

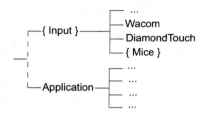

Figure 5. The set of input devices in the tree

In conformance with the choice to make event communication the core mechanism of control in the application tree, the dynamicity of input devices is handled through

events. IntuiKit has *Set* elements, that contain other elements; adding or removing an element from a set triggers an event. By subscribing to a Set as an event source, one can associate an action to the addition or the removal. The set of all input devices is accessible through the global name 'input'; subscribing to it allows to be notified of all new devices connected to the computer:

```
new Binding(-source => 'input', -spec => 'add', ...);
```

3.4 Hierarchical devices

So far we have been indiscriminate about the exact nature of input devices, referring to multiple mice in the same way as multiple pointers on a tabletop. However, there are differences. When using mice, every of them is an input device of its own. When using a Wacom Intuos 2 tablet, which is able to handle two styluses, the tablet itself is the device: plugging it on the computer is a legitimate hot-plugging event, and one may wish to subscribe to all events from the tablet. Nevertheless, one would still be interested in being notified when a new stylus is used on the tablet, and to subscribe to events from this stylus. The same holds for a DiamondTouch and its four users; it gets even more complex when one uses a tracking algorithm to distinguish among multiple pointer from a same user on the DiamondTouch.

The application tree provides a framework for describing this. By considering devices as elements that can contain other elements, one can build a model of devices that takes into account all of the above situations: devices are either atomic or made of subdevices, like interaction components can be made of subcomponents. For instance, a mouse is made of a locator and several buttons. A Wacom Intuos 2 contains a set of pointers. A DiamondTouch contains a set of users, which each possibly contain a set of pointers. One can subscribe to the apparition of a new pointer by subscribing to the set of all devices in the first case, or the set of pointers contained in the device in the two other cases.

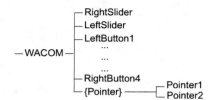

Figure 6. Internal structure of a Wacom device

This hierarchical view of devices not only matches the underlying application tree model where all interactive components can be made of sub-components. It also matches theoretical models of input devices [3] and provides a useful basis for dealing with device equivalence and combination when detecting and adapting the input configuration for reusing components or applications.

4 Input configuration

The gist of software reuse is the ability to reuse a piece of code or a component in contexts that did not need to be explicit at the time of writing it. For instance, a sorting function can be used to sort all types of lists. This usually requires a way to impose constraints on the context of reuse. A type system is often used for that purpose in programming languages. This also requires that the reusing programmer be proposed a way to adapt the original code to a context that is not exactly compatible. Functional languages make it easy to create wrapper functions or to pass functions as arguments to the original code, for instance.

With tabletops, the central reuse issue is currently that of device structure and specification. There is no standard for devices as there has been, explicitly or not, for mice and keyboards. Whatever its actual protocol, a basic mouse always consists of a locator and one or more two-state buttons. A tabletop device can distinguish users or not, detect proximity or not, provide X and Y histograms of the contact surface or contours of all contact points, etc. Furthermore, these devices are still expensive and programmers often have to simulate them with mice when developing applications. And finally, there is no reason why an interactive component developed for a touch screen or a desktop computer could not be reused on a tabletop. For all these reasons, the ability to detect and adapt the input configuration is important for reusing applications or components. Concepts such as equivalence, adaptation, and complementarity [15] play important roles in this.

4.1 Device inspection and encapsulation

Detecting the input configuration available to an application on a computer starts with being able to locate the devices plugged onto the computer. We have seen earlier how this can be done and how typing constraints can be applied. But we have seen that there is no standard on how tabletops are structured. In addition, several devices from the same brand may have different features. For instance, a Wacom Intuos 2 tablet accepts two styluses at a time, whereas a Wacom Cintiq has a similar protocol and can be managed with the same driver but can only handle one stylus. Therefore, in order to use a given device to an application, one needs to access its structure to inspect it or to connect to it.

The component encapsulation mechanism provides support for this. The programmer of a component can choose what properties and children of the component are visible to the outside, and under what name. Programmers who use an element can list its exported properties, children and events. It is also possible to directly access the events by directly subscribing, and the properties and children as follows:

```
$set = $dev->get (-child => 'pointers');
$x = $pointer->get (-property => 'x');
```

This allows application programmers to check that the element they are using is as expected, and to access its parts so as to subscribe from them or connect to them. It is also planned for the future to check that the sequence of events that an element may emit (and declared as a regular language for instance) is compatible with the input language of a component that subscribes to it, as in [1]. This would provide an equivalent of type checking for the event-driven architecture, and would help detect if a given device can be used with a given application.

Accessing the internal structure of a device, when it exports it, also allows to perform source selection. On a Wacom Intuos 2 or a DiamondTouch, if one is interested in a given stylus or user one can directly subscribe to events from this stylus or user rather than using a complex event specification or subscribing to all events and performing a test afterward. Finally, one can use component encapsulation to masquerade a device as another type of device. For instance, given a DiamondTouch device, one can create a component that contains it as the only child, and that exports only the events and properties from the child of the DiamondTouch that represent one user. The result is a component that emulates a touch screen.

4.2 Source filtering

Encapsulation works when the equivalence between devices can be obtained by simple renamings and information hiding. However, most often the situation is more complex: to make a given device compatible with another, one often needs to combine event attributes, to memorise information from one event to the next, or to perform computations. For instance, the locator in a mouse is a relative device. To make the mouse compatible with a component that expects events from a touch screen, one needs to apply an acceleration law to translations of the mouse, to store an absolute position that is incremented at each move, to apply a scaling function, and to crop the result so as to stay within the bounding box of the screen. To simulate a multi-user touchscreen with a DiamondTouch, one needs to compute the barycentres of the X and Y histograms it provides for each user. One even sometimes needs to combine several devices to simulate another, for instance four mice to simulate a DiamondTouch.

The architecture proposed for this in IntuiKit is *source filtering*. It uses the fact that all elements can be event sources to have an organisation similar to data-flow connections: an element stands as a front end for another element and acts as a relay for event subscriptions. Filtering can be combined with encapsulation: a filter can be a component that encapsulates the original source, thus hiding it from the rest of the application. In all cases, the filter element has its own event specification format, which allows it to give its own version of what types of events are available. For instance, a filter for a DiamondTouch may provide the subscription language of a mouse if it applies the barycentre computation mentioned above. Some filters just relay event subscriptions and do not perform any operation on events: they just provide another way of subscribing. But most filters apply transformation to events: renaming of event attributes, or computations to create new attributes. Those transformations are performed in an action similar to the Watcher's action in a data-flow element.

Filtering is the mechanism used in IntuiKit to account for gesture recognition: the positions provided in events by pointer devices are memorised in the filter, then a classification algorithm is applied when the button or pressure is released. Filtering also accounts for picking, the operation in which each pointer event is associated to a graphical object based on geometrical considerations, and which allows to subscribe to pointer events by addressing graphical objects themselves. Having this mechanism explicit is important in multi-touch systems: it allows all pointers to be associated with the graphical scene, by connecting them to the picking filter as soon as they are detected. Filtering is also used to perform input configuration. As already mentioned, a DiamondTouch can be filtered by applying a barycentre computation to its events so as to simulate the behaviour of a mouse or touch screen. It can also be filtered by using a tracking algorithm that extracts multiple contact points from the data provided by the DiamondTouch, thus providing into a multi-user multi-touch source.

4.3 Remote devices

Interaction designers sometimes wish to access input devices through inter-process communications. This may be because the device is actually remote, for instance when experimenting with two remote tables coupled with a video-conferencing system [7]. This may be because there is no driver available yet for a given device on the target platform. Or this may be because a given application has been built without support for changing the configuration, and the configuration needs to be adapted from the outside. For these situations, IntuiKit's ability to transport events over message buses such as the Ivy software bus [2] or Open Sound Control [18] is appropriate. One can build, with IntuiKit or with their tool of choice, a software agent that implements IntuiKit's text protocol for input devices. The software agent can represent the actual device or use source filtering to simulate the device expected by the application.

5 Interacting in parallel

The device addressing and input configuration mechanisms described above provide programmers with a flexible way of accessing and managing multiple input devices. However, the programmer's main goal is to implement interaction styles and not only access devices. What makes multiple input special regarding interaction is obviously the ability to have several interactions in parallel, and sometimes to combine several input flows to produced synergistic interaction. As the models used in IntuiKit are aimed at multimodal interaction, we will see how these possibilities are built in its core mechanisms.

The first requirement for interacting in parallel is that the programming framework provide a way of adding new input sources that can emit events asynchronously. Most modern frameworks or toolkits, including IntuiKit, have this feature either through a multi-threading system or through an extensible "main loop". This has the consequence of providing a parallel execution semantics for the application tree.

Then the software architecture promoted by the framework must allow programmers to build interactors that can be manipulated in parallel. The event communication model is intrisically parallel, but any incitation to store interaction state globally, for instance in global variables, is fatal. It is even worse if the framework itself proposes interactors that do store state globally. The architecture based on a tree of components that contain properties and communicate through events is a strong incitation to building programs as a collection of components that store their state locally and behave as parallel agents. When dialogue control requires that some state is shared by several components, such as the state of a dialogue box, the hierarchical organisation of the application tree incites to manage this by storing the state in a parent common to all components concerned; here, for instance, the dialogue box would managed the "global" state and its children (buttons for instance) would manage their local states and communicate with it through events that change its "global" state. Elements such as FSMs provide help for creating such locally managed behaviours, at different levels in the tree if need be. By cloning a component one clones all its subcomponents and properties, and thus several identical components will be able to work in parallel.

Finally, one sometimes needs to merge input flows: zooming with two fingers, button that is only triggered when two users press it together, etc. The two main ways of describing interactive behaviours in IntuiKit provide for such combined behaviours. On the one hand, data flows can come from two origins and end up connected to different properties of the same element, like in the Whizz or ICon toolkits [4, 9]. This allows for instance to control one angle of a rectangle with one finger and the opposed angle with another finger. On the other hand, the transitions of FSMs can be labelled with any event specification from any event source. This allows to build FSMs that rely on events from different pointers, for instance a three-state button that is fully pressed only when two fingers have pressed it.

6 Example application

IntuiKit is used in several research or commercial projects using tabletops. We describe here the Multi-Actor Man Machine Interface (MAMMI) project carried out for Eurocontrol in the domain of air traffic control. The project aims at designing a large horizontal surface where two or more controllers could share tools and data, exchange information (figure 7). The sought benefit is for them to be able to adjust their repartition of tasks in real-time so as to adapt to situations and improve their overall performance.

Figure 7. A tabletop for air traffic control

Two hardware devices have been investigated: the DiamondTouch and a prototype built by a European company. Both have input resolutions that enable to test realistic solutions, and can be plugged to display devices that support rich graphics. Each has advantages and drawbacks regarding interaction. The DiamondTouch distinguishes between up to four users. The other device detects an indefinite number of inputs represented by sets of points.

The project team was composed of a graphic designer, UI designers and hardware experts. The model-based architecture of IntuiKit allowed us to apply iterative and concurrent design. First, participatory design led to producing paper prototypes that explored design variations based on the features of each device: with and without user identification, with and without multi-touch for each user. The paper prototypes then served as a reference to split the interface into a tree of components that represent the software architecture of the application as well as its graphical structure. The tree then served as a contract between all project actors, especially between UI designers and the graphic designer. From then on, team members started to work independently. The hardware expert exploited IntuiKit's ability

to handle devices as remote sources: he produced a software agent for handling the prototype device remotely, because no driver was available on the target platform. The graphic designer produced graphical elements using a professional drawing tool (Figure 8).

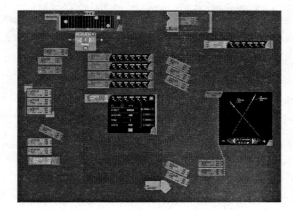

Figure 8. The designer's work

Meanwhile, the UI designers programmed the interaction. For each component, they defined the behaviours and connection to the functional core. Because they used mice for testing, they used IntuiKit's device encapsulation mechanism to emulate the target devices with several mice. Using device inspection, their were able to test the two design variants: the application checks if user identification is available and adapts the way it handles conflicts. If the device does not identify users, the application solely relies on existing social protocols to prevent and resolve conflicts. With user identification, the application activates software

Figure 9. Different feedback for each user

coordination policies, such as access permission or explicit sharing, and provides different feedback for each user (Figure 9) to improve mutual awareness. They also used a gesture recognition filter to implement gestures in the interface.

Finally, after a period of graphic design, test and integration, the final application was operational and able to run with multiple mice, a DiamondTouch, and the prototype device. Switching devices is just a matter of changing a reference in a configuration file.

7 Related work

Interaction libraries such as DiamondSpin [17], or the Grouplab DiamondTouch Toolkit [8] have been developed for tabletop interaction, but they are focused on one particular hardware or on graphical features such as rotation.

The Input Extension to the X Window Server protocol [10] provides inspection of devices, but no support for dynamicity, input configuration and interaction description. More recently, the TUIO protocol [13] addressed tabletops and tangible user interfaces, with a low level of asbtraction. Multiple input has been addressed in the Whizz [4] and ICon [9] toolkits, using the data-flow paradigm to support interaction description. ICon addresses the issues of input configuration, by allowing users to edit the data-flow graph. However, these toolkits do not address the dynamicity of devices and the data-flow paradigm alone sometimes makes state-based interaction complex to handle.

Concurrency in user interaction tools has been studied as early as in Sassafras [11]. The architecture model in IntuiKit also has some similarities with interactors in Garnet [14] or with VRED [12]. Its originality lies in the model-driven architecture, the unifying tree structure, and the unification of events and data-flow.

8 Conclusion

In this article, we have described how the models of interactive software used in the IntuiKit framework support device adressing and detection, input configuration and the description of parallel interaction in tabletop systems. Beyond the mere ability to produce a given type of interaction, what makes an interaction style available to the large public of users is the ability to manage this style according to basic software engineering criteria: reusability, encapsulation, orthogonality. The proposed models were extended to support tabletops without having to introduce additional concepts. This strongly suggests that the properties already demonstrated by IntuiKit in terms of reusability, customisation and concurrent engineering are transferred to application development for tabletops.

Acknowlegements

This work was supported by the French *Agence Nationale de la Recherche* (project DigiTable), and by *Eurocontrol* (project MAMMI). The source model was designed with P.Dragicevic and D.Thevenin. The tracking algorithm mentioned in section 4 is by F.Bérard at LGI/IIHM and has not yet been published. C.Dupré and S.Meunier have helped with examples. IntuiLab is seeking patent protection for some solutions described in this article.

References

[1] J. Accot, S. Chatty, S. Maury, and P. Palanque. Formal transducers: models of devices and building bricks for the design of highly interactive systems. In *Proc. of the 4th Eurographics DSVIS workshop (DSVIS'97)*. Springer-Verlag, 1997.

[2] M. Buisson, A. Bustico, S. Chatty, F.-R. Colin, Y. Jestin, S. Maury, C. Mertz, and P. Truillet. Ivy: un bus logiciel au service du développement de prototypes de systèmes interactifs. In *Proc. of IHM'02*, pp. 223–226. ACM Press, 2002.

[3] S. Card, J. Mackinlay, and G. Robertson. A morphological analysis of the design space of input devices. *ACM Trans. on Office Information Systems*, 9(2):99–122, 1991.

[4] S. Chatty. Extending a graphical toolkit for two-handed interaction. In *Proceedings of the ACM UIST*, pages 195–204. Addison-Wesley, Nov. 1994.

[5] S. Chatty. Programs = data + algorithms + architecture. Consequences for interactive software. In *Proceedings of the 2007 joint conference on Engineering Interactive Software*. Springer-Verlag, Mar. 2007.

[6] S. Chatty, S. Sire, J. Vinot, P. Lecoanet, C. Mertz, and A. Lemort. Revisiting visual interface programming: Creating GUI tools for designers and programmers. In *Proceedings of the ACM UIST*. Addison-Wesley, Oct. 2004.

[7] F. Coldefy and S. Louis-dit-Picard. Digitable: an interactive multiuser table for collocated and remote collaboration enabling remote gesture visualization. In *Proceedings of the 4th IEEE workshop on projector-camera systems*, 2007.

[8] R. Diaz-Marino, E. Tse, and S. Greenberg. The GroupLab DiamondTouch toolkit. In *Video Proceedings of the ACM CSCW 2004 conference*, 2004.

[9] P. Dragicevic and J.-D. Fekete. Support for input adaptability in the icon toolkit. In *Proceedings of the Sixth International Conference on Multimodal Interfaces (ICMI'04)*, pages 212–219. ACM Press, 2004.

[10] P. Ferguson. The X11 Input extension: Reference pages. *The X Resource*, 4(1):195–270, 1992.

[11] R. Hill. Supporting concurrency, communication and synchronization in human-computer interaction - the Sassafras UIMS. *ACM Trans. on Graphics*, 5(2):179–210, 1986.

[12] R. Jacob, L. Deligiannidis, and S. Morrison. A software model and specification language for non-WIMP user interfaces. *ACM Trans. on Computer-Human Interaction*, 6(1):1–46, 1999.

[13] M. Kaltenbrunner, T. Bovermann, R. Bencina, and E. Costanza. TUIO: A protocol for table-top tangible user interfaces. In *Proceedings of Gesture Workshop 2005*.

[14] B. A. Myers. A new model for handling input. *ACM Trans. on Office Information Systems*, pages 289–320, July 1990.

[15] L. Nigay and J. Coutaz. Multifeature systems: The CARE properties and their impact on software design intelligence and multimodality. In J. Lee, editor, *Multimedia Interfaces: Research and Applications*, chapter 9. AAAI Press, 1997.

[16] X. Ren and S. Moriya. Efficient strategies for selecting small targets on pen-based systems: an evaluation experiment for selection strategies and strategy classifications. In *Proceedings of the EHCI conference*, IFIP Transactions series, pages 19–37. Kluwer Academic Publishers, 1998.

[17] C. Shen, F. D. Vernier, C. Forlines, and M. Ringel. DiamondSpin: an extensible toolkit for around-the-table interaction. In *Proceedings of the CHI'04 conference*, pages 167–174. ACM Press, 2004.

[18] M. Wright, A. Freed, and A. Momeni. OpenSound Control: State of the art 2003. In *Proceedings of the NIME-03 conference*, 2003.

Gadgets & Gizmos: 'Notable' Tabletop Hardware

EmiTable: A Tabletop Surface Pervaded with Imperceptible Metadata

Sho Kimura, Masahiko Kitamura, Takeshi Naemura
The University of Tokyo
{kimura, kitamura, naemura}@hc.ic.i.u-tokyo.ac.jp

Abstract

This paper proposes a novel tabletop display named "EmiTable" that can emit imperceptible metadata along with the tabletop image. Actually, our system displays a visual image on the tabletop whose pixels contain metadata as bit patterns for dedicated receivers. Since the bit patterns are embedded as high-speed flickers, the users would not perceive the hidden signal behind the image. However, we can read out the metadata by putting stand-alone receivers on the tabletop. Since the hidden signal is embedded independently in each pixel, different metadata can be drawn according to the position on the tabletop. The advantage of our system is that it can superimpose metadata which are strongly related to the image content in an imperceptible way. This paper presents the detailed design and several applications.

1. Introduction

Tabletop displays can support group works as an effective workspace for users. This is because the users can put physical objects on it as an intuitive tangible input method. This paper focuses on how to transmit data or information from the tabletop surface to the objects.

The concept of Display-based Computing (DBC)[1] has been proposed to utilize a display as a method for controlling machines (physical objects). Basically, it displays visible images for the users and markers for the machines, simultaneously. We can achieve position-dependent control which is strongly related to the image content, and simultaneous control of several numbers of machines. However, the visible markers obstruct the view, and we cannot display images for the users at the position where the markers are displayed.

This paper adopts the concept of DBC to realize a new tabletop system, and proposes a new method for invisible (imperceptible) data transmission. For this purpose, the concept of position-dependent visible light communication (PVLC)[2] which the authors have developed is applied. It displays a visual image whose pixels contain bit patterns for dedicated receivers. By utilizing this technology, we have realized a new tabletop system named EmiTable, which is a smart tabletop environment that can emit imperceptible metadata along with the tabletop image.

This paper describes the mechanism of PVLC, design of EmiTable, and several applications.

2. Related Works

Many researches on the tabletop display have been investigated. Among them, the methods for detecting the position of tabletop objects have been one of the essential topics for achieving natural and intuitive interaction [3, 4]. The authors believe that it is also very important to realize data transmission between the tabletop surface and the tabletop objects. If the tabletop surface itself emits some metadata, the tabletop object can get to know its position by simply receiving the emitted metadata. In addition, we can also send textual, acoustic or visual data and control signals as well as the position data.

For this purpose, the concept of DBC is useful. As mentioned above, this paper focuses on an imperceptible way of controlling the physical objects. Researches on utilizing projectors to embed imperceptible patterns have been also reported [5, 6]. While they concentrate on how to measure the 3D shape of the scene, our aim is to transmit more versatile metadata. Apart from the image projection, visible light communication (VLC) [7] is a practical method for embedding imperceptible data into illumination. Smart Light [8] is an array of VLC to realize visual pattern projection with the function of VLC, but it is still limited to very low resolution. Our approach is adding the function of VCL to an image projector with XGA resolution.

3. Core Technology

3.1. Fundamental Principle

PVLC can display a visual image containing metadata as bit patterns decodable by dedicated receivers. The method

0-7695-3013-3/07 $25.00 © 2007 IEEE
DOI 10.1109/TABLETOP.2007.26

is basically based on the pixel-by-pixel pulse width modulation (PWM). Figure 1(a) illustrates the fundamental principle for embedding imperceptible metadata into the visual image. When two inverted patterns are displayed alternatively at high-frequency, we would see just a flat gray image because of our persistence of vision. Though we cannot perceive and distinguish each image, the receiver with a photo sensor can detect them as different signals.

On the other hand, the problem of flickering is important for this mechanism. It is known that we can perceive flickering when the refresh rate is under 60 Hz. Therefore, we need to switch the images at a rate higher than 60 Hz to realize flicker-free displaying.

In PWM, the luminance of a pixel on the screen is expressed by the ratio of time between ON and OFF period. In other words, the luminance does not depend on the order of ON and OFF. Consequently, we can embed some data (bit patterns) by replacing the order of ON and OFF. For example, each pattern shown in Figure 1(b) cannot be distinguished by the users, but can be detected as different signals by the receivers.

To implement PVLC, we developed a new projector installing digital micro-mirror device (DMD) which is widely used in commercially available DLP projectors. We introduced the DMD discovery 1100 Starter Kit and ALP which has 1024 x 768 mirrors and can switch ON and OFF at 8kHz. Thus, the new projector has an XGA resolution with PWM function at each pixel.

3.2. Embedding Algorithm

To achieve PVLC, we need to design the effective method for locating ON and OFF period. Although several methods of on-off keying (OOK) are studied, it is difficult to simply adapt them, because of strict requirements such as keeping luminance and avoiding flickers.

Considering these points, the authors have implemented an algorithm shown in Figure 2. It introduces three kinds of blocks for synchronization, embedding information and luminance compensation for each pixel. The details of the blocks are as follows:

- **Block for synchronizing:** This block indicates the start of signal.

- **Block for embedding information:** This block contains the metadata.

- **Block for compensating for luminance:** This block is used to keep the time ratio of ON and OFF periods for the luminance of each pixel.

To avoid the flicker, the embedding block and the compensation block are allocated alternately. Thus, we can su-

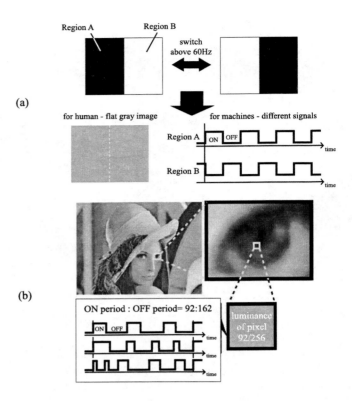

(a)

(b)

Figure 1. Fundamental Principle.

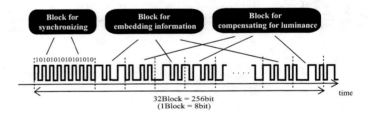

Figure 2. Embedding Algorithm.

perimpose the metadata along with the visual image pixel-by-pixel in an imperceptible way.

4. Implementation and Applications

4.1. EmiTable

By utilizing the implemented PVLC projector, we developed a smart tabletop surface named "EmiTable" as shown in Figure 3. Figure 4 illustrates the diagram of the prototype system. When the users put stand-alone receivers onto the tabletop, the receivers can read out the position-dependent metadata. The features of EmiTable are as follows:

- Our embedding method doesn't modulate the luminance of visual image, but modulate the process of dis-

Figure 3. EmiTable.

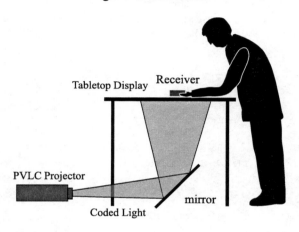

Figure 4. System overview of EmiTable.

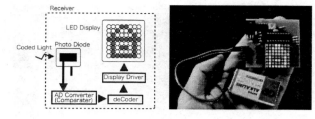

Figure 5. Receiver.

Figure 6. Application:Crossword Puzzle.

playing the image. So the users would not perceive the hidden signal behind the image.

- Since the metadata is embedded independently in each pixel, this system is applicable to pixel-by-pixel precision control.

- We do not need any prior adjustment and alignment of complex systems: display units, sensing units, and so on. This is because the tabletop surface (projector light) itself emits the metadata. Thus, EmiTable is very robust.

- We can use many physical objects (receivers) at a time. This feature is not easily achieved by the camera and recognition approach.

- The physical object does not need to be a complex hardware like PDAs, but it could be just a simple receiver.

4.2. Receiver

The authors impremended the receiver shown in Figure 5. The receiver consists of a photo diode, a comparator, a PIC micro controller and a small LED display. The photo diode receives the digital signal sequence, the comparator converts digital state for the post processing, and the controller and the LED display the received data. The wire seen in Figure 5 is used only for power supply.

4.3. Applications

Figure 6 shows a crossword puzzle as an application. When the user puts a receiver in a blank square on the tabletop, the answer is displayed. In addition, the user can put several receivers at a time to solve the puzzle.

Another application is the weather forecast as shown in Figure 7. The users can see a pictogram indicating the

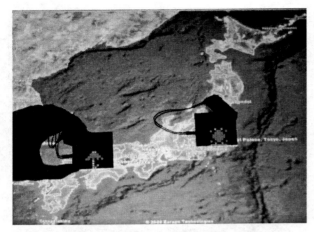

Figure 7. Application:Weather Forecast.

weather at the place on the map.

In these applications, we send 64 bit metadata because pictograms consist of 64 pixels. ON/OFF of each pixel of LED display corresponds to 0/1 of signal(1 bit). In fact ! $we send 2 blocks for synchronizing, 8 blocks for embedding information and 22 blocks for compensating for luminance.

In addition, to overcome the disparity of position between the receiver and the display on the table, we embed the same metadata onto a sufficiently large blocks of pixels.

Thus, EmiTable can handle versatile metadata including pictogram as well as textural data. Moreover, we can also embed other types of metadata such as sound, force and magnetic field in principle.

5. Conclusion and Future Works

This paper presents the new system EmiTable which offers a novel human-to-computer interaction on tabletop environment.

In the future works, the authors plan to develop more applications embedding other metadata such as sound and force and various kinds of receivers with which those metadata can be decoded. In addition, multiplexing the metadata at a pixel is also an important extension of the system. By multiplexing the metadata, different receivers can read out the different metadata at the same position on the tabletop. Moreover, the authors are planing to improve the embedding algorithm. In the present algorithm, we cannot embed

the metadata in such pixels with very high luminance or very low luminance.

Finally, we would like to thank Prof. Hiroshi Harashima and members of our laboratory for giving us a lot of useful advices.

6. References

[1] M.Kojima, M.Sugimoto, A.Nakamura, M.Tomita, H.Nii and M.Inami: "Augmented Coliseum:An Augmented Game Environment with Small Vehicles", The First IEEE Intern. Workshop on Horizontal Interactive Human-Computer Systems(TableTop2006), pp.3–8, 2006.

[2] M.Kitamura, T.Naemura: "A study on Position-dependent Visible Light Communication using DMD for ProCam", IPSJ CVIM-156, pp.17–24, 2006. (in Japanese)

[3] B.Ullmer and H.Ishii: "The metaDESK: Models nd Prototypes for Tangible User Interfaces", In Symposium on User Interface Software and Technology(UIST'97), pp.223–232, 1997.

[4] Y.Kakehi, M.Iida, T.Naemura and M.Matsushita: "Tablescape Plus: Upstanding Tiny Displays on Tabletop Display," SIGGRAPH2006 Emerging Technologies, 2006.

[5] Q.Chen, T.Wada:"A light modulation/demodulation method for real-time 3d imaging", IEEE 3DIM 2005, pp.15–21, 2005.

[6] Daniel Cotting, Martin Naef, Markus Gross and Henry Fuchs:"Embedding Imperceptible Patterns into Projected Images for Simultaneous Acquisition and Display", Proc. International Symposium on Mixed and Augmented Reality(ISMAR2004), pp.100–109, 2004.

[7] Toshihiko Komine and Masao Nakagawa:"Integrated System of White LED Visible-Light Communication and Power-Line Communication", IEEE Trans. on Consumer Electronics , Vol. 49, No. 1, pp.71–79, 2003.

[8] H.Nii, M.Sugimoto and M.Inami:"Smart Light:Ultra High Speed Projector for Spatial Multiplexing Optical Transmission", IEEE Conference on Computer Vision and Pattern Recognition(CVPR'05), p.95–102, 2005.

Ortholumen: Using Light for Direct Tabletop Input

Tommaso Piazza[‡,*]
‡Institut National Polytechnique de Grenoble
ENSIMAG
F-38402 St Martin d'Heres, France
E-mail: tommaso.piazza@gmail.com

Morten Fjeld*
*TableTop Interaction Lab (t2i Lab), www.t2i.se
CSE, Chalmers University of Technology
SE-41296 Gothenburg, Sweden
E-mail: morten@fjeld.ch

Abstract

Ortholumen is a light pen based tabletop interaction system that can employ all the pen's spatial degrees of freedom (DOF). The pen's light is projected from above onto a horizontal translucent screen and tracked by a webcam sitting underneath, facing upwards; system output is projected back onto the same screen. The elliptic light spot cast by the pen informs the system of pen position, orientation, and direction. While this adds up to six DOFs, we have used up to four at a time. In order to better separate input and output light we employ polarizing filters on the webcam and on the projector lens. Two applications, painting and map navigation, are presented. Ortholumen can be expanded to track multiple pens of the same or different colors. This would enable bi-manual input, collaboration, and placed pens as external memory. Visible light, as opposed to infrared or radio, may be perceived more directly by users. Ortholumen employs only low-cost parts, making the system affordable to home users.

1. Introduction

Most tabletop interaction relies exclusively on horizontal input. Recently, some efforts have been made to incorporate the third dimension above [1] and below [2] the table. While our work is an attempt to further explore interaction possibilities above the table surface, some of the solutions suggested here may also work for input underneath the table. Ortholumen[1], the system presented in this tech paper, is based on using visible light source(s) that are manipulated in the space above the table. Since light sources are defined by their position, orientation, and direction in space, they may give additional degrees of freedom (DOFs) to tabletop input. Our approach differs

---

[1] This work was carried out at the t2i Lab, CSE, Chalmers. Project web site, including video: http://www.t2i.se/projects.php?project=ol

from laser pointer interaction [3]. As opposed to the light we use, laser is coherent collimated light.

To assure coinciding input and output spaces, any input device manipulated apart from the tabletop display surface should provide immediately perceivable meaningful mappings of its input cues, preferably in the output space. Such mappings can more easily be created employing visible light than alternative invisible media such as radio, ultrasound, or infrared. Using these alternatives may also be cumbersome due to their complex set-up. An added benefit of visible light is that it is perceived equally well by the human eye as by camera-based tracking systems.

By using visible light instead of invisible alternatives, Ortholumen complies with three of the five *direct manipulation* criteria [4] (two criteria, reversibility of actions and syntactic correctness, are less related to input technique):

- **visibility of the objects of interest**
  light does not in any way impede the visibility of the object of interest, except when concentrated

- **incremental action at the interface with rapid feedback for all actions**
  shape, size, and position of the elliptic light spot can be changed in a continuous way with just a small effort by the user and with immediate feedback

- **replacement of complex commands languages with actions to manipulate directly the visible object**
  all characteristics of the elliptic light spot can be used as parts of an interaction schemata

In the case of a handheld light source, there is a connection between perceiving projected light and sensing cues of the source. Capitalizing on this connection, Ortholumen allows for meaningful ways to combine intuitive handling of the tangible source with immediately perceived feedback to the user. Our work is focused on exploring potential

0-7695-3013-3/07 $25.00 © 2007 IEEE
DOI 10.1109/TABLETOP.2007.23

benefits of using distance and angle between the input device and table top. Since the most common handheld input device in a tabletop context is the pen, we chose a light source of similar size and form. Instead of tracking the yaw, pitch, roll, and position of the light emitting pen, the system relies on the elliptic light spot projected onto the table surface. Such a solution provides for marker-less tracking of untethered input devices with low power consumption.

2. Related Work

Horizontal interactive systems have garnered increasing attention from researchers and system designers. Device based, direct touch, and gesture [5][6] input possibilities are among those that have been widely explored as alternatives for interaction with objects at both close and far distances [7]. Local and remote pointing using laser or invisible media, such as radio, have also been explored [3][8]. Still, the physical space for interaction in most tabletop systems is restricted to the table surface; exceptionally, the spaces above [1] or below it [2] are employed. Only a few projects have employed the space between the user's body and the table surface [1][5]. In the first of these projects, two-handed gestures were combined with a vertical screen as an output device [5]. In the second project, offering multi-layer interaction on a horizontal screen, the space was divided into layers that the user can select and interact with by controlling distance between input device and table [1]. Inspired by these projects, we adopted a continuous approach to the space above the table. This is achieved by drawing on polarization techniques for image segmentation [9].

3. System Requirements and Set-Up

Ortholumen is designed to give the user immediate visual feedback. It integrates interaction and visualization spaces defined by the user's reach. Moreover, to avoid user obstruction of the system output, back projection was adopted. To enable better tracking of the light source we chose a webcam placed below the table top. Such camera placement combined with back-projection minimizes glare and bright disturbances caused by the projector. To further enhance tracking, we employed linear polarizing filter(s); one in front of the projector, in the case of a non-LCD projector, and one in front of the webcam lens.

The fixed parts of the set-up consist of a table, holding a translucent screen, an LCD projector, a mirror, and a low-cost web camera (Fig. 1). In this installation, one or multiple LED pens are held by hand in the space above the table or in direct contact with the surface. The light

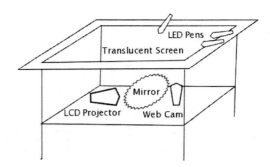

Figure 1. The set-up including table with translucent screen, LCD projector, mirror, web cam, and LED pens.

of the LCD projector is reflected by the mirror onto the translucent screen. The webcam, mounted next to the mirror, captures the screen image combining pen input and projector output. In front of the camera lens there is a polarizing filter. The filter is aligned orthogonally to the polarization direction of the projector's light. All components are of consumer quality, making the system affordable to most users:

- **Projector**
  The video projector used is of the LCD type, a *Sony VPL-CS5* 1800 lumen.

- **Camera**
  The web camera used is of the CCD type, an *Apple iSight* with 640x480 pixel resolution.

- **Polarizing Filters**
  A neutral gray linear polarizing film with 99% polarizing efficiency, 38% single, 30.1% parallel, and 0.0045% transmittance efficiency was chosen because of its superior transmissive characteristics between 400 and 700 nm.

- **Light Emitting Pen**
  The LED pen used has tip-mounted color LEDs which can be activated one at a time or in combination by pressing a side-mounted button (Fig. 2). The LED light employed is incoherent, not collimated, and mostly monochromatic which benefits tracking. Solid state light sources require no external reflector to collect light because the solid package can be designed to concentrate light. This, in addition to its solid-state nature, provides for resistance to shock and vibration.

4. Tracking

One of the first problems approached was how to track a pen's light as it would mix with the projector and

Figure 2. Side and front view of the LED pen.

environmental light. Since the light coming from the pen is colored and blends with projected images from the system, plain color histogram tracking is generally not precise enough to allow our system to work well.

The goal is to track the position, orientation, and size of the elliptic light spot cast by the pen. In a scenario where the pen's light is mostly diffuse and often of the same color as the background, tracking according only to color is unsatisfactory. For this reason we adopted the HSV color space, which enables the system to distinguish between color and brightness. A two-dimensional hue-value histogram of the region of the image known to be the pen is computed and then back-projected to the image's two planes of interest (H and V). The CamShift algorithm [10] as implemented in the OpenCV[2] library is then applied.

The primary assumption made is that the pen's light spot would appear as one of the brightest sources in the image. This assumption should also hold while lifting or lowering the pen and for small pen surface distances. Still, once the light spot becomes too weak, due to pen distance, tracking terminates. Interference by other sources of light present in the environment is prevented by the hue-value tracking combination since normal light is of neutral color and the tracked light has specific hue values. As the system has no learning capacities start-up involves manual selection of the light spot to be tracked.

5. Polarizing Filters

The role of the filter(s) is to enhance tracking sensitivity and precision. Following the principles of polarization the idea is to prevent as much light as possible from interfering with the tracking system. Interference is extra bright zone(s) in the image or glare(s), making the camera unable to discriminate the pen's light spot. For these reasons, one polarizing filter is laid in front of the projector lens, in the case of a non LCD projector, and a second one orthogonal to the first one in front of the camera lens. Since the projector lens used to focalize the light could alter the polarization, the filter sits after the lens. For the camera, there is no need to preserve polarization after the lens.

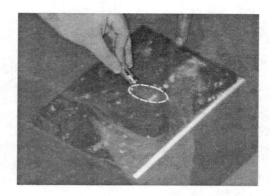

Figure 3. A view of the map application.

6. Applications

As a proof-of-concept, we built two single-user applications employing one up to four of the pen's six DOFs. Firstly, we designed a *painting application* where the pen plays the role of a brush. The light spot's x and y coordinates determine the brush coordinates. The pen's distance from the table top, inferred from the characteristics of the elliptic light spot, determines the size of the brush. Hence, it is possible to interpret the pen's distance from the table top either in a visually-coherent (VC) mode or in a position-coherent (PC) mode. In VC mode, lifting the pen increases the size of the brush just as the user-perceived size of the light gets bigger; lowering the pen reduces the size of the brush. In PC mode distance affects size in the opposite way. Secondly, we built a *map navigation application* by connecting Ortholumen and Google Earth[3] (Fig. 3). Here the pen acts much like a joystick: distance and angle to the center of the display jointly activate and control horizontal map movement; elevation determines the zoom factor. Tilt around the display's x axis controls tilt in the map. Much like in the painting application, leaving or approaching the table surface affects zoom according to one of two alternative modes. In PC mode leaving the surface results in zooming out the map while approaching results in zooming in. In VC mode the pen works like a magnifying glass. When lifting the pen the system reacts as if a magnifying glass was lifted from the surface, zooming in the map.

7. Discussion and Future work

Ortholumen derives much of its value from a three-dimensional interaction space and the use of light as interactive media. While this is less complex than other tabletop interaction technologies, our approach also has a number of limitations.

---

[2]http://www.intel.com/technology/computing/opencv/

[3]http://earth.google.com/

Since the approach relies on visual tracking and interpretation of the light's color and brightness in order to determine changes in position, size, and shape, the detection of the correct light source representing the pen depends on the quality of the image's segmentation. While segmentation as such is difficult, it becomes even more a challenge in uncontrolled viewing circumstances such as mobile scenarios (e.g. map navigation). While our prototype facilitates segmentation by using polarization, back projection and the use of LCD projector technology limit the power of the technique. Very bright zones are likely to fool the system.

The overall quality of the estimation of the pen's distance from the table greatly depends on the diffusion of the light reaching the table top. At a certain height, typically above 10 cm, light beamed to the surface becomes too diffuse to be tracked by a webcam-based system. Small angles, however, are less of an issue as long as the pen projects onto the surface. The use of a more concentrated light source could partially help solving these issues in future prototypes.

Tilting the pen to change the shape of the projection radically influences the size in most cases. This becomes an issue if there is a need to use both size and other characteristics of the shape simultaneously, because it relies on the user's ability to keep one parameter constant while varying the other. To avoid such problems in future prototypes decoupling of size and tilt may be reached by introducing color coding. Finally, tracking the pen's rotation around its main axis remains a challenge in realizing full six DOFs input.

In future work, multiple pen realization of Ortholumen may enable bi-manual input, collaboration, and pens placed upright as external memory. Connecting multiple DOFs with a set of active and placed pens will require a systematic investigation. Infrared light could be added to the system by integrating two infrared LEDs into the pen. This would make computation of the pen's rotation around its main axis easier.

8. Conclusion

We have realized a tabletop interaction technique based on visible light which extends interaction to the space above the table surface. This gives meaning to user input actions such as lifting or lowering a hand held device, as well as changing its yaw, pitch, and roll. Unlike other techniques, our technique does not involve specialized hardware and gives the user immediate visual feedback. Two applications using up to four DOFs have been realized. We would like to further explore the Ortholumen technique in multiuser environments and other contexts where multiple tangible input devices can be of use.

9. Acknowledgments

Andreas Kunz and Martin Kuechler gave good advice on the use of polarization for image segmentation. Erik Tobin, Fredrik Gustafsson, Sven Berg Ryen, and Wayne Brailsford helped in proofreading.

References

[1] Subramanian, S., Aliakseyeu, D., and Lucero, A. "Multi-layer interaction for digital tables". In Proc. UIST'06, 2006, pp. 269-272.

[2] Wigdor, D., Leigh, D., Forlines, C., Shipman, S., Barnwell, J., Balakrishnan, R., and Shen, C. "Under the table interaction". In Proc. UIST'06, 2006, pp. 259-268.

[3] Olsen, D. R. and Nielsen, T. "Laser pointer interaction". In Proc. CHI'01, 2001, pp. 17-22.

[4] Shneiderman, Ben. "Direct manipulation: a step beyond programming languages". In IEEE Computer 16(8), 1983, pp. 57-69.

[5] Wilson, A. D. "Robust computer vision-based detection of pinching for one and two-handed gesture input". In Proc. UIST'06, 2006, pp. 255-258.

[6] Wu, M. and Balakrishnan, R. "Multi-finger and whole hand gestural interaction techniques for multi-user tabletop displays". In Proc. UIST'03, 2003, pp. 193-202.

[7] Vogel, D. and Balakrishnan, R. "Distant freehand pointing and clicking on very large, high resolution displays". In Proc. UIST'05, 2005, pp. 33-42.

[8] Parker, J. K., Mandryk, R. L., and Inkpen, K. M. "TractorBeam: seamless integration of local and remote pointing for tabletop displays". In Proc. Graphics interface 2005, 2005, pp. 33-40.

[9] Kuechler, M., Kunz, A. "Imperceptible projection blanking for reliable segmentation within mixed reality applications". In Proc. 9th IPT/11th EGVE, 2005, pp. 23-30.

[10] Bradski, G. R. "Computer vision face tracking tor use in a perceptual user interface". In Intel Technology Journal Q2'98, 1998.

High Precision Multi-touch Sensing on Surfaces using Overhead Cameras

Ankur Agarwal, Shahram Izadi, Manmohan Chandraker, Andrew Blake

Microsoft Research Cambridge, 7 J J Thomson Avenue, Cambridge, CB3 0FB

Abstract

We present a method to enable multi-touch interactions on an arbitrary flat surface using a pair of cameras mounted above the surface. Current systems in this domain mostly make use of special touch-sensitive hardware, require cameras to be mounted behind the display, or are based on infrared sensors used in various configurations. The very few that use ordinary cameras mounted overhead for touch detection fail to do so accurately due to the difficulty in computing the proximity of fingertips to the surface with a precision that would match the behaviour of a truly touch-sensitive surface. This paper describes a novel computer vision algorithm that can robustly identify finger tips and detect touch with a precision of a few millimetres above the surface. The algorithm relies on machine learning methods and a geometric finger model to achieve the required precision, and can be 'trained' to work in different physical settings. We provide a quantitative evaluation of the method and demonstrate its use for gesture based interactions with ordinary tablet displays, both in single user and remote collaboration scenarios.

Keywords: Interactive surfaces, bimanual interaction, multi-touch detection, hand gestures, computer vision

1. Introduction

Developing multi-touch technologies for interaction on tabletop surfaces is a very active area of research [1], the goal of which is to enable users to seamlessly interact with electronic media using finger touches and hand gestures. Several systems have been developed in this domain (*e.g.* [15,5,6,11]) and a large variety of configurations of sensing mechanisms and surfaces have been studied and experimented in this context. The most common of these include using specially designed surfaces with embedded sensors (*e.g.* using capacitive sensing [3,13]), cameras mounted behind a custom surface (*e.g.* [17]), cameras mounted in front of the surface (*e.g.* [9,10,18]) or on the surface peripheri (*e.g.* [14]). This paper addresses the case of overhead cameras mounted on top of a horizontal surface, using ordinary cameras that operate in the visible spectrum of light.

The overhead camera configuration has several advantages as it can be used to convert any arbitrary surface into an interactive one, thus allowing for smaller form-factor possibilities, easy installation and customization, and reduced

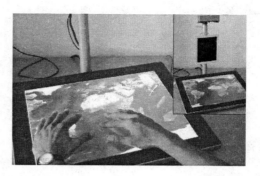

Figure 1. Our multi-touch sensing mechanism allows for enhanced gesture based interactions with an ordinary tablet display, simply by using an overhead stereo camera. The high precision is critical to giving the feel of a real touch-screen.

costs. The use of ordinary cameras allows for various computer vision techniques to enable recognition of day-to-day objects or hand gestures [2] as well as to overlay physical objects from one workspace onto another in the case of remote collaboration setups, *e.g.* [8]. This can create a very rich and multipurpose workspace on the interactive surface.

One of the major shortcomings of current overhead camera based systems, however, is the difficulty in accurately sensing contact with the surface. This limits the fluidity of interactions possible, *e.g.* the Visual Touchpad of [10] that uses two cameras for depth computation may report a touch event even if a finger is within approximately 1cm from the surface; in [9], the single camera system has no way to detect contact of a finger with the surface, so relies on detecting pauses in finger trajectories to report mouse *button* events. The PlayAnywhere system of [18] makes use of an infrared camera and a simple analysis of the shape of shadow of a finger to achieve good touch detection. This works well with projection based displays on opaque surfaces and when a finger is pointing in a direction almost perpedicular to that of the infrared light source, but we find that sensing multiple finger tips on top of an LCD display in the absence of directional lighting causes shadow based cues to be less reliable due to occlusions and lighting factors.

The contribution of this paper is a novel computer vision based algorithm that can robustly detect finger tips and sense touch for each finger with high precision using an overhead stereo camera. Unlike previous attempts to solve this problem [10,19], we present a quantitative analysis of both the finger detection and touch sensing components of our sys-

0-7695-3013-3/07 $25.00 © 2007 IEEE
DOI 10.1109/TABLETOP.2007.29

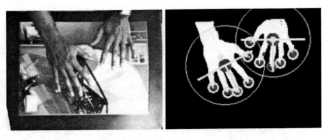

Figure 2. Fingertip detection and multi-touch sensing using stereo vision. *(left)* Input image from one camera after homography transformation; *(right)* Segmentation mask showing orientations of each hand and detected finger tips (bold circles indicate touch).

tem. We use the algorithm for enabling multi-touch interactions on tablet displays.

2. Physical Setup

Our system consists of a stereo camera mounted above a horizontal surface, viewing the surface at a slightly oblique angle to avoid interference within the working volume. The sensing algorithm can convert any surface into an interactive one, though this paper focusses on horizontal tablet displays to augment stylus input with multi-touch sensitivity. Figure 1 (inset) shows a prototype of the setup.

Calibration. In order to transform the camera view into the physical coordinates of the working surface, a corner detection algorithm is used to automatically detect the 4 corners of the working area in both the camera views. These may be the corners of the display screen as in our case, or pre-marked points on any surface. A homographic transformation and depth plane equation of the surface are then computed and stored for use during the main algorithm.

3. High Precision Touch Sensing

We develop a machine learning based approach to sense touching fingers on the surface. Labelled images of several different finger tips touching and not touching the surface are used as training data and a mathematical model is developed that *learns* to (a) detect multiple finger tips in an image, and (b) compute for each tip whether it touches the surface.

3.1. Image Segmentation

Before proceeding with fingertip detection, we first segment the hands from the rest of the image, which is referred to as the *background*. Other systems have used image differencing [9] or infrared filters [18] to suppress the background. Recent computer vision techniques that model the appearance statistics of the background [2] have proved very effective in dealing with arbitrary backgrounds. In this work, the background surface is an LCD screen. We exploit the fact that the light emitted by LCDs is polarized and make use of appropriately rotated polarizing filters on the stereo camera to cancel out

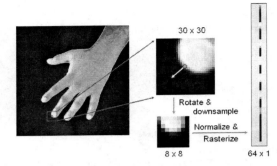

Figure 3. Encoding process that converts each point on the boundary of a hand into a signature vector. These are used to classify each edge-point as a *tip* or *non-tip* point, which are then spatially clustered to locate individual finger tips.

the contents of the screen [7]. As a result, the display screen always appears to be 'switched off' to the cameras and the highly complex dynamic background can be suppressed by simple thresholding (figure 2).

3.2. Fingertip Detection

Fingertip detection in the past has been done using shape filtering on binary images [9], finding strong peaks along hand blob perimeters [10] or using shadow based methods with heuristics that return a single fingertip detection per hand when the finger points in an appropriate direction [18]. In contrast, we make use of machine learning to develop a classifier that combines shape and appearance cues to robustly identify points having high probability of lying on a finger tip. These are called *tip points*, and are then clustered to obtain multiple fingertip detections in the image. Fingertips are thus detected only when there is a substantial evidence in the form of several tip points.

A few hundred points from the database of training images are marked as *tip* points or *non-tip* points (depending on whether or not they lie on a finger tip). These are encoded, using local image patches of 8×8 pixels, as 64-dimensional *signature* vectors. A linear decision rule in the form of a Support Vector Machine [16] is then learned that allows any new point to be classified as a tip point based on its signature. The signature computation process consists of normalizing each image patch with respect to rotation using the image gradient at that point, and scaling its intensity values to have unit variance. The matrix of intensities in this patch is then raster-scanned into a 64-dimensional vector. The process is illustrated in figure 3. This encoding allows the detection to be independent of the rotation of the finger and also quite robust to lighting variations. Individual finger tips are located and counted by performing a connected component analysis based clustering on the detected tip-points.

3.3. Touch and Hover Detection

Distinguishing events of touch from those where a finger is hovering a few millimeters above the screen requires very high precision stereo information. Conventional stereo algorithms that compute disparity images fail to provide this. In our physical setup, for instance, where the cameras have a baseline of 12cm and are mounted roughly 50cm above the tablet surface, depth near the screen is quantized every 5mm, so disparity images provide centimetre level precision at best. Here we develop an algorithm that probabilistically aggregates stereo cues from several points at each fingertip and uses a finger-specific model to achieve millimetre level precision.

Geometrically, the touching criterion is a function of the orientation and height of the finger tip above the screen. We extract this information by computing the equation of a plane that passes through points detected on the boundary of the finger – the plane that slices the finger to form its silhouette as shown in figure 4. However, in place of actual height above the screen, we use disparity values d_i relative to the screen surface for each pixel. At each point $\mathbf{x_i} \equiv (x_i, y_i)$ on the boundary of the finger tip (the *tip* points from above), the disparity is expressed as

$$d_i = \alpha^\top \mathbf{x}_i + \beta \qquad (1)$$

where (α, β) are the parameters of the desired plane. $\alpha = [\alpha_1\ \alpha_2]^\top$. $\mathbf{x_i}$ are measured in a local coordinate system attached to the finger, for rotation and translation invariance, and d_i is measured from stereo matching. With each disparity measure d_i, we also associate an uncertainty measure σ_i^2 which is obtained by modelling the stereo match likelihood [4] along each scan line as a normal distribution $\mathcal{N}(d_i, \sigma_i^2)$. This allows for a significant increase in the precision of estimated plane parameters (as compared to using *winner-take-all* stereo) since the optimal (α, β) may be estimated via a weighted least squares regression:

$$(\alpha^*, \beta^*) = \arg\min_{(\alpha,\beta)} \sum \frac{1}{\sigma_i^2} [d_i - (\alpha^\top \mathbf{x}_i + \beta)]^2 \qquad (2)$$

In order to detect touch from the α and β values for each fingertip, we learn a linear decision rule on these parameters in the form of a discriminative classifier. The condition for touch thus takes the form

$$w_1 \alpha_1 + w_2 \alpha_2 + w_3 \beta + w_4 > 0 \qquad (3)$$

where $\{w_1 \ldots w_4\}$ are weights that are learned using a second Support Vector Machine, taking labeled instances of touching and non-touching finger tips as training data. The linear form of a rule for detecting touch is motivated by geometrically approximating the finger tip as an ellipsoid that makes a rolling contact with the screen (see figure 4). In this case, the touching criterion may be expressed as the height of the centre of ellipsoid being less than a threshold:

$$[\alpha_1\ \alpha_2] \begin{bmatrix} 0 \\ r \end{bmatrix} + \beta < r' \qquad (4)$$

which is a special case of the condition in (3) with $w_1 = 0$. Learning the generic rule (3) directly from data rather than

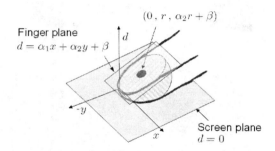

Figure 4. Geometric model of a finger on the screen-plane. The orientation and height of a finger is summarized by a plane computed from the detected tip points; and the surface of the finger tip is well-approximated as an ellipsoid to detect instances of touch.

	Tips	Non-tips	Combined
average accuracy (%)	96.10	92.12	92.48
standard deviation	2.21	1.05	0.98

Figure 5. Classification accuracy of points as tip points or non-tip points without incorporating spatial information. More tip points are correctly classified than non-tip points. Although 92.48% represents a decent performance in itself, most mis-classifications are corrected during the spatial clustering step that follows (see text).

	Disparity histograms	Geometric finger model
average accuracy %	80.50	98.48
standard deviation	6.91	1.38

Figure 6. Classification accuracy of detected tips as touching or not touching the surface using two different stereo features.

explicity modelling the geometry as in (4) allows for the model to accomodate deformability of the finger. Futhermore, it allows us to compute the probability that a fingertip touches the surface [12], and obtain more reliable information by incorporating temporal information.

4. Performance Evaluation

This section presents a quantitative evaluation of the fingertip detection and touch sensing accuracy of our system, followed by a qualitative description of its use for multi-touch and gesture-based interactions on tablet displays.

Sensing Accuracy. We conducted experiments with a database of 500 stereo images of a few different people's hands taken with the setup described in section 2. About 3 tip points were marked per visible finger on each image (each image had between 2 and 5 visible fingers) and 150 non-tip points marked per image. Figure 5 shows the classification accuracy of points as tip points or non-tip points in the form of an average over 100 trials with random 90%-10% splits into training and test data for cross-validation. The average accuracy of classifying points in this manner is 92.48%, but our clustering step removes almost all of

Figure 7. Our high precision algorithm allows seemless multi-touch interactions with an ordinary tablet display. *(left)* zooming into a map using a bimanual gesture *(centre)* using the non-dominant hand to rotate an electronic canvas while drawing with the stylus, and *(right)* a remote user zooms into a figure and highlights text in a collaborative work scenario where the workspace is shared multiple tablets. The stereo camera is used to render a remote user's hands on the tablet with depth-senstive transparency; we call this *phantom presence* [8].

the mis-classifications and individual finger tips are detected with almost 100% accuracy. For learning the touch-detection classifier, we define a finger tip that is roughly 2mm or more from the surface as non-touching. Figure 6 shows the accuracy of our touch-detection algorithm. Using the method described in section 3.3, detected fingertips were correctly classified as touching or not with an accuracy of 98.48%. As a benchmark, the table also shows the performance of a classifier than uses an alternate set of features based on simple disparity estimates from each fingertip as opposed to the geometric model of section 3.3.

Interaction on tablet displays. We implemented our algorithm to support bimanual interactions on tablet displays, as well as complement standard stylus input with gestures from the non-dominant hand. The sensing algorithm works at up to 20 fps on a 3.4GHz processor and our applications use interpolation to allow for seamless interactions. Figure 7 shows some of the interactions we currently support. The complete system is called the *Collaborative Slate* (C-Slate) and is described in [8]. Besides single-user interactions, it enables enhanced remote collaboration between multiple users on shared workspaces across more than one tablet; and supports object sensing and *phantom presence* [8].

5. Conclusion

This paper has presented a novel algorithm for multi-touch sensing on surfaces using an overhead stereo camera that supports multiple users. We have combined the use of machine learning with a geometrical intuition of the problem to robustly detect multiple finger tips in an image and sense touch with a precision of 2-3mm. This is a significant advancement over existing systems using stereo vision, which are restricted to centimetre level precision. The approach is also envisaged to be useful in other setups, *e.g.* using infrared images. The performance of the algorithm falls in adverse lighting conditions and is also currently susceptible to strong reflections on the screen surface. Although vision-based systems are often associated with such drawbacks, resolving these issues will be the focus of our future work.

[1] W. Buxton. Multi-Touch Systems I Have Known & Loved. 2007. http://www.billbuxton.com/multitouchOverview.html.

[2] T. Deselaers, A. Criminisi, J. Winn, and A. Agarwal. Incorporating On-demand Stereo for Real Time Recognition. In *Proc. Computer Vision and Pattern Recognition*, 2007.

[3] P. Dietz and D. Lehigh. DiamondTouch: a Multi-User Touch Technology. In *Proceedings of UIST*, 2001.

[4] V. Kolmogorov et al. Bi-layer segmentation of binocular stereo video. In *Proc. Computer Vision and Pattern Recognition*, 2005.

[5] J. Y. Han. Low-Cost Multi-Touch Sensing through Frustrated Total Internal Reflection. In *Proceedings of UIST*, 2005.

[6] Tactex Controls Inc. http://www.tactex.com/products_array.php.

[7] H. Ishii, M. Kobayashi, and J. Grudin. Integration of Interpersonal Space and Shared Workspace: ClearBoard Design and Experiments. *ACM Trans. Information Systems*, 1993.

[8] S. Izadi, A. Agarwal, A. Criminisi, J. Winn, A. Blake, and A. Fitzgibbon. C-Slate: A Multi-Touch and Object Recognition System for Remote Collaboration using Horizontal Surfaces. In *IEEE TableTop Workshop*, 2007.

[9] J. Letessier and F. Berard. Visual Tracking of Bare Fingers for Interactive Surfaces. In *Proceedings of UIST*, 2004.

[10] Shahzad Malik and Joe Laszlo. Visual Touchpad: A Two-handed Gestural Input Device. In *Proc. ICMI*, 2004.

[11] Microsoft Surface Computing. http://www.surface.com.

[12] John Platt. Probabilities for Support Vector Machines. *Advances in Large Margin Classifiers*, pages 61–74, 1999.

[13] J. Rekimoto. SmartSkin: An infrastructure for freehand manipulation on interactive surfaces. In *Proc. CHI*, 2002.

[14] SMART Technologies. http://www.smarttech.com.

[15] TactaPad. http://www.tactiva.com/tactapad.html.

[16] V. Vapnik. *The Nature of Statistical Learning Theory.* Springer, 1995.

[17] A. Wilson. TouchLight: An Imaging Touch Screen and Display for Gesture-Based Interaction. In *Proc. ICMI*, 2004.

[18] A. Wilson. PlayAnywhere: A Compact Interactive Tabletop Projection-Vision System. In *Proceedings of UIST*, 2005.

[19] C. Wren and Y. Ivanov. Volumetric Operations with Surface Margins. In *Computer Vision and Pattern Recognition Conference: Technical Sketches*, 2001.

Depth-Sensing Video Cameras for 3D Tangible Tabletop Interaction

Andrew D. Wilson
Microsoft Research
Redmond, WA
awilson@microsoft.com

Abstract

Recently developed depth-sensing video camera technologies provide precise per-pixel range data in addition to color video. Such cameras will find application in robotics and vision-based human computer interaction scenarios such as games and gesture input systems. We present an interactive tabletop system which uses a depth-sensing camera to build a height map of the objects on the table surface. This height map is used in a driving simulation game that allows players to drive a virtual car over real objects placed on the table. Players can use folded bits of paper, for example, to lay out a course of ramps and other obstacles. A projector displays the position of the car on the surface, such that when the car is driven over a ramp, for example, it jumps appropriately. A second display shows a synthetic graphical view of the entire surface, or a traditional arcade view from behind the car. Micromotorcross is a fun initial investigation into the applicability of depth-sensing cameras to tabletop interfaces. We present details on its implementation, and speculate on how this technology will enable new tabletop interactions.

1. Introduction

Tabletops distinguish themselves from other surfaces in the everyday world by their ability to support objects placed on them. This property lends tabletops to a wide variety of complex, productive tasks involving physical objects. A garage workbench, for example, is often the site of intricate assembly tasks, while architects still build physical models of buildings and landscapes on horizontal surfaces. Accordingly, many interactive tabletop systems include some ability to sense and use physical objects placed on them. Often these capabilities are based on capacitive sensing, RFID, active infrared emitting devices, generic computer vision-based object recognition, or visual barcode recognition.

However, while these objects live in a 3D world, interactions with them on interactive surfaces are typically 2D in nature. For example, a game piece placed on the surface would typically indicate the 2D position of a player on a board game. Beyond tabletop interfaces, the field of augmented reality offers sophisticated techniques to reason about 3D objects, but these efforts are often based on manipulating some aspect of the physical object, or are primarily concerned with determining camera position.

A few interactive tabletop systems deal with 3D objects more generally. Illuminating Clay [2], for example, uses a laser scanner, while SandScape[1] uses infrared illumination, an infrared camera, and translucent beads to deduce a height map of the surface. The Perceptive Workbench [3] combines views of objects placed on its surface to perform 3D reconstruction. Meanwhile, 3D gesture interfaces over tabletops are typically based on augmented reality or VR techniques such as magnetic trackers or other motion capture techniques.

In this paper we propose the use of recently developed depth-sensing video cameras to support a wide range of 3D interactions on interactive tabletops. This new camera technology enables the real-time 3D capture of everyday objects placed on the surface for example. We present an early demonstration system which uses the calculated height map in a driving simulation that allows the player to drive a virtual car over real objects placed on the table.

2. Depth-sensing cameras

We refer to camera systems which recover depth information throughout the captured scene (i.e., depth per pixel) as *depth-sensing*. While we acknowledge the utility of other camera-based means of 3D capture for interactive surfaces, such as recognizing an object from

---

[1] http://tangible.media.mit.edu/projects/sandscape

0-7695-3013-3/07 $25.00 © 2007 IEEE
DOI 10.1109/TABLETOP.2007.35

two views [4], a fully detailed range image permits a great deal of flexibility.

Laser scanners have been used in robotics and other fields to calculate accurate depth images. Despite being available for many years, such technology is still expensive, and often is barely fast enough for interactive applications (Illuminating Clay reports 3Hz scan rate).

Correlation-based stereo is another old approach which suffers from a number of difficulties. For example, stereo matching typically fails on regions of the scene with little or no texture. Secondly, even today stereo matching requires a great deal of computational power to obtain interactive rates at reasonable resolution. Finally, stereo camera setups typically require fine calibration.

New camera technologies under development observe depth information in a more direct fashion, and so address many of the drawbacks of previous approaches.

In the present work we use the ZSense camera by 3DV Systems, Ltd [1]. The ZSense times the return of pulsed infrared light: reflected light from nearer objects will arrive sooner. A Gallium-Arsenide (GaAs) solid-state shutter makes this possible (see Figure 1). The result is an 8 bit depth image, over a variable dynamic range (70cm to 3m). Figure 1d illustrates an example ZSense depth image. The ZSense camera also includes a separate color camera. The output of the color camera is registered with the depth image to obtain a complete "RGBZ" image at 30Hz.

3. Micromotocross

3.1 Motivation

To explore the application of depth-sensing cameras to interactive tabletops, we built a projection-vision system which uses the camera to recover the height map of the table surface and the objects placed on it. Graphics are then projected on the same surface.

We are interested in exploring the range of interactions made possible by this configuration. To begin, we implemented a simple driving simulation using the XNA game development platform. Players drive a virtual dune buggy around and over any objects placed on the table surface. The players can arrange folded bits of construction paper, for example, to lay out a course of ramps and other obstacles. A projector is used to display the position of the car on the surface, such that when the car drives over a ramp, for example, the car jumps appropriately. Players control their cars with a wireless Xbox 360 controller.

3.2 Terrain model

The 320x240 depth image is returned by the camera at a frame rate of 30Hz. The camera is configured to place its depth-sensing dynamic range at the height of the table and about 70cm above the table.

Because the focal length of the camera is known, it is possible to calculate the 3D position (in centimeters, for example) indicated at each pixel in the depth image. It is straightforward to then construct a vertex buffer for this height map, and it is similarly easy to texture map this mesh with the color image also returned by the camera.

In the present implementation, instead of converting the mesh to world coordinates as suggested above, the depth image is normalized between a minimum depth image collected offline when the surface is clear of objects, and a maximum depth image, collected when the surface is raised about 20cm.

The ZSense depth image is somewhat noisy. For some applications it will be necessary to smooth the image to mitigate the effects of shot noise. In Micromotocross, where every bump due to noise is potentially a huge pothole, we found it necessary to use a mixture of spatial and temporal smoothing. This has the effect of adding a significant delay from when an object on the surface is moved, to when this change is reflected in the modeled terrain.

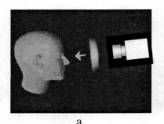 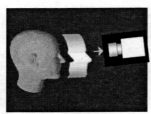 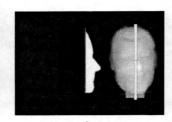 

| a. | b. | c. | d. |

Figure 1. 3DV ZSense uses pulsed infrared light (a) and solid state shutter to compute depth image. Reflected light from closer surfaces arrives sooner (b). Fast shutter truncates light (c) while imaging sensor integrates more light from closer surfaces. A second captured image is used to normalize for differences in reflectance. Example depth image (d). Illustrations adapted from [1].

3.3 Projection-vision system

In order to project graphics that are correctly registered with the sensed image, it is necessary to model the coordinate transform that relates a position in the sensed image to a position in the projected image. In the common case of a 2D camera and projection on a 2D surface, this can be handled using a projective transform and a simple calibration procedure which maps the four corners of the table surface in the camera view to display coordinates [5].

When using a 3D camera to sense objects and various depths, projected graphics need further correction such that, for example, the virtual dune buggy appears the same size whether it is on the table surface or on some object of significant height placed on the table surface.

We use a simple extension of the 2D case which allows an easy two step calibration process. Offline, the calibration of the 2D projective transform mapping image coordinates to display coordinates is run twice: first when the table is clear, and second with the table raised about 20cm from its normal height. In each calibration, the user clicks on 4 projected points in the color video image. This yields two 2D projective transforms, one for each table height.

The display coordinates of any point in the normalized depth image can then be determined by interpolating between the results of both projective transforms, at an amount given by the depth value. It is convenient to incorporate these calculations in the graphics vertex shader, replacing the usual graphics camera projection, so that the application developer need not be aware of such details when constructing the graphics scene, and so that this transformation imparts no overhead to the system. Figure 2 illustrates the tabletop with projection and extracted terrain.

In addition to the table projection display, the Micromotocross system includes a secondary LCD display which shows a purely synthetic overview of the

Figure 3. Traditional arcade view for blue player shows other player and ramp ahead.

scene. In this view, the terrain is textured with the color image. Players can switch to a conventional arcade view, in which the graphics camera is placed just behind the car (Figure 3). A player can toggle this view by hitting a button on the controller. The second player can switch the display back to the overview by hitting the same button on their controller.

3.4 Physics model

Two players can control their dune buggies using standard driving controls on wireless Xbox 360 controllers. The car's movement is calculated by the Newton physics library, which includes a detailed vehicle dynamics model of acceleration, steering, tire friction effects and chassis rigid body dynamics. Figure 2 shows a car airborne after a jump, for example.

Most physics libraries include facilities for collision detection that are specialized to efficiently handle many separate rigid bodies. Typically the geometry of each object is constrained to be static, so that various structures such as convex hulls and BSP trees can be pre-computed to speed collision detection. In Micromotocross, however, these techniques are inappropriate when detecting the collision of the cars

Figure 2. Micromotocross demonstration. Left: Tabletop with paper ramps and obstacles, and top-down projected cars. Middle: Synthetic (graphics) overview of tabletop, showing extracted terrain model, two cars, synthetic shadows, and user's hand in the scene. Right: In the synthetic view, a car is airborne after taking a jump.

with the dynamically changing height map. Fortunately, because the height field is a regular grid of points, determining which parts of the mesh are potentially in contact with the car's tires, for example, is a simple lookup operation.

Unfortunately, most available physics libraries do not support dynamically changing meshes in the calculation of collision response. Fast changes in the mesh can result in unpredictable dynamics. If the player moves an object quickly against the virtual car, the response of the car may not look convincing, or may even penetrate the terrain mesh.

Finally, it is important to note that a height map-based terrain model is indifferent to the motion of distinct objects as it relates to the simulation of friction. For example, if the car is sitting on a physical object that the user then moves across the table, the car will not stay on the object (even if its brakes are on). An appropriate analogy may be moving one's hand under a bed sheet, with objects sitting on the sheet: the objects are likely to stay in place.

3.5 User experiences

Micromotocross has been experienced by hundreds of people of a wide variety of ages and backgrounds. People have fun manipulating objects on the table, setting up ramps and bridges from one object to another. Many are impressed by the magical quality of the interaction.

Some users prefer to look at the synthetic view (overview or behind-car), while others prefer to look at the table projection. Some may prefer the synthetic view because it is easier to see the car as it goes through the air over a jump, or because it has higher resolution.

Many people are amused to find that the system will incorporate their hands into the scene when they are placed on the table. Some try to drive their buggy over their friend's hand, or even up their arm, while a few try to hold the car in the palm of their hand to move it (if the hand cupped and moved slowly, this is often successful). Children often will have fun knocking the car driven by their friend off the table, but are annoyed when this happens when it is their turn to drive.

4. Further interactions

It is interesting to watch people attempt to interact with the virtual cars directly with their hands. Once they realize that the system sees their hands, and that the virtual objects tend to react in somewhat appropriate ways to real physical objects on the table, many people try to pick up and move the car. These observations suggest that users would be able to use a gesture-based interface to manipulate virtual objects, just as they would manipulate real objects on the table.

In fact, it has been our goal all along to explore the use of gestures in the 3D space on and above the table surface. The depth image will make certain gestures potentially easier to recognize, and the 3D information should ease interactions with the physical objects.

The current prototype supports an initial implementation of a pinching gesture that may be suitable for picking up objects (see [6]). Presently, this gesture must be done well above the surface of the table, and instead of grasping a virtual object, the gesture creates an obstacle (a heavy block) which is dropped into the scene.

We envision the ability to pick up a virtual object with this grasping gesture, place it on a physical object sitting on the table, or even hold the virtual object in the palm of the hand. So that such interactions behave in the way that users expect, it may be desirable to drive such interactions from the physics engine (in contrast to recognizing the hand as a special object, for example). Such an approach will require significant upgrades to the physics simulation's support of dynamic meshes.

4. Acknowledgements

Thanks to 3DV Systems, Ltd., for providing the ZSense prototype which made this work possible.

5. References

[1] G. J. Iddan and G. Yahav, "3D Imaging in the Studio," *SPIE*, vol. 4298, pp. 48, 2001.

[2] B. Piper, C. Ratti, and H. Ishii, "Illuminating Clay: A 3-D Tangible Interface for Landscape Analysis," presented at CHI 2002 Conference on Human Factors in Computing Systems, 2002.

[3] T. Starner, B. Leibe, D. Minnen, T. Westeyn, A. Hurst, and J. Weeks, "The perceptive workbench: Computer-vision-based gesture tracking, object tracking, and 3D reconstruction for augmented desks," *Machine Vision and Applications*, vol. 14, pp. 51-71, 2003.

[4] A. Wilson, "TouchLight: An Imaging Touch Screen and Display for Gesture-Based Interaction," presented at International Conference on Multimodal Interfaces, 2004.

[5] A. Wilson, "PlayAnywhere: A Compact Tabletop Computer Vision System," presented at Symposium on User Interface Software and Technology (UIST), 2005.

[6] A. Wilson, "Robust computer vision-based detection of pinching for one and two-handed gesture input," presented at UIST, 2006.

Low-Cost Malleable Surfaces with Multi-Touch Pressure Sensitivity

J. David Smith, T.C. Nicholas Graham
School of Computing
Queen's University
Kingston, Ontario, Canada
{smith, graham} @cs.queensu.ca

David Holman, Jan Borchers
Media Computing Group
RWTH Aachen University
Aachen, Germany
holman@cs.rwth-aachen.de; jan@rwth-aachen.de

Abstract

While touch sensitivity has today become commonplace, it is oftentimes limited to a single point of contact with a hard, rigid surface. We present a novel technique for the construction of a malleable surface with multi-touch sensitivity. The sensor is pressure sensitive and responds to near zero-force touch from any object. The technique is an extension of previous work based on frustrated total internal reflection.

1. Introduction

Touch screens have become a common input device; how-ever, most of today's systems can only detect a single point of contact. Multi-touch sensors exist, but are typically ex-pensive and difficult to construct. These systems also tend to be hard, rigid, flat surfaces which provide no haptic feedback. A recent development is the malleable touch surface [3][10][11]. These surfaces are characterized by a softer touch interface that provide passive haptic feedback and are pressure sensitive. They also provide a feeling of depth and tangibility that makes them well suited for 3D applications such as sculpting, molding, terrain deformation, etc.

We present a simple technique for the construction of a multi-touch sensitive display with a malleable surface. The technique detects near zero-force touch with any object and is highly sensitive to pressure. Additionally the surface can be made to a variable degree of softness and thickness, lending well to usage requiring deformability and feed-back, such as sculpting and massaging applications. The technique is an extension of Han's multi-touch sensor de-sign based on frustrated total internal reflection (FTIR), which is a technique commonly used in fingerprint readers [2].

2. Related Work

Multi-touch sensitive surfaces are found in various forms in many different technologies. A simple approach for multi-touch sensing is to deploy an array of discrete sensors. These sensors can operate entirely independently [9], through a connected set of independent active elements [4][12], or through a matrix of purely passive sensors [7][8]. However these approaches tend to suffer from poor resolution and are typically very complex to construct.

Vision-based systems have been proposed to provide higher resolution and support for malleable surface materials. These systems either approximate the 3D position of the user's hand through pixel intensity [6], stereoscopy [5][13], or through markers attached to a deformable material [3][10][11]. Using a deformable material has the added advantage of providing passive

Figure 1: Multi-touch sensitive surfaces are particularly useful for collaboration on large displays such as multi-user tabletops.

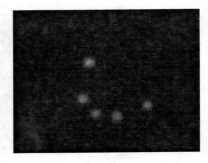

Figure 2: The pixel intensity grows as touch pressure grows. The left image is a zero-force touch, center is a light press, and right is a hard press.

haptic feedback and adds an element of depth to the interaction surface. Additionally, these surfaces typically report pressure as a vector, meaning touch pressure can be interpreted in directions not necessarily perpendicular to the interaction surface. However the markers on the deformable material must be opaque, meaning the system must be top-projected.

2.1. FTIR-Based Multi-touch Sensing

Han proposed a low-cost, simple FTIR-based sensor. The system introduces infrared (IR) light into a medium (typically acrylic) with an index of refraction significantly different than the air around it. When the light reaches the interface between the two mediums at an appropriate angle of incidence, it is reflected. However when the sensor is touched, the difference in the index of refraction between the two interfacing mediums (acrylic and skin/oil/sweat in this case) is reduced and the reflection is frustrated, causing the light to escape out the opposite side. This light can then been detected with an optical sensor such as an IR filtered camera or photodiode.

This approach suffers from a number of drawbacks. First, the system gives only a rough sense of pressure. The intensity of the frustration does not change significantly as the user presses more firmly; however the elasticity of the user's skin causes the radius of the touch contour to grow with pressure. This is effective for very coarse pressure sensitivity, but is severely limited by the resolution of the camera. Additionally, performance is severely degraded when the users' hands are dry. For example, we deployed an FTIR surface in the demo session of a large academic conference held in a cold, dry, mountainous region. We found the technique performed poorly for approximately half of users.

To address these issues Han proposed the use of a surface overlay with an FTIR sensor. Additionally the overlay material can serve as the display surface,

removing the distance between the screen and the point at which the users' touch is sensed. Also, the use of a proper overlay reports touch as a continuous range of intensity rather than a binary value, which leads to greatly increased pressure sensitivity.

However Han suggests the use of simple vinyl rear projection screen as an overlay. We have found this material to be ineffective. The user must press quite hard to cause even minimal frustration, and the system suffers from severe hysteresis upon relaxation. Han reports a hysteresis of up to a full second; however our tests have yielded hysteresis up to 5 seconds. Additionally the material is flat and assumes the rigidity of the underlying acrylic.

3. FTIR with Malleable Surface Overlay

Our technique builds on Han's design by including a thick, soft surface overlay. The softness of the surface amplifies the pressure sensitivity of the sensor while providing an inviting user experience with passive feedback. Addition-ally, because users can "dig their hands" into the surface, the technique provides an interaction surface with a feeling of tangible depth. The surface is also sensitive to touch from any object, not just those with the appropriate optical properties. Additionally, the sensor will report the contour of the touch, enabling rough shape recognition.

The softness, scalability, and sensitivity to touch with any object are useful for tangible drawing applications. Finger-paint Plus (Figure 3) is a simple painting application that allows the user to paint using not only their hands, but also paint brushes, stamps, cookie cutters, etc. The large surface naturally supports collaborative painting, and the softness of the surface makes the sensor well suited for deployment into usage scenarios involving small children.

Figure 3: *Fingerpaint Plus* is an application that allows users to paint with any object. For example a user can perform strokes using a simple paintbrush.

Other potential applications of the surface include 3D terrain deformations, where users can tangibly create mountains and valleys by performing whole handed gestures while digging into the table surface. For example, a user could perform a "gathering" gesture where she draws her hands towards each other to create a mountain. Alternatively she could perform a "spreading" gesture by moving her hands apart to create a valley. Additionally use of familiar physical tools would be possible, such as using a spatula or whisk to "smooth" and "stir" the terrain, or heavy objects such as rocks and weights could be dropped onto the surface to create virtual impact craters.

3.1. Implementation

We chose to construct our surface overlay with silicone rubber. The material is inexpensive and widely available at most hobby shops. It is typically sold in liquid form as a molding material for physical product prototyping, but is also available in sheets. The material can be mixed to varying degrees of softness, comes in a variety of colors (including transparent), and forms to the shape of the mold in which it is poured. Silicone rubber makes an effective surface overlay for many reasons:

- **Malleable** – It can be mixed to practically any thickness and softness and will perform properly. Therefore soft, malleable touch surfaces similar in feel to a sponge or gym mat can be created as well as thin, rigid surfaces.
- **Moldable** – It is primarily sold as a casting material for plastic molds and therefore holds shape well. This makes the material well suited for applications where a non-planar or textured touch surface is desirable.
- **Improved Performance** – It is remarkably effective at causing the frustration effect when used with acrylic. When molded properly the system has effectively no hysteresis, a high sense of pressure sensitivity, and senses touches of near zero force.

On top of the rubber we placed a sheet of simple vinyl rear projection screen to serve at the display surface. Also, we found it necessary to mold a rough texture to the side of the surface overlay that touches the acrylic to reduce false positives and hysteresis. Implementations have been produced using both top and rear projection.

4. Performance

Informal evaluations have been used to determine system performance. Two separate tabletops were created: a thick, soft top-projected system and a thin, hard, rear-projected system. The top-projected system had an overlay approximately 1 cm thick and the softness of a gym mat. The thin system had an overlay less than 1 mm thick and felt as hard as a piece of acrylic. The thick system was top projected because even reportedly clear silicone rubber is partially cloudy and was found to distort the projection when poured to a thickness over a centimeter.

Both systems were found to provide touch sensitivity much more reliably than Han's technique. Both systems could detect touches near zero-force. Additionally, the thickness and softness of the top projected system provided considerably more pressure sensitivity. The thick system could detect distinct pressures ranging from a light touch with a paint brush to a hard press with the thumb. However the thick system caused the contour of the contact to become "fuzzy", making the thin system more appropriate for applications in need of shape recognition. Additionally, the poured silicone rubber was found to be rather heavy (~1 kilogram per Liter) and excessively thick systems might reduce the portability of the surface.

5. Future Work

Our future work will continue along two paths. First, we will explore new interactive surface designs that are now made possible through application of our technique. Additionally, we will seek to make the design more portable.

5.1. Textured Surfaces

An advantage to using a cast material is that the surface can be molded to fit any shape. This presents the possibility of some interesting design options. For example, regions of the screen can be given different textures. But-tons, for example, could be raised above the surrounding screen, or the texture of the material could be manipulated to represent the texture of the displayed content underneath it. For example, a 2D terrain might include a patch of ice which could be given a smooth texture, while a patch of dirt might be given a rough texture. More ambitiously, the shape of the surface could even be made to reflect a 3D terrain; such has having large mountains physically protruding up from the interaction surface.

5.2. Portable Displays

Currently the system requires a camera positioned behind the interaction surface, along with a means of projecting the display image. This makes the system somewhat large and requires an active calibration step upon setup. Han reports that a common LCD panel allows IR light to pass through [1]. We have verified this finding and are working to integrate an IR sensing device directly into the casing of an LCD display. A current promising approach is to re-place the camera with a mesh of IR sensitive photodiodes. This approach is similar in design to the device described in Lee et al. [4], and is analogous to embedding a very large monochrome Color Capture Device (CCD) directly into the display. The photodiode mesh would be the same size as the LCD panel, porous, and placed between the LCD and the backlight. This would increase system port-ability and greatly simplify system deployment by eliminating the need for a calibration step. A further refinement might include integration with an OLED display that re-quires no backlighting. Additionally, the photodiode mesh could be made flexible, allowing for possible integration with IR transparent flexible displays.

6. Acknowledgements

We wish to thank NECTAR and NSERC for funding sup-port of this work, along with the EQUIS Group at Queen's University and Gerald Morrison from Smart Technologies.

7. References

[1] Fingerworks. iGesturePad. www.fingerworks.com

[2] Han, J. Y. 2005. Low-cost multi-touch sensing through frustrated total internal reflection. In Proceedings of the 18th Annual ACM Symposium on User interface Software and Technology (Seattle, WA, USA, October 23 - 26, 2005). UIST '05. ACM Press, New York, NY, 115-118.

[3] Kamiyama, K., Vlack, K., Mizota, T., Kajimoto, H., Kawakami, N., and Tachi, S. 2005. Vision-Based Sen-sor for Real-Time Measuring of Surface Traction Fields. IEEE Comput. Graph. Appl. 25, 1 (Jan. 2005), 68-75.

[4] Lee, S., Buxton, W., and Smith, K. C. 1985. A Multi-Touch Three Dimensional Touch-Sensitive Tablet. In Proceedings of the SIGCHI Conference on Human Factors in Computing Systems (San Francisco, Califor-nia, United States). CHI '85. ACM Press, New York, NY, 21-25.

[5] Malik, S. and Laszlo, J. 2004. Visual Touchpad: A Two-Handed Gestural Input Device. In Proceedings of the 6th International Conference on Multimodal Inter-faces (State College, PA, USA, October 13 - 15, 2004). ICMI '04. ACM Press, New York, NY, 289-296.

[6] Matsushita, N. and Rekimoto, J. 1997. HoloWall: De-signing a Finger, Hand, Body, and Object Sensitive Wall. In Proceedings of the 10th Annual ACM Sympo-sium on User Interface Software and Technology (Banff, Alberta, Canada, October 14 - 17, 1997). UIST '97. ACM Press, New York, NY, 209-210.

[7] Nicol, K., and Hennig, E. M. C. 1979. Apparatus for the Time- Dependant Measurement of Physical Quanti-ties. U.S. Patent 4,134,063. Jan. 1979.

[8] Rekimoto, J. 2002. SmartSkin: An Infrastructure for Freehand Manipulation on Interactive Surfaces. In Pro-ceedings of the SIGCHI Conference on Human Factors in Computing Systems. CHI '02. ACM Press, New York, NY, 113-120.

[9] Tactex. Smart Fabric Technology. www.tactex.com

[10] Vlack, K., Mizota, T., Kawakami, N., Kamiyama, K., Kajimoto, H., and Tachi, S. 2005. GelForce: a vision-based traction field computer interface. In CHI '05 Ex-tended Abstracts on Human Factors in Computing Sys-tems (Portland, OR, USA, April 02 - 07, 2005). CHI '05. ACM Press, New York, NY, 1154-1155.

[11] Vogt, F., Chen, T., Hoskinson, R., and Fels, S. 2004. A malleable surface touch interface. In ACM SIGGRAPH 2004 Sketches (Los Angeles, California, August 08 - 12, 2004). R. Barzel, Ed. SIGGRAPH '04. ACM Press, New York, NY, 36.

[12] Westerman, W. and Elias, J. G. 2001. Method and Ap-paratus for Integrating Manual Input. U.S. Patent 6,323,846. Nov. 2001.

[13] Wilson, A. D. 2004. TouchLight: An Imaging Touch Screen and Display for Gesture-Based Interaction. In Proceedings of the 6th International Conference on Multimodal Interfaces (State College, PA, USA, Octo-ber 13 - 15, 2004). ICMI '04. ACM Press, New York, NY, 69-76.

Author Index

IEEE Computer Society
Conference Publications
Operations Committee

CPOC Chair

Phillip Laplante
Professor, Penn State University

Board Members

Thomas Baldwin, *Manager, Conference Publishing Services* (CPS)
Mike Hinchey, *Director, Software Engineering Lab, NASA Goddard*
Paolo Montuschi, *Professor, Politecnico di Torino*
Linda Shafer, *Professor Emeritus, University of Texas at Austin*
Jeffrey Voas, *Director, Systems Assurance Technologies, SAIC*
Wenping Wang, *Associate Professor, University of Hong Kong*

IEEE Computer Society Executive Staff

Angela Burgess, *Publisher*

IEEE Computer Society Publications

The world-renowned IEEE Computer Society publishes, promotes, and distributes a wide variety of authoritative computer science and engineering texts. These books are available from most retail outlets. Visit the CS Store at *http://www.computer.org/portal/site/store/index.jsp* for a list of products.

IEEE Computer Society *Conference Publishing Services* (CPS)

The IEEE Computer Society produces conference publications for more than 200 acclaimed international conferences each year in a variety of formats, including books, CD-ROMs, USB Drives, and on-line publications. For information about the IEEE Computer Society's *Conference Publishing Services* (CPS), please e-mail: cps@computer.org or telephone +1-714-821-8380. Fax +1-714-761-1784. Additional information about *Conference Publishing Services* (CPS) can be accessed from our web site at: *http://www.computer.org/cps*

IEEE Computer Society / Wiley Partnership

The IEEE Computer Society and Wiley partnership allows the CS Press *Authored Book* program to produce a number of exciting new titles in areas of computer science and engineering with a special focus on software engineering. IEEE Computer Society members continue to receive a 15% discount on these titles when purchased through Wiley or at: *http://wiley.com/ieeecs*. To submit questions about the program or send proposals, please e-mail dplummer@computer.org or telephone +1-714-821-8380. Additional information regarding the Computer Society's authored book program can also be accessed from our web site at:
http://www.computer.org/portal/pages/ieeecs/publications/books/about.html

Revised: 16 March 2007

 New *CPS Online* Workspace

An IEEE Online Collaborative Publishing Environment

CPS Online is a new IEEE online collaborative conference publishing environment designed to speed the delivery of price quotations and provide conferences with real-time access to all of a project's publication materials during production, including the final papers. The *CPS Online* workspace gives a conference the opportunity to upload files through any Web browser, check status and scheduling on their project, make changes to the Table of Contents and Front Matter, approve editorial changes and proofs, and communicate with their CPS editor through discussion forums, chat tools, commenting tools and e-mail.

The following is the URL link to the CPS Online Publishing Inquiry Form:
http://www.ieeeconfpublishing.org/cpir/inquiry/cps_inquiry.html